C0-AWU-485

# CONTEMPORARY DRAMA
# EUROPEAN PLAYS
# II

# CONTEMPORARY DRAMA

## AMERICAN PLAYS

### I

| | |
|---|---|
| The New York Idea | Mitchell |
| The Emperor Jones | O'Neill |
| Processional | Lawson |
| Beggar on Horseback | Kaufman and Connelly |
| The Silver Cord | Howard |

## ENGLISH AND IRISH PLAYS

### I

| | |
|---|---|
| Riders to the Sea | Synge |
| Hyacinth Halvey | Gregory |
| What Every Woman Knows | Barrie |
| Mid-Channel | Pinero |
| The Glittering Gate | Dunsany |
| Justice | Galsworthy |

### II

| | |
|---|---|
| Mr. Pim Passes By | Milne |
| The Circle | Maugham |
| Loyalties | Galsworthy |
| Hassan | Flecker |
| Juno and the Paycock | O'Casey |

## EUROPEAN PLAYS

### I

| | |
|---|---|
| A Doll's House | Ibsen |
| The Vultures | Becque |
| The Fossils | de Curel |
| The Beaver Coat | Hauptmann |
| Light-o'-Love | Schnitzler |

### II

| | |
|---|---|
| Hedda Gabler | Ibsen |
| Pelleas and Melisande | Maeterlinck |
| Magda | Sudermann |
| Cyrano de Bergerac | Rostand |
| Uncle Vanya | Chekhov |

### III

| | |
|---|---|
| The Sea Gull | Chekhov |
| The Lower Depths | Gorki |
| Francesca da Rimini | D'Annunzio |
| The Dream Play | Strindberg |
| The Passion Flower | Benavente |

### IV

| | |
|---|---|
| The Cherry Orchard | Chekhov |
| He Who Gets Slapped | Andreyev |
| Man and the Masses | Toller |
| R. U. R. | Capek |
| Henry IV | Pirandello |

# CONTEMPORARY DRAMA

# EUROPEAN PLAYS

# II

## HEDDA GABLER
Henrik Ibsen

## PÉLLÉAS AND MÉLISANDE
Maurice Maeterlinck

## MAGDA
Hermann Sudermann

## CYRANO DE BERGERAC
Edmond Rostand

## UNCLE VANYA
Anton P. Chekhov

SELECTED BY

E. BRADLEE WATSON
*Professor of English, Dartmouth College*
*and*
BENFIELD PRESSEY
*Professor of English, Dartmouth College*

CHARLES SCRIBNER'S SONS

NEW YORK CHICAGO BOSTON ATLANTA
SAN FRANCISCO DALLAS

Printed in the United States of America

## PREFACE

The plays in this volume represent some of the fruits of that flowering of the dramatic impulse that came to Europe immediately after Ibsen and the Free Theatre groups had broken the ground. How and with what aims they broke the ground is shown in the first volume of European plays in this series. In this second volume Ibsen himself again appears, with his most impartial work. The old carpentry of the "well-made" play, as skilfully done as possible, may be seen in Sudermann's *Magda,* which nevertheless has borrowed some of the more modern values of the social drama. Perhaps the grandest romantic play of our time, *Cyrano de Bergerac,* shows that, despite the noise and power of the naturalists and the Ibsenites, audiences could still be charmed by poetry and idealization. Another aspect of the movement away from mere rationality can be seen in Maeterlinck's play, and in the theories that governed its creation. And, rising independently, but soon to interact with the West, the Russian theatre is represented here by Chekhov.

These plays then, with those in the previous European volume, give the background from which the contemporary drama of America and England was still to emerge. Various in intention and method though they are, each of them has its important place, not merely in the history of the drama, but also in the mind and memory of every intelligent worker in the theatre to-day. Before to-day could be what it is, these must have been.

E. B. W.<br>B. P.

## WORKING BOOK LIST IN THE DRAMA AND THEATRE, ESPECIALLY OF THE LATE NINETEENTH CENTURY


Archer, William: *Playmaking.* 1912.

Archer, William: *The Theatrical World.* 1894–1898.

Baker, G. P.: *Technique of the Drama.* 1915.

Balmforth, R.: *The Problem-Play and Its Influence.* 1928.

Chandler, F. W.: *Aspects of the Modern Drama.* 1914.

Chandler, F. W.: *Modern Continental Playwrights.* 1931.

Cheney, Sheldon: *Stage Decoration.* 1928.

Cheney, Sheldon: *The New Movement in the Theatre.* 1914.

Clark, B. H.: *A Study of the Modern Drama.* 1928.

Clark, B. H.: *European Theories of the Drama.* 1925.

Clark, B. H.: *The Continental Drama of Today.* 1914.

Courtney, W. L.: *The Idea of Tragedy.* 1900.

Dickinson, T. H.: *An Outline of Contemporary Drama.* 1927.

Doumic, R.: *De Scribe à Ibsen.* 1893.

Doumic, R.: *Essais sur le Théâtre Contemporain.* 1896.

Dukes, Ashley: *Drama.* 1926.

Dukes, Ashley: *Modern Dramatists.* 1912.

Faguet, Emile: *Drame ancien : Drame moderne.* 1898.

Filon, A.: *Modern French Drama.* 1898.

Friedmann, S.: *Das Deutsche Drama des neunzehnten Jahrhunderts.* 1903.

Fuerst, W. R., and Hume, S. J.: *Twentieth Century Stage Decoration.* 1928.

Gregor, J., and Fülöp-Miller, R.: *The Russian Theatre.* 1930.

Hale, E. E.: *Dramatists of Today.* 1911.

Hamilton, Clayton: *The Theory of the Theatre.* 1910.

Hughes, Glenn: *The Story of the Theatre.* 1928.

Huneker, James: *Iconoclasts.* 1905.
Jameson, Storm: *Modern Drama in Europe.* 1920.
Lemaître, Jules: *Theatrical Impressions.* 1924.
Lewisohn, Ludwig: *The Modern Drama.* 1915.
Matthews, Brander: *The Development of the Drama.* 1908.
Miller, Anna I.: *The Independent Theatre in Europe* 1931.
Nicoll, Allardyce: *The Development of the Theatre.* 1927.
Nicoll, Allardyce: *The Theory of Drama.* 1931.
Pollard, P.: *Masks and Minstrels of New Germany.* 1911.
Sarcey, F.: *Quarante Ans de Théâtre.* 1900.
Sayler, O. M.: *Inside the Moscow Art Theatre.* 1925.
Sayler, O. M.: *The Russian Theatre.* 1922.
Shaw, G. B.: *Dramatic Opinions and Essays.* 1907.
Stanislavsky, C.: *My Life in Art.* 1924.
Stoeckius, A.: *Naturalism in Recent German Drama.* 1903.
Stuart, D. C.: *The Development of Dramatic Art.* 1928.
Wiener, Leo: *The Contemporary Drama of Russia.* 1924.
Winter, W.: *The Wallet of Time.* 1913.
Witkowski: *German Drama in the Nineteenth Century.* 1909.

### Henrik Ibsen

Archer, William: Introductions to his editions of Ibsen. 1891. 1908. 1912.
Brandes, Georg: *Henrik Ibsen.* 1898.
Brandes, Georg: *Creative Spirits of the Nineteenth Century.* 1923.
Campbell, T. M.: *Hebbel, Ibsen, and the Analytic Exposition.*
Chater, A. G.: *From Ibsen's Workshop.* 1912.
Dowden, Edward: *Essays, Modern and Elizabethan.* 1910.
Firkins, I. T. E.: *Henrik Ibsen: a Bibliography of Criticism and Biography.* 1921.
Gosse, Edmund: *Henrik Ibsen.* 1907.
Heller, Otto: *Henrik Ibsen: Plays and Problems.* 1912.
Henderson, A.: *European Dramatists.* 1913.
Huneker, J.: *Egoists.* 1909.

Huneker, J.: *Ivory Apes and Peacocks.* 1915.
Ibsen, Henrik: *Letters.* 1905.
Koht, Halvdan: *Life of Henrik Ibsen.* 1931.
Lavrin, Janko: *Ibsen and His Creation.* 1921.
Lee, J.: *The Ibsen Secret.* 1907.
Merejkowski, D.: *The Life Work of Henrik Ibsen.* 1915.
Moses, M. J.: *Henrik Ibsen.* 1908.
Roberts, R. E.: *Henrik Ibsen.* 1912.
Shaw, G. B.: *The Quintessence of Ibsenism.* 1915.
Weigand, H. J.: *The Modern Ibsen.* 1925.
Zucker, A. E.: *Ibsen, the Master Builder.* 1929.

### Maurice Maeterlinck

Bithell, Jethro: *Life and Writings of Maurice Maeterlinck.* 1913.
Bithell, Jethro: *Contemporary Belgian Literature.* 1915.
Chesterton, G. K.: *Books and Personalities.* 1905.
Clark, Macdonald: *Maurice Maeterlinck.* 1915.
Courtney, W. L.: *The Development of Maurice Maeterlinck.* 1904.
Harry, Gerard: *Maurice Maeterlinck.* 1910.
Hills, E. C.: *Evolution of Maeterlinck's Dramatic Theory.* 1907.
Jackson, Holbrook: *Maurice Maeterlinck.* 1910.
Leblanc, Georgette: *Mes Souvenirs.* 1930.
Le Sidanier, L.: *Maurice Maeterlinck.* 1928.
Moses, M. J.: *Maurice Maeterlinck.* 1911.
Sturgis, G. F.: *The Psychology of Maeterlinck.* 1914.
Taylor, Una: *Maurice Maeterlinck.* 1914.
Thomas, Edward: *Maurice Maeterlinck.* 1911.
Turquet-Milnes, G.: *Some Modern Belgian Writers.* 1917.

### Hermann Sudermann

Busse, Kurt: *Hermann Sudermann, sein Werk und sein Leben.* 1927.
Harris, Frank: *Contemporary Portraits.* 1919.

Henderson, A.: *The Changing Drama.* 1919.

Hawerau, Waldemar: *Hermann Sudermann, eine kritische Studie.* 1898.

Seibel, George: *Hauptmann and Sudermann.* 1925.

### Edmond Rostand

Beerbohm, Max: *Around Theatres.* 1930.

Chandler, F. W.: *The Contemporary Drama of France.* 1920.

Clark, Barrett H.: *Contemporary French Dramatists.* 1915.

Eliot, T. S.: *The Sacred Wood.* 1921.

Faure, Paul: *Vingt Ans d'intimité avec Edmond Rostand.* 1928.

Grein, J. T.: *Premieres of the Year.* 1900.

Hamilton, C.: Preface to Brian Hooker's translation of *Cyrano de Bergerac.* 1924.

Phelps, W. L.: *Essays on Modern Dramatists.* 1921.

Smith, H. A.: *Main Currents of Modern French Drama.* 1926.

### Anton P. Chekhov

Bakshy, A.: *The Path of the Russian Stage.* 1918.

Chekhov, A. P.: *Letters of Anton Tchekoff to his Family and Friends,* tr. by Constance Garnett. 1920.

Chekhov, A. P.: *Letters on the Short Story, the Drama, and Other Literary Topics,* ed. by L. S. Friedland. 1924.

Efros, N.: *The Moscow Art Theatre, 1898–1923.* 1924.

Fell, Marian: Preface to *Plays of Anton Tchekoff, First Series.* 1912.

Fovitsky, A. L.: *The Moscow Art Theatre and Its Distinguishing Characteristics.* 1922.

Gerhardi, William: *Anton Chehov.* 1923.

Gorky, M.: *Reminiscences of Anton Chekhov,* tr. by S. S. Koteliansky and L. Woolf. 1921.

Koteliansky, S. S., and Tomlinson, P.: *Life and Letters of A. Tchekhov.* 1925.

Koteliansky, S. S.: Preface to *The Wood Demon.* 1926.

Koteliansky, S. S.: *Anton Tchekhov: Literary and Theatrical Reminiscences.* 1927.

Kropotkin, P.: *Russian Literature.* 1905.

Mirsky, D. S.: *Contemporary Russian Literature.* 1926.

Sayler, O. M.: *The Russian Theatre under the Revolution.* 1920.

Shestov, L.: *Anton Tchekhov and Other Essays*, tr. by S. S. Koteliansky and J. M. Murry. 1916.

West, Julius: Preface to *Plays by Anton Tchekoff, Second Series.* 1916.

## CONTENTS

# HEDDA GABLER

BY

HENRIK IBSEN

*Translated by* EDMUND GOSSE *and* WILLIAM ARCHER.

## Henrik Ibsen

b. 1828, Skien, Norway.
Apprenticed to an apothecary.
1850, University of Christiania. First play, *Catiline*, published.
1851, "Theater-poet" at Bergen.
1857, Manager and artistic adviser of theaters at Christiania.
1862, *Love's Comedy* violently criticized for its individualism.
1864, Pension refused him. He withdrew to Italy.
1866, *Brand* won him a poet's pension.
1868-1891, Resident in Germany.
1869, *The League of Youth,* the first of his modern prose dramas.
1877-1899, Period of the great social prose dramas.
1891-1906, In Christiania.
d. 1906.

## Plays

1850 *Catiline.*
1850 *The Viking's Barrow.*
1853 *St. John's Night.*
1855 *Lady Inger of Ostrat.*
1856 *The Feast of Solhaug.*
1857 *Olaf Liljekrans.*
1858 *Vikings of Helgeland.*
1862 *Love's Comedy.*
1864 *The Pretenders.*
1866 *Brand.*

1867 *Peer Gynt.*
1869 *The League of Youth.*
1873 *Emperor and Galilean.*
1877 *Pillars of Society.*
1879 *A Doll's House.*
1881 *Ghosts.*
1882 *An Enemy of the People.*
1884 *The Wild Duck.*
1886 *Rosmersholm.*
1888 *The Lady from the Sea.*
1890 *Hedda Gabler.*
1892 *The Master Builder.*
1894 *Little Eyolf.*
1896 *John Gabriel Borkman.*
1899 *When We Dead Awaken.*

## HEDDA GABLER

Ibsen wrote of *Hedda Gabler*: "My intention in giving it this name was to indicate that Hedda, as a personality, is to be regarded rather as her father's daughter than as her husband's wife. It was not my desire to deal in this play with so-called problems. What I principally wanted to do was to depict human beings, human emotions, and human destinies, upon a groundwork of certain of the social conditions and principles of the present day."

The strange qualities of the Ibsen mind and soul emerge amusingly and pathetically in the encounter that gave rise to *Hedda Gabler* and *The Master Builder*. In the autumn of 1889 Ibsen met Emilie Bardach, a miss of eighteen. He was sixty, married, a parent, and famous; she was pretty, gay, and a head-hunter. She came from Austria to meet and captivate him, and by smiling at him from a park bench as he passed on his walks, she aroused his timid interest. Thereafter they had long talks, always in public places, for Ibsen was careful. Yet he was impressed; one can imagine that short stiff figure, with the aureole of white fringe about the face and the spectacles glittering in the light, turned attentively toward the slight vivacious girl, chattering and posing for him—in the lobby of a hotel. She seems to have thought herself a "new" woman, an "Ibsen woman," in fact; and he must have been both fascinated and repelled at this embodiment of his influence. Here, in a way, was posterity, the judge to which every artist appeals, and it was already impregnated with what it thought were his ideas. Here he found the courage in action that he himself had always lacked and wished for, but it was directed and reenforced by a flippant ruthlessness. Emilie professed to wish never to marry; she would capture other women's husbands. Yet she strangely invited boredom: she was clever, she had talent for music and painting, but she would do nothing with them. She preferred to pose as mysterious, tired, aloof. Ibsen once wrote to her, sadly, "You and the Christmas season do not quite fit together."

But she fired his imagination. Since *The Wild Duck* the use of the symbol as substitute for actuality had been a growing habit with him. He had always used life itself as his material, but in his shyness and seclusion he had tended to take it second or third hand, and compensate for lack of closely observed outline by lending depth and shadow. Emilie Bardach, so closely listened to and studied, gave him actuality first hand. At least, she gave him a character, or rather many characters, for it may be guessed that she was the prototype not only of Hedda, but also of Hilda Wangel and even of Kaia Fosli. With his hard mind and stern artistic eye, he lifted from the living girl those qualities she had displayed in their variety to charm him, and poured each into its appropriate mold. She gave him no incident, to be sure; at eighteen, what incident could there be? But fortunately he heard, at about the same time, of a brilliant but dissipated young professor who lost a manuscript; of the wife of a composer who in jealousy burned her husband's just completed symphony; and of another wife who tempted her husband, cured of alcoholism, by leaving brandy in his room. Then came the fusion, and *Hedda Gabler*. As soon as he began work on the play, early in 1890, Ibsen forbade Emilie to write to him or see him. But he remembered her, and sent her a copy of *Hedda Gabler* as a Christmas gift.

For a discussion of Ibsen's development and significance as a dramatist, see the preface to *A Doll's House*, in *Contemporary Drama, European Plays*, volume 1.

## CHARACTERS

GEORGE TESMAN.[1]
HEDDA TESMAN, *his wife.*
MISS JULIANA TESMAN, *his aunt.*
MRS. ELVSTED.
JUDGE[2] BRACK.
EILERT LÖVBORG.
BERTA, *servant at the Tesmans.*

*The scene of the action is Tesman's villa, in the west end of Christiania.*

[1] Tesman, whose Christian name in the original is "Jörgen," is described as "stipendiat i kulturhistorie"—that is to say, the holder of a scholarship for purposes of research into the History of Civilization.

[2] In the original "Assessor."

# HEDDA GABLER

## ACT FIRST

*A spacious, handsome, and tastefully furnished drawing-room, decorated in dark colors. In the back, a wide doorway with curtains drawn back, leading into a smaller room decorated in the same style as the drawing-room. In the right-hand wall of the front room, a folding door leading out to the hall. In the opposite wall, on the left, a glass door, also with curtains drawn back. Through the panes can be seen part of a veranda outside, and trees covered with autumn foliage. An oval table, with a cover on it, and surrounded by chairs, stands well forward. In front, by the wall on the right, a wide stove of dark porcelain, a high-backed arm-chair, a cushioned foot-rest, and two footstools. A settee, with a small round table in front of it, fills the upper right-hand corner. In front, on the left, a little way from the wall, a sofa. Further back than the glass door, a piano. On either side of the doorway at the back a what-not with terra-cotta and majolica ornaments.—Against the back wall of the inner room a sofa, with a table, and one or two chairs. Over the sofa hangs a portrait of a handsome elderly man in a General's uniform. Over the table a hanging lamp, with an opal glass shade. —A number of bouquets are arranged about the drawing-room, in vases and glasses. Others lie upon the tables. The floors in both rooms are cov-*

*ered with thick carpets.—Morning light. The sun shines in through the glass door.*

[MISS JULIANA TESMAN, *with her bonnet on and carrying a parasol, comes in from the hall, followed by* BERTA, *who carries a bouquet wrapped in paper.* MISS TESMAN *is a comely and pleasant-looking lady of about sixty-five. She is nicely but simply dressed in a gray walking-costume.* BERTA *is a middle-aged woman of plain and rather countrified appearance.*

MISS TESMAN. [*Stops close to the door, listens, and says softly.*] Upon my word, I don't believe they are stirring yet!

BERTA. [*Also softly.*] I told you so, Miss. Remember how late the steamboat got in last night. And then, when they got home!—good Lord, what a lot the young mistress had to unpack before she could get to bed.

MISS TESMAN. Well well—let them have their sleep out. But let us see that they get a good breath of the fresh morning air when they do appear.

[*She goes to the glass door and throws it open.*

BERTA. [*Beside the table, at a loss what to do with the bouquet in her hand.*] I declare there isn't a bit of room left. I think I'll put it down here, Miss.

[*She places it on the piano.*

MISS TESMAN. So you've got a new mistress now, my dear Berta. Heaven knows it was a wrench to me to part with you.

BERTA. [*On the point of weeping.*] And do you think it wasn't hard for me too, Miss? After all the blessed years I've been with you and Miss Rina.[1]

MISS TESMAN. We must make the best of it, Berta. There was nothing else to be done. George can't do

[1] Pronounce *Reena.*

without you, you see—he absolutely can't. He has had you to look after him ever since he was a little boy.

BERTA. Ah but, Miss Julia, I can't help thinking of Miss Rina lying helpless at home there, poor thing. And with only that new girl too! She'll never learn to take proper care of an invalid.

MISS TESMAN. Oh, I shall manage to train her. And of course, you know, I shall take most of it upon myself. You needn't be uneasy about my poor sister, my dear Berta.

BERTA. Well, but there's another thing, Miss. I'm so mortally afraid I shan't be able to suit the young mistress.

MISS TESMAN. Oh well—just at first there may be one or two things——

BERTA. Most like she'll be terrible grand in her ways.

MISS TESMAN. Well, you can't wonder at that—General Gabler's daughter! Think of the sort of life she was accustomed to in her father's time. Don't you remember how we used to see her riding down the road along with the General? In that long black habit—and with feathers in her hat?

BERTA. Yes indeed—I remember well enough!—But, good Lord, I should never have dreamt in those days that she and Master George would make a match of it.

MISS TESMAN. Nor I.—But by-the-bye, Berta—while I think of it: in future you mustn't say Master George. You must say Dr. Tesman.

BERTA. Yes, the young mistress spoke of that too—last night—the moment they set foot in the house. Is it true then, Miss?

MISS TESMAN. Yes, indeed it is. Only think, Berta—some foreign university has made him a doctor—

while he has been abroad, you understand. I hadn't heard a word about it, until he told me himself upon the pier.

BERTA. Well, well, he's clever enough for anything, he is. But I didn't think he'd have gone in for doctoring people too.

MISS TESMAN. No no, it's not that sort of doctor he is. [*Nods significantly.*] But let me tell you, we may have to call him something still grander before long.

BERTA. You don't say so! What can that be, Miss?

MISS TESMAN. [*Smiling.*] H'm—wouldn't you like to know! [*With emotion.*] Ah, dear, dear—if my poor brother could only look up from his grave now, and see what his little boy has grown into! [*Looks around.*] But bless me, Berta—why have you done this? Taken the chintz covers off all the furniture?

BERTA. The mistress told me to. She can't abide covers on the chairs, she says.

MISS TESMAN. Are they going to make this their everyday sitting-room then?

BERTA. Yes, that's what I understood—from the mistress. Master George—the doctor—he said nothing.

[GEORGE TESMAN *comes from the right into the inner room, humming to himself, and carrying an unstrapped empty portmanteau. He is a middle-sized, young-looking man of thirty-three, rather stout, with a round, open, cheerful face, fair hair and beard. He wears spectacles, and is somewhat carelessly dressed in comfortable indoor clothes.*

MISS TESMAN. Good morning, good morning, George.

TESMAN. [*In the doorway between the rooms.*] Aunt Julia! Dear Aunt Julia! [*Goes up to her and shakes hands warmly.*] Come all this way—so early! Eh?

MISS TESMAN. Why, of course I had to come and see how you were getting on.

TESMAN. In spite of your having had no proper night's rest?

MISS TESMAN. Oh, that makes no difference to me.

TESMAN. Well, I suppose you got home all right from the pier? Eh?

MISS TESMAN. Yes, quite safely, thank goodness. Judge Brack was good enough to see me right to my door.

TESMAN. We were so sorry we couldn't give you a seat in the carriage. But you saw what a pile of boxes Hedda had to bring with her.

MISS TESMAN. Yes, she had certainly plenty of boxes.

BERTA. [*To* TESMAN.] Shall I go in and see if there's anything I can do for the mistress?

TESMAN. No, thank you, Berta—you needn't. She said she would ring if she wanted anything.

BERTA. [*Going towards the right.*] Very well.

TESMAN. But look here—take this portmanteau with you.

BERTA. [*Taking it.*] I'll put it in the attic.

[*She goes out by the hall door.*

TESMAN. Fancy, Auntie—I had the whole of that portmanteau chock full of copies of documents. You wouldn't believe how much I have picked up from all the archives I have been examining—curious old details that no one has had any idea of——

MISS TESMAN. Yes, you don't seem to have wasted your time on your wedding trip, George.

TESMAN. No, that I haven't. But do take off your bonnet, Auntie. Look here! Let me untie the strings—eh?

MISS TESMAN. [*While he does so.*] Well, well—this is just as if you were still at home with us.

TESMAN. [*With the bonnet in his hand, looks at it from all sides.*] Why, what a gorgeous bonnet you've been investing in!

MISS TESMAN. I bought it on Hedda's account.

TESMAN. On Hedda's account? Eh?

MISS TESMAN. Yes, so that Hedda needn't be ashamed of me if we happened to go out together.

TESMAN. [*Patting her cheek.*] You always think of everything, Aunt Julia. [*Lays the bonnet on a chair beside the table.*] And now, look here—suppose we sit comfortably on the sofa and have a little chat, till Hedda comes.

[*They seat themselves. She places her parasol in the corner of the sofa.*

MISS TESMAN. [*Takes both his hands and looks at him.*] What a delight it is to have you again, as large as life, before my very eyes, George! My George—my poor brother's own boy!

TESMAN. And it's a delight for me, too, to see you again, Aunt Julia! You, who have been father and mother in one to me.

MISS TESMAN. Oh yes, I know you will always keep a place in your heart for your old aunts.

TESMAN. And what about Aunt Rina? No improvement—eh?

MISS TESMAN. Oh no—we can scarcely look for any improvement in her case, poor thing. There she lies, helpless, as she has lain for all these years. But heaven grant I may not lose her yet awhile! For if I did, I don't know what I should make of my life, George—especially now that I haven't you to look after any more.

TESMAN. [*Patting her back.*] There, there, there——!

MISS TESMAN. [*Suddenly changing her tone.*] And

to think that here are you a married man, George!—And that you should be the one to carry off Hedda Gabler—the beautiful Hedda Gabler! Only think of it—she, that was so beset with admirers!

TESMAN. [*Hums a little and smiles complacently.*] Yes, I fancy I have several good friends about town who would like to stand in my shoes—eh?

MISS TESMAN. And then this fine long wedding-tour you have had! More than five—nearly six months——

TESMAN. Well, for me it has been a sort of tour of research as well. I have had to do so much grubbing among old records—and to read no end of books too, Auntie.

MISS TESMAN. Oh yes, I suppose so. [*More confidentially, and lowering her voice a little.*] But listen now, George,—have you nothing—nothing special to tell me?

TESMAN. As to our journey?

MISS TESMAN. Yes.

TESMAN. No, I don't know of anything except what I have told you in my letters. I had a doctor's degree conferred on me—but that I told you yesterday.

MISS TESMAN. Yes, yes, you did. But what I mean is—haven't you any—any—expectations——?

TESMAN. Expectations?

MISS TESMAN. Why you know, George—I'm your old auntie!

TESMAN. Why, of course I have expectations.

MISS TESMAN. Ah!

TESMAN. I have every expectation of being a professor one of these days.

MISS TESMAN. Oh yes, a professor——

TESMAN. Indeed, I may say I am certain of it. But my dear Auntie—you know all about that already!

MISS TESMAN. [*Laughing to herself.*] Yes, of course I do. You are quite right there. [*Changing the subject.*] But we were talking about your journey. It must have cost a great deal of money, George?

TESMAN. Well, you see—my handsome traveling-scholarship went a good way.

MISS TESMAN. But I can't understand how you can have made it go far enough for two.

TESMAN. No, that's not so easy to understand—eh?

MISS TESMAN. And especially traveling with a lady —they tell me that makes it ever so much more expensive.

TESMAN. Yes, of course—it makes it a little more expensive. But Hedda had to have this trip, Auntie. She really had to. Nothing else would have done.

MISS TESMAN. No, no, I suppose not. A wedding-tour seems to be quite indispensable nowadays.—But tell me now—have you gone thoroughly over the house yet?

TESMAN. Yes, you may be sure I have. I have been afoot ever since daylight.

MISS TESMAN. And what do you think of it all?

TESMAN. I'm delighted! Quite delighted! Only I can't think what we are to do with the two empty rooms between this inner parlor and Hedda's bedroom.

MISS TESMAN. [*Laughing.*] Oh my dear George, I daresay you may find some use for them—in the course of time.

TESMAN. Why of course, you are quite right, Aunt Julia! You mean as my library increases—eh?

MISS TESMAN. Yes, quite so, my dear boy. It was your library I was thinking of.

TESMAN. I am specially pleased on Hedda's account. Often and often, before we were engaged, she said that she would never care to live anywhere but in Secretary Falk's villa.[1]

MISS TESMAN. Yes, it was lucky that this very house should come into the market, just after you had started.

TESMAN. Yes, Aunt Julia, the luck was on our side, wasn't it—eh?

MISS TESMAN. But the expense, my dear George! You will find it very expensive, all this.

TESMAN. [*Looks at her, a little cast down.*] Yes, I suppose I shall, Aunt!

MISS TESMAN. Oh, frightfully!

TESMAN. How much do you think? In round numbers?—Eh?

MISS TESMAN. Oh, I can't even guess until all the accounts come in.

TESMAN. Well, fortunately, Judge Brack has secured the most favorable terms for me,—so he said in a letter to Hedda.

MISS TESMAN. Yes, don't be uneasy, my dear boy.—Besides, I have given security for the furniture and all the carpets.

TESMAN. Security? You? My dear Aunt Julia—what sort of security could you give?

MISS TESMAN. I have given a mortgage on our annuity.

TESMAN. [*Jumps up.*] What! On your—and Aunt Rina's annuity!

MISS TESMAN. Yes, I knew of no other plan, you see.

TESMAN. [*Placing himself before her.*] Have you gone out of your senses, Auntie! Your annuity—it's all that you and Aunt Rina have to live upon.

MISS TESMAN. Well, well—don't get so excited about

[1] In the original, "Statsrådinde Falks villa"—showing that it had belonged to the widow of a cabinet minister.

it. It's only a matter of form you know—Judge Brack assured me of that. It was he that was kind enough to arrange the whole affair for me. A mere matter of form, he said.

TESMAN. Yes, that may be all very well. But nevertheless——

MISS TESMAN. You will have your own salary to depend upon now. And, good heavens, even if we did have to pay up a little——! To eke things out a bit at the start——! Why, it would be nothing but a pleasure to us.

TESMAN. Oh Auntie—will you never be tired of making sacrifices for me!

MISS TESMAN. [*Rises and lays her hand on his shoulders.*] Have I any other happiness in this world except to smooth your way for you, my dear boy? You, who have had neither father nor mother to depend on. And now we have reached the goal, George! Things have looked black enough for us, sometimes; but, thank heaven, now you have nothing to fear.

TESMAN. Yes, it is really marvellous how everything has turned out for the best.

MISS TESMAN. And the people who opposed you—who wanted to bar the way for you—now you have them at your feet. They have fallen, George. Your most dangerous rival—his fall was the worst.—And now he has to lie on the bed he has made for himself—poor misguided creature.

TESMAN. Have you heard anything of Eilert? Since I went away, I mean.

MISS TESMAN. Only that he is said to have published a new book.

TESMAN. What! Eilert Lövborg! Recently—eh?

MISS TESMAN. Yes, so they say. Heaven knows whether it can be worth anything! Ah, when your new book appears—that will be another story, George! What is it to be about?

TESMAN. It will deal with the domestic industries of Brabant during the Middle Ages.

MISS TESMAN. Fancy—to be able to write on such a subject as that!

TESMAN. However, it may be some time before the book is ready. I have all these collections to arrange first, you see.

MISS TESMAN. Yes, collecting and arranging—no one can beat you at that. There you are my poor brother's own son.

TESMAN. I am looking forward eagerly to setting to work at it; especially now that I have my own delightful home to work in.

MISS TESMAN. And, most of all, now that you have got the wife of your heart, my dear George.

TESMAN. [*Embracing her.*] Oh yes, yes, Aunt Julia! Hedda—she is the best part of it all! [*Looks towards the doorway.*] I believe I hear her coming—eh?

[HEDDA *enters from the left through the inner room. She is a woman of nine-and-twenty. Her face and figure show refinement and distinction. Her complexion is pale and opaque. Her steel-gray eyes express a cold, unruffled repose. Her hair is of an agreeable medium brown, but not particularly abundant. She is dressed in a tasteful, somewhat loose-fitting morning gown.*

MISS TESMAN. [*Going to meet* HEDDA.] Good morning, my dear Hedda! Good morning, and a hearty welcome.

HEDDA. [*Holds out her hand.*] Good morning, dear Miss Tesman! So early a call! That is kind of you.

MISS TESMAN. [*With some embarrassment.*] Well—has the bride slept well in her new home?

HEDDA. Oh yes, thanks. Passably.

TESMAN. [*Laughing.*] Passably! Come, that's good, Hedda! You were sleeping like a stone when I got up.

HEDDA. Fortunately. Of course one has always to accustom one's self to new surroundings, Miss Tesman—little by little. [*Looking towards the left.*] Oh—there the servant has gone and opened the veranda door, and let in a whole flood of sunshine.

MISS TESMAN. [*Going towards the door.*] Well, then we will shut it.

HEDDA. No no, not that! Tesman, please draw the curtains. That will give a softer light.

TESMAN. [*At the door.*] All right—all right.—There now, Hedda, now you have both shade and fresh air.

HEDDA. Yes, fresh air we certainly must have, with all these stacks of flowers——. But—won't you sit down, Miss Tesman?

MISS TESMAN. No, thank you. Now that I have seen that everything is all right here—thank heaven!—I must be getting home again. My sister is lying longing for me, poor thing.

TESMAN. Give her my very best love, Auntie; and say I shall look in and see her later in the day.

MISS TESMAN. Yes, yes, I'll be sure to tell her. But by-the-bye, George—[*Feeling in her dress pocket*]—I had almost forgotten—I have something for you here.

TESMAN. What is it, Auntie? Eh?

MISS TESMAN. [*Produces a flat parcel wrapped in newspaper and hands it to him.*] Look here, my dear boy.

TESMAN. [*Opening the parcel.*] Well, I declare!—Have you really saved them for me, Aunt Julia! Hedda! isn't this touching—eh?

HEDDA. [*Beside the whatnot on the right.*] Well, what is it?

TESMAN. My old morning-shoes! My slippers.

HEDDA. Indeed. I remember you often spoke of them while we were abroad.

TESMAN. Yes, I missed them terribly. [*Goes up to her.*] Now you shall see them, Hedda!

HEDDA. [*Going towards the stove.*] Thanks, I really don't care about it.

TESMAN. [*Following her.*] Only think—ill as she was, Aunt Rina embroidered these for me. Oh you can't think how many associations cling to them.

HEDDA. [*At the table.*] Scarcely for me.

MISS TESMAN. Of course not for Hedda, George.

TESMAN. Well, but now that she belongs to the family, I thought——

HEDDA. [*Interrupting.*] We shall never get on with this servant, Tesman.

MISS TESMAN. Not get on with Berta?

TESMAN. Why, dear, what puts that in your head? Eh?

HEDDA. [*Pointing.*] Look there! She has left her old bonnet lying about on a chair.

TESMAN. [*In consternation, drops the slippers on the floor.*] Why, Hedda——

HEDDA. Just fancy, if any one should come in and see it!

TESMAN. But Hedda—that's Aunt Julia's bonnet.

HEDDA. Is it!

MISS TESMAN. [*Taking up the bonnet.*] Yes, indeed it's mine. And, what's more, it's not old, Madam Hedda.

HEDDA. I really did not look closely at it, Miss Tesman.

MISS TESMAN. [*Tying on the bonnet.*] Let me tell

you it's the first time I have worn it—the very first time.

TESMAN. And a very nice bonnet it is too—quite a beauty!

MISS TESMAN. Oh, it's no such great thing, George. [*Looks around her.*] My parasol——? Ah, here. [*Takes it.*] For this is mine too—[*mutters*]—not Berta's.

TESMAN. A new bonnet and a new parasol! Only think, Hedda!

HEDDA. Very handsome indeed.

TESMAN. Yes, isn't it? Eh? But Auntie, take a good look at Hedda before you go! See how handsome she is!

MISS TESMAN. Oh, my dear boy, there's nothing new in that. Hedda was always lovely.

[*She nods and goes towards the right.*

TESMAN. [*Following.*] Yes, but have you noticed what splendid condition she is in? How she has filled out on the journey?

HEDDA. [*Crossing the room.*] Oh, do be quiet——!

MISS TESMAN. [*Who has stopped and turned.*] Filled out?

TESMAN. Of course you don't notice it so much now that she has that dress on. But I, who can see——

HEDDA. [*At the glass door, impatiently.*] Oh, you can't see anything.

TESMAN. It must be the mountain air in the Tyrol——

HEDDA. [*Curtly, interrupting.*] I am exactly as I was when I started.

TESMAN. So you insist; but I'm quite certain you are not. Don't you agree with me, Auntie?

MISS TESMAN. [*Who has been gazing at her with folded hands.*] Hedda is lovely—lovely—lovely. [*Goes *up to her, takes her head between both hands, draws it downwards, and kisses her hair.*] God bless and preserve Hedda Tesman—for George's sake.

HEDDA. [*Gently freeing herself.*] Oh—! Let me go.

MISS TESMAN. [*In quiet emotion.*] I shall not let a day pass without coming to see you.

TESMAN. No, you won't, will you, Auntie? Eh?

MISS TESMAN. Good-bye—good-bye!

[*She goes out by the hall door.* TESMAN *accompanies her. The door remains half open.* TESMAN *can be heard repeating his message to Aunt Rina and his thanks for the slippers.*

[*In the meantime,* HEDDA *walks about the room, raising her arms and clenching her hands as if in desperation. Then she flings back the curtains from the glass door, and stands there looking out.*

[*Presently* TESMAN *returns and closes the door behind him.*

TESMAN. [*Picks up the slippers from the floor.*] What are you looking at, Hedda?

HEDDA. [*Once more calm and mistress of herself.*] I am only looking at the leaves. They are so yellow—so withered.

TESMAN. [*Wraps up the slippers and lays them on the table.*] Well you see, we are well into September now.

HEDDA. [*Again restless.*] Yes, to think of it!—Already in—in September.

TESMAN. Don't you think Aunt Julia's manner was strange, dear? Almost solemn? Can you imagine what was the matter with her? Eh?

HEDDA. I scarcely know her, you see. Is she not often like that?

TESMAN. No, not as she was to-day.

HEDDA. [*Leaving the glass door.*] Do you think she was annoyed about the bonnet?

TESMAN. Oh, scarcely at all. Perhaps a little, just at the moment——

HEDDA. But what an idea, to pitch her bonnet about in the drawing-room! No one does that sort of thing.

TESMAN. Well, you may be sure Aunt Julia won't do it again.

HEDDA. In any case, I shall manage to make my peace with her.

TESMAN. Yes, my dear, good Hedda, if you only would.

HEDDA. When you call this afternoon, you might invite her to spend the evening here.

TESMAN. Yes, that I will. And there's one thing more you could do that would delight her heart.

HEDDA. What is it?

TESMAN. If you could only prevail on yourself to say *du*[1] to her. For my sake, Hedda? Eh?

HEDDA. No no, Tesman—you really mustn't ask that of me. I have told you so already. I shall try to call her "Aunt"; and you must be satisfied with that.

TESMAN. Well well. Only I think now that you belong to the family, you——

HEDDA. H'm—I can't in the least see why——

[*She goes up towards the middle doorway.*

TESMAN. [*After a pause.*] Is there anything the matter with you, Hedda? Eh?

HEDDA. I'm only looking at my old piano. It doesn't go at all well with all the other things.

TESMAN. The first time I draw my salary, we'll see about exchanging it.

[1] *Du* = thou; Tesman means, "If you could persuade yourself to *tutoyer* her."

HEDDA. No, no—no exchanging. I don't want to part with it. Suppose we put it there in the inner room, and then get another here in its place. When it's convenient, I mean.

TESMAN. [*A little taken aback.*] Yes—of course we could do that.

HEDDA. [*Takes up the bouquet from the piano.*] These flowers were not here last night when we arrived.

TESMAN. Aunt Julia must have brought them for you.

HEDDA. [*Examining the bouquet.*] A visiting-card. [*Takes it out and reads:*] "Shall return later in the day." Can you guess whose card it is?

TESMAN. No. Whose? Eh?

HEDDA. The name is "Mrs. Elvsted."

TESMAN. Is it really? Sheriff Elvsted's wife? Miss Rysing that was.

HEDDA. Exactly. The girl with the irritating hair, that she was always showing off. An old flame of yours, I've been told.

TESMAN. [*Laughing.*] Oh, that didn't last long; and it was before I knew you, Hedda. But fancy her being in town!

HEDDA. It's odd that she should call upon us. I have scarcely seen her since we left school.

TESMAN. I haven't seen her either for—heaven knows how long. I wonder how she can endure to live in such an out-of-the-way-hole—eh?

HEDDA. [*After a moment's thought, says suddenly.*] Tell me, Tesman—isn't it somewhere near there that he—that—Eilert Lövborg is living?

TESMAN. Yes, he is somewhere in that part of the country.

[BERTA *enters by the hall door.*

BERTA. That lady, ma'am, that brought some flowers a little while ago, is here again. [*Pointing.*] The flowers you have in your hand, ma'am.

HEDDA. Ah, is she? Well, please show her in.

[BERTA *opens the door for* MRS. ELVSTED, *and goes out herself.*—MRS. ELVSTED *is a woman of fragile figure, with pretty, soft features. Her eyes are light blue, large, round, and somewhat prominent, with a startled, inquiring expression. Her hair is remarkably light, almost flaxen, and unusually abundant and wavy. She is a couple of years younger than* HEDDA. *She wears a dark visiting dress, tasteful, but not quite in the latest fashion.*

HEDDA. [*Receives her warmly.*] How do you do, my dear Mrs. Elvsted? It's delightful to see you again.

MRS. ELVSTED. [*Nervously, struggling for self-control.*] Yes, it's a very long time since we met.

TESMAN. [*Gives her his hand.*] And we too—eh?

HEDDA. Thanks for your lovely flowers——

MRS. ELVSTED. Oh, not at all——. I would have come straight here yesterday afternoon; but I heard that you were away——

TESMAN. Have you just come to town? Eh?

MRS. ELVSTED. I arrived yesterday, about midday. Oh, I was quite in despair when I heard that you were not at home.

HEDDA. In despair! How so?

TESMAN. Why, my dear Mrs. Rysing—I mean Mrs. Elvsted——

HEDDA. I hope that you are not in any trouble?

MRS. ELVSTED. Yes, I am. And I don't know another living creature here that I can turn to.

HEDDA. [*Laying the bouquet on the table.*] Come—let us sit here on the sofa——

MRS. ELVSTED. Oh, I am too restless to sit down.

HEDDA. Oh no, you're not. Come here.

[*She draws* MRS. ELVSTED *down upon the sofa and sits at her side.*

TESMAN. Well? What is it, Mrs. Elvsted——?

HEDDA. Has anything particular happened to you at home?

MRS. ELVSTED. Yes—and no. Oh—I am so anxious you should not misunderstand me——

HEDDA. Then your best plan is to tell us the whole story, Mrs. Elvsted.

TESMAN. I suppose that's what you have come for—eh?

MRS. ELVSTED. Yes, yes—of course it is. Well then, I must tell you—if you don't already know—that Eilert Lövborg is in town, too.

HEDDA. Lövborg——!

TESMAN. What! Has Eilert Lövborg come back? Fancy that, Hedda!

HEDDA. Well well—I hear it.

MRS. ELVSTED. He has been here a week already. Just fancy—a whole week! In this terrible town, alone! With so many temptations on all sides.

HEDDA. But, my dear Mrs. Elvsted—how does *he* concern you so much?

MRS. ELVSTED. [*Looks at her with a startled air, and says rapidly.*] He was the children's tutor.

HEDDA. Your children's?

MRS. ELVSTED. My husband's. I have none.

HEDDA. Your step-children's, then?

MRS. ELVSTED. Yes.

TESMAN. [*Somewhat hesitatingly.*] Then was he—I don't know how to express it—was he—regular enough in his habits to be fit for the post? Eh?

Mrs. Elvsted. For the last two years his conduct has been irreproachable.

Tesman. Has it indeed? Fancy that, Hedda!

Hedda. I hear it.

Mrs. Elvsted. Perfectly irreproachable, I assure you! In every respect. But all the same—now that I know he is here—in this great town—and with a large sum of money in his hands—I can't help being in mortal fear for him.

Tesman. Why did he not remain where he was? With you and your husband? Eh?

Mrs. Elvsted. After his book was published he was too restless and unsettled to remain with us.

Tesman. Yes, by-the-bye, Aunt Julia told me he had published a new book.

Mrs. Elvsted. Yes, a big book, dealing with the march of civilization—in broad outline, as it were. It came out about a fortnight ago. And since it has sold so well, and been so much read—and made such a sensation——

Tesman. Has it indeed? It must be something he has had lying by since his better days.

Mrs. Elvsted. Long ago, you mean?

Tesman. Yes.

Mrs. Elvsted. No, he has written it all since he has been with us—within the last year.

Tesman. Isn't that good news, Hedda? Think of that!

Mrs. Elvsted. Ah yes, if only it would last!

Hedda. Have you seen him here in town?

Mrs. Elvsted. No, not yet. I have had the greatest difficulty in finding out his address. But this morning I discovered it at last.

Hedda. [*Looks searchingly at her.*] Do you know, it seems to me a little odd of your husband—h'm——

MRS. ELVSTED. [*Starting nervously.*] Of my husband! What?

HEDDA. That he should send *you* to town on such an errand—that he does not come himself and look after his friend.

MRS. ELVSTED. Oh no, no—my husband has no time. And besides, I—I had some shopping to do.

HEDDA. [*With a slight smile.*] Ah, that is a different matter.

MRS. ELVSTED. [*Rising quickly and uneasily.*] And now I beg and implore you, Mr. Tesman—receive Eilert Lövborg kindly if he comes to you! And that he is sure to do. You see you were such great friends in the old days. And then you are interested in the same studies—the same branch of science—so far as I can understand.

TESMAN. We used to be, at any rate.

MRS. ELVSTED. That is why I beg so earnestly that you—you too—will keep a sharp eye upon him. Oh, you will promise me that, Mr. Tesman—won't you?

TESMAN. With the greatest of pleasure, Mrs. Rysing——

HEDDA. Elvsted.

TESMAN. I assure you I shall do all I possibly can for Eilert. You may rely upon me.

MRS. ELVSTED. Oh, how very, very kind of you! [*Presses his hands.*] Thanks, thanks, thanks! [*Frightened.*] You see, my husband is so very fond of him!

HEDDA. [*Rising.*] You ought to write to him, Tesman. Perhaps he may not care to come to you of his own accord.

TESMAN. Well, perhaps it would be the right thing to do, Hedda? Eh?

HEDDA. And the sooner the better. Why not at once?

MRS. ELVSTED. [*Imploringly.*] Oh, if you only would!

TESMAN. I'll write this moment. Have you his address, Mrs.—Mrs. Elvsted?

MRS. ELVSTED. Yes. [*Takes a slip of paper from her pocket and hands it to him.*] Here it is.

TESMAN. Good, good. Then I'll go in—— [*Looks about him.*] By-the-bye,—my slippers? Oh, here.

[*Takes the packet, and is about to go.*

HEDDA. Be sure you write him a cordial, friendly letter. And a good long one too.

TESMAN. Yes, I will.

MRS. ELVSTED. But please, please don't say a word to show that I have suggested it.

TESMAN. No, how could you think I would? Eh?

[*He goes out to the right, through the inner room.*

HEDDA. [*Goes up to* MRS. ELVSTED, *smiles, and says in a low voice.*] There! We have killed two birds with one stone.

MRS. ELVSTED. What do you mean?

HEDDA. Could you not see that I wanted him to go?

MRS. ELVSTED. Yes, to write the letter——

HEDDA. And that I might speak to you alone.

MRS. ELVSTED. [*Confused.*] About the same thing?

HEDDA. Precisely.

MRS. ELVSTED. [*Apprehensively.*] But there is nothing more, Mrs. Tesman! Absolutely nothing!

HEDDA. Oh yes, but there is. There is a great deal more—I can see that. Sit here—and we'll have a cosy, confidential chat.

[*She forces* MRS. ELVSTED *to sit in the easy-chair beside the stove, and seats herself on one of the footstools.*

MRS. ELVSTED. [*Anxiously, looking at her watch.*]

But, my dear Mrs. Tesman—I was really on the point of going.

HEDDA. Oh, you can't be in such a hurry.—Well? Now tell me something about your life at home.

MRS. ELVSTED. Oh, that is just what I care least to speak about.

HEDDA. But to me, dear——? Why, weren't we schoolfellows?

MRS. ELVSTED. Yes, but you were in the class above me. Oh, how dreadfully afraid of you I was then!

HEDDA. Afraid of me?

MRS. ELVSTED. Yes, dreadfully. For when we met on the stairs you used always to pull my hair.

HEDDA. Did I, really?

MRS. ELVSTED. Yes, and once you said you would burn it off my head.

HEDDA. Oh that was all nonsense, of course.

MRS. ELVSTED. Yes, but I was so silly in those days. —And since then, too—we have drifted so far—far apart from each other. Our circles have been so entirely different.

HEDDA. Well then, we must try to drift together again. Now listen! At school we said *du* to each other; and we called each other by our Christian names——

MRS. ELVSTED. No, I am sure you must be mistaken.

HEDDA. No, not at all! I can remember quite distinctly. So now we are going to renew our old friendship. [*Draws the footstool close to* MRS. ELVSTED.] There now! [*Kisses her cheek.*] You must say *du* to me and call me Hedda.

MRS. ELVSTED. [*Presses and pats her hands.*] Oh, how good and kind you are! I am not used to such kindness.

HEDDA. There, there, there! And I shall say *du* to you, as in the old days, and call you my dear Thora.

MRS. ELVSTED. My name is Thea.[1]

HEDDA. Why, of course! I meant Thea. [*Looks at her compassionately.*] So you are not accustomed to goodness and kindness, Thea? Not in your own home?

MRS. ELVSTED. Oh, if I only had a home! But I haven't any; I have never had a home.

HEDDA. [*Looks at her for a moment.*] I almost suspected as much.

MRS. ELVSTED. [*Gazing helplessly before her.*] Yes—yes—yes.

HEDDA. I don't quite remember—was it not as housekeeper that you first went to Mr. Elvsted's?

MRS. ELVSTED. I really went as governess. But his wife—his late wife—was an invalid,—and rarely left her room. So I had to look after the housekeeping as well.

HEDDA. And then—at last—you became mistress of the house.

MRS. ELVSTED. [*Sadly.*] Yes, I did.

HEDDA. Let me see—about how long ago was that?

MRS. ELVSTED. My marriage?

HEDDA. Yes.

MRS. ELVSTED. Five years ago.

HEDDA. To be sure; it must be that.

MRS. ELVSTED. Oh those five years——! Or at all events the last two or three of them! Oh, if you[2] could only imagine——

HEDDA. [*Giving her a little slap on the hand.*] *De?* Fie, Thea!

MRS. ELVSTED. Yes, yes, I will try—— Well, if—you could only imagine and understand——

[1] Pronounce *Tora* and *Taya.*

[2] Mrs. Elvsted here uses the formal pronoun *De,* whereupon Hedda rebukes her. In her next speech Mrs. Elvsted says *du.*

Hedda. [*Lightly.*] Eilert Lövborg has been in your neighborhood about three years, hasn't he?

Mrs. Elvsted. [*Looks at her doubtfully.*] Eilert Lövborg? Yes—he has.

Hedda. Had you known him before, in town here?

Mrs. Elvsted. Scarcely at all. I mean—I knew him by name of course.

Hedda. But you saw a good deal of him in the country?

Mrs. Elvsted. Yes, he came to us every day. You see, he gave the children lessons; for in the long run I couldn't manage it all myself.

Hedda. No, that's clear.—And your husband——? I suppose he is often away from home?

Mrs. Elvsted. Yes. Being sheriff, you know, he has to travel about a good deal in his district.

Hedda. [*Leaning against the arm of the chair.*] Thea—my poor, sweet Thea—now you must tell me everything—exactly as it stands.

Mrs. Elvsted. Well then, you must question me.

Hedda. What sort of a man is your husband, Thea? I mean—you know—in everyday life. Is he kind to you?

Mrs. Elvsted. [*Evasively.*] I am sure he means well in everything.

Hedda. I should think he must be altogether too old for you. There is at least twenty years' difference between you, is there not?

Mrs. Elvsted. [*Irritably.*] Yes, that is true, too. Everything about him is repellent to me! We have not a thought in common. We have no single point of sympathy—he and I.

Hedda. But is he not fond of you all the same? In his own way?

Mrs. Elvsted. Oh I really don't know. I think he

regards me simply as a useful property. And then it doesn't cost much to keep me. I am not expensive.

Hedda. That is stupid of you.

Mrs. Elvsted. [*Shakes her head.*] It cannot be otherwise—not with him. I don't think he really cares for any one but himself—and perhaps a little for the children.

Hedda. And for Eilert Lövborg, Thea.

Mrs. Elvsted. [*Looking at her.*] For Eilert Lövborg? What puts that into your head?

Hedda. Well, my dear—I should say, when he sends you after him all the way to town—— [*Smiling almost imperceptibly.*] And besides, you said so yourself, to Tesman.

Mrs. Elvsted. [*With a little nervous twitch.*] Did I? Yes, I suppose I did. [*Vehemently, but not loudly.*] No—I may just as well make a clean breast of it at once! For it must all come out in any case.

Hedda. Why, my dear Thea——?

Mrs. Elvsted. Well, to make a long story short: My husband did not know that I was coming.

Hedda. What! Your husband didn't know it!

Mrs. Elvsted. No, of course not. For that matter, he was away from home himself—he was traveling. Oh, I could bear it no longer, Hedda! I couldn't indeed—so utterly alone as I should have been in the future.

Hedda. Well? And then?

Mrs. Elvsted. So I put together some of my things—what I needed most—as quietly as possible. And then I left the house.

Hedda. Without a word?

Mrs. Elvsted. Yes—and took the train straight to town.

Hedda. Why, my dear, good Thea—to think of you daring to do it!

MRS. ELVSTED. [*Rises and moves about the room.*] What else could I possibly do?

HEDDA. But what do you think your husband will say when you go home again?

MRS. ELVSTED. [*At the table, looks at her.*] Back to *him*?

HEDDA. Of course.

MRS. ELVSTED. I shall never go back to him again.

HEDDA. [*Rising and going towards her.*] Then you have left your home—for good and all?

MRS. ELVSTED. Yes. There was nothing else to be done.

HEDDA. But then—to take flight so openly.

MRS. ELVSTED. Oh, it's impossible to keep things of that sort secret.

HEDDA. But what do you think people will say of you, Thea?

MRS. ELVSTED. They may say what they like, for aught *I* care. [*Seats herself wearily and sadly on the sofa.*] I have done nothing but what I *had* to do.

HEDDA. [*After a short silence.*] And what are your plans now? What do you think of doing?

MRS. ELVSTED. I don't know yet. I only know this, that I must live here, where Eilert Lövborg is—if I am to live at all.

HEDDA. [*Takes a chair from the table, seats herself beside her, and strokes her hands.*] My dear Thea—how did this—this friendship—between you and Eilert Lövborg come about?

MRS. ELVSTED. Oh it grew up gradually. I gained a sort of influence over him.

HEDDA. Indeed?

MRS. ELVSTED. He gave up his old habits. Not because I asked him to, for I never dared do that. But of course he saw how repulsive they were to me; and so he dropped them.

HEDDA. [*Concealing an involuntary smile of scorn.*] Then you have reclaimed him—as the saying goes—my little Thea.

MRS. ELVSTED. So he says himself, at any rate. And he, on his side, has made a real human being of me—taught me to think, and to understand so many things.

HEDDA. Did he give *you* lessons too, then?

MRS. ELVSTED. No, not exactly lessons. But he talked to me—talked about such an infinity of things. And then came the lovely, happy time when I began to share in his work—when he allowed me to help him!

HEDDA. Oh he did, did he?

MRS. ELVSTED. Yes! He never wrote anything without my assistance.

HEDDA. You were two good comrades, in fact?

MRS. ELVSTED. [*Eagerly.*] Comrades! Yes, fancy, Hedda—that is the very word he used!—Oh, I ought to feel perfectly happy; and yet I cannot; for I don't know how long it will last.

HEDDA. Are you no surer of him than that?

MRS. ELVSTED. [*Gloomily.*] A woman's shadow stands between Eilert Lövborg and me.

HEDDA. [*Looks at her anxiously.*] Who can *that* be?

MRS. ELVSTED. I don't know. Some one he knew in his—in his past. Some one he has never been able wholly to forget.

HEDDA. What has he told you—about this?

MRS. ELVSTED. He has only once—quite vaguely—alluded to it.

HEDDA. Well! And what did he say?

MRS. ELVSTED. He said that when they parted, she threatened to shoot him with a pistol.

HEDDA. [*With cold composure.*] Oh nonsense! No one does that sort of thing here.

MRS. ELVSTED. No. And that is why I think it must have been that red-haired singing-woman whom he once——

HEDDA. Yes, very likely.

MRS. ELVSTED. For I remember they used to say of her that she carried loaded firearms.

HEDDA. Oh—then of course it must have been she.

MRS. ELVSTED. [*Wringing her hands.*] And now just fancy, Hedda—I hear that this singing-woman—that she is in town again! Oh, I don't know what to do——

HEDDA. [*Glancing towards the inner room.*] Hush! Here comes Tesman. [*Rises and whispers.*] Thea—all this must remain between you and me.

MRS. ELVSTED. [*Springing up.*] Oh yes—yes! For heaven's sake——!

[GEORGE TESMAN, *with a letter in his hand, comes from the right through the inner room.*

TESMAN. There now—the epistle is finished.

HEDDA. That's right. And now Mrs. Elvsted is just going. Wait a moment—I'll go with you to the garden gate.

TESMAN. Do you think Berta could post the letter, Hedda dear?

HEDDA. [*Takes it.*] I will tell her to.

[BERTA *enters from the hall.*

BERTA. Judge Brack wishes to know if Mrs. Tesman will receive him.

HEDDA. Yes, ask Judge Brack to come in. And look here—put this letter in the post.

BERTA. [*Taking the letter.*] Yes, ma'am.

[*She opens the door for* JUDGE BRACK *and goes out herself.* BRACK *is a man of forty-five; thick-*

*set, but well-built and elastic in his movements. His face is roundish with an aristocratic profile. His hair is short, still almost black, and carefully dressed. His eyes are lively and sparkling. His eyebrows thick. His moustaches are also thick, with short-cut ends. He wears a well-cut walking-suit, a little too youthful for his age. He uses an eye-glass, which he now and then lets drop.*

JUDGE BRACK. [*With his hat in his hand, bowing.*] May one venture to call so early in the day?

HEDDA. Of course one may.

TESMAN. [*Presses his hand.*] You are welcome at any time. [*Introducing him.*] Judge Brack—Miss Rysing——

HEDDA. Oh——!

BRACK. [*Bowing.*] Ah—delighted——

HEDDA. [*Looks at him and laughs.*] It's nice to have a look at you by daylight, Judge!

BRACK. Do you find me—altered?

HEDDA. A little younger, I think.

BRACK. Thank you so much.

TESMAN. But what do you think of Hedda—eh? Doesn't she look flourishing? She has actually——

HEDDA. Oh, do leave me alone. You haven't thanked Judge Brack for all the trouble he has taken——

BRACK. Oh, nonsense—it was a pleasure to me——

HEDDA. Yes, you are a friend indeed. But here stands Thea all impatience to be off—so *au revoir*, Judge. I shall be back again presently.

[*Mutual salutations.* MRS. ELVSTED *and* HEDDA *go out by the hall door.*

BRACK. Well,—is your wife tolerably satisfied——

TESMAN. Yes, we can't thank you sufficiently. Of course she talks of a little re-arrangement here and there; and one or two things are still wanting. We shall have to buy some additional trifles.

BRACK. Indeed!

TESMAN. But we won't trouble you about these things. Hedda says she herself will look after what is wanting.—Shan't we sit down? Eh?

BRACK. Thanks, for a moment. [*Seats himself beside the table.*] There is something I wanted to speak to you about, my dear Tesman.

TESMAN. Indeed? Ah, I understand! [*Seating himself.*] I suppose it's the serious part of the frolic that is coming now. Eh?

BRACK. Oh, the money question is not so very pressing; though, for that matter, I wish we had gone a little more economically to work.

TESMAN. But that would never have done, you know! Think of Hedda, my dear fellow! You, who know her so well——. I couldn't possibly ask her to put up with a shabby style of living!

BRACK. No, no—that is just the difficulty.

TESMAN. And then—fortunately—it can't be long before I receive my appointment.

BRACK. Well, you see—such things are often apt to hang fire for a time.

TESMAN. Have you heard anything definite? Eh?

BRACK. Nothing exactly definite——. [*Interrupting himself.*] But by-the-bye—I have one piece of news for you.

TESMAN. Well?

BRACK. Your old friend, Eilert Lövborg, has returned to town.

TESMAN. I know that already.

BRACK. Indeed! How did you learn it?

TESMAN. From that lady who went out with Hedda.

BRACK. Really? What was her name? I didn't quite catch it.

TESMAN. Mrs. Elvsted.

BRACK. Aha—Sheriff Elvsted's wife? Of course—he has been living up in their regions.

TESMAN. And fancy—I'm delighted to hear that he is quite a reformed character!

BRACK. So they say.

TESMAN. And then he has published a new book—eh?

BRACK. Yes, indeed he has.

TESMAN. And I hear it has made some sensation!

BRACK. Quite an unusual sensation.

TESMAN. Fancy—isn't that good news! A man of such extraordinary talents——. I felt so grieved to think that he had gone irretrievably to ruin.

BRACK. That was what everybody thought.

TESMAN. But I cannot imagine what he will take to now! How in the world will he be able to make his living? Eh?

[*During the last words,* HEDDA *has entered by the hall door.*

HEDDA. [*To* BRACK, *laughing with a touch of scorn.*] Tesman is forever worrying about how people are to make their living.

TESMAN. Well you see, dear—we were talking about poor Eilert Lövborg.

HEDDA. [*Glancing at him rapidly.*] Oh, indeed? [*Seats herself in the arm-chair beside the stove and asks indifferently:*] What is the matter with *him*?

TESMAN. Well—no doubt he has run through all his property long ago; and he can scarcely write a new book every year—eh? So I really can't see what is to become of him.

BRACK. Perhaps I can give you some information on that point.

TESMAN. Indeed!

BRACK. You must remember that his relations have a good deal of influence.

TESMAN. Oh, his relations, unfortunately, have entirely washed their hands of him.

BRACK. At one time they called him the hope of the family.

TESMAN. At one time, yes! But he has put an end to all that.

HEDDA. Who knows? [*With a slight smile.*] I hear they have reclaimed him up at Sheriff Elvsted's——

BRACK. And then this book that he has published——

TESMAN. Well, well, I hope to goodness they may find something for him to do. I have just written to him. I asked him to come and see us this evening, Hedda dear.

BRACK. But my dear fellow, you are booked for my bachelors' party this evening. You promised on the pier last night.

HEDDA. Had you forgotten, Tesman?

TESMAN. Yes, I had utterly forgotten.

BRACK. But it doesn't matter, for you may be sure he won't come.

TESMAN. What makes you think that? Eh?

BRACK. [*With a little hesitation, rising and resting his hands on the back of his chair.*] My dear Tesman—and you too, Mrs. Tesman—I think I ought not to keep you in the dark about something that—that——

TESMAN. That concerns Eilert——?

BRACK. Both you and him.

TESMAN. Well, my dear Judge, out with it.

BRACK. You must be prepared to find your appointment deferred longer than you desired or expected.

TESMAN. [*Jumping up uneasily.*] Is there some hitch about it? Eh?

BRACK. The nomination may perhaps be made conditional on the result of a competition——

TESMAN. Competition! Think of that, Hedda!

HEDDA. [*Leans further back in the chair.*] Aha—aha!

TESMAN. But who can my competitor be? Surely not——?

BRACK. Yes, precisely—Eilert Lövborg.

TESMAN. [*Clasping his hands.*] No, no—it's quite inconceivable! Quite impossible! Eh?

BRACK. H'm—that is what it may come to, all the same.

TESMAN. Well but, Judge Brack—it would show the most incredible lack of consideration for me. [*Gesticulates with his arms.*] For—just think—I'm a married man! We have married on the strength of these prospects, Hedda and I; and run deep into debt; and borrowed money from Aunt Julia too. Good heavens, they had as good as promised me the appointment. Eh?

BRACK. Well, well, well—no doubt you will get it in the end; only after a contest.

HEDDA. [*Immovable in her arm-chair.*] Fancy, Tesman, there will be a sort of sporting interest in that.

TESMAN. Why, my dearest Hedda, how can you be so indifferent about it?

HEDDA. [*As before.*] I am not at all indifferent. I am most eager to see who wins.

BRACK. In any case, Mrs. Tesman, it is best that you should know how matters stand. I mean—before you set about the little purchases I hear you are threatening.

HEDDA. This can make no difference.

BRACK. Indeed! Then I have no more to say. Good-bye! [*To* TESMAN.] I shall look in on my way back from my afternoon walk, and take you home with me.

TESMAN. Oh yes, yes—your news has quite upset me.

HEDDA. [*Reclining, holds out her hand.*] Good-bye, Judge; and be sure you call in the afternoon.

BRACK. Many thanks. Good-bye, good-bye!

TESMAN. [*Accompanying him to the door.*] Good-bye, my dear Judge! You must really excuse me——

[JUDGE BRACK *goes out by the hall door.*

TESMAN. [*Crosses the room.*] Oh Hedda—one should never rush into adventures. Eh?

HEDDA. [*Looks at him, smiling.*] Do *you* do *that*?

TESMAN. Yes, dear—there is no denying—it *was* adventurous to go and marry and set up house upon mere expectations.

HEDDA. Perhaps you are right there.

TESMAN. Well—at all events, we have our delightful home, Hedda! Fancy, the home we both dreamed of—the home we were in love with, I may almost say. Eh?

HEDDA. [*Rising slowly and wearily.*] It was part of our compact that we were to go into society—to keep open house.

TESMAN. Yes, if you only knew how I had been looking forward to it! Fancy—to see you as hostess—in a select circle! Eh? Well, well, well—for the present we shall have to get on without society, Hedda—only to invite Aunt Julia now and then.—Oh, I intended you to lead such an utterly different life, dear——!

HEDDA. Of course I cannot have my man in livery just yet.

TESMAN. Oh no, unfortunately. It would be out of the question for us to keep a footman, you know.

HEDDA. And the saddle-horse I was to have had——

TESMAN. [*Aghast.*] The saddle-horse!

HEDDA. ——I suppose I must not think of that now.

TESMAN. Good heavens, no!—that's as clear as daylight.

HEDDA. [*Goes up the room.*] Well, I shall have one thing at least to kill time with in the meanwhile.

TESMAN. [*Beaming.*] Oh thank heaven for that! What is it, Hedda? Eh?

HEDDA. [*In the middle doorway, looks at him with covert scorn.*] My pistols, George.

TESMAN. [*In alarm.*] Your pistols!

HEDDA. [*With cold eyes.*] General Gabler's pistols.

[*She goes out through the inner room, to the left.*

TESMAN. [*Rushes up to the middle doorway and calls after her:*] No, for heaven's sake, Hedda darling —don't touch those dangerous things! For my sake, Hedda! Eh?

CURTAIN

## ACT SECOND

*The room at the* Tesmans' *as in the first Act, except that the piano has been removed, and an elegant little writing-table with book-shelves put in its place. A smaller table stands near the sofa on the left. Most of the bouquets have been taken away.* Mrs. Elvsted's *bouquet is upon the large table in front.—It is afternoon.*

[Hedda *dressed to receive callers, is alone in the room. She stands by the open glass door, loading a revolver. The fellow to it lies in an open pistol-case on the writing-table.*

Hedda. [*Looks down the garden, and calls:*] So you are here again, Judge!

Brack. [*Is heard calling from a distance.*] As you see, Mrs. Tesman!

Hedda. [*Raises the pistol and points.*] Now I'll shoot you, Judge Brack!

Brack. [*Calling unseen.*] No, no, no! Don't stand aiming at me!

Hedda. This is what comes of sneaking in by the back way.[1] [*She fires.*

Brack. [*Nearer.*] Are you out of your senses——?

Hedda. Dear me—did I happen to hit you?

Brack. [*Still outside.*] I wish you would let these pranks alone!

Hedda. Come in then, Judge.

[Judge Brack, *dressed as though for a men's*

[1] "Bagveje" means both "back ways" and "underhand courses."

*party, enters by the glass door. He carries a light overcoat over his arm.*

BRACK. What the deuce—haven't you tired of that sport, yet? What are you shooting at?

HEDDA. Oh, I am only firing in the air.

BRACK. [*Gently takes the pistol out of her hand.*] Allow me, madam! [*Looks at it.*] Ah—I know this pistol well! [*Looks around.*] Where is the case? Ah, here it is. [*Lays the pistol in it, and shuts it.*] Now we won't play at that game any more to-day.

HEDDA. Then what in heaven's name would you have me do with myself?

BRACK. Have you had no visitors?

HEDDA. [*Closing the glass door.*] Not one. I suppose all our set are still out of town.

BRACK. And is Tesman not at home either?

HEDDA. [*At the writing-table, putting the pistol-case in a drawer which she shuts.*] No. He rushed off to his aunt's directly after lunch; he didn't expect you so early.

BRACK. H'm—how stupid of me not to have thought of that!

HEDDA. [*Turning her head to look at him.*] Why stupid?

BRACK. Because if I had thought of it I should have come a little—earlier.

HEDDA. [*Crossing the room.*] Then you would have found no one to receive you; for I have been in my room changing my dress ever since lunch.

BRACK. And is there no sort of little chink that we could hold a parley through?

HEDDA. You have forgotten to arrange one.

BRACK. That was another piece of stupidity.

HEDDA. Well, we must just settle down here—and wait. Tesman is not likely to be back for some time yet.

BRACK. Never mind; I shall not be impatient.

[HEDDA *seats herself in the corner of the sofa.* BRACK *lays his overcoat over the back of the nearest chair, and sits down, but keeps his hat in his hand. A short silence. They look at each other.*

HEDDA. Well?

BRACK. [*In the same tone.*] Well?

HEDDA. I spoke first.

BRACK. [*Bending a little forward.*] Come, let us have a cosy little chat, Mrs. Hedda.[1]

HEDDA. [*Leaning further back in the sofa.*] Does it not seem like a whole eternity since our last talk? Of course I don't count those few words yesterday evening and this morning.

BRACK. You mean since our last confidential talk? Our last *tête-à-tête*?

HEDDA. Well yes—since you put it so.

BRACK. Not a day has passed but I have wished that you were home again.

HEDDA. And I have done nothing but wish the same thing.

BRACK. You? Really, Mrs. Hedda? And I thought you had been enjoying your tour so much!

HEDDA. Oh yes, you may be sure of that!

BRACK. But Tesman's letters spoke of nothing but happiness.

HEDDA. Oh, *Tesman*! You see, he thinks nothing so delightful as grubbing in libraries and making copies of old parchments, or whatever you call them.

[1] As this form of address is contrary to English usage, and as the note of familiarity would be lacking in "Mrs. Tesman," Brack may, in stage representation, say "Miss Hedda," thus ignoring her marriage and reverting to the form of address no doubt customary between them of old.

BRACK. [*With a spice of malice.*] Well, that is his vocation in life—or part of it at any rate.

HEDDA. Yes, of course; and no doubt when it's your vocation——. But *I*! Oh, my dear Mr. Brack, how mortally bored I have been.

BRACK. [*Sympathetically.*] Do you really say so? In downright earnest?

HEDDA. Yes, you can surely understand it——! To go for six whole months without meeting a soul that knew anything of our circle, or could talk about the things we are interested in.

BRACK. Yes, yes—I too should feel that a deprivation.

HEDDA. And then, what I found most intolerable of all——

BRACK. Well?

HEDDA. ——was being everlastingly in the company of—one and the same person——

BRACK. [*With a nod of assent.*] Morning, noon, and night, yes—at all possible times and seasons.

HEDDA. I said "everlastingly."

BRACK. Just so. But I should have thought, with our excellent Tesman, one could——

HEDDA. Tesman is—a specialist, my dear Judge.

BRACK. Undeniably.

HEDDA. And specialists are not at all amusing to travel with. Not in the long run at any rate.

BRACK. Not even—the specialist one happens to *love*?

HEDDA. Faugh—don't use that sickening word!

BRACK. [*Taken aback.*] What do you say, Mrs. Hedda?

HEDDA. [*Half laughing, half irritated.*] You should just try it! To hear of nothing but the history of civilization, morning, noon, and night——

BRACK. Everlastingly.

HEDDA. Yes, yes, yes! And then all this about the domestic industry of the middle ages——! That's the most disgusting part of it!

BRACK. [*Looks searchingly at her.*] But tell me—in that case, how am I to understand your——? H'm——

HEDDA. My accepting George Tesman, you mean?

BRACK. Well, let us put it so.

HEDDA. Good heavens, do you see anything so wonderful in that?

BRACK. Yes and no—Mrs. Hedda.

HEDDA. I had positively danced myself tired, my dear Judge. My day was done—— [*With a slight shudder.*] Oh no—I won't say that; nor think it either!

BRACK. You have assuredly no reason to.

HEDDA. Oh, reasons—— [*Watching him closely.*] And George Tesman—after all, you must admit that he is correctness itself.

BRACK. His correctness and respectability are beyond all question.

HEDDA. And I don't see anything absolutely ridiculous about him.—Do you?

BRACK. Ridiculous? N—no—I shouldn't exactly say so——

HEDDA. Well—and his powers of research, at all events, are untiring.—I see no reason why he should not one day come to the front, after all.

BRACK. [*Looks at her hesitatingly.*] I thought that you, like every one else, expected him to attain the highest distinction.

HEDDA. [*With an expression of fatigue.*] Yes, so I did.—And then, since he was bent, at all hazards, on being allowed to provide for me—I really don't know why I should not have accepted his offer?

BRACK. No—if you look at it in *that* light——

HEDDA. It was more than my other adorers were prepared to do for me, my dear Judge.

BRACK. [*Laughing.*] Well, I can't answer for all the rest; but as for myself, you know quite well that I have always entertained a—a certain respect for the marriage tie—for marriage as an institution, Mrs. Hedda.

HEDDA. [*Jestingly.*] Oh, I assure you I have never cherished any hopes with respect to *you.*

BRACK. All I require is a pleasant and intimate interior, where I can make myself useful in every way, and am free to come and go as—as a trusted friend——

HEDDA. Of the master of the house, do you mean?

BRACK. [*Bowing.*] Frankly—of the mistress first of all; but of course of the master too, in the second place. Such a triangular friendship—if I may call it so—is really a great convenience for all parties, let me tell you.

HEDDA. Yes, I have many a time longed for some one to make a third on our travels. Oh—those railway-carriage *tête-à-têtes*——!

BRACK. Fortunately your wedding journey is over now.

HEDDA. [*Shaking her head.*] Not by a long—long way. I have only arrived at a station on the line.

BRACK. Well, then the passengers jump out and move about a little, Mrs. Hedda.

HEDDA. I never jump out.

BRACK. Really?

HEDDA. No—because there is always some one standing by to——

BRACK. [*Laughing.*] To look at your ankles, do you mean?

HEDDA. Precisely.

BRACK. Well but, dear me——

HEDDA. [*With a gesture of repulsion.*] I won't have it. I would rather keep my seat where I happen to be—and continue the *tête-à-tête.*

BRACK. But suppose a third person were to jump in and join the couple.

HEDDA. Ah—that is quite another matter!

BRACK. A trusted, sympathetic friend——

HEDDA. ——with a fund of conversation on all sorts of lively topics——

BRACK. ——and not the least bit of a specialist!

HEDDA. [*With an audible sigh.*] Yes, that would be a relief indeed.

BRACK. [*Hears the front door open, and glances in that direction.*] The triangle is completed.

HEDDA. [*Half aloud.*] And on goes the train.

[GEORGE TESMAN, *in a gray walking-suit, with a soft felt hat, enters from the hall. He has a number of unbound books under his arm and in his pockets.*

TESMAN. [*Goes up to the table beside the corner settee.*] Ouf—what a load for a warm day—all these books. [*Lays them on the table.*] I'm positively perspiring, Hedda. Hallo—are you there already, my dear Judge? Eh? Berta didn't tell me.

BRACK. [*Rising.*] I came in through the garden.

HEDDA. What books have you got there?

TESMAN. [*Stands looking them through.*] Some new books on my special subjects—quite indispensable to me.

HEDDA. Your special subjects?

BRACK. Yes, books on his special subjects, Mrs. Tesman.

[BRACK *and* HEDDA *exchange a confidential smile.*

HEDDA. Do you need still more books on your special subjects?

TESMAN. Yes, my dear Hedda, one can never have too many of them. Of course one must keep up with all that is written and published.

HEDDA. Yes, I suppose one must.

TESMAN. [*Searching among his books.*] And look here—I have got hold of Eilert Lövborg's new book too. [*Offering it to her.*] Perhaps you would like to glance through it, Hedda? Eh?

HEDDA. No, thank you. Or rather—afterwards perhaps.

TESMAN. I looked into it a little on the way home.

BRACK. Well, what do you think of it—as a specialist?

TESMAN. I think it shows quite remarkable soundness of judgment. He never wrote like that before. [*Putting the books together.*] Now I shall take all these into my study. I'm longing to cut the leaves——! And then I must change my clothes. [*To* BRACK.] I suppose we needn't start just yet? Eh?

BRACK. Oh, dear no—there is not the slightest hurry.

TESMAN. Well then, I will take my time. [*Is going with his books, but stops in the doorway and turns.*] By-the-bye, Hedda—Aunt Julia is not coming this evening.

HEDDA. Not coming? Is it that affair of the bonnet that keeps her away?

TESMAN. Oh, not at all. How could you think such a thing of Aunt Julia? Just fancy——! The fact is, Aunt Rina is very ill.

HEDDA. She always is.

TESMAN. Yes, but to-day she is much worse than usual, poor dear.

HEDDA. Oh, then it's only natural that her sister should remain with her. I must bear my disappointment.

TESMAN. And you can't imagine, dear, how delighted Aunt Julia seemed to be—because you had come home looking so flourishing!

HEDDA. [*Half aloud, rising.*] Oh, those everlasting Aunts!

TESMAN. What?

HEDDA. [*Going to the glass door.*] Nothing.

TESMAN. Oh, all right.

[*He goes through the inner room, out to the right.*

BRACK. What bonnet were you talking about?

HEDDA. Oh, it was a little episode with Miss Tesman this morning. She had laid down her bonnet on the chair there—[*Looks at him and smiles.*]—and I pretended to think it was the servant's.

BRACK. [*Shaking his head.*] Now my dear Mrs. Hedda, how could you do such a thing? To that excellent old lady, too!

HEDDA. [*Nervously crossing the room.*] Well, you see—these impulses come over me all of a sudden; and I cannot resist them. [*Throws herself down in the easy-chair by the stove.*] Oh, I don't know how to explain it.

BRACK. [*Behind the easy-chair.*] You are not really happy—that is at the bottom of it.

HEDDA. [*Looking straight before her.*] I know of no reason why I should be—happy. Perhaps you can give me one?

BRACK. Well—amongst other things, because you have got exactly the home you had set your heart on.

HEDDA. [*Looks up at him and laughs.*] Do you too believe in that legend?

BRACK. Is there nothing in it, then?

HEDDA. Oh yes, there is *something* in it.

BRACK. Well?

HEDDA. There is this in it, that I made use of Tesman to see me home from evening parties last summer——

BRACK. I, unfortunately, had to go quite a different way.

HEDDA. That's true. I know you were going a different way last summer.

BRACK. [*Laughing.*] Oh fie, Mrs. Hedda! Well, then—you and Tesman——?

HEDDA. Well, we happened to pass here one evening; Tesman, poor fellow, was writhing in the agony of having to find conversation; so I took pity on the learned man——

BRACK. [*Smiles doubtfully.*] *You* took pity? H'm——

HEDDA. Yes, I really did. And so—to help him out of his torment—I happened to say, in pure thoughtlessness, that I should like to live in this villa.

BRACK. No more than that?

HEDDA. Not *that* evening.

BRACK. But afterwards?

HEDDA. Yes, my thoughtlessness had consequences, my dear Judge.

BRACK. Unfortunately that too often happens, Mrs. Hedda.

HEDDA. Thanks! So you see it was this enthusiasm for Secretary Falk's villa that first constituted a bond of sympathy between George Tesman and me. From that came our engagement and our marriage, and our wedding journey, and all the rest of it. Well, well, my dear Judge—as you make your bed so you must lie, I could almost say.

BRACK. This is exquisite! And you really cared not a rap about it all the time?

HEDDA. No, heaven knows I didn't.

BRACK. But now? Now that we have made it so homelike for you?

HEDDA. Uh—the rooms all seem to smell of lavender and dried rose-leaves.—But perhaps it's Aunt Julia that has brought that scent with her.

BRACK. [*Laughing.*] No, I think it must be a legacy from the late Mrs. Secretary Falk.

HEDDA. Yes, there is an odor of mortality about it. It reminds me of a bouquet—the day after the ball. [*Clasps her hands behind her head, leans back in her chair and looks at him.*] Oh, my dear Judge—you cannot imagine how horribly I shall bore myself here.

BRACK. Why should not you, too, find some sort of vocation in life, Mrs. Hedda?

HEDDA. A vocation—that should attract me?

BRACK. If possible, of course.

HEDDA. Heaven knows what sort of a vocation that could be. I often wonder whether—— [*Breaking off.*] But that would never do either.

BRACK. Who can tell? Let me hear what it is.

HEDDA. Whether I might not get Tesman to go into politics, I mean.

BRACK. [*Laughing.*] Tesman? No, really now, political life is not the thing for him—not at all in his line.

HEDDA. No, I daresay not.—But if I could get him into it all the same?

BRACK. Why—what satisfaction could you find in that? If he is not fitted for that sort of thing, why should you want to drive him into it?

HEDDA. Because I am bored, I tell you! [*After a*

*pause.*] So you think it quite out of the question that Tesman should ever get into the ministry?

BRACK. H'm—you see, my dear Mrs. Hedda—to get into the ministry, he would have to be a tolerably rich man.

HEDDA. [*Rising impatiently.*] Yes, there we have it! It is this genteel poverty I have managed to drop into——! [*Crosses the room.*] *That* is what makes life so pitiable! So utterly ludicrous!—For that's what it is.

BRACK. Now *I* should say the fault lay elsewhere.

HEDDA. Where, then?

BRACK. You have never gone through any really stimulating experience.

HEDDA. Anything serious, you mean?

BRACK. Yes, you may call it so. But now you may perhaps have one in store.

HEDDA. [*Tossing her head.*] Oh, you're thinking of the annoyances about this wretched professorship! But that must be Tesman's own affair. I assure you I shall not waste a thought upon it.

BRACK. No, no, I daresay not. But suppose now that what people call—in elegant language—a solemn responsibility were to come upon you? [*Smiling.*] A new responsibility, Mrs. Hedda?

HEDDA. [*Angrily.*] Be quiet! Nothing of that sort will ever happen.

BRACK. [*Warily.*] We will speak of this again a year hence—at the very outside.

HEDDA. [*Curtly.*] I have no turn for anything of the sort, Judge Brack. No responsibilities for me!

BRACK. Are you so unlike the generality of women as to have no turn for duties which——?

HEDDA. [*Beside the glass door.*] Oh, be quiet, I

tell you!—I often think there is only one thing in the world I have any turn for.

BRACK. [*Drawing near to her.*] And what is that, if I may ask?

HEDDA. [*Stands looking out.*] Boring myself to death. Now you know it. [*Turns, looks towards the inner room, and laughs.*] Yes, as I thought! Here comes the Professor.

BRACK. [*Softly, in a tone of warning.*] Come, come, come, Mrs. Hedda!

[GEORGE TESMAN, *dressed for the party, with his gloves and hat in his hand, enters from the right through the inner room.*

TESMAN. Hedda, has no message come from Eilert Lövborg? Eh?

HEDDA. No.

TESMAN. Then you'll see he'll be here presently.

BRACK. Do you really think he will come?

TESMAN. Yes, I am almost sure of it. For what you were telling us this morning must have been a mere floating rumor.

BRACK. You think so?

TESMAN. At any rate, Aunt Julia said she did not believe for a moment that he would ever stand in my way again. Fancy that!

BRACK. Well then, that's all right.

TESMAN. [*Placing his hat and gloves on a chair on the right.*] Yes, but you must really let me wait for him as long as possible.

BRACK. We have plenty of time yet. None of my guests will arrive before seven or half-past.

TESMAN. Then meanwhile we can keep Hedda company, and see what happens. Eh?

HEDDA. [*Placing* BRACK's *hat and overcoat upon the*

*corner settee.*] And at the worst Mr. Lövborg can remain here with me.

BRACK. [*Offering to take his things.*] Oh, allow me, Mrs. Tesman!—What do you mean by "at the worst"?

HEDDA. If he won't go with you and Tesman.

TESMAN. [*Looks dubiously at her.*] But, Hedda dear—do you think it would quite do for him to remain with you? Eh? Remember, Aunt Julia can't come.

HEDDA. No, but Mrs. Elvsted is coming. We three can have a cup of tea together.

TESMAN. Oh yes, *that* will be all right.

BRACK. [*Smiling.*] And that would perhaps be the safest plan for him.

HEDDA. Why so?

BRACK. Well, you know, Mrs. Tesman, how you used to gird at my little bachelor parties. You declared they were adapted only for men of the strictest principles.

HEDDA. But no doubt Mr. Lövborg's principles are strict enough now. A converted sinner——

[BERTA *appears at the hall door.*

BERTA. There's a gentleman asking if you are at home, ma'am——

HEDDA. Well, show him in.

TESMAN. [*Softly.*] I'm sure it is he! Fancy that!

[EILERT LÖVBORG *enters from the hall. He is slim and lean; of the same age as* TESMAN, *but looks older and somewhat worn-out. His hair and beard are of a blackish brown, his face long and pale, but with patches of color on the cheekbones. He is dressed in a well-cut black visiting suit, quite new. He has dark gloves and a silk hat. He stops near the door, and makes a rapid bow, seeming somewhat embarrassed.*

TESMAN. [*Goes up to him and shakes him warmly by*

*the hand.*] Well, my dear Eilert—so at last we meet again!

LÖVBORG. [*Speaks in a subdued voice.*] Thanks for your letter, Tesman. [*Approaching* HEDDA.] Will you too shake hands with me, Mrs. Tesman?

HEDDA. [*Taking his hand.*] I am glad to see you, Mr. Lövborg. [*With a motion of her hand.*] I don't know whether you two gentlemen——?

LÖVBORG. [*Bowing slightly.*] Judge Brack, I think.

BRACK. [*Doing likewise.*] Oh yes,—in the old days——

TESMAN. [*To* LÖVBORG, *with his hands on his shoulders.*] And now you must make yourself entirely at home, Eilert! Mustn't he, Hedda?—For I hear you are going to settle in town again? Eh?

LÖVBORG. Yes, I am.

TESMAN. Quite right, quite right. Let me tell you, I have got hold of your new book; but I haven't had time to read it yet.

LÖVBORG. You may spare yourself the trouble.

TESMAN. Why so?

LÖVBORG. Because there is very little in it.

TESMAN. Just fancy—how can you say so?

BRACK. But it has been very much praised, I hear.

LÖVBORG. That was what I wanted; so I put nothing into the book but what every one would agree with.

BRACK. Very wise of you.

TESMAN. Well but, my dear Eilert——!

LÖVBORG. For now I mean to win myself a position again—to make a fresh start.

TESMAN. [*A little embarrassed.*] Ah, that is what you wish to do? Eh?

LÖVBORG. [*Smiling, lays down his hat, and draws a packet, wrapped in paper, from his coat pocket.*] But when this one appears, George Tesman, you will have to read it. For *this* is the real book—the book I have put my true self into.

TESMAN. Indeed? And what is it?

LÖVBORG. It is the continuation.

TESMAN. The continuation? Of what?

LÖVBORG. Of the book.

TESMAN. Of the new book?

LÖVBORG. Of course.

TESMAN. Why, my dear Eilert—does it not come down to our own days?

LÖVBORG. Yes, it does; and this one deals with the future.

TESMAN. With the future! But, good heavens, we know nothing of the future!

LÖVBORG. No; but there is a thing or two to be said about it all the same. [*Opens the packet.*] Look here——

TESMAN. Why, that's not your handwriting.

LÖVBORG. I dictated it. [*Turning over the pages.*] It falls into two sections. The first deals with the civilizing forces of the future. And here is the second —[*running through the pages towards the end*]—forecasting the probable line of development.

TESMAN. How odd now! I should never have thought of writing anything of that sort.

HEDDA. [*At the glass door, drumming on the pane.*] H'm——. I daresay not.

LÖVBORG. [*Replacing the manuscript in its paper and laying the packet on the table.*] I brought it, thinking I might read you a little of it this evening.

TESMAN. That was very good of you, Eilert. But this evening——? [*Looking at* BRACK.] I don't quite see how we can manage it——

LÖVBORG. Well then, some other time. There is no hurry.

BRACK. I must tell you, Mr. Lövborg—there is a little gathering at my house this evening—mainly in honor of Tesman, you know——

LÖVBORG. [*Looking for his hat.*] Oh—then I won't detain you——

BRACK. No, but listen—will you not do me the favor of joining us?

LÖVBORG. [*Curtly and decidedly.*] No, I can't—thank you very much.

BRACK. Oh, nonsense—do! We shall be quite a select little circle. And I assure you we shall have a "lively time," as Mrs. Hed—as Mrs. Tesman says.

LÖVBORG. I have no doubt of it. But nevertheless——

BRACK. And then you might bring your manuscript with you, and read it to Tesman at my house. I could give you a room to yourselves.

TESMAN. Yes, think of that, Eilert,—why shouldn't you? Eh?

HEDDA. [*Interposing.*] But, Tesman, if Mr. Lövborg would really rather not! I am sure Mr. Lövborg is much more inclined to remain here and have supper with me.

LÖVBORG. [*Looking at her.*] With you, Mrs. Tesman?

HEDDA. And with Mrs. Elvsted.

LÖVBORG. Ah—— [*Lightly.*] I saw her for a moment this morning.

HEDDA. Did you? Well, she is coming this evening. So you see you are almost bound to remain, Mr. Lövborg, or she will have no one to see her home.

LÖVBORG. That's true. Many thanks, Mrs. Tesman—in that case I will remain.

HEDDA. Then I have one or two orders to give the servant——

[*She goes to the hall door and rings.* BERTA *enters.* HEDDA *talks to her in a whisper, and points towards the inner room.* BERTA *nods and goes out again.*

TESMAN. [*At the same time, to* LÖVBORG.] Tell me, Eilert—is it this new subject—the future—that you are going to lecture about?

LÖVBORG. Yes.

TESMAN. They told me at the bookseller's that you are going to deliver a course of lectures this autumn.

LÖVBORG. That is my intention. I hope you won't take it ill, Tesman.

TESMAN. Oh no, not in the least! But——?

LÖVBORG. I can quite understand that it must be disagreeable to you.

TESMAN. [*Cast down.*] Oh, I can't expect you, out of consideration for me, to——

LÖVBORG. But I shall wait till you have received your appointment.

TESMAN. Will you wait? Yes but—yes but—are you not going to compete with me? Eh?

LÖVBORG. No; it is only the moral victory I care for.

TESMAN. Why, bless me—then Aunt Julia was right after all! Oh yes—I knew it! Hedda! Just fancy—Eilert Lövborg is not going to stand in our way!

HEDDA. [*Curtly.*] *Our* way? Pray leave *me* out of the question.

[*She goes up towards the inner room, where* BERTA *is placing a tray with decanters and glasses on the table.* HEDDA *nods approval, and comes forward again.* BERTA *goes out.*

TESMAN. [*At the same time.*] And you, Judge Brack—what do you say to this? Eh?

BRACK. Well, I say that a moral victory—h'm—may be all very fine——

TESMAN. Yes, certainly. But all the same——

HEDDA. [*Looking at* TESMAN *with a cold smile.*] You stand there looking as if you were thunder-struck——

TESMAN. Yes—so I am—I almost think——

BRACK. Don't you see, Mrs. Tesman, a thunderstorm has just passed over?

HEDDA. [*Pointing towards the inner room.*] Will you not take a glass of cold punch, gentlemen?

BRACK. [*Looking at his watch.*] A stirrup-cup? Yes, it wouldn't come amiss.

TESMAN. A capital idea, Hedda! Just the thing! Now that the weight has been taken off my mind——

HEDDA. Will you not join them, Mr. Lövborg?

LÖVBORG. [*With a gesture of refusal.*] No, thank you. Nothing for me.

BRACK. Why bless me—cold punch is surely not poison.

LÖVBORG. Perhaps not for every one.

HEDDA. I will keep Mr. Lövborg company in the meantime.

TESMAN. Yes, yes, Hedda dear, do.

[*He and* BRACK *go into the inner room, seat themselves, drink punch, smoke cigarettes, and carry on a lively conversation during what follows.* EILERT LÖVBORG *remains standing beside the stove.* HEDDA *goes to the writing-table.*

HEDDA. [*Raising her voice a little.*] Do you care to look at some photographs, Mr. Lövborg? You know Tesman and I made a tour in the Tyrol on our way home?

[*She takes up an album, and places it on the table beside the sofa, in the further corner of which she seats herself.* EILERT LÖVBORG *approaches, stops, and looks at her. Then he takes a chair and seats himself to her left, with his back towards the inner room.*

HEDDA. [*Opening the album.*] Do you see this range of mountains, Mr. Lövborg? It's the Ortler group. Tesman has written the name underneath. Here it is: "The Ortler group near Meran."

LÖVBORG. [*Who has never taken his eyes off her, says softly and slowly:*] Hedda—Gabler!

HEDDA. [*Glancing hastily at him.*] Ah! Hush!

LÖVBORG. [*Repeats softly.*] Hedda Gabler!

HEDDA. [*Looking at the album.*] That was my name in the old days—when we two knew each other.

LÖVBORG. And I must teach myself never to say Hedda Gabler again—never, as long as I live.

HEDDA. [*Still turning over the pages.*] Yes, you must. And I think you ought to practise in time. The sooner the better, I should say.

LÖVBORG. [*In a tone of indignation.*] Hedda Gabler married? And married to—George Tesman!

HEDDA. Yes—so the world goes.

LÖVBORG. Oh, Hedda, Hedda—how could you[1] throw yourself away!

HEDDA. [*Looks sharply at him.*] What? I can't allow this!

LÖVBORG. What do you mean?

[TESMAN *comes into the room and goes towards the sofa.*

HEDDA. [*Hears him coming and says in an indifferent tone.*] And this is a view from the Val d'Ampezzo, Mr. Lövborg. Just look at these peaks! [*Looks affectionately up at* TESMAN.] What's the name of these curious peaks, dear?

TESMAN. Let me see. Oh, those are the Dolomites.

[1] He uses the familiar *du.*

HEDDA. Yes, that's it!—Those are the Dolomites, Mr. Lövborg.

TESMAN. Hedda dear,—I only wanted to ask whether I shouldn't bring you a little punch after all? For yourself at any rate—eh?

HEDDA. Yes, do, please; and perhaps a few biscuits.

TESMAN. No cigarettes?

HEDDA. No.

TESMAN. Very well.

[*He goes into the inner room and out to the right.* BRACK *sits in the inner room, and keeps an eye from time to time on* HEDDA *and* LÖVBORG.

LÖVBORG. [*Softly, as before.*] Answer me, Hedda—how could you go and do this?

HEDDA. [*Apparently absorbed in the album.*] If you continue to say *du* to me I won't talk to you.

LÖVBORG. May I not say *du* even when we are alone?

HEDDA. No. You may think it; but you mustn't say it.

LÖVBORG. Ah, I understand. It is an offense against George Tesman, whom you[1]—love.

HEDDA. [*Glances at him and smiles.*] Love? What an idea!

LÖVBORG. You don't love him then!

HEDDA. But I won't hear of any sort of unfaithfulness. Remember that.

LÖVBORG. Hedda—answer me one thing——

HEDDA. Hush!

[TESMAN *enters with a small tray from the inner room.*

TESMAN. Here you are! Isn't this tempting?

[*He puts the tray on the table.*

[1] From this point onward Lövborg uses the formal *De.*

HEDDA. Why do you bring it yourself?

TESMAN. [*Filling the glasses.*] Because I think it's such fun to wait upon you, Hedda.

HEDDA. But you have poured out two glasses. Mr. Lövborg said he wouldn't have any——

TESMAN. No, but Mrs. Elvsted will soon be here, won't she?

HEDDA. Yes, by-the-bye—Mrs. Elvsted——

TESMAN. Had you forgotten her? Eh?

HEDDA. We were so absorbed in these photographs. [*Shows him a picture.*] Do you remember this little village?

TESMAN. Oh, it's that one just below the Brenner Pass. It was there we passed the night——

HEDDA. ——and met that lively party of tourists.

TESMAN. Yes, that was the place. Fancy—if we could only have had *you* with us, Eilert! Eh?

[*He returns to the inner room and sits beside* BRACK.

LÖVBORG. Answer me this one thing, Hedda——

HEDDA. Well?

LÖVBORG. Was there no love in your friendship for *me* either? Not a spark—not a tinge of love in it?

HEDDA. I wonder if there was? To me it seems as though we were two good comrades—two thoroughly intimate friends. [*Smilingly.*] You especially were frankness itself.

LÖVBORG. It was you that made me so.

HEDDA. As I look back upon it all, I think there was really something beautiful, something fascinating—something daring—in—in that secret intimacy—that comradeship which no living creature so much as dreamed of.

LÖVBORG. Yes, yes, Hedda! Was there not?—When I used to come to your father's in the afternoon—and the General sat over at the window reading his papers—with his back towards us——

HEDDA. And we two on the corner sofa——

LÖVBORG. Always with the same illustrated paper before us——

HEDDA. For want of an album, yes.

LÖVBORG. Yes, Hedda, and when I made my confessions to you—told you about myself, things that at that time no one else knew! There I would sit and tell you of my escapades—my days and nights and devilment. Oh, Hedda—what was the power in you that forced me to confess these things?

HEDDA. Do you think it was any power in me?

LÖVBORG. How else can I explain it? And all those—those roundabout questions you used to put to me——

HEDDA. Which you understood so particularly well——

LÖVBORG. How could you sit and question me like that? Question me quite frankly——

HEDDA. In roundabout terms, please observe.

LÖVBORG. Yes, but frankly nevertheless. Cross-question me about—all that sort of thing?

HEDDA. And how could you answer, Mr. Lövborg?

LÖVBORG. Yes, that is just what I can't understand—in looking back upon it. But tell me now, Hedda—was there not love at the bottom of our friendship? On your side, did you not feel as though you might purge my stains away—if I made you my confessor? Was it not so?

HEDDA. No, not quite.

LÖVBORG. What was your motive, then?

HEDDA. Do you think it quite incomprehensible that a young girl—when it can be done—without any one knowing——

LÖVBORG. Well?

HEDDA. ——should be glad to have a peep, now and then, into a world which——

LÖVBORG. Which——?

HEDDA. ——which she is forbidden to know anything about?

LÖVBORG. So *that* was it?

HEDDA. Partly. Partly—I almost think.

LÖVBORG. Comradeship in the thirst for life. But why should not *that*, at any rate, have continued?

HEDDA. The fault was yours.

LÖVBORG. It was you that broke with me.

HEDDA. Yes, when our friendship threatened to develop into something more serious. Shame upon you, Eilert Lövborg! How could you think of wronging your —your frank comrade?

LÖVBORG. [*Clenching his hands.*] Oh, why did you not carry out your threat? Why did you not shoot me down?

HEDDA. Because I have such a dread of scandal.

LÖVBORG. Yes, Hedda, you are a coward at heart.

HEDDA. A terrible coward. [*Changing her tone.*] But it was a lucky thing for you. And now you have found ample consolation at the Elvsteds'.

LÖVBORG. I know what Thea has confided to you.

HEDDA. And perhaps you have confided to her something about us?

LÖVBORG. Not a word. She is too stupid to understand anything of that sort.

HEDDA. Stupid?

LÖVBORG. She is stupid about matters of that sort.

HEDDA. And I am cowardly. [*Bends over towards him, without looking him in the face, and says more softly:*] But now I will confide something to *you*.

LÖVBORG. [*Eagerly.*] Well?

HEDDA. The fact that I dared not shoot you down——

LÖVBORG. Yes!

HEDDA. ——*that* was not my most arrant cowardice—that evening.

LÖVBORG. [*Looks at her a moment, understands, and whispers passionately.*] Oh, Hedda! Hedda Gabler! Now I begin to see a hidden reason beneath our comradeship! You[1] and I——! After all, then, it was your craving for life——

HEDDA. [*Softly, with a sharp glance.*] Take care! Believe nothing of the sort!

[*Twilight has begun to fall. The hall door is opened from without by* BERTA.

HEDDA. [*Closes the album with a bang and calls smilingly:*] Ah, at last! My darling Thea,—come along!

[MRS. ELVSTED *enters from the hall. She is in evening dress. The door is closed behind her.*

HEDDA. [*On the sofa, stretches out her arms towards her.*] My sweet Thea—you can't think how I have been longing for you!

[MRS. ELVSTED, *in passing, exchanges slight salutations with the gentlemen in the inner room, then goes up to the table and gives* HEDDA *her hand.* EILERT LÖVBORG *has risen. He and* MRS. ELVSTED *greet each other with a silent nod.*

MRS. ELVSTED. Ought I to go in and talk to your husband for a moment?

HEDDA. Oh, not at all. Leave those two alone. They will soon be going.

MRS. ELVSTED. Are they going out?

[1] In this speech he once more says *du.* Hedda addresses him throughout as *De.*

HEDDA. Yes, to a supper-party.

MRS. ELVSTED. [*Quickly, to* LÖVBORG.] Not *you*?

LÖVBORG. No.

HEDDA. Mr. Lövborg remains with us.

MRS. ELVSTED. [*Takes a chair and is about to seat herself at his side.*] Oh, how nice it is here!

HEDDA. No, thank you, my little Thea! Not *there*! You'll be good enough to come over here to me. I will sit between you.

MRS. ELVSTED. Yes, just as you please.

[*She goes round the table and seats herself on the sofa on* HEDDA'S *right.* LÖVBORG *re-seats himself on his chair.*

LÖVBORG. [*After a short pause, to* HEDDA.] Is not she lovely to look at?

HEDDA. [*Lightly stroking her hair.*] Only to look at?

LÖVBORG. Yes. For *we* two—she and I—*we* are two real comrades. We have absolute faith in each other; so we can sit and talk with perfect frankness——

HEDDA. Not roundabout, Mr. Lövborg?

LÖVBORG. Well——

MRS. ELVSTED. [*Softly clinging close to* HEDDA.] Oh, how happy I am, Hedda! For, only think, he says I have inspired him too.

HEDDA. [*Looks at her with a smile.*] Ah! Does he say that, dear?

LÖVBORG. And then she is so brave, Mrs. Tesman!

MRS. ELVSTED. Good heavens—am I brave?

LÖVBORG. Exceedingly—where your comrade is concerned.

HEDDA. Ah yes—courage! If one only had *that*!

LÖVBORG. What then? What do you mean?

HEDDA. Then life would perhaps be livable, after all. [*With a sudden change of tone.*] But now, my dearest Thea, you really must have a glass of cold punch.

MRS. ELVSTED. No, thanks—I never take anything of that kind.

HEDDA. Well then, *you*, Mr. Lövborg.

LÖVBORG. Nor I, thank you.

MRS. ELVSTED. No, he doesn't either.

HEDDA. [*Looks fixedly at him.*] But if I say you *shall*?

LÖVBORG. It would be no use.

HEDDA. [*Laughing.*] Then I, poor creature, have no sort of power over you?

LÖVBORG. Not in *that* respect.

HEDDA. But seriously, I think you ought to—for your own sake.

MRS. ELVSTED. Why, Hedda——!

LÖVBORG. How so?

HEDDA. Or rather on account of other people.

LÖVBORG. Indeed?

HEDDA. Otherwise people might be apt to suspect that—in your heart of hearts—you did not feel quite secure—quite confident in yourself.

MRS. ELVSTED. [*Softly.*] Oh please, Hedda——

LÖVBORG. People may suspect what they like—for the present.

MRS. ELVSTED. [*Joyfully.*] Yes, let them!

HEDDA. I saw it plainly in Judge Brack's face a moment ago.

LÖVBORG. What did you see?

HEDDA. His contemptuous smile, when you dared not go with them into the inner room.

LÖVBORG. Dared not? Of course I preferred to stop here and talk to *you*.

MRS. ELVSTED. What could be more natural, Hedda?

HEDDA. But the Judge could not guess that. And I

saw, too, the way he smiled and glanced at Tesman when you dared not accept his invitation to this wretched little supper-party of his.

LÖVBORG. Dared not! Do you say I dared not?

HEDDA. *I* don't say so. But that was how Judge Brack understood it.

LÖVBORG. Well, let him.

HEDDA. Then you are not going with them?

LÖVBORG. I will stay here with you and Thea.

MRS. ELVSTED. Yes, Hedda—how can you doubt that?

HEDDA. [*Smiles and nods approvingly to* LÖVBORG.] Firm as a rock! Faithful to your principles, now and forever! Ah, that is how a man should be! [*Turns to* MRS. ELVSTED *and caresses her.*] Well now, what did I tell you, when you came to us this morning in such a state of distraction——

LÖVBORG. [*Surprised.*] Distraction!

MRS. ELVSTED. [*Terrified.*] Hedda—oh Hedda——!

HEDDA. You can see for yourself! You haven't the slightest reason to be in such mortal terror—— [*Interrupting herself.*] There! Now we can all three enjoy ourselves!

LÖVBORG. [*Who has given a start.*] Ah—what is all this, Mrs. Tesman?

MRS. ELVSTED. Oh my God, Hedda! What are you saying? What are you doing?

HEDDA. Don't get excited! That horrid Judge Brack is sitting watching you.

LÖVBORG. So she was in mortal terror! On my account!

MRS. ELVSTED. [*Softly and piteously.*] Oh, Hedda—now you have ruined everything!

LÖVBORG. [*Looks fixedly at her for a moment. His*

*face is distorted.*] So *that* was my comrade's frank confidence in me?

MRS. ELVSTED. [*Imploringly.*] Oh, my dearest friend—only let me tell you——

LÖVBORG. [*Takes one of the glasses of punch, raises it to his lips, and says in a low, husky voice.*] Your health, Thea!

[*He empties the glass, puts it down, and takes the second.*

MRS. ELVSTED. [*Softly.*] Oh, Hedda, Hedda—how *could* you do this?

HEDDA. *I* do it? *I?* Are you crazy?

LÖVBORG. Here's to your health too, Mrs. Tesman. Thanks for the truth. Hurrah for the truth!

[*He empties the glass and is about to refill it.*

HEDDA. [*Lays her hand on his arm.*] Come, come—no more for the present. Remember you are going out to supper.

MRS. ELVSTED. No, no, no!

HEDDA. Hush! They are sitting watching you.

LÖVBORG. [*Putting down the glass.*] Now, Thea—tell me the truth——

MRS. ELVSTED. Yes.

LÖVBORG. Did your husband know that you had come after me?

MRS. ELVSTED. [*Wringing her hands.*] Oh, Hedda—do you hear what he is asking?

LÖVBORG. Was it arranged between you and him that you were to come to town and look after me? Perhaps it was the Sheriff himself that urged you to come? Aha, my dear—no doubt he wanted my help in his office! Or was it at the card-table that he missed me?

MRS. ELVSTED. [*Softly, in agony.*] Oh, Lövborg, Lövborg——!

Lövborg. [*Seizes a glass and is on the point of filling it.*] Here's a glass for the old Sheriff too!

Hedda. [*Preventing him.*] No more just now. Remember, you have to read your manuscript to Tesman.

Lövborg. [*Calmly, putting down the glass.*] It was stupid of me, all this, Thea—to take it in this way, I mean. Don't be angry with me, my dear, dear comrade. You shall see—both you and the others—that if I was fallen once—now I have risen again! Thanks to *you*, Thea.

Mrs. Elvsted. [*Radiant with joy.*] Oh, heaven be praised——!

[Brack *has in the meantime looked at his watch. He and* Tesman *rise and come into the drawing-room.*

Brack. [*Takes his hat and overcoat.*] Well, Mrs. Tesman, our time has come.

Hedda. I suppose it has.

Lövborg. [*Rising.*] Mine too, Judge Brack.

Mrs. Elvsted. [*Softly and imploringly.*] Oh, Lövborg, don't do it!

Hedda. [*Pinching her arm.*] They can hear you!

Mrs. Elvsted. [*With a suppressed shriek.*] Ow!

Lövborg. [*To* Brack.] You were good enough to invite me.

Brack. Well, are you coming after all?

Lövborg. Yes, many thanks.

Brack. I'm delighted——

Lövborg. [*To* Tesman, *putting the parcel of MS. in his pocket.*] I should like to show you one or two things before I send it to the printers.

Tesman. Fancy—that will be delightful. But, Hedda dear, how is Mrs. Elvsted to get home? Eh?

Hedda. Oh, that can be managed somehow.

LÖVBORG. [*Looking towards the ladies.*] Mrs. Elvsted? Of course, I'll come again and fetch her. [*Approaching.*] At ten or thereabouts, Mrs. Tesman? Will that do?

HEDDA. Certainly. That will do capitally.

TESMAN. Well, then, that's all right. But you must not expect *me* so early, Hedda.

HEDDA. Oh, you may stop as long—as long as ever you please.

MRS. ELVSTED. [*Trying to conceal her anxiety.*] Well then, Mr. Lövborg—I shall remain here until you come.

LÖVBORG. [*With his hat in his hand.*] Pray do, Mrs. Elvsted.

BRACK. And now off goes the excursion train, gentlemen! I hope we shall have a lively time, as a certain fair lady puts it.

HEDDA. Ah, if only the fair lady could be present unseen——!

BRACK. Why unseen?

HEDDA. In order to hear a little of your liveliness at first hand, Judge Brack.

BRACK. [*Laughing.*] I should not advise the fair lady to try it.

TESMAN. [*Also laughing.*] Come, you're a nice one, Hedda! Fancy that!

BRACK. Well, good-bye, good-bye, ladies.

LÖVBORG. [*Bowing.*] About ten o'clock, then.

> [BRACK, LÖVBORG, *and* TESMAN *go out by the hall door. At the same time,* BERTA *enters from the inner room with a lighted lamp, which she places on the drawing-room table; she goes out by the way she came.*

MRS. ELVSTED. [*Who has risen and is wandering*

*restlessly about the room.*] Hedda—Hedda—what will come of all this?

HEDDA. At ten o'clock—he will be here. I can see him already—with vine-leaves in his hair—flushed and fearless——

MRS. ELVSTED. Oh, I hope he may.

HEDDA. And then, you see—then he will have regained control over himself. Then he will be a free man for all his days.

MRS. ELVSTED. Oh God!—if he would only come as you see him now!

HEDDA. He will come as I see him—so, and not otherwise! [*Rises and approaches* THEA.] You may doubt him as long as you please; *I* believe in him. And now we will try——

MRS. ELVSTED. You have some hidden motive in this, Hedda!

HEDDA. Yes, I have. I want for once in my life to have power to mold a human destiny.

MRS. ELVSTED. Have you not the power?

HEDDA. I have not—and have never had it.

MRS. ELVSTED. Not your husband's?

HEDDA. Do you think *that* is worth the trouble? Oh, if you could only understand how poor I am. And fate has made *you* so rich! [*Clasps her passionately in her arms.*] I think I must burn your hair off, after all.

MRS. ELVSTED. Let me go! Let me go! I am afraid of you, Hedda!

BERTA. [*In the middle doorway.*] Tea is laid in the dining-room, ma'am.

HEDDA. Very well. We are coming.

MRS. ELVSTED. No, no, no! I would rather go home alone! At once!

HEDDA. Nonsense! First you shall have a cup of tea, you little stupid. And then—at ten o'clock—Eilert Lövborg will be here—with vine-leaves in his hair.

[*She drags* MRS. ELVSTED *almost by force towards the middle doorway.*

CURTAIN

## ACT THIRD

*The room at the* Tesmans'. *The curtains are drawn over the middle doorway, and also over the glass door. The lamp, half turned down, and with a shade over it, is burning on the table. In the stove, the door of which stands open, there has been a fire, which is now nearly burnt out.*

[Mrs. Elvsted, *wrapped in a large shawl, and with her feet upon a foot-rest, sits close to the stove, sunk back in the arm-chair.* Hedda, *fully dressed, lies sleeping upon the sofa, with a sofa-blanket over her.*

Mrs. Elvsted. [*After a pause, suddenly sits up in her chair, and listens eagerly. Then she sinks back again wearily, moaning to herself.*] Not yet!—Oh God—oh God—not yet!

[Berta *slips cautiously in by the hall door. She has a letter in her hand.*

Mrs. Elvsted. [*Turns and whispers eagerly.*] Well—has any one come?

Berta. [*Softly.*] Yes, a girl has just brought this letter.

Mrs. Elvsted. [*Quickly, holding out her hand.*] A letter! Give it to me!

Berta. No, it's for Dr. Tesman, ma'am.

Mrs. Elvsted. Oh, indeed.

Berta. It was Miss Tesman's servant that brought it. I'll lay it here on the table.

Mrs. Elvsted. Yes, do.

BERTA. [*Laying down the letter.*] I think I had better put out the lamp. It's smoking.

MRS. ELVSTED. Yes, put it out. It must soon be daylight now.

BERTA. [*Putting out the lamp.*] It is daylight already, ma'am.

MRS. ELVSTED. Yes, broad day! And no one come back yet——!

BERTA. Lord bless you, ma'am—I guessed how it would be.

MRS. ELVSTED. You guessed?

BERTA. Yes, when I saw that a certain person had come back to town—and that he went off with them. For we've heard enough about that gentleman before now.

MRS. ELVSTED. Don't speak so loud. You will waken Mrs. Tesman.

BERTA. [*Looks towards the sofa and sighs.*] No, no—let her sleep, poor thing. Shan't I put some wood on the fire?

MRS. ELVSTED. Thanks, not for me.

BERTA. Oh, very well.

[*She goes softly out by the hall door.*

HEDDA. [*Is wakened by the shutting of the door, and looks up.*] What's that——?

MRS. ELVSTED. It was only the servant——

HEDDA. [*Looking about her.*] Oh, we're here——! Yes, now I remember. [*Sits erect upon the sofa, stretches herself, and rubs her eyes.*] What o'clock is it, Thea?

MRS. ELVSTED. [*Looks at her watch.*] It's past seven.

HEDDA. When did Tesman come home?

MRS. ELVSTED. He has not come.

HEDDA. Not come home yet?

Mrs. Elvsted. [*Rising.*] No one has come.

Hedda. Think of our watching and waiting here till four in the morning——

Mrs. Elvsted. [*Wringing her hands.*] And *how* I watched and waited for him!

Hedda. [*Yawns, and says with her hand before her mouth:*] Well, well—we might have spared ourselves the trouble.

Mrs. Elvsted. Did you get a little sleep?

Hedda. Oh yes; I believe I have slept pretty well. Have you not?

Mrs. Elvsted. Not for a moment. I couldn't, Hedda!—not to save my life.

Hedda. [*Rises and goes towards her.*] There, there, there! There's nothing to be so alarmed about. I understand quite well what has happened.

Mrs. Elvsted. Well, what do you think? Won't you tell me?

Hedda. Why, of course it has been a very late affair at Judge Brack's——

Mrs. Elvsted. Yes, yes—that is clear enough. But all the same——

Hedda. And then, you see, Tesman hasn't cared to come home and ring us up in the middle of the night. [*Laughing.*] Perhaps he wasn't inclined to show himself either—immediately after a jollification.

Mrs. Elvsted. But in that case—where can he have gone?

Hedda. Of course he has gone to his Aunts' and slept there. They have his old room ready for him.

Mrs. Elvsted. No, he can't be with *them*; for a letter has just come for him from Miss Tesman. There it lies.

Hedda. Indeed? [*Looks at the address.*] Why yes, it's addressed in Aunt Julia's own hand. Well then, he has remained at Judge Brack's. And as for Eilert Lövborg—he is sitting, with vine leaves in his hair, reading his manuscript.

MRS. ELVSTED. Oh Hedda, you are just saying things you don't believe a bit.

HEDDA. You really are a little blockhead, Thea.

MRS. ELVSTED. Oh yes, I suppose I am.

HEDDA. And how mortally tired you look.

MRS. ELVSTED. Yes, I am mortally tired.

HEDDA. Well then, you must do as I tell you. You must go into my room and lie down for a little while.

MRS. ELVSTED. Oh no, no—I shouldn't be able to sleep.

HEDDA. I am sure you would.

MRS. ELVSTED. Well, but your husband is certain to come soon now; and then I want to know at once——

HEDDA. I shall take care to let you know when he comes.

MRS. ELVSTED. Do you promise me, Hedda?

HEDDA. Yes, rely upon me. Just you go in and have a sleep in the meantime.

MRS. ELVSTED. Thanks; then I'll try to.

[*She goes off through the inner room.*

[HEDDA *goes up to the glass door and draws back the curtains. The broad daylight streams into the room. Then she takes a little hand-glass from the writing-table, looks at herself in it, and arranges her hair. Next she goes to the hall door and presses the bell-button.* BERTA *presently appears at the hall door.*

BERTA. Did you want anything, ma'am?

HEDDA. Yes; you must put some more wood in the stove. I am shivering.

BERTA. Bless me—I'll make up the fire at once. [*She rakes the embers together and lays a piece of wood upon them; then stops and listens.*] That was a ring at the front door, ma'am.

HEDDA. Then go to the door. I will look after the fire.

BERTA. It'll soon burn up.

[*She goes out by the hall door.*

[HEDDA *kneels on the foot-rest and lays some more pieces of wood in the stove. After a short pause,* GEORGE TESMAN *enters from the hall. He looks tired and rather serious. He steals on tiptoe towards the middle doorway and is about to slip through the curtains.*

HEDDA. [*At the stove, without looking up.*] Good morning.

TESMAN. [*Turns.*] Hedda! [*Approaching her.*] Good heavens—are you up so early? Eh?

HEDDA. Yes, I am up very early this morning.

TESMAN. And I never doubted you were still sound asleep. Fancy that, Hedda!

HEDDA. Don't speak so loud. Mrs. Elvsted is resting in my room.

TESMAN. Has Mrs. Elvsted been here all night?

HEDDA. Yes, since no one came to fetch her.

TESMAN. Ah, to be sure.

HEDDA. [*Closes the door of the stove and rises.*] Well, did you enjoy yourselves at Judge Brack's?

TESMAN. Have you been anxious about me? Eh?

HEDDA. No, I should never think of being anxious. But I asked if you had enjoyed yourself.

TESMAN. Oh yes,—for once in a way. Especially the beginning of the evening; for then Eilert read me part of his book. We arrived more than an hour too early—fancy that! And Brack had all sorts of arrangements to make—so Eilert read to me.

HEDDA. [*Seating herself by the table on the right.*] Well? Tell me, then——

TESMAN. [*Sitting on a footstool near the stove.*] Oh Hedda, you can't conceive what a book that is going to be! I believe it is one of the most remarkable things that have ever been written. Fancy that!

HEDDA. Yes, yes; I don't care about that——

TESMAN. I must make a confession to you, Hedda. When he had finished reading—a horrid feeling came over me.

HEDDA. A horrid feeling?

TESMAN. I felt jealous of Eilert for having had it in him to write such a book. Only think, Hedda!

HEDDA. Yes, yes, I am thinking!

TESMAN. And then how pitiful to think that he—with all his gifts—should be irreclaimable, after all.

HEDDA. I suppose you mean that he has more courage than the rest?

TESMAN. No, not at all—I mean that he is incapable of taking his pleasures in moderation.

HEDDA. And what came of it all—in the end?

TESMAN. Well, to tell the truth, I think it might best be described as an orgy, Hedda.

HEDDA. Had he vine-leaves in his hair?

TESMAN. Vine-leaves? No, I saw nothing of the sort. But he made a long, rambling speech in honor of the woman who had inspired him in his work—that was the phrase he used.

HEDDA. Did he name her?

TESMAN. No, he didn't; but I can't help thinking he meant Mrs. Elvsted. You may be sure he did.

HEDDA. Well—where did you part from him?

TESMAN. On the way to town. We broke up—the last of us at any rate—all together; and Brack came with us to get a breath of fresh air. And then, you see, we agreed to take Eilert home; for he had had far more than was good for him.

HEDDA. I daresay.

TESMAN. But now comes the strange part of it, Hedda; or, I should rather say, the melancholy part of it. I declare I am almost ashamed—on Eilert's account—to tell you——

HEDDA. Oh, go on——!

TESMAN. Well, as we were getting near town, you see, I happened to drop a little behind the others. Only for a minute or two—fancy that!

HEDDA. Yes, yes, yes, but——?

TESMAN. And then, as I hurried after them—what do you think I found by the wayside? Eh?

HEDDA. Oh, how should I know!

TESMAN. You mustn't speak of it to a soul, Hedda! Do you hear? Promise me, for Eilert's sake. [*Draws a parcel, wrapped in paper, from his coat pocket.*] Fancy, dear—I found this.

HEDDA. Is not that the parcel he had with him yesterday?

TESMAN. Yes, it is the whole of his precious, irreplaceable manuscript! And he had gone and lost it, and knew nothing about it. Only fancy, Hedda! So deplorably——

HEDDA. But why did you not give him back the parcel at once?

TESMAN. I didn't dare to—in the state he was then in——

HEDDA. Did you not tell any of the others that you had found it?

TESMAN. Oh, far from it! You can surely understand that, for Eilert's sake, I wouldn't do that.

HEDDA. So no one knows that Eilert Lövborg's manuscript is in your possession?

TESMAN. No. And no one *must* know it.

HEDDA. Then what did you say to him afterwards?

TESMAN. I didn't talk to him again at all; for when we got in among the streets, he and two or three of the others gave us the slip and disappeared. Fancy that!

HEDDA. Indeed! They must have taken him home then.

TESMAN. Yes, so it would appear. And Brack, too, left us.

HEDDA. And what have you been doing with yourself since?

TESMAN. Well, I and some of the others went home with one of the party, a jolly fellow, and took our morning coffee with him; or perhaps I should rather call it our night coffee—eh? But now, when I have rested a little, and given Eilert, poor fellow, time to have his sleep out, I must take this back to him.

HEDDA. [*Holds out her hand for the packet.*] No—don't give it to him! Not in such a hurry, I mean. Let me read it first.

TESMAN. No, my dearest Hedda, I mustn't, I really mustn't.

HEDDA. You must not?

TESMAN. No—for you can imagine what a state of despair he will be in when he wakens and misses the manuscript. He has no copy of it, you must know! He told me so.

HEDDA. [*Looking searchingly at him.*] Can such a thing not be reproduced? Written over again?

TESMAN. No, I don't think that would be possible. For the inspiration, you see——

HEDDA. Yes, yes—I suppose it depends on that—— [*Lightly.*] But, by-the-bye—here is a letter for you.

TESMAN. Fancy——!

HEDDA. [*Handing it to him.*] It came early this morning.

TESMAN. It's from Aunt Julia! What can it be? [*He lays the packet on the other footstool, opens the letter, runs his eye through it, and jumps up.*] Oh, Hedda—she says that poor Aunt Rina is dying!

HEDDA. Well, we were prepared for that.

TESMAN. And that if I want to see her again, I must make haste. I'll run in to them at once.

HEDDA. [*Suppressing a smile.*] Will you run?

TESMAN. Oh, my dearest Hedda—if you could only make up your mind to come with me! Just think!

HEDDA. [*Rises and says wearily, repelling the idea:*] No, no, don't ask me. I *will* not look upon sickness and death. I loathe all sorts of ugliness.

TESMAN. Well, well, then——! [*Bustling around.*] My hat——? My overcoat——? Oh, in the hall——. I do hope I mayn't come too late, Hedda! Eh?

HEDDA. Oh, if you run——

[BERTA *appears at the hall door.*

BERTA. Judge Brack is at the door, and wishes to know if he may come in.

TESMAN. At this time! No, I can't possibly see him.

HEDDA. But I can. [*To* BERTA.] Ask Judge Brack to come in. [BERTA *goes out.*

HEDDA. [*Quickly, whispering.*] The parcel, Tesman! [*She snatches it up from the stool.*

TESMAN. Yes, give it to me!

HEDDA. No, no, I will keep it till you come back.

[*She goes to the writing-table and places it in the bookcase.* TESMAN *stands in a flurry of haste, and cannot get his gloves on.* JUDGE BRACK *enters from the hall.*

HEDDA. [*Nodding to him.*] You are an early bird, I must say.

BRACK. Yes, don't you think so? [*To* TESMAN.] Are you on the move, too?

TESMAN. Yes, I *must* rush off to my aunts'. Fancy—the invalid one is lying at death's door, poor creature.

BRACK. Dear me, is she indeed? Then on no account let me detain you. At such a critical moment——

TESMAN. Yes, I must really rush—— Good-bye! Good-bye! [*He hastens out by the hall door.*

HEDDA. [*Approaching.*] You seem to have made a particularly lively night of it at your rooms, Judge Brack.

BRACK. I assure you I have not had my clothes off, Mrs. Hedda.

HEDDA. Not you, either?

BRACK. No, as you may see. But what has Tesman been telling you of the night's adventures?

HEDDA. Oh, some tiresome story. Only that they went and had coffee somewhere or other.

BRACK. I have heard about that coffee-party already. Eilert Lövborg was not with them, I fancy?

HEDDA. No, they had taken him home before that.

BRACK. Tesman too?

HEDDA. No, but some of the others, he said.

BRACK. [*Smiling.*] George Tesman is really an ingenuous creature, Mrs. Hedda.

HEDDA. Yes, heaven knows he is. Then is there something behind all this?

BRACK. Yes, perhaps there may be.

HEDDA. Well then, sit down, my dear Judge, and tell your story in comfort.

[*She seats herself to the left of the table.*

BRACK *sits near her, at the long side of the table.*

HEDDA. Now then?

BRACK. I had special reasons for keeping track of my guests—or rather of some of my guests—last night.

HEDDA. Of Eilert Lövborg among the rest, perhaps?

BRACK. Frankly—yes.

HEDDA. Now you make me really curious——

BRACK. Do you know where he and one or two of the others finished the night, Mrs. Hedda?

HEDDA. If it is not quite unmentionable, tell me.

BRACK. Oh no, it's not at all unmentionable. Well, they put in an appearance at a particularly animated soirée.

HEDDA. Of the lively kind?

BRACK. Of the very liveliest——

HEDDA. Tell me more of this, Judge Brack——

BRACK. Lövborg, as well as the others, had been invited in advance. I knew all about it. But he had declined the invitation; for now, as you know, he has become a new man.

HEDDA. Up at the Elvsteds', yes. But he went after all, then?

BRACK. Well, you see, Mrs. Hedda—unhappily the spirit moved him at my rooms last evening——

HEDDA. Yes, I hear he found inspiration.

BRACK. Pretty violent inspiration. Well, I fancy that altered his purpose; for we menfolk are unfortunately not always so firm in our principles as we ought to be.

HEDDA. Oh, I am sure *you* are an exception, Judge Brack. But as to Lövborg——?

BRACK. To make a long story short—he landed at last in Mademoiselle Diana's rooms.

HEDDA. Mademoiselle Diana's?

BRACK. It was Mademoiselle Diana that was giving the soirée, to a select circle of her admirers and her lady friends.

HEDDA. Is she a red-haired woman?

BRACK. Precisely.

HEDDA. A sort of a—singer?

BRACK. Oh yes—in her leisure moments. And moreover a mighty huntress—of men—Mrs. Hedda. You have no doubt heard of her. Eilert Lövborg was one of her most enthusiastic protectors—in the days of his glory.

HEDDA. And how did all this end?

BRACK. Far from amicably, it appears. After a most tender meeting, they seem to have come to blows——

HEDDA. Lövborg and she?

BRACK. Yes. He accused her or her friends of having robbed him. He declared that his pocket-book had disappeared—and other things as well. In short, he seems to have made a furious disturbance.

HEDDA. And what came of it all?

BRACK. It came to a general scrimmage, in which the ladies as well as the gentlemen took part. Fortunately the police at last appeared on the scene.

HEDDA. The police too?

BRACK. Yes. I fancy it will prove a costly frolic for Eilert Lövborg, crazy being that he is.

HEDDA. How so?

BRACK. He seems to have made a violent resistance—to have hit one of the constables on the head and torn the coat off his back. So they had to march him off to the police-station with the rest.

HEDDA. How have you learnt all this?

BRACK. From the police themselves.

HEDDA. [*Gazing straight before her.*] So that is what happened. Then he had no vine-leaves in his hair.

BRACK. Vine-leaves, Mrs. Hedda?

HEDDA. [*Changing her tone.*] But tell me now, Judge—what is your real reason for tracking out Eilert Lövborg's movements so carefully?

BRACK. In the first place, it could not be entirely indifferent to me if it should appear in the police-court that he came straight from my house.

HEDDA. Will the matter come into court, then?

BRACK. Of course. However, I should scarcely have troubled so much about that. But I thought that, as a friend of the family, it was my duty to supply you and Tesman with a full account of his nocturnal exploits.

HEDDA. Why so, Judge Brack?

BRACK. Why, because I have a shrewd suspicion that he intends to use you as a sort of blind.

HEDDA. Oh, how can you think such a thing!

BRACK. Good heavens, Mrs. Hedda—we have eyes in our head. Mark my words! This Mrs. Elvsted will be in no hurry to leave town again.

HEDDA. Well, even if there should be anything between them, I suppose there are plenty of other places where they could meet.

BRACK. Not a single *home*. Henceforth, as before, every respectable house will be closed against Eilert Lövborg.

HEDDA. And so ought mine to be, you mean?

BRACK. Yes. I confess it would be more than painful to me if this personage were to be made free of your house. How superfluous, how intrusive, he would be, if he were to force his way into——

HEDDA. ——into the triangle?

BRACK. Precisely. It would simply mean that I should find myself homeless.

HEDDA. [*Looks at him with a smile.*] So you want to be the one cock in the basket[1]—that is your aim.

BRACK. [*Nods slowly and lowers his voice.*] Yes, that is my aim. And for that I will fight—with every weapon I can command.

HEDDA. [*Her smile vanishing.*] I see you are a dangerous person—when it comes to the point.

BRACK. Do you think so?

HEDDA. I am beginning to think so. And I am exceedingly glad to think—that you have no sort of hold over me.

BRACK. [*Laughing equivocally.*] Well, well, Mrs. Hedda—perhaps you are right there. If I had, who knows what I might be capable of!

HEDDA. Come, come now, Judge Brack! That sounds almost like a threat.

BRACK. [*Rising.*] Oh, not at all! The triangle, you know, ought, if possible, to be spontaneously constructed.

HEDDA. There I agree with you.

BRACK. Well, now I have said all I had to say; and I had better be getting back to town. Good-bye, Mrs. Hedda. [*He goes towards the glass door.*

HEDDA. [*Rising.*] Are you going through the garden?

BRACK. Yes, it's a short cut for me.

HEDDA. And then it is a back way, too.

BRACK. Quite so. I have no objection to back ways. They may be piquant enough at times.

HEDDA. When there is ball practice going on, you mean?

[1] "Eneste hane i kurven"—a proverbial saying.

BRACK. [*In the doorway, laughing to her.*] Oh, people don't shoot their tame poultry, I fancy.

HEDDA. [*Also laughing.*] Oh no, when there is only one cock in the basket——

[*They exchange laughing nods of farewell. He goes. She closes the door behind him.*

[HEDDA, *who has become quite serious, stands for a moment looking out. Presently she goes and peeps through the curtain over the middle doorway. Then she goes to the writing-table, takes* LÖVBORG'S *packet out of the bookcase, and is on the point of looking through its contents.* BERTA *is heard speaking loudly in the hall.* HEDDA *turns and listens. Then she hastily locks up the packet in the drawer, and lays the key on the inkstand.*

[EILERT LÖVBORG, *with his greatcoat on and his hat in his hand, tears open the hall door. He looks somewhat confused and irritated.*

LÖVBORG. [*Looking towards the hall.*] And I tell you I must and will come in! There!

[*He closes the door, turns, sees* HEDDA, *at once regains his self-control, and bows.*

HEDDA. [*At the writing-table.*] Well, Mr. Lövborg, this is rather a late hour to call for Thea.

LÖVBORG. You mean rather an early hour to call on you. Pray pardon me.

HEDDA. How do you know that she is still here?

LÖVBORG. They told me at her lodgings that she had been out all night.

HEDDA. [*Going to the oval table.*] Did you notice anything about the people of the house when they said that?

LÖVBORG. [*Looks inquiringly at her.*] Notice anything about them?

HEDDA. I mean, did they seem to think it odd?

LÖVBORG. [*Suddenly understanding.*] Oh, yes, of course! I am dragging her down with me! However, I didn't notice anything.—I suppose Tesman is not up yet?

HEDDA. No—I think not——

LÖVBORG. When did he come home?

HEDDA. Very late.

LÖVBORG. Did he tell you anything?

HEDDA. Yes, I gathered that you had had an exceedingly jolly evening at Judge Brack's.

LÖVBORG. Nothing more?

HEDDA. I don't think so. However, I was so dreadfully sleepy——

[MRS. ELVSTED *enters through the curtains of the middle doorway.*

MRS. ELVSTED. [*Going towards him.*] Ah, Lövborg! At last——!

LÖVBORG. Yes, at last. And too late!

MRS. ELVSTED. [*Looks anxiously at him.*] What is too late?

LÖVBORG. Everything is too late now. It is all over with me.

MRS. ELVSTED. Oh no, no—don't say that!

LÖVBORG. You will say the same when you hear——

MRS. ELVSTED. I won't hear anything!

HEDDA. Perhaps you would prefer to talk to her alone? If so, I will leave you.

LÖVBORG. No, stay—you too. I beg you to stay.

MRS. ELVSTED. Yes, but I won't hear anything, I tell you.

LÖVBORG. It is not last night's adventures that I want to talk about.

MRS. ELVSTED. What is it then——?

LÖVBORG. I want to say that now our ways must part.

MRS. ELVSTED. Part!

HEDDA. [*Involuntarily.*] I knew it!

LÖVBORG. You can be of no more service to me, Thea.

MRS. ELVSTED. How can you stand there and say that! No more service to you! Am I not to help you now, as before? Are we not to go on working together?

LÖVBORG. Henceforward I shall do no work.

MRS. ELVSTED. [*Despairingly.*] Then what am I to do with my life?

LÖVBORG. You must try to live your life as if you had never known me.

MRS. ELVSTED. But you know I cannot do that!

LÖVBORG. Try if you cannot, Thea. You must go home again——

MRS. ELVSTED. [*In vehement protest.*] Never in this world! Where you are, there will I be also! I will not let myself be driven away like this! I will remain here! I will be with you when the book appears.

HEDDA. [*Half aloud, in suspense.*] Ah yes—the book!

LÖVBORG. [*Looks at her.*] My book and Thea's; for *that* is what it is.

MRS. ELVSTED. Yes, I feel that it is. And that is why I have a right to be with you when it appears! I will see with my own eyes how respect and honor pour in upon you afresh. And the happiness—the happiness—oh, I must share it with you!

LÖVBORG. Thea—our book will never appear.

HEDDA. Ah!

MRS. ELVSTED. Never appear!

LÖVBORG. *Can* never appear.

MRS. ELVSTED. [*In agonized foreboding.*] Lövborg —what have you done with the manuscript?

HEDDA. [*Looks anxiously at him.*] Yes, the manuscript——?

MRS. ELVSTED. Where is it?

LÖVBORG. Oh Thea—don't ask me about it!

MRS. ELVSTED. Yes, yes, I *will* know. I demand to be told at once.

LÖVBORG. The manuscript——. Well then—I have torn the manuscript into a thousand pieces.

MRS. ELVSTED. [*Shrieks.*] Oh no, no——!

HEDDA. [*Involuntarily.*] But that's not——

LÖVBORG. [*Looks at her.*] Not true, you think?

HEDDA. [*Collecting herself.*] Oh well, of course—since you say so. But it sounded so improbable——

LÖVBORG. It is true, all the same.

MRS. ELVSTED. [*Wringing her hands.*] Oh God—oh God, Hedda—torn his own work to pieces!

LÖVBORG. I have torn my own life to pieces. So why should I not tear my life-work too——?

MRS. ELVSTED. And you did this last night?

LÖVBORG. Yes, I tell you! Tore it into a thousand pieces—and scattered them on the fiord—far out. There, there is cool sea-water at any rate—let them drift upon it—drift with the current and the wind. And then presently they will sink—deeper and deeper—as I shall, Thea.

MRS. ELVSTED. Do you know, Lövborg, that what you have done with the book—I shall think of it to my dying day as though you had killed a little child.

LÖVBORG. Yes, you are right. It is a sort of child-murder.

MRS. ELVSTED. How could you, then——! Did not the child belong to me too?

HEDDA. [*Almost inaudibly.*] Ah, the child——

MRS. ELVSTED. [*Breathing heavily.*] It is all over, then. Well, well, now I will go, Hedda.

HEDDA. But you are not going away from town?

MRS. ELVSTED. Oh, I don't know what I shall do. I see nothing but darkness before me.

[*She goes out by the hall door.*

HEDDA. [*Stands waiting for a moment.*] So you are not going to see her home, Mr. Lövborg?

LÖVBORG. I? Through the streets? Would you have people see her walking with me?

HEDDA. Of course I don't know what else may have happened last night. But is it so utterly irretrievable?

LÖVBORG. It will not end with last night—I know that perfectly well. And the thing is that now I have no taste for that sort of life either. I won't begin it anew. She has broken my courage and my power of braving life out.

HEDDA. [*Looking straight before her.*] So that pretty little fool has had her fingers in a man's destiny. [*Looks at him.*] But all the same, how could you treat her so heartlessly?

LÖVBORG. Oh, don't say that it was heartless!

HEDDA. To go and destroy what has filled her whole soul for months and years! You do not call that heartless!

LÖVBORG. To you I can tell the truth, Hedda.

HEDDA. The truth?

LÖVBORG. First promise me—give me your word—that what I now confide to you Thea shall never know.

HEDDA. I give you my word.

LÖVBORG. Good. Then let me tell you that what I said just now was untrue.

HEDDA. About the manuscript?

LÖVBORG. Yes. I have not torn it to pieces—nor thrown it into the fiord.

HEDDA. No, no——. But—where is it then?

LÖVBORG. I have destroyed it none the less—utterly destroyed it, Hedda!

HEDDA. I don't understand.

LÖVBORG. Thea said that what I had done seemed to her like a child-murder.

HEDDA. Yes, so she said.

LÖVBORG. But to kill his child—that is not the worst thing a father can do to it.

HEDDA. Not the worst?

LÖVBORG. No. I wanted to spare Thea from hearing the worst.

HEDDA. Then what is the worst?

LÖVBORG. Suppose now, Hedda, that a man—in the small hours of the morning—came home to his child's mother after a night of riot and debauchery, and said: "Listen—I have been here and there—in this place and in that. And I have taken our child with me—to this place and to that. And I have lost the child—utterly lost it. The devil knows into what hands it may have fallen—who may have had their clutches on it."

HEDDA. Well—but when all is said and done, you know—this was only a book——

LÖVBORG. Thea's pure soul was in that book.

HEDDA. Yes, so I understand.

LÖVBORG. And you can understand, too, that for her and me together no future is possible.

HEDDA. What path do you mean to take, then?

LÖVBORG. None. I will only try to make an end of it all—the sooner the better.

HEDDA. [*A step nearer him.*] Eilert Lövborg—listen to me.—Will you not try to—to do it beautifully?

LÖVBORG. Beautifully? [*Smiling.*] With vine-leaves in my hair, as you used to dream in the old days——?

HEDDA. No, no. I have lost my faith in the vine-leaves. But beautifully nevertheless! For once in a way!—Good-bye! You must go now—and do not come here any more.

LÖVBORG. Good-bye, Mrs. Tesman. And give George Tesman my love. [*He is on the point of going.*

HEDDA. No, wait! I must give you a memento to take with you.

[*She goes to the writing-table and opens the drawer and the pistol-case; then returns to* LÖVBORG *with one of the pistols.*

LÖVBORG. [*Looks at her.*] This? Is *this* the memento?

HEDDA. [*Nodding slowly.*] Do you recognize it? It was aimed at you once.

LÖVBORG. You should have used it then.

HEDDA. Take it—and do *you* use it now.

LÖVBORG. [*Puts the pistol in his breast pocket.*] Thanks!

HEDDA. And beautifully, Eilert Lövborg. Promise me that!

LÖVBORG. Good-bye, Hedda Gabler.

[*He goes out by the hall door.*

[HEDDA *listens for a moment at the door. Then she goes up to the writing-table, takes out the packet of manuscript, peeps under the cover, draws a few of the sheets half out, and looks at them. Next she goes over and seats herself in the arm-chair beside the stove, with the packet in her lap. Presently she opens the stove door, and then the packet.*

HEDDA. [*Throws one of the quires into the fire and

*whispers to herself.*] Now I am burning your child, Thea!—Burning it, curly-locks! [*Throwing one or two more quires into the stove.*] Your child and Eilert Lövborg's. [*Throws the rest in.*] I am burning—I am burning your child.

**CURTAIN**

## ACT FOURTH

*The same rooms at the* TESMANS'. *It is evening. The drawing-room is in darkness. The back room is lighted by the hanging lamp over the table. The curtains over the glass door are drawn close.*

HEDDA, *dressed in black, walks to and fro in the dark room. Then she goes into the back room and disappears for a moment to the left. She is heard to strike a few chords on the piano. Presently she comes in sight again, and returns to the drawing-room.*

BERTA *enters from the right, through the inner room, with a lighted lamp, which she places on the table in front of the corner settee in the drawing-room. Her eyes are red with weeping, and she has black ribbons in her cap. She goes quietly and circumspectly out to the right.* HEDDA *goes up to the glass door, lifts the curtain a little aside, and looks out into the darkness.*

*Shortly afterwards,* MISS TESMAN, *in mourning, with a bonnet and veil on, comes in from the hall.* HEDDA *goes towards her and holds out her hand.*

MISS TESMAN. Yes, Hedda, here I am, in mourning and forlorn; for now my poor sister has at last found peace.

HEDDA. I have heard the news already, as you see. Tesman sent me a card.

MISS TESMAN. Yes, he promised me he would. But nevertheless I thought that to Hedda—here in the house of life—I ought myself to bring the tidings of death.

HEDDA. That was very kind of you.

MISS TESMAN. Ah, Rina ought not to have left us just *now*. This is not the time for Hedda's house to be a house of mourning.

HEDDA. [*Changing the subject.*] She died quite peacefully, did she not, Miss Tesman?

MISS TESMAN. Oh, her end was so calm, so beautiful. And then she had the unspeakable happiness of seeing George once more—and bidding him good-bye.—Has he not come home yet?

HEDDA. No. He wrote that he might be detained. But won't you sit down?

MISS TESMAN. No thank you, my dear, dear Hedda. I should like to, but I have so much to do. I must prepare my dear one for her rest as well as I can. She shall go to her grave looking her best.

HEDDA. Can I not help you in any way?

MISS TESMAN. Oh, you must not think of it! Hedda Tesman must have no hand in such mournful work. Nor let her thoughts dwell on it either—not at this time.

HEDDA. One is not always mistress of one's thoughts——

MISS TESMAN. [*Continuing.*] Ah, yes, it is the way of the world. At home we shall be sewing a shroud; and here there will soon be sewing too, I suppose—but of another sort, thank God!

[GEORGE TESMAN *enters by the hall door.*

HEDDA. Ah, you have come at last!

TESMAN. You here, Aunt Julia? With Hedda? Fancy that!

MISS TESMAN. I was just going, my dear boy. Well, have you done all you promised?

TESMAN. No; I'm really afraid I have forgotten half of it. I must come to you again to-morrow. To-day my brain is all in a whirl. I can't keep my thoughts together.

MISS TESMAN. Why, my dear George, you mustn't take it in this way.

TESMAN. Mustn't——? How do you mean?

MISS TESMAN. Even in your sorrow you must rejoice, as I do—rejoice that she is at rest.

TESMAN. Oh yes, yes—you are thinking of Aunt Rina.

HEDDA. You will feel lonely now, Miss Tesman.

MISS TESMAN. Just at first, yes. But that will not last very long, I hope. I daresay I shall soon find an occupant for poor Rina's little room.

TESMAN. Indeed? Who do you think will take it? Eh?

MISS TESMAN. Oh, there's always some poor invalid or other in want of nursing, unfortunately.

HEDDA. Would you really take such a burden upon you again?

MISS TESMAN. A burden! Heaven forgive you, child—it has been no burden to me.

HEDDA. But suppose you had a total stranger on your hands——

MISS TESMAN. Oh, one soon makes friends with sick folk; and it's such an absolute necessity for me to have some one to live for. Well, heaven be praised, there may soon be something in this house, too, to keep an old aunt busy.

HEDDA. Oh, don't trouble about anything here.

TESMAN. Yes, just fancy what a nice time we three might have together, if——?

HEDDA. If——?

TESMAN. [*Uneasily.*] Oh, nothing. It will all come right. Let us hope so—eh?

MISS TESMAN. Well, well, I daresay you two want

to talk to each other. [*Smiling.*] And perhaps Hedda may have something to tell you too, George. Good-bye! I must go home to Rina. [*Turning at the door.*] How strange it is to think that now Rina is with me and with my poor brother as well!

TESMAN. Yes, fancy that, Aunt Julia! Eh?

[MISS TESMAN *goes out by the hall door.*

HEDDA. [*Follows* TESMAN *coldly and searchingly with her eyes.*] I almost believe your Aunt Rina's death affects *you* more than it does your Aunt Julia.

TESMAN. Oh, it's not that alone. It's Eilert I am so terribly uneasy about.

HEDDA. [*Quickly.*] Is there anything new about him?

TESMAN. I looked in at his rooms this afternoon, intending to tell him the manuscript was in safe keeping.

HEDDA. Well, did you not find him?

TESMAN. No. He wasn't at home. But afterwards I met Mrs. Elvsted, and she told me that he had been here early this morning.

HEDDA. Yes, directly after you had gone.

TESMAN. And he said that he had torn his manuscript to pieces—eh?

HEDDA. Yes, so he declared.

TESMAN. Why, good heavens, he must have been completely out of his mind! And I suppose you thought it best not to give it back to him, Hedda?

HEDDA. No, he did not get it.

TESMAN. But of course you told him that we had it?

HEDDA. No. [*Quickly.*] Did you tell Mrs. Elvsted?

TESMAN. No; I thought I had better not. But you ought to have told him. Fancy, if, in desperation, he should go and do himself some injury! Let me have the manuscript, Hedda! I will take it to him at once. Where is it?

HEDDA. [*Cold and immovable, leaning on the arm-chair.*] I have not got it.

TESMAN. Have not got it? What in the world do you mean?

HEDDA. I have burnt it—every line of it.

TESMAN. [*With a violent movement of terror.*] Burnt! Burnt Eilert's manuscript!

HEDDA. Don't scream so. The servant might hear you.

TESMAN. Burnt! Why, good God——! No, no, no! It's impossible!

HEDDA. It is so, nevertheless.

TESMAN. Do you know what you have done, Hedda? It's unlawful appropriation of lost property. Fancy that! Just ask Judge Brack, and he'll tell you what it is.

HEDDA. I advise you not to speak of it—either to Judge Brack, or to any one else.

TESMAN. But how could you do anything so unheard-of? What put it into your head? What possessed you? Answer me that—eh?

HEDDA. [*Suppressing an almost imperceptible smile.*] I did it for your sake, George.

TESMAN. For my sake!

HEDDA. This morning, when you told me about what he had read to you——

TESMAN. Yes, yes—what then?

HEDDA. You acknowledged that you envied him his work.

TESMAN. Oh, of course I didn't mean that literally.

HEDDA. No matter—I could not bear the idea that any one should throw you into the shade.

TESMAN. [*In an outburst of mingled doubt and joy.*]

Hedda! Oh, is this true? But—but—I never knew you show your love like that before. Fancy that!

HEDDA. Well, I may as well tell you that—just at this time—— [*Impatiently, breaking off.*] No, no; you can ask Aunt Julia. *She* will tell you, fast enough.

TESMAN. Oh, I almost think I understand you, Hedda! [*Clasps his hands together.*] Great heavens! do you really mean it! Eh?

HEDDA. Don't shout so. The servant might hear.

TESMAN. [*Laughing in irrepressible glee.*] The servant! Why, how absurd you are, Hedda. It's only my old Berta! Why, I'll tell Berta myself.

HEDDA. [*Clenching her hands together in desperation.*] Oh, it is killing me,—it is killing me, all this!

TESMAN. What is, Hedda? Eh?

HEDDA. [*Coldly, controlling herself.*] All this—absurdity—George.

TESMAN. Absurdity! Do you see anything absurd in my being overjoyed at the news! But after all—perhaps I had better not say anything to Berta.

HEDDA. Oh——why not that too?

TESMAN. No, no, not yet! But I must certainly tell Aunt Julia. And then that you have begun to call me George too! Fancy that! Oh, Aunt Julia will be so happy—so happy!

HEDDA. When she hears that I have burnt Eilert Lövborg's manuscript—for your sake?

TESMAN. No, by-the-bye—that affair of the manuscript—of course nobody must know about that. But that you love me so much,[1] Hedda—Aunt Julia must really share my joy in that! I wonder, now, whether this sort of thing is usual in young wives? Eh?

HEDDA. I think you had better ask Aunt Julia that question too.

[1] Literally, "That you burn for me."

TESMAN. I will indeed, some time or other. [*Looks uneasy and downcast again.*] And yet the manuscript—the manuscript! Good God! it is terrible to think what will become of poor Eilert now.

[MRS. ELVSTED, *dressed as in the first Act, with hat and cloak, enters by the hall door.*

MRS. ELVSTED. [*Greets them hurriedly, and says in evident agitation:*] Oh, dear Hedda, forgive my coming again.

HEDDA. What is the matter with you, Thea?

TESMAN. Something about Eilert Lövborg again—eh?

MRS. ELVSTED. Yes! I am dreadfully afraid some misfortune has happened to him.

HEDDA. [*Seizes her arm.*] Ah,—do you think so?

TESMAN. Why, good Lord—what makes you think that, Mrs. Elvsted?

MRS. ELVSTED. I heard them talking of him at my boarding-house—just as I came in. Oh, the most incredible rumors are afloat about him to-day.

TESMAN. Yes, fancy, so I heard too! And I can bear witness that he went straight home to bed last night. Fancy that!

HEDDA. Well, what did they say at the boarding-house?

MRS. ELVSTED. Oh, I couldn't make out anything clearly. Either they knew nothing definite, or else——. They stopped talking when they saw me; and I did not dare to ask.

TESMAN. [*Moving about uneasily.*] We must hope—we must hope that you misunderstood them, Mrs. Elvsted.

MRS. ELVSTED. No, no; I am sure it was of him they were talking. And I heard something about the hospital or——

TESMAN. The hospital?

HEDDA. No—surely that cannot be!

MRS. ELVSTED. Oh, I was in such mortal terror! I went to his lodgings and asked for him there.

HEDDA. *You* could make up your mind to that, Thea!

MRS. ELVSTED. What else could I do? I really could bear the suspense no longer.

TESMAN. But you didn't find him either—eh?

MRS. ELVSTED. No. And the people knew nothing about him. He hadn't been home since yesterday afternoon, they said.

TESMAN. Yesterday! Fancy, how could they say that?

MRS. ELVSTED. Oh, I am sure something terrible must have happened to him.

TESMAN. Hedda dear—how would it be if I were to go and make inquiries——?

HEDDA. No, no—don't you mix yourself up in this affair.

[JUDGE BRACK, *with his hat in his hand, enters by the hall door, which* BERTA *opens, and closes behind him. He looks grave and bows in silence.*

TESMAN. Oh, is that you, my dear Judge? Eh?

BRACK. Yes. It was imperative I should see you this evening.

TESMAN. I can see you have heard the news about Aunt Rina?

BRACK. Yes, that among other things.

TESMAN. Isn't it sad—eh?

BRACK. Well, my dear Tesman, that depends on how you look at it.

TESMAN. [*Looks doubtfully at him.*] Has anything else happened?

BRACK. Yes.

HEDDA. [*In suspense.*] Anything sad, Judge Brack?

BRACK. That, too, depends on how you look at it, Mrs. Tesman.

MRS. ELVSTED. [*Unable to restrain her anxiety.*] Oh! it is something about Eilert Lövborg!

BRACK. [*With a glance at her.*] What makes you think that, Madam? Perhaps you have already heard something——?

MRS. ELVSTED. [*In confusion.*] No, nothing at all, but——

TESMAN. Oh, for heaven's sake, tell us!

BRACK. [*Shrugging his shoulders.*] Well, I regret to say Eilert Lövborg has been taken to the hospital. He is lying at the point of death.

MRS. ELVSTED. [*Shrieks.*] Oh God! oh God——!

TESMAN. To the hospital! And at the point of death!

HEDDA. [*Involuntarily.*] So soon then——

MRS. ELVSTED. [*Wailing.*] And we parted in anger, Hedda!

HEDDA. [*Whispers.*] Thea—Thea—be careful!

MRS. ELVSTED. [*Not heeding her.*] I must go to him! I must see him alive!

BRACK. It is useless, Madam. No one will be admitted.

MRS. ELVSTED. Oh, at least tell me what has happened to him? What is it?

TESMAN. You don't mean to say that he has himself——. Eh?

HEDDA. Yes, I am sure he has.

TESMAN. Hedda, how can you——?

BRACK. [*Keeping his eyes fixed upon her.*] Unfortunately you have guessed quite correctly, Mrs. Tesman.

MRS. ELVSTED. Oh, how horrible!

TESMAN. Himself, then! Fancy that!

HEDDA. Shot himself!

BRACK. Rightly guessed again, Mrs. Tesman.

MRS. ELVSTED. [*With an effort at self-control.*] When did it happen, Mr. Brack?

BRACK. This afternoon—between three and four.

TESMAN. But, good Lord, where did he do it? Eh?

BRACK. [*With some hesitation.*] Where? Well—I suppose at his lodgings.

MRS. ELVSTED. No, that cannot be; for I was there between six and seven.

BRACK. Well then, somewhere else. I don't know exactly. I only know that he was found——. He had shot himself—in the breast.

MRS. ELVSTED. Oh, how terrible! That he should die like that!

HEDDA. [*To* BRACK.] Was it in the breast?

BRACK. Yes—as I told you.

HEDDA. Not in the temple?

BRACK. In the breast, Mrs. Tesman.

HEDDA. Well, well—the breast is a good place, too.

BRACK. How do you mean, Mrs. Tesman?

HEDDA. [*Evasively.*] Oh, nothing—nothing.

TESMAN. And the wound is dangerous, you say—eh?

BRACK. Absolutely mortal. The end has probably come by this time.

MRS. ELVSTED. Yes, yes, I feel it. The end! The end! Oh, Hedda——!

TESMAN. But tell me, how have you learnt all this?

BRACK. [*Curtly.*] Through one of the police. A man I had some business with.

HEDDA. [*In a clear voice.*] At last a deed worth doing!

TESMAN. [*Terrified.*] Good heavens, Hedda! what are you saying?

HEDDA. I say there is beauty in this.

BRACK. H'm, Mrs. Tesman——

TESMAN. Beauty! Fancy that!

MRS. ELVSTED. Oh, Hedda, how can you talk of beauty in such an act!

HEDDA. Eilert Lövborg has himself made up his account with life. He has had the courage to do—the one right thing.

MRS. ELVSTED. No, you must never think *that* was how it happened! It must have been in delirium that he did it.

TESMAN. In despair!

HEDDA. That he did not. I am certain of that.

MRS. ELVSTED. Yes, yes! In delirium! Just as when he tore up our manuscript.

BRACK. [*Starting.*] The manuscript? Has he torn that up?

MRS. ELVSTED. Yes, last night.

TESMAN. [*Whispers softly.*] Oh, Hedda, we shall never get over this.

BRACK. H'm, very extraordinary.

TESMAN. [*Moving about the room.*] To think of Eilert going out of the world in this way! And not leaving behind him the book that would have immortalized his name——

MRS. ELVSTED. Oh, if only it could be put together again!

TESMAN. Yes, if it only could! I don't know what I would not give——

MRS. ELVSTED. Perhaps it can, Mr. Tesman.

TESMAN. What do you mean?

MRS. ELVSTED. [*Searches in the pocket of her dress.*]

Look here. I have kept all the loose notes he used to dictate from.

HEDDA. [*A step forward.*] Ah——!

TESMAN. You have kept them, Mrs. Elvsted! Eh?

MRS. ELVSTED. Yes, I have them here. I put them in my pocket when I left home. Here they still are——

TESMAN. Oh, do let me see them!

MRS. ELVSTED. [*Hands him a bundle of papers.*] But they are in such disorder—all mixed up.

TESMAN. Fancy, if we could make something out of them, after all! Perhaps if we two put our heads together——

MRS. ELVSTED. Oh yes, at least let us try——

TESMAN. We *will* manage it! We *must!* I will dedicate my life to this task.

HEDDA. You, George? Your life?

TESMAN. Yes, or rather all the time I can spare. My own collections must wait in the meantime. Hedda—you understand, eh? I owe this to Eilert's memory.

HEDDA. Perhaps.

TESMAN. And so, my dear Mrs. Elvsted, we will give our whole minds to it. There is no use in brooding over what can't be undone—eh? We must try to control our grief as much as possible, and——

MRS. ELVSTED. Yes, yes, Mr. Tesman, I will do the best I can.

TESMAN. Well then, come here. I can't rest until we have looked through the notes. Where shall we sit? Here? No, in there, in the back room. Excuse me, my dear Judge. Come with me, Mrs. Elvsted.

MRS. ELVSTED. Oh, if only it were possible!

[TESMAN *and* MRS. ELVSTED *go into the back room. She takes off her hat and cloak. They both sit at the table under the hanging lamp, and are soon deep in an eager examination of the papers.* HEDDA *crosses to the stove and sits in the arm-chair. Presently* BRACK *goes up to her.*

HEDDA. [*In a low voice.*] Oh, what a sense of freedom it gives one, this act of Eilert Lövborg's.

BRACK. Freedom, Mrs. Hedda? Well, of course, it is a release for him——

HEDDA. I mean for me. It gives me a sense of freedom to know that a deed of deliberate courage is still possible in this world—a deed of spontaneous beauty.

BRACK. [*Smiling.*] H'm—my dear Mrs. Hedda——

HEDDA. Oh, I know what you are going to say. For you are a kind of specialist too, like—you know!

BRACK. [*Looking hard at her.*] Eilert Lövborg was more to you than perhaps you are willing to admit to yourself. Am I wrong?

HEDDA. I don't answer such questions. I only know that Eilert Lövborg has had the courage to live his life after his own fashion. And then—the last great act, with its beauty! Ah! that he should have the will and the strength to turn away from the banquet of life—so early.

BRACK. I am sorry, Mrs. Hedda,—but I fear I must dispel an amiable illusion.

HEDDA. Illusion?

BRACK. Which could not have lasted long in any case.

HEDDA. What do you mean?

BRACK. Eilert Lövborg did not shoot himself—voluntarily.

HEDDA. Not voluntarily?

BRACK. No. The thing did not happen exactly as I told it.

HEDDA. [*In suspense.*] Have you concealed something? What is it?

BRACK. For poor Mrs. Elvsted's sake I idealized the facts a little.

HEDDA. What are the facts?

BRACK. First, that he is already dead.

HEDDA. At the hospital?

BRACK. Yes—without regaining consciousness.

HEDDA. What more have you concealed?

BRACK. This—the event did not happen at his lodgings.

HEDDA. Oh, that can make no difference.

BRACK. Perhaps it may. For I must tell you—Eilert Lövborg was found shot in—in Mademoiselle Diana's boudoir.

HEDDA. [*Makes a motion as if to rise, but sinks back again.*] That is impossible, Judge Brack! He cannot have been *there* again to-day.

BRACK. He was there this afternoon. He went there, he said, to demand the return of something which they had taken from him. Talked wildly about a lost child——

HEDDA. Ah—so that was why——

BRACK. I thought probably he meant his manuscript; but now I hear he destroyed that himself. So I suppose it must have been his pocket-book.

HEDDA. Yes, no doubt. And there—there he was found?

BRACK. Yes, there. With a pistol in his breast-pocket, discharged. The ball had lodged in a vital part.

HEDDA. In the breast—yes.

BRACK. No—in the bowels.

HEDDA. [*Looks up at him with an expression of loathing.*] That too! Oh, what curse is it that makes everything I touch turn ludicrous and mean?

BRACK. There is one point more, Mrs. Hedda—another disagreeable feature in the affair.

HEDDA. And what is that?

BRACK. The pistol he carried——

HEDDA. [*Breathless.*] Well? What of it?

BRACK. He must have stolen it.

HEDDA. [*Leaps up.*] Stolen it? That is not true! He did not steal it!

BRACK. No other explanation is possible. He *must* have stolen it——. Hush!

[TESMAN *and* MRS. ELVSTED *have risen from the table in the back room, and come into the drawing-room.*

TESMAN. [*With the papers in both his hands.*] Hedda dear, it is almost impossible to see under that lamp. Think of that!

HEDDA. Yes, I am thinking.

TESMAN. Would you mind our sitting at your writing-table—eh?

HEDDA. If you like. [*Quickly.*] No, wait! Let me clear it first!

TESMAN. Oh, you needn't trouble, Hedda. There is plenty of room.

HEDDA. No, no, let me clear it, I say! I will take these things in and put them on the piano. There!

[*She has drawn out an object, covered with sheet music, from under the bookcase, places several other pieces of music upon it, and carries the whole into the inner room, to the left.* TESMAN *lays the scraps of paper on the writing-table, and moves the lamp there from the corner table. He and* MRS. ELVSTED *sit down and proceed with their work.* HEDDA *returns.*

HEDDA. [*Behind* MRS. ELVSTED'S *chair, gently ruf-*

*fling her hair.*] Well, my sweet Thea,—how goes it with Eilert Lövborg's monument?

MRS. ELVSTED. [*Looks dispiritedly up at her.*] Oh, it will be terribly hard to put in order.

TESMAN. We *must* manage it. I am determined. And arranging other people's papers is just the work for me.

[HEDDA *goes over to the stove, and seats herself on one of the footstools.* BRACK *stands over her, leaning on the arm-chair.*

HEDDA. [*Whispers.*] What did you say about the pistol?

BRACK. [*Softly.*] That he must have stolen it.

HEDDA. Why stolen it?

BRACK. Because every other explanation *ought* to be impossible, Mrs. Hedda.

HEDDA. Indeed?

BRACK. [*Glances at her.*] Of course Eilert Lövborg was here this morning. Was he not?

HEDDA. Yes.

BRACK. Were you alone with him?

HEDDA. Part of the time.

BRACK. Did you not leave the room whilst he was here?

HEDDA. No.

BRACK. Try to recollect. Were you not out of the room a moment?

HEDDA. Yes, perhaps just a moment—out in the hall.

BRACK. And where was your pistol-case during that time?

HEDDA. I had it locked up in——

BRACK. Well, Mrs. Hedda?

HEDDA. The case stood there on the writing-table.

BRACK. Have you looked since, to see whether both the pistols are there?

HEDDA. No.

BRACK. Well, you need not. I saw the pistol found in Lövborg's pocket, and I knew it at once as the one I had seen yesterday—and before, too.

HEDDA. Have you it with you?

BRACK. No; the police have it.

HEDDA. What will the police do with it?

BRACK. Search till they find the owner.

HEDDA. Do you think they will succeed?

BRACK. [*Bends over her and whispers.*] No, Hedda Gabler—not so long as I say nothing.

HEDDA. [*Looks frightened at him.*] And if you do *not* say nothing—what then?

BRACK. [*Shrugs his shoulders.*] There is always the possibility that the pistol was stolen.

HEDDA. [*Firmly.*] Death rather than that.

BRACK. [*Smiling.*] People say such things—but they don't *do* them.

HEDDA. [*Without replying.*] And supposing the pistol was not stolen, and the owner is discovered? What then?

BRACK. Well, Hedda—then comes the scandal.

HEDDA. The scandal!

BRACK. Yes, the scandal—of which you are so mortally afraid. You will, of course, be brought before the court—both you and Mademoiselle Diana. She will have to explain how the thing happened—whether it was an accidental shot or murder. Did the pistol go off as he was trying to take it out of his pocket, to threaten her with? Or did she tear the pistol out of his hand, shoot him, and push it back into his pocket? That would be quite like her; for she is an able-bodied young person, this same Mademoiselle Diana.

HEDDA. But *I* have nothing to do with all this repulsive business.

BRACK. No. But you will have to answer the question: Why did you give Eilert Lövborg the pistol? And what conclusions will people draw from the fact that you did give it to him?

HEDDA. [*Lets her head sink.*] That is true. I did not think of that.

BRACK. Well, fortunately, there is no danger, so long as I say nothing.

HEDDA. [*Looks up at him.*] So I am in your power, Judge Brack. You have me at your beck and call, from this time forward.

BRACK. [*Whispers softly.*] Dearest Hedda—believe me—I shall not abuse my advantage.

HEDDA. I am in your power none the less. Subject to your will and your demands. A slave, a slave then! [*Rises impetuously.*] No, I cannot endure the thought of that! Never!

BRACK. [*Looks half-mockingly at her.*] People generally get used to the inevitable.

HEDDA. [*Returns his look.*] Yes, perhaps. [*She crosses to the writing-table. Suppressing an involuntary smile, she imitates* TESMAN'S *intonations.*] Well? Are you getting on, George? Eh?

TESMAN. Heaven knows, dear. In any case it will be the work of months.

HEDDA. [*As before.*] Fancy that! [*Passes her hands softly through* MRS. ELVSTED'S *hair.*] Doesn't it seem strange to you, Thea? Here are you sitting with Tesman—just as you used to sit with Eilert Lövborg.

MRS. ELVSTED. Ah, if I could only inspire your husband in the same way!

HEDDA. Oh, that will come too—in time.

TESMAN. Yes, do you know, Hedda—I really think I begin to feel something of the sort. But won't you go and sit with Brack again?

HEDDA. Is there nothing I can do to help you two?

TESMAN. No, nothing in the world. [*Turning his head.*] I trust to you to keep Hedda company, my dear Brack.

BRACK. [*With a glance at* HEDDA.] With the very greatest of pleasure.

HEDDA. Thanks. But I am tired this evening. I will go in and lie down a little on the sofa.

TESMAN. Yes, do, dear—eh?

[HEDDA *goes into the back room and draws the curtains. A short pause. Suddenly she is heard playing a wild dance on the piano.*

MRS. ELVSTED. [*Starts from her chair.*] Oh—what is that?

TESMAN. [*Runs to the doorway.*] Why, my dearest Hedda—don't play dance-music to-night! Just think of Aunt Rina! And of Eilert too!

HEDDA. [*Puts her head out between the curtains.*] And of Aunt Julia. And of all the rest of them.—After this, I will be quiet. [*Closes the curtains again.*]

TESMAN. [*At the writing-table.*] It's not good for her to see us at this distressing work. I'll tell you what, Mrs. Elvsted,—you shall take the empty room at Aunt Julia's, and then I will come over in the evenings, and we can sit and work *there*—eh?

HEDDA. [*In the inner room.*] I hear what you are saying, Tesman. But how am *I* to get through the evenings out here?

TESMAN. [*Turning over the papers.*] Oh, I daresay Judge Brack will be so kind as to look in now and then, even though I am out.

BRACK. [*In the arm-chair, calls out gaily.*] Every

blessed evening, with all the pleasure in life, Mrs. Tesman! We shall get on capitally together, we two!

HEDDA. [*Speaking loud and clear.*] Yes, don't you flatter yourself we will, Judge Brack? Now that you are the one cock in the basket——

[*A shot is heard within.* TESMAN, MRS. ELVSTED, *and* BRACK *leap to their feet.*

TESMAN. Oh, now she is playing with those pistols again.

[*He throws back the curtains and runs in, followed by* MRS. ELVSTED. HEDDA *lies stretched on the sofa, lifeless. Confusion and cries.* BERTA *enters in alarm from the right.*

TESMAN. [*Shrieks to* BRACK.] Shot herself! Shot herself in the temple! Fancy that!

BRACK. [*Half-fainting in the arm-chair.*] Good God!—people don't do such things!

CURTAIN

# PÉLLÉAS AND MÉLISANDE

BY

MAURICE MAETERLINCK

*Translated by* RICHARD HOVEY.

## Maurice Maeterlinck

b. 1862, Ghent, Belgium.
University of Ghent.
1887, associated in Paris with the French symbolists.
1911, awarded Nobel prize for literature.
Poet, mystic, entomologist.

### Plays

1889 *La Princesse Maleine* (translated as *The Princess Maleine*).
1890 *Les Aveugles* (translated as *The Blind* and *The Sightless*).
1890 *L'Intruse* (translated as *The Intruder*).
1891 *Les Sept Princesses* (translated as *The Seven Princesses*).
1892 *Pélléas et Mélisande* (translated as *Pélléas and Mélisande*).
1894 *Alladine et Palomides* (translated as *Alladine and Palomides*).
1894 *L'Intérieur* (translated as *Interior* and *Home*).
1894 *La Mort de Tintagile* (translated as *The Death of Tintagiles*).
1895 *Annabella* (translation of Ford's *'Tis Pity She's a Whore*).
1896 *Aglavaine et Sélysette* (translated as *Aglavaine and Selysette*).
1900 *Soeur Béatrice* (translated as *Sister Beatrice*).
1901 *Ariane et Barbe Bleu* (translated as *Ardiane and Barbe Bleu*).
1902 *Monna Vanna* (translated as *Mónna Vanna*).

1903 *Joyzelle* (translated as *Joyzelle*).
1904 *Le Miracle de Saint Antoine* (translated as *The Miracle of Saint Anthony*).
1908 *L'Oiseau Bleu* (translated as *The Blue Bird*).
1910 *Marie Magdeleine* (translated as *Mary Magdalene*).
1910 *Macbeth* (translation of Shakespeare).
1918 *Les Fiançailles* (translated as *The Betrothal,* sequel to *The Blue Bird*).
1918 *Le Bourgmestre de Stilemonde* (translated as *The Burgomaster of Stilemonde*).
1920 *Le Sel de la Vie* (sequel to *The Burgomaster of Stilemonde,* not translated).
1923 *La Puissance des Morts* (translated as *The Power of the Dead*).
1923 *The Cloud that Lifted* (translated, but not published or produced in French).
1925 *Le Malheur Passe* (not translated).
1927 *Marie-Victoire* (not translated).
1929 *Juda de Kerioth* (not translated).

WRITINGS ABOUT THE DRAMA

*The Treasure of the Humble,* translated by Alfred Sutro, 1898, especially *The Tragical in Daily Life.*
*The Modern Drama,* in *The Double Garden,* translated by A. T. de Mattos. 1904.

## PÉLLÉAS AND MÉLISANDE

Maurice Maeterlinck's first play, *La Princesse Maleine,* attracted to him the attention of the theatrical world, largely because Octave Mirbeau, the distinguished critic and novelist, wrote of it as "comparable and—dare I say it?—superior in beauty to what is most beautiful in Shakespeare . . . more tragic than *Macbeth,* more extraordinary in thought than *Hamlet.*" That obviously extravagant judgment could scarcely be thought today, when Maeterlinck's dramas are rarely played, and he is no longer a force in the theatre. But in 1889, and in the years following, Maeterlinck was to bring to the stage work that was distinctly fresh and original, based on a theory of drama that was startling and fructifying and at the same time poetic. The theory is stated most clearly in *The Treasure of the Humble,* where Maeterlinck himself gives it the name "static." He found the theatre of his time "primitive, arid, and brutal; . . . I was yearning for one of the strange moments of a higher life that flit unperceived through my dreariest hours; whereas, almost invariably, all that I beheld was but a man who would tell me, at wearisome length, why he was jealous, why he poisoned, or why he killed. . . . I have grown to believe that an old man, seated in his arm chair, waiting patiently with his lamp beside him; giving unconscious ear to all the eternal laws that reign about his house, interpreting, without comprehending, the silence of doors and windows and the quivering voice of the light, submitting with bent head to the presence of his soul and of destiny . . . motionless as he is, does yet in reality live a deeper, more human, and more universal life than the lover who strangles his mistress, the captain who conquers in battle, or 'the husband who avenges his honor.' . . . Indeed, it is not in the actions but in the words that are found the beauty and greatness of tragedies that are truly beautiful and great; and this not solely in the words that accompany and explain the action, for there must perforce be another dialogue besides the one which is superficially necessary. And indeed the only words that count in the play are those that at first seemed useless, for it is therein that the essence lies. Side by side with the necessary dialogue you will almost always find another dialogue that seems superfluous; but examine it carefully, and it will be borne home to you that this is the only one that the soul can listen to profoundly, for here alone is it the soul that is being addressed. . . . One may even affirm that a poem draws the nearer to beauty and loftier truth in the measure that it eliminates words that explain the action, and substitutes for them others that reveal, not the so-called 'soul-state,' but I know not what intangible and unceasing striving of the soul towards its own beauty and truth."

This striving for the atmospheric and intangible, together with Maeterlinck's fatalistic prepossessions, barred him, in his plays, from the study of character, and made his people phantoms, though he called them marionettes. Actors have always found the parts in the early plays difficult: so much that is left unsaid and undone must nevertheless be conveyed. *Pélléas and Mélisande* is a typical play of Maeterlinck's first period in its atmospheric quality and the tenuousness of its people, and in its abundance of literary echoes, such as the first scene, reminiscent of *Macbeth*, and the main situation, reminiscent of the Francesca da Rimini story.

For a widely different treatment of the same theme, see D'Annunzio's *Francesca da Rimini,* in *Contemporary Drama, European Plays III.*

Pélléas and Mélisande has had many interesting productions. It was first played in English in London under the management of Johnston Forbes-Robertson, who played Golaud, with Mrs. Patrick Campbell as Mélisande, in 1898. A gauze curtain was hung between audience and players, in order, perhaps, to heighten the unreality. Later Mrs. Campbell played Mélisande to Mme. Sarah Bernhardt's Pélléas, in French. A most unusual production of the play took place in 1910 at Maeterlinck's country home in Normandy, the Abbaye de Saint-Wandrille. Under the direction of Mme. Georgette Leblanc, then Maeterlinck's wife, who played Mélisande, the rooms and grounds of the Abbaye were used as settings and the invited audience followed the players about, carrying camp-stools. Reports of the occasion pronounced it most successful.

*Pélléas and Mélisande* was performed in America by Mrs. Patrick Campbell in 1902. It was revived in 1923, when Miss Jane Cowl played Mélisande for a short run. Debussy's opera of the same name, which uses an abbreviated version of the play as libretto, was first produced in New York in 1908, under the direction of Oscar Hammerstein at the Manhattan Opera House. Mary Garden created Mélisande. The opera is now occasionally included in the repertory of the Metropolitan Opera Company, and is considered one of the greatest music-dramas since Wagner.

## PERSONS

ARKËL, *King of Allemonde.*
GENEVIÈVE, *mother of Pélléas and Golaud.*
PÉLLÉAS, } *grandsons of Arkël.*
GOLAUD, }
MÉLISANDE.
LITTLE YNIOLD, *son of Golaud (by a former marriage).*
A PHYSICIAN.
THE PORTER.
*Servants, Beggars, etc.*

# PÉLLÉAS AND MÉLISANDE

## ACT FIRST

### SCENE I.—*The gate of the castle.*

MAIDSERVANTS. [*Within.*] Open the gate! Open the gate!

PORTER. [*Within.*] Who is there? Why do you come and wake me up? Go out by the little gates; there are enough of them! . . .

A MAIDSERVANT. [*Within.*] We have come to wash the threshold, the gate, and the steps; open, then! open!

ANOTHER MAIDSERVANT. [*Within.*] There are going to be great happenings!

THIRD MAIDSERVANT. [*Within.*] There are going to be great fêtes! Open quickly! . . .

THE MAIDSERVANTS. Open! open!

PORTER. Wait! wait! I do not know whether I shall be able to open it; . . . it is never opened. . . . Wait till it is light. . . .

FIRST MAIDSERVANT. It is light enough without; I see the sunlight through the chinks. . . .

PORTER. Here are the great keys. . . . Oh! oh! how the bolts and the locks grate! . . . Help me! help me! . . .

MAIDSERVANTS. We are pulling; we are pulling. . . .

SECOND MAIDSERVANT. It will not open. . . .

FIRST MAIDSERVANT. Ah! ah! It is opening! it is opening slowly!

PORTER. How it shrieks! how it shrieks! It will wake up everybody. . . .

SECOND MAIDSERVANT. [*Appearing on the threshold.*] Oh, how light it is already out-of-doors!

FIRST MAIDSERVANT. The sun is rising on the sea!

PORTER. It is open. . . . It is wide open! . . .

[*All the maidservants appear on the threshold and pass over it.*

FIRST MAIDSERVANT. I am going to wash the sill first. . . .

SECOND MAIDSERVANT. We shall never be able to clean all this.

OTHER MAIDSERVANTS. Fetch the water! fetch the water!

PORTER. Yes, yes; pour on water; pour on water; pour on all the water of the Flood! You will never come to the end of it. . . .

SCENE II.—*A forest.* MÉLISANDE *discovered at the brink of a spring.*

[*Enter* GOLAUD.

GOLAUD. I shall never be able to get out of this forest again.—God knows where that beast has led me. And yet I thought I had wounded him to death; and here are traces of blood. But now I have lost sight of him; I believe I am lost myself—my dogs can no longer find me—I shall retrace my steps. . . .—I hear weeping . . . Oh! oh! what is there yonder by the water's edge? . . . A little girl weeping by the water's edge? [*He coughs.*]—She does not hear me. I cannot see her face. [*He approaches and touches* MÉLISANDE *on the shoulder.*] Why weepest thou? [MÉLISANDE *trembles, starts up, and would flee.*]—Do not be afraid. You have nothing to fear. Why are you weeping here all alone?

MÉLISANDE. Do not touch me! do not touch me!

GOLAUD. Do not be afraid. . . . I will not do you any . . . Oh, you are beautiful!

MÉLISANDE. Do not touch me! do not touch me! or I throw myself in the water! . . .

GOLAUD. I will not touch you. . . . See, I will stay here, against the tree. Do not be afraid. Has any one hurt you?

MÉLISANDE. Oh! yes! yes! yes! . . . [*She sobs profoundly.*]

GOLAUD. Who has hurt you?

MÉLISANDE. Every one! every one!

GOLAUD. What hurt have they done you?

MÉLISANDE. I will not tell! I cannot tell! . . .

GOLAUD. Come; do not weep so. Whence come you?

MÉLISANDE. I have fled! . . . fled . . . fled. . . .

GOLAUD. Yes; but whence have you fled?

MÉLISANDE. I am lost! . . . lost! . . . Oh! oh! lost here. . . . I am not of this place. . . . I was not born here. . . .

GOLAUD. Whence are you? Where were you born?

MÉLISANDE. Oh! oh! far away from here! . . . far away . . . far away. . . .

GOLAUD. What is it shining so at the bottom of the water?

MÉLISANDE. Where?—Ah! it is the crown he gave me. It fell as I was weeping. . . .

GOLAUD. A crown?—Who was it gave you a crown? —I will try to get it. . . .

MÉLISANDE. No, no; I will have no more of it! I will have no more of it! . . . I had rather die . . . die at once. . . .

GOLAUD. I could easily pull it out. The water is not very deep.

MÉLISANDE. I will have no more of it! If you take it out, I throw myself in its place! . . .

GOLAUD. No, no; I will leave it there. It could be reached without difficulty, nevertheless. It seems very beautiful.—Is it long since you fled?

MÉLISANDE. Yes, yes! . . . Who are you?

GOLAUD. I am Prince Golaud,—grandson of Arkël, the old King of Allemonde. . . .

MÉLISANDE. Oh, you have gray hairs already. . . .

GOLAUD. Yes; some, here, by the temples . . .

MÉLISANDE. And in your beard, too. . . . Why do you look at me so?

GOLAUD. I am looking at your eyes.—Do you never shut your eyes?

MÉLISANDE. Oh, yes; I shut them at night. . . .

GOLAUD. Why do you look so astonished?

MÉLISANDE. You are a giant?

GOLAUD. I am a man like the rest. . . .

MÉLISANDE. Why have you come here?

GOLAUD. I do not know, myself. I was hunting in the forest. I was chasing a wild boar. I mistook the road.—You look very young. How old are you?

MÉLISANDE. I am beginning to be cold. . . .

GOLAUD. Will you come with me?

MÉLISANDE. No, no; I will stay here. . . .

GOLAUD. You cannot stay here all alone. You cannot stay here all night long. . . . What is your name?

MÉLISANDE. Mélisande.

GOLAUD. You cannot stay here, Mélisande. Come with me. . . .

MÉLISANDE. I will stay here. . . .

GOLAUD. You will be afraid, all alone. We do not know what there may be here . . . all night long . . . all alone . . . it is impossible. Mélisande, come, give me your hand. . . .

MÉLISANDE. Oh, do not touch me! . . .

GOLAUD. Do not scream. . . . I will not touch you

again. But come with me. The night will be very dark and very cold. Come with me. . . .

MÉLISANDE. Where are you going? . . .

GOLAUD. I do not know. . . . I am lost too. . . .

[*Exeunt.*

SCENE III.—*A hall in the castle.* ARKËL *and* GENEVIÈVE *discovered.*

GENEVIÈVE. Here is what he writes to his brother Pélléas: "I found her all in tears one evening, beside a spring in the forest where I had lost myself. I do not know her age, nor who she is, nor whence she comes, and I dare not question her, for she must have had a sore fright; and when you ask her what has happened to her, she falls at once a-weeping like a child, and sobs so heavily you are afraid. Just as I found her by the springs, a crown of gold had slipped from her hair and fallen to the bottom of the water. She was clad, besides, like a princess, though her garments had been torn by the briers. It is now six months since I married her and I know no more about it than on the day of our meeting. Meanwhile, dear Pélléas, thou whom I love more than a brother, although we were not born of the same father; meanwhile make ready for my return. . . . I know my mother will willingly forgive me. But I am afraid of the King, our venerable grandsire, I am afraid of Arkël, in spite of all his kindness, for I have undone by this strange marriage all his plans of state, and I fear the beauty of Mélisande will not excuse my folly to eyes so wise as his. If he consents nevertheless to receive her as he would receive his own daughter, the third night following this letter, light a lamp at the top of the tower that overlooks the sea. I shall perceive it from the bridge of our ship; otherwise I shall go far away again and come back no more. . . ." What say you of it?

ARKËL. Nothing. He has done what he probably must have done. I am very old, and nevertheless I have not yet seen clearly for one moment into myself; how would you that I judge what others have done? I am not far from the tomb and do not succeed in judging myself. . . . One always mistakes when one does not close his eyes. That may seem strange to us; but that is all. He is past the age to marry and he weds, like a child, a little girl he finds by a spring. . . . That may seem strange to us, because we never see but the reverse of destinies . . . the reverse even of our own. . . . He has always followed my counsels hitherto; I had thought to make him happy in sending him to ask the hand of Princess Ursula. . . . He could not remain alone; since the death of his wife he has been sad to be alone; and that marriage would have put an end to long wars and old hatreds. . . . He would not have it so. Let it be as he would have it; I have never put myself athwart a destiny; and he knows better than I his future. There happen perhaps no useless events. . . .

GENEVIÈVE. He has always been so prudent, so grave and so firm. . . . If it were Pélléas, I should understand. . . . But he . . . at his age. . . . Who is it he is going to introduce here?—An unknown found along the roads. . . . Since his wife's death, he has no longer lived for aught but his son, the little Yniold, and if he were about to marry again, it was because you had wished it. . . . And now . . . a little girl in the forest. . . . He has forgotten everything. . . .—What shall we do? . . .

[*Enter* PÉLLÉAS.

ARKËL. Who is coming in there?

GENEVIÈVE. It is Pélléas. He has been weeping.

ARKËL. Is it thou, Pélléas?—Come a little nearer, that I may see thee in the light. . . .

PÉLLÉAS. Grandfather, I received another letter at the same time as my brother's; a letter from my friend Marcellus. . . . He is about to die and calls for me. He would see me before dying. . . .

ARKËL. Thou wouldst leave before thy brother's return?—Perhaps thy friend is less ill than he thinks. . . .

PÉLLÉAS. His letter is so sad you can see death between the lines. . . . He says he knows the very day when death must come. . . . He tells me I can arrive before it if I will, but that there is no more time to lose. The journey is very long, and if I await Golaud's return, it will be perhaps too late. . . .

ARKËL. Thou must wait a little while, nevertheless. . . . We do not know what this return has in store for us. And besides, is not thy father here, above us, more sick perhaps than thy friend? . . . Couldst thou choose between the father and the friend? . . . [*Exit.*

GENEVIÈVE. Have a care to keep the lamp lit from this evening, Pélléas. . . . [*Exeunt severally.*

SCENE IV.—*Before the castle. Enter* GENEVIÈVE *and* MÉLISANDE.

MÉLISANDE. It is gloomy in the gardens. And what forests, what forests all about the palaces! . . .

GENEVIÈVE. Yes; that astonished me too when I came hither; it astonishes everybody. There are places where you never see the sun. But one gets used to it so quickly. . . . It is long ago, it is long ago. . . . It is nearly forty years that I have lived here. . . . Look toward the other side, you will have the light of the sea. . . .

MÉLISANDE. I hear a noise below us. . . .

GENEVIÈVE. Yes; it is some one coming up toward us. . . . Ah! it is Pélléas. . . . He seems still tired from having waited so long for you. . . .

MÉLISANDE. He has not seen us.

GENEVIÈVE. I think he has seen us but does not know what he should do. . . . Pélléas, Pélléas, is it thou? . . .

[*Enter* PÉLLÉAS.

PÉLLÉAS. Yes! . . . I was coming toward the sea. . . .

GENEVIÈVE. So were we; we were seeking the light. It is a little lighter here than elsewhere; and yet the sea is gloomy.

PÉLLÉAS. We shall have a storm to-night. There has been one every night for some time, and yet it is so calm now. . . . One might embark unwittingly and come back no more.

MÉLISANDE. Something is leaving the port. . . .

PÉLLÉAS. It must be a big ship. . . . The lights are very high, we shall see it in a moment, when it enters the band of light. . . .

GENEVIÈVE. I do not know whether we shall be able to see it . . . there is still a fog on the sea. . . .

PÉLLÉAS. The fog seems to be rising slowly. . . .

MÉLISANDE. Yes; I see a little light down there, which I had not seen. . . .

PÉLLÉAS. It is a lighthouse; there are others we cannot see yet.

MÉLISANDE. The ship is in the light. . . . It is already very far away. . . .

PÉLLÉAS. It is a foreign ship. It looks larger than ours. . . .

MÉLISANDE. It is the ship that brought me here! . . .

PÉLLÉAS. It flies away under full sail. . . .

MÉLISANDE. It is the ship that brought me here. It has great sails. . . . I recognized it by its sails.

PÉLLÉAS. There will be a rough sea to-night.

MÉLISANDE. Why does it go away to-night? . . . You can hardly see it any longer. . . . Perhaps it will be wrecked. . . .

PÉLLÉAS. The night falls very quickly. . . .

[*A silence.*

GENEVIÈVE. No one speaks any more? . . . You have nothing more to say to each other? . . . It is time to go in. Pélléas, show Mélisande the way. I must go see little Yniold a moment. [*Exit.*

PÉLLÉAS. Nothing can be seen any longer on the sea. . . .

MÉLISANDE. I see more lights.

PÉLLÉAS. It is the other lighthouses. . . . Do you hear the sea? . . . It is the wind rising. . . . Let us go down this way. Will you give me your hand?

MÉLISANDE. See, see, my hands are full. . . .

PÉLLÉAS. I will hold you by the arm, the road is steep and it is very gloomy there. . . . I am going away perhaps to-morrow. . . .

MÉLISANDE. Oh! . . . why do you go away?

[*Exeunt.*

# ACT SECOND

## SCENE I.—*A fountain in the park.*

[*Enter* PÉLLÉAS *and* MÉLISANDE.

PÉLLÉAS. You do not know where I have brought you?—I often come to sit here, toward noon, when it is too hot in the gardens. It is stifling to-day, even in the shade of the trees.

MÉLISANDE. Oh, how clear the water is! . . .

PÉLLÉAS. It is as cool as winter. It is an old abandoned spring. It seems to have been a miraculous spring,—it opened the eyes of the blind,—they still call it "Blind Man's Spring."

MÉLISANDE. It no longer opens the eyes of the blind?

PÉLLÉAS. Since the King has been nearly blind himself, no one comes any more. . . .

MÉLISANDE. How alone one is here! . . . There is no sound.

PÉLLÉAS. There is always a wonderful silence here. . . . One could hear the water sleep. . . . Will you sit down on the edge of the marble basin? There is one linden where the sun never comes. . . .

MÉLISANDE. I am going to lie down on the marble.—I should like to see the bottom of the water. . . .

PÉLLÉAS. No one has ever seen it.—It is as deep, perhaps, as the sea.—It is not known whence it comes.—Perhaps it comes from the bottom of the earth. . . .

MÉLISANDE. If there were anything shining at the bottom, perhaps one could see it. . . .

PÉLLÉAS. Do not lean over so. . . .

MÉLISANDE. I would like to touch the water. . . .

PÉLLÉAS. Have a care of slipping. . . . I will hold your hand. . . .

MÉLISANDE. No, no, I would plunge both hands in it. . . . You would say my hands were sick to-day. . . .

PÉLLÉAS. Oh! oh! take care! take care! Mélisande! . . . Mélisande! . . .—Oh! your hair! . . .

MÉLISANDE. [*Starting upright.*] I cannot, . . . I cannot reach it. . . .

PÉLLÉAS. Your hair dipped in the water. . . .

MÉLISANDE. Yes, it is longer than my arms. . . . It is longer than I. . . . [*A silence.*

PÉLLÉAS. It was at the brink of a spring, too, that he found you?

MÉLISANDE. Yes. . . .

PÉLLÉAS. What did he say to you?

MÉLISANDE. Nothing;—I no longer remember. . . .

PÉLLÉAS. Was he quite near you?

MÉLISANDE. Yes; he would have kissed me.

PÉLLÉAS. And you would not?

MÉLISANDE. No.

PÉLLÉAS. Why would you not?

MÉLISANDE. Oh! oh! I saw something pass at the bottom of the water. . . .

PÉLLÉAS. Take care! take care!—You will fall! What are you playing with?

MÉLISANDE. With the ring he gave me. . . .

PÉLLÉAS. Take care; you will lose it. . . .

MÉLISANDE. No, no; I am sure of my hands. . . .

PÉLLÉAS. Do not play so, over so deep a water. . . .

MÉLISANDE. My hands do not tremble.

PÉLLÉAS. How it shines in the sunlight!—Do not throw it so high in the air. . . .

MÉLISANDE. Oh! . . .

PÉLLÉAS. It has fallen?

MÉLISANDE. It has fallen into the water! . . .

PÉLLÉAS. Where is it? where is it? . . .

MÉLISANDE. I do not see it sink. . . .

PÉLLÉAS. I think I see it shine. . . .

MÉLISANDE. My ring?

PÉLLÉAS. Yes, yes; down yonder. . . .

MÉLISANDE. Oh! oh! It is so far away from us! . . . no, no, that is not it . . . that is not it . . . It is lost . . . lost. . . . There is nothing any more but a great circle on the water. . . . What shall we do? What shall we do now? . . .

PÉLLÉAS. You need not be so troubled for a ring. It is nothing. . . . We shall find it again, perhaps. Or else we will find another. . . .

MÉLISANDE. No, no; we shall never find it again; we shall never find any others either. . . . And yet I thought I had it in my hands. . . . I had already shut my hands, and it is fallen in spite of all. . . . I threw it too high, toward the sun. . . .

PÉLLÉAS. Come, come, we will come back another day; . . . come, it is time. They will come to meet us. It was striking noon at the moment the ring fell.

MÉLISANDE. What shall we say to Golaud if he ask where it is?

PÉLLÉAS. The truth, the truth, the truth. . . .

[*Exeunt.*

SCENE II.—*An apartment in the castle.* GOLAUD *discovered, stretched upon his bed;* MÉLISANDE, *by his bedside.*

GOLAUD. Ah! ah! all goes well; it will amount to nothing. But I cannot understand how it came to pass. I was hunting quietly in the forest. All at once my horse ran away, without cause. Did he see anything unusual? . . . I had just heard the twelve strokes of noon. At the twelfth stroke he suddenly took fright and ran like a blind madman against a tree. I heard no more. I do not yet know what happened. I fell, and he must have fallen on me. I thought I had the whole forest on my breast; I thought my heart was crushed. But my heart is sound. It is nothing, apparently. . . .

MÉLISANDE. Would you like a little water?

GOLAUD. Thanks, thanks; I am not thirsty.

MÉLISANDE. Would you like another pillow? . . . There is a little spot of blood on this.

GOLAUD. No, no; it is not worth while. I bled at the mouth just now. I shall bleed again perhaps. . . .

MÉLISANDE. Are you quite sure? . . . You are not suffering too much?

GOLAUD. No, no; I have seen a good many more like this. I was made of iron and blood. . . . These are not the little bones of a child; do not alarm yourself. . . .

MÉLISANDE. Close your eyes and try to sleep. I shall stay here all night. . . .

GOLAUD. No, no; I do not wish you to tire yourself so. I do not need anything; I shall sleep like a child. . . . What is the matter, Mélisande? Why do you weep all at once? . . .

MÉLISANDE. [*Bursting into tears.*] I am . . . I am ill too. . . .

GOLAUD. Thou art ill? . . . What ails thee, then; what ails thee, Mélisande? . . .

MÉLISANDE. I do not know. . . . I am ill here. . . . I had rather tell you to-day; my lord, my lord, I am not happy here. . . .

GOLAUD. Why, what has happened, Mélisande? What is it? . . . And I suspecting nothing. . . . What has happened? . . . Some one has done thee harm? . . . Some one has given thee offense?

MÉLISANDE. No, no; no one has done me the least

harm. . . . It is not that. . . . It is not that. . . . But I can live here no longer. I do not know why. . . . I would go away, go away! . . . I shall die if I am left here. . . .

GOLAUD. But something has happened? You must be hiding something from me? . . . Tell me the whole truth, Mélisande. . . . Is it the King? . . . Is it my mother? . . . Is it Pélléas? . . .

MÉLISANDE. No, no; it is not Pélléas. It is not anybody. . . . You could not understand me. . . .

GOLAUD. Why should I not understand? . . . If you tell me nothing, what will you have me do? . . . Tell me everything and I shall understand everything.

MÉLISANDE. I do not know myself what it is. . . . I do not know just what it is. . . . If I could tell you, I would tell you. . . . It is something stronger than I. . . .

GOLAUD. Come; be reasonable, Mélisande.—What would you have me do?—You are no longer a child.—Is it I whom you would leave?

MÉLISANDE. Oh! no, no; it is not that. . . . I would go away with you. . . . It is here that I can live no longer. . . . I feel that I shall not live a long while. . . .

GOLAUD. But there must be a reason nevertheless. You will be thought mad. It will be thought child's dreams.—Come, is it Pélléas, perhaps?—I think he does not often speak to you.

MÉLISANDE. Yes, yes; he speaks to me sometimes. I think he does not like me; I have seen it in his eyes. . . . But he speaks to me when he meets me. . . .

GOLAUD. You must not take it ill of him. He has always been so. He is a little strange. And just now he is sad; he thinks of his friend Marcellus, who is at the point of death, and whom he cannot go to see. . . . He will change, he will change, you will see; he is young. . . .

MÉLISANDE. But it is not that . . . it is not that. . . .

GOLAUD. What is it, then?—Can you not get used to the life one leads here? Is it too gloomy here?—It is true the castle is very old and very sombre. . . . It is very cold, and very deep. And all those who dwell in it are already old. And the country may seem gloomy too, with all its forests, all its old forests without light. But that may all be enlivened if we will. And then, joy, joy, one does not have it every day; we must take things as they come. But tell me something; no matter what; I will do everything you could wish. . . .

MÉLISANDE. Yes, yes; it is true. . . . You never see the sky here. I saw it for the first time this morning. . . .

GOLAUD. It is that, then, that makes you weep, my poor Mélisande?—It is only that, then?—You weep, not to see the sky?—Come, come, you are no longer at the age when one may weep for such things. . . . And then, is not the summer yonder? You will see the sky every day.—And then, next year. . . . Come, give me your hand; give me both your little hands. [*He takes her hands.*] Oh! oh! these little hands that I could crush like flowers. . . .—Hold! where is the ring I gave you?

MÉLISANDE. The ring?

GOLAUD. Yes; our wedding-ring, where is it?

MÉLISANDE. I think . . . I think it has fallen. . . .

GOLAUD. Fallen?—Where has it fallen?—You have not lost it?

MÉLISANDE. No, no; it fell . . . it must have fallen . . . but I know where it is. . . .

Golaud. Where is it?

Mélisande. You know . . . you know well . . . the grotto by the seashore? . . .

Golaud. Yes.

Mélisande. Well then, it is there. . . . It must be it is there. . . . Yes, yes; I remember. . . . I went there this morning to pick up shells for little Yniold. . . . There were some very fine ones. . . . It slipped from my finger . . . then the sea came in; and I had to go out before I had found it.

Golaud. Are you sure it is there?

Mélisande. Yes, yes; quite sure. . . . I felt it slip . . . then, all at once, the noise of the waves. . . .

Golaud. You must go look for it at once.

Mélisande. I must go look for it at once?

Golaud. Yes.

Mélisande. Now?—at once?—in the dark?

Golaud. Now, at once, in the dark. You must go look for it at once. I had rather have lost all I have than have lost that ring. You do not know what it is. You do not know whence it came. The sea will be very high to-night. The sea will come to take it before you. . . . Make haste. You must go look for it at once. . . .

Mélisande. I dare not. . . . I dare not go alone. . . .

Golaud. Go, go with no matter whom. But you must go at once, do you understand?—Make haste; ask Pélléas to go with you.

Mélisande. Pélléas?—With Pélléas?—But Pélléas would not. . . .

Golaud. Pélléas will do all you ask of him. I know Pélléas better than you do. Go, go; hurry! I shall not sleep until I have the ring.

MÉLISANDE. Oh! oh! I am not happy! . . . I am not happy! . . . [*Exit, weeping.*

SCENE III.—*Before a grotto.*

[*Enter* PÉLLÉAS *and* MÉLISANDE.

PÉLLÉAS. [*Speaking with great agitation.*] Yes; it is here; we are there. It is so dark you cannot tell the entrance of the grotto from the rest of the night. . . . There are no stars on this side. Let us wait till the moon has torn through that great cloud; it will light up the whole grotto, and then we can enter without danger. There are dangerous places, and the path is very narrow between two lakes whose bottom has not yet been found. I did not think to bring a torch or a lantern, but I think the light of the sky will be enough for us.—You have never gone into this grotto?

MÉLISANDE. No. . . .

PÉLLÉAS. Let us go in; let us go in. . . . You must be able to describe the place where you lost the ring, if he questions you. . . . It is very big and very beautiful. There are stalactites that look like plants and men. It is full of blue darks. It has not yet been explored to the end. There are great treasures hidden there, it seems. You will see the remains of ancient shipwrecks there. But you must not go far in it without a guide. There have been some who never have come back. I myself dare not go forward too far. We will stop the moment we no longer see the light of the sea or the sky. When you strike a little light there, you would say the vault was covered with stars like the sky. It is bits of crystal or salt, they say, that shine so in the rock. —Look, look, I think the sky is going to clear. . . . Give me your hand; do not tremble, do not tremble so. There is no danger; we will stop the moment we no longer see the light of the sea. . . . Is it the noise of the grotto that frightens you? It is the noise of night or the noise of silence. . . . Do you hear the sea behind us?—It does not seem happy to-night. . . . Ah! look, the light! . . .

[*The moon lights up abundantly the entrance and part of the darkness of the grotto; and at a certain depth are seen three old beggars with white hair, seated side by side, leaning upon each other and asleep against a bowlder.*

MÉLISANDE. Ah!

PÉLLÉAS. What is it?

MÉLISANDE. There are . . . there are . . .

[*She points out the three beggars.*

PÉLLÉAS. Yes, yes; I have seen them too. . . .

MÉLISANDE. Let us go! . . . Let us go! . . .

PÉLLÉAS. Yes . . . it is three old poor men fallen asleep. . . . There is a famine in the country. . . . Why have they come to sleep here? . . .

MÉLISANDE. Let us go! . . . Come, come. . . . Let us go! . . .

PÉLLÉAS. Take care; do not speak so loud. . . . Let us not wake them. . . . They are still sleeping heavily. . . . Come.

MÉLISANDE. Leave me, leave me; I prefer to walk alone. . . .

PÉLLÉAS. We will come back another day. . . .

[*Exeunt.*

SCENE IV.—*An apartment in the castle.* ARKËL *and* PÉLLÉAS *discovered.*

ARKËL. You see that everything retains you here just now and forbids you this useless journey. We have concealed your father's condition from you until now; but it is perhaps hopeless; and that alone should suffice to stop you on the threshold. But there are so many other reasons. . . . And it is not in the day when our enemies awake, and when the people are dying of hunger and murmur about us, that you have the right to desert us. And why this journey? Marcellus is dead; and life has graver duties than the visit to a tomb. You are weary, you say, of your inactive life; but activity and duty are not found on the highways. They must be waited for upon the threshold, and let in as they go by; and they go by every day. You have never seen them? I hardly see them any more myself; but I will teach you to see them, and I will point them out to you the day when you would make them a sign. Nevertheless, listen to me; if you believe it is from the depths of your life this journey is exacted, I do not forbid your undertaking it, for you must know better than I the events you must offer to your being or your fate. I shall ask you only to wait until we know what must take place ere long. . . .

PÉLLÉAS. How long must I wait?

ARKËL. A few weeks; perhaps a few days. . . .

PÉLLÉAS. I will wait. . . .

## ACT THIRD

SCENE I.—*An apartment in the castle.* PÉLLÉAS *and* MÉLISANDE *discovered.* MÉLISANDE *plies her distaff at the back of the room.*

PÉLLÉAS. Yniold does not come back; where has he gone?

MÉLISANDE. He had heard something in the corridor; he has gone to see what it is.

PÉLLÉAS. Mélisande. . . .

MÉLISANDE. What is it?

PÉLLÉAS. . . . Can you see still to work there? . . .

MÉLISANDE. I work as well in the dark. . . .

PÉLLÉAS. I think everybody is already asleep in the castle. Golaud does not come back from the chase. It is late, nevertheless. . . . He no longer suffers from his fall? . . .

MÉLISANDE. He said he no longer suffered from it.

PÉLLÉAS. He must be more prudent; his body is no longer as supple as at twenty years. . . . I see the stars through the window and the light of the moon on the trees. It is late; he will not come back now. [*Knocking at the door.*] Who is there? . . . Come in! . . .

[*Little* YNIOLD *opens the door and enters the room.*

It was you knocking so? . . . That is not the way to knock at doors. It is as if a misfortune had arrived; look, you have frightened little mother.

LITTLE YNIOLD. I only knocked a tiny little bit.

PÉLLÉAS. It is late; little father will not come back to-night; it is time for you to go to bed.

LITTLE YNIOLD. I shall not go to bed before you do.

PÉLLÉAS. What? . . . What is that you are saying?

LITTLE YNIOLD. I say . . . not before you . . . not before you . . .

[*Bursts into sobs and takes refuge by* MÉLISANDE.

MÉLISANDE. What is it, Yniold? . . . What is it? . . . why do you weep all at once?

YNIOLD. [*Sobbing.*] Because . . . oh! oh! because . . .

MÉLISANDE. Because what? . . . Because what? . . . Tell me . . .

YNIOLD. Little mother . . . little mother . . . you are going away. . . .

MÉLISANDE. But what has taken hold of you, Yniold? . . . I have never dreamed of going away. . . .

YNIOLD. Yes, you have; yes, you have; little father has gone away. . . . Little father does not come back, and you are going to go away too. . . . I have seen it . . . I have seen it. . . .

MÉLISANDE. But there has never been any idea of that, Yniold. . . . Why, what makes you think that I would go away? . . .

YNIOLD. I have seen it . . . I have seen it. . . . You have said things to uncle that I could not hear . . .

PÉLLÉAS. He is sleepy. . . . He has been dreaming. . . . Come here, Yniold; asleep already? . . . Come and look out at the window; the swans are fighting with the dogs. . . .

YNIOLD. [*At the window.*] Oh! oh! they are chasing the dogs! . . . They are chasing them! . . . Oh! oh! the water! . . . the wings! . . . the wings! . . . they are afraid. . . .

PÉLLÉAS. [*Coming back by* MÉLISANDE.] He is sleepy; he is struggling against sleep; his eyes were closing. . . .

MÉLISANDE. [*Singing softly as she spins.*]

Saint Daniel and Saint Michaël. . . .
Saint Michaël and Saint Raphaël. . . .

YNIOLD. [*At the window.*] Oh! oh! little mother! . . .

MÉLISANDE. [*Rising abruptly.*] What is it, Yniold? . . . What is it? . . .

YNIOLD. I saw something at the window? . . .

[PÉLLÉAS *and* MÉLISANDE *run to the window.*

PÉLLÉAS. What is there at the window? . . . What have you seen? . . .

YNIOLD. Oh! oh! I saw something! . . .

PÉLLÉAS. But there is nothing. I see nothing. . . .

MÉLISANDE. Nor I. . . .

PÉLLÉAS. Where did you see something? Which way? . . .

YNIOLD. Down there, down there! . . . It is no longer there. . . .

PÉLLÉAS. He does not know what he is saying. He must have seen the light of the moon on the forest. There are often strange reflections, . . . or else something must have passed on the highway . . . or in his sleep. For see, see, I believe he is quite asleep. . . .

YNIOLD. [*At the window.*] Little father is there! little father is there!

PÉLLÉAS. [*Going to the window.*] He is right; Golaud is coming into the courtyard. . . .

YNIOLD. Little father! . . . little father! . . . I am going to meet him! . . .

[*Exit, running.—A silence.*

PÉLLÉAS. They are coming up the stair. . . .

[*Enter* GOLAUD *and little* YNIOLD *with a lamp.*

GOLAUD. You are still waiting in the dark?

YNIOLD. I have brought a light, little mother, a big light! . . . [*He lifts the lamp and looks at* MÉLISANDE.] You have been weeping, little mother? . . . You have been weeping? . . . [*He lifts the lamp toward* PÉLLÉAS *and looks in turn at him.*] You too, you too, you have been weeping? . . . Little father, look, little father; they have both been weeping. . . .

GOLAUD. Do not hold the light under their eyes so. . . .

SCENE II.—*One of the towers of the castle.—A watchman's round passes under a window in the tower.*

MÉLISANDE. [*At the window, combing her unbound hair.*]

My long locks fall foaming
To the threshold of the tower,—
My locks await your coming
All along the tower,
And all the long, long hour,
And all the long, long hour.

*Saint Daniel and Saint Michaël,*
*Saint Michaël and Saint Raphaël.*

I was born on a Sunday,
A Sunday at high noon. . . .

[*Enter* PÉLLÉAS *by the watchman's round.*

PÉLLÉAS. Holà! Holà! ho! . . .

MÉLISANDE. Who is there?

PÉLLÉAS. I, I, and I! . . . What art thou doing

there at the window, singing like a bird that is not native here?

MÉLISANDE. I am doing my hair for the night. . . .

PÉLLÉAS. Is it that I see upon the wall? . . . I thought you had some light. . . .

MÉLISANDE. I have opened the window; it is too hot in the tower. . . . It is beautiful to-night. . . .

PÉLLÉAS. There are innumerable stars; I have never seen so many as to-night; . . . but the moon is still upon the sea. . . . Do not stay in the shadow, Mélisande; lean forward a little till I see your unbound hair. . . .

MÉLISANDE. I am frightful so. . . .

[*She leans out at the window.*

PÉLLÉAS. Oh! oh! Mélisande! . . . oh, thou art beautiful! . . . thou art beautiful so! . . . Lean out! lean out! . . . Let me come nearer thee . . .

MÉLISANDE. I cannot come nearer thee. . . . I am leaning out as far as I can. . . .

PÉLLÉAS. I cannot come up higher; . . . give me at least thy hand to-night . . . before I go away. . . . I leave to-morrow. . . .

MÉLISANDE. No, no, no! . . .

PÉLLÉAS. Yes, yes, yes; I leave, I shall leave to-morrow. . . . Give me thy hand, thy hand, thy little hand upon my lips. . . .

MÉLISANDE. I give thee not my hand if thou wilt leave. . . .

PÉLLÉAS. Give, give, give! . . .

MÉLISANDE. Thou wilt not leave? . . .

PÉLLÉAS. I will wait; I will wait. . . .

MÉLISANDE. I see a rose in the shadows. . .

PÉLLÉAS. Where? . . . I see only the boughs of the willow hanging over the wall. . . .

MÉLISANDE. Further down, further down, in the garden; further down, in the somber green. . . .

PÉLLÉAS. It is not a rose. . . . I will go see by and by, but give me thy hand first; first thy hand. . . .

MÉLISANDE. There, there; . . . I cannot lean out further. . . .

PÉLLÉAS. I cannot reach thy hand with my lips. . . .

MÉLISANDE. I cannot lean out further. . . . I am on the point of falling. . . .—Oh! oh! my hair is falling down the tower! . . .

[*Her tresses fall suddenly over her head, as she is leaning out so, and stream over* PÉLLÉAS.]

PÉLLÉAS. Oh! oh! what is it? . . . Thy hair, thy hair is falling down to me! . . . All thy locks, Mélisande, all thy locks have fallen down the tower! . . . I hold them in my hands; I hold them in my mouth. . . . I hold them in my arms; I put them about my neck. . . . I will not open my hands again to-night. . . .

MÉLISANDE. Let me go! let me go! . . . Thou wilt make me fall! . . .

PÉLLÉAS. No, no, no; . . . I have never seen such hair as thine, Mélisande! . . . See, see, see; it comes from so high and yet it floods me to the heart! . . . And yet it floods me to the knees! . . . And it is sweet, sweet as if it fell from heaven! . . . I see the sky no longer through thy locks. Thou seest, thou seest? . . . I can no longer hold them with both hands; there are some on the boughs of the willow. . . . They are alive like birds in my hands, . . . and they love me, they love me more than thou! . . .

MÉLISANDE. Let me go; let me go! . . . Some one might come. . . .

PÉLLÉAS. No, no, no; I shall not set thee free to-night. . . . Thou art my prisoner to-night; all night, all night! . . .

MÉLISANDE. Pélléas! Pélléas! . . .

PÉLLÉAS. I tie them, I tie them to the willow boughs. . . . Thou shalt not go away now; . . . thou shalt not go away now. . . . Look, look, I am kissing thy hair. . . . I suffer no more in the midst of thy hair. . . . Hearest thou my kisses along thy hair? . . . They mount along thy hair. . . . Each hair must bring thee some. . . . Thou seest, thou seest, I can open my hands. . . . My hands are free, and thou canst not leave me now. . . .

MÉLISANDE. Oh! oh! thou hurtest me. . . . [*Doves come out of the tower and fly about them in the night.*] —What is that, Pélléas?—What is it flying about me?

PÉLLÉAS. It is the doves coming out of the tower. . . . I have frightened them; they are flying away. . . .

MÉLISANDE. It is my doves, Pélléas.—Let us go away, let me go; they will not come back again. . . .

PÉLLÉAS. Why will they not come back again?

MÉLISANDE. They will be lost in the dark. . . . Let me go; let me lift my head. . . . I hear a noise of footsteps. . . . Let me go!—It is Golaud! . . . I believe it is Golaud! . . . He has heard us. . . .

PÉLLÉAS. Wait! Wait! . . . Thy hair is about the boughs. . . . It is caught there in the darkness. . . . Wait, wait! . . . It is dark. . . .

[*Enter* GOLAUD, *by the watchman's round.*

GOLAUD. What do you here?

PÉLLÉAS. What do I here? . . . I . . .

GOLAUD. You are children. . . . Mélisande, do not lean out so at the window; you will fall. . . . Do you not know it is late?—It is nearly midnight.—Do not play so in the darkness.—You are children. . . .

[*Laughing nervously.*] What children! . . . What children! . . . [*Exit, with* PÉLLÉAS.

SCENE III.—*The vaults of the castle.*

[*Enter* GOLAUD *and* PÉLLÉAS.

GOLAUD. Take care; this way, this way.—You have never penetrated into these vaults?

PÉLLÉAS. Yes; once, of old; but it was long ago. . . .

GOLAUD. They are prodigious great; it is a succession of enormous crypts that end, God knows where. The whole castle is builded on these crypts. Do you smell the deathly odor that reigns here?—That is what I wished to show you. In my opinion, it comes from the little underground lake I am going to have you see. Take care; walk before me, in the light of my lantern. I will warn you when we are there. [*They continue to walk in silence.*] Hey! hey! Pélléas! stop! stop!—[*He seizes him by the arm.*] For God's sake! . . . Do you not see?—One step more, and you had been in the gulf! . . .

PÉLLÉAS. But I did not see it! . . . The lantern no longer lighted me. . . .

GOLAUD. I made a misstep, . . . but if I had not held you by the arm . . . Well, this is the stagnant water that I spoke of to you. . . . Do you perceive the smell of death that rises?—Let us go to the end of this overhanging rock, and do you lean over a little. It will strike you in the face.

PÉLLÉAS. I smell it already; . . . you would say a smell of the tomb.

GOLAUD. Further, further. . . . It is this that on certain days has poisoned the castle. The King will not believe it comes from here.—The crypt should be walled up in which this standing water is found. It is time, besides, to examine these vaults a little. Have you noticed those lizards on the walls and pillars of the vaults?—There is a labor hidden here you would not suspect; and the whole castle will be swallowed up one of these nights, if it is not looked out for. But what will you have? nobody likes to come down this far. . . . There are strange lizards in many of the walls. . . . Oh! here . . . do you perceive the smell of death that rises?

PÉLLÉAS. Yes; there is a smell of death rising about us. . . .

GOLAUD. Lean over; have no fear. . . . I will hold you . . . give me . . . no, no, not your hand . . . it might slip . . . your arm, your arm! . . . Do you see the gulf? [*Moved.*]—Pélléas? Pélléas? . . .

PÉLLÉAS. Yes; I think I see the bottom of the gulf. . . . Is it the light that trembles so? . . . You . . . [*He straightens up, turns, and looks at* GOLAUD.]

GOLAUD. [*With a trembling voice.*] Yes; it is the lantern. . . . See, I shook it to lighten the walls. . . .

PÉLLÉAS. I stifle here; . . . let us go out. . . .

GOLAUD. Yes; let us go out. . . .

[*Exeunt in silence.*

SCENE IV.—*A terrace at the exit of the vaults. Enter* GOLAUD *and* PÉLLÉAS.

PÉLLÉAS. Ah! I breathe at last! . . . I thought, one moment, I was going to be ill in those enormous crypts; I was on the point of falling. . . . There is a damp air there, heavy as a leaden dew, and darkness thick as a poisoned paste. . . . And now, all the air of all the sea! . . . There is a fresh wind, see; fresh as a leaf that has just opened, over the little green waves. . . . Hold! the flowers have just been watered at the foot of the terrace, and the smell of the verdure and the wet roses comes up to us. . . . It must be nearly noon; they are already in the shadow of the tower. . . . It is noon; I hear the bells ringing, and the children are going down to the beach to bathe. . . . I did not know that we had stayed so long in the caverns. . . .

GOLAUD. We went down towards eleven o'clock. . . .

PÉLLÉAS. Earlier; it must have been earlier; I heard it strike half-past ten.

GOLAUD. Half-past ten or a quarter to eleven. . . .

PÉLLÉAS. They have opened all the windows of the castle. It will be unusually hot this afternoon. . . . Look, there is mother with Mélisande at a window of the tower. . . .

GOLAUD. Yes; they have taken refuge on the shady side.—Speaking of Mélisande, I heard what passed and what was said last night. I am quite aware all that is but child's play; but it need not be repeated. Mélisande is very young and very impressionable; and she must be treated the more circumspectly that she is perhaps with child at this moment. . . . She is very delicate, hardly woman; and the least emotion might bring on a mishap. It is not the first time I have noticed there might be something between you. . . . You are older than she; it will suffice to have told you. . . . Avoid her as much as possible; without affectation moreover; without affectation. . . . —What is it I see yonder on the highway toward the forest? . . .

PÉLLÉAS. Some herds they are leading to the city. . . .

GOLAUD. They cry like lost children; you would say they smelt the butcher already.—It will be time for dinner.—What a fine day! What a capital day for the harvest! . . .

[*Exeunt.*

SCENE V.—*Before the castle.*

[*Enter* GOLAUD *and little* YNIOLD.

GOLAUD. Come, we are going to sit down here, Yniold; sit on my knee; we shall see from here what passes in the forest. I do not see you any more at all now. You abandon me too; you are always at little mother's. . . . Why, we are sitting just under little mother's windows.—Perhaps she is saying her evening prayer at this moment. . . . But tell me, Yniold, she is often with your uncle Pélléas, isn't she?

YNIOLD. Yes, yes; always, little father; when you are not there, little father. . . .

GOLAUD. Ah!—look; some one is going by with a lantern in the garden.—But I have been told they did not like each other. . . . It seems they often quarrel; . . . no? Is it true?

YNIOLD. Yes, yes; it is true.

GOLAUD. Yes?—Ah! ah!—But what do they quarrel about?

YNIOLD. About the door.

GOLAUD. What? about the door?—What are you talking about?—No, come, explain yourself; why do they quarrel about the door?

YNIOLD. Because it won't stay open.

GOLAUD. Who wants it to stay open?—Come, why do they quarrel?

YNIOLD. I don't know, little father; about the light.

GOLAUD. I am not talking to you about the light; we will talk of that by and by. I am talking to you about the door. Answer what I ask you; you must learn to talk; it is time. . . . Do not put your hand in your mouth so; . . . come. . . .

YNIOLD. Little father! little father! . . . I won't do it any more. . . . [*He cries.*]

GOLAUD. Come; what are you crying for now? What has happened?

YNIOLD. Oh! oh! little father, you hurt me. . . .

GOLAUD. I hurt you?—Where did I hurt you? I did not mean to. . . .

YNIOLD. Here, here; on my little arm. . . .

GOLAUD. I did not mean to; come, don't cry any more, and I will give you something to-morrow.

YNIOLD. What, little father?

GOLAUD. A quiver and some arrows; but tell me what you know about the door.

YNIOLD. Big arrows?

GOLAUD. Yes, yes; very big arrows.—But why don't they want the door to be open?—Come, answer me sometime!—no, no; do not open your mouth to cry. I am not angry. We are going to have a quiet talk, like Pélléas and little mother when they are together. What do they talk about when they are together?

YNIOLD. Pélléas and little mother?

GOLAUD. Yes; what do they talk about?

YNIOLD. About me; always about me.

GOLAUD. And what do they say about you?

YNIOLD. They say I am going to be very big.

GOLAUD. Oh, plague of my life! . . . I am here like a blind man searching for his treasure at the bottom of the ocean! . . . I am here like a new-born child lost in the forest, and you . . . Come, come, Yniold, I was wandering; we are going to talk seriously. Do Pélléas and little mother never speak of me when I am not there? . . .

YNIOLD. Yes, yes, little father; they are always speaking of you.

GOLAUD. Ah! . . . And what do they say of me?

YNIOLD. They say I shall grow as big as you are.

GOLAUD. You are always by them?

YNIOLD. Yes, yes, always, always, little father.

GOLAUD. They never tell you to go play somewhere else?

YNIOLD. No, little father; they are afraid when I am not there.

GOLAUD. They are afraid? . . . What makes you think they are afraid?

YNIOLD. Little mother always says, "Don't go away; don't go away!" . . . They are unhappy, but they laugh. . . .

GOLAUD. But that does not prove they are afraid.

YNIOLD. Yes, yes, little father; she is afraid. . . .

GOLAUD. Why do you say she is afraid?

YNIOLD. They always weep in the dark.

GOLAUD. Ah! ah! . . .

YNIOLD. That makes one weep too.

GOLAUD. Yes, yes! . . .

YNIOLD. She is pale, little father.

GOLAUD. Ah! ah! . . . patience, my God, patience! . . .

YNIOLD. What, little father?

GOLAUD. Nothing, nothing, my child.—I saw a wolf go by in the forest.—Then they get on well together?—I am glad to learn they are on good terms.—They kiss each other sometimes?—No? . . .

YNIOLD. Kiss each other, little father?—No, no,—ah! yes, little father, yes, yes; once . . . once when it rained. . . .

GOLAUD. They kissed?—But how, how did they kiss?

YNIOLD. So, little father, so! . . . [*He gives him a*

*kiss on the mouth, laughing.*] Ah! ah! your beard, little father! . . . It pricks! it pricks! it pricks! It is getting all gray, little father, and your hair, too; all gray, all gray, all gray. . . . [*The window under which they are sitting is lighted up at this moment, and the light falls upon them.*] Ah ah! little mother has lit her lamp. It is light, little father; it is light. . . .

GOLAUD. Yes; it is beginning to be light. . . .

YNIOLD. Let us go there too, little father; let us go there too. . . .

GOLAUD. Where do you want to go?

YNIOLD. Where it is light, little father.

GOLAUD. No, no, my child; let us stay in the dark a little longer. . . . One cannot tell, one cannot tell yet. . . . Do you see those poor people down there trying to kindle a little fire in the forest?—It has rained. And over there, do you see the old gardener trying to lift that tree the wind has blown down across the road?—He cannot; the tree is too big; the tree is too heavy, and it will lie where it fell. All that cannot be helped. . . . I think Péllèas is mad. . . .

YNIOLD. No, little father, he is not mad; he is very good.

GOLAUD. Do you want to see little mother?

YNIOLD. Yes, yes; I want to see her!

GOLAUD. Don't make any noise; I am going to hoist you up to the window. It is too high for me, for all I am so big. . . . [*He lifts the child.*] Do not make the least noise; little mother would be terribly afraid. . . . Do you see her?—Is she in the room?

YNIOLD. Yes. . . . Oh, how light it is!

GOLAUD. She is alone?

YNIOLD. Yes; . . . no, no; Uncle Péllèas is there, too.

GOLAUD. He— . . . !

YNIOLD. Ah! ah! little father! you have hurt me! . . .

GOLAUD. It is nothing; be still; I will not do it any more; look, look, Yniold! . . . I stumbled; speak lower. What are they doing?—

YNIOLD. They are not doing anything, little father; they are waiting for something.

GOLAUD. Are they near each other?

YNIOLD. No, little father.

GOLAUD. And . . . and the bed? are they near the bed?

YNIOLD. The bed, little father?—I can't see the bed.

GOLAUD. Lower, lower; they will hear you. Are they speaking?

YNIOLD. No, little father; they do not speak.

GOLAUD. But what are they doing?—They must be doing something. . . .

YNIOLD. They are looking at the light.

GOLAUD. Both?

YNIOLD. Yes, little father.

GOLAUD. They do not say anything?

YNIOLD. No, little father; they do not close their eyes.

GOLAUD. They do not come near each other?

YNIOLD. No, little father; they do not stir.

GOLAUD. They are sitting down?

YNIOLD. No, little father; they are standing upright against the wall.

GOLAUD. They make no gestures?—They do not look at each other?—They make no signs? . . .

YNIOLD. No, little father.—Oh! oh! little father; they never close their eyes. . . . I am terribly afraid. . . .

GOLAUD. Be still. They do not stir yet?

YNIOLD. No, little father.—I am afraid, little father; let me come down! . . .

GOLAUD. Why, what are you afraid of?—Look! look! . . .

YNIOLD. I dare not look any more, little father! . . . Let me come down! . . .

GOLAUD. Look! look! . . .

YNIOLD. Oh! oh! I am going to cry, little father!—Let me come down; let me come down! . . .

GOLAUD. Come; we will go see what has happened.

[*Exeunt.*

## ACT FOURTH

### SCENE I.—*A corridor in the castle.*

[*Enter* Pélléas *and* Mélisande, *meeting.*

Pélléas. Where goest thou? I must speak to thee to-night. Shall I see thee?

Mélisande. Yes.

Pélléas. I have just left my father's room. He is getting better. The physician has told us he is saved. . . . And yet this morning I had a presentiment this day would end ill. I have had a rumor of misfortune in my ears for some time. . . . Then, all at once there was a great change; to-day it is no longer anything but a question of time. All the windows in his room have been thrown open. He speaks; he seems happy. He does not speak yet like an ordinary man, but already his ideas no longer all come from the other world. . . . He recognized me. He took my hand and said with that strange air he has had since he fell sick: "Is it thou, Pélléas? Why, why, I had not noticed it before, but thou hast the grave and friendly look of those who will not live long. . . . You must travel; you must travel. . . ." It is strange; I shall obey him. . . . My mother listened to him and wept for joy.—Hast thou not been aware of it?—The whole house seems already to revive, you hear breathing, you hear speaking, you hear walking. . . . Listen; I hear some one speaking behind that door. Quick, quick! answer quickly! where shall I see thee?

Mélisande. Where wouldst thou?

PÉLLÉAS. In the park; near "Blind Man's Spring."—Wilt thou?—Wilt thou come?

MÉLISANDE. Yes.

PÉLLÉAS. It will be the last night;—I am going to travel, as my father said. Thou wilt not see me more. . . .

MÉLISANDE. Do not say that, Pélléas. . . . I shall see thee always; I shall look upon thee always. . . .

PÉLLÉAS. Thou wilt look in vain. . . . I shall be so far away thou couldst no longer see me. . . . I shall try to go very far away. . . . I am full of joy, and you would say I had all the weight of heaven and earth on my body to-day. . .

MÉLISANDE. What has happened, Pélléas?—I no longer understand what you say. . . .

PÉLLÉAS. Go, go; let us separate. I hear some one speaking behind that door. . . . It is the strangers who came to the castle this morning. . . . They are going out. . . . Let us go; it is the strangers. . . .

[*Exeunt severally.*

SCENE II.—*An apartment in the castle.*

[ARKËL *and* MÉLISANDE *discovered.*

ARKËL. Now that Pélléas's father is saved, and sickness, the old handmaid of Death, has left the castle, a little joy and a little sunlight will at last come into the house again. . . . It was time!—For, since thy coming, we have only lived here whispering about a closed room. . . . And truly I have pitied thee, Mélisande. . . . Thou camest here all joyous, like a child seeking a gala-day, and at the moment thou enteredst in the vestibule I saw thy face change, and probably thy soul, as the face changes in spite of us when we enter at noon into a grotto too gloomy and too cold. . . . And since,—since, on account of all that, I have often no longer understood thee. . . . I observed thee, thou wert there, listless perhaps, but with the strange, astray look of one awaiting ever a great trouble, in the sunlight, in a beautiful garden. . . . I cannot explain. . . . But I was sad to see thee so; for thou art too young and too beautiful to live already day and night under the breath of death. . . . But now all that will change. At my age,—and there perhaps is the surest fruit of my life,—at my age I have gained I know not what faith in the fidelity of events, and I have always seen that every young and beautiful being creates about itself young, beautiful, and happy events. . . . And it is thou who wilt now open the door for the new era I have glimpses of. . . . Come here; why dost thou stay there without answering and without lifting thine eyes?—I have kissed thee but once only hitherto,—the day of thy coming; and yet old men need sometimes to touch with their lips a woman's forehead or a child's cheek, to believe still in the freshness of life and avert awhile the menaces. . . . Art thou afraid of my old lips? How I have pitied thee these months! . . .

MÉLISANDE. Grandfather, I have not been unhappy. . .

ARKËL. Perhaps you were of those who are unhappy without knowing it, . . . and they are the most unhappy. . . . Let me look at thee, so, quite near, a moment; . . . we have such need of beauty beside Death. . . .

[*Enter* GOLAUD.

GOLAUD. Pélléas leaves to-night.

ARKËL. Thou hast blood on thy forehead.—What hast thou done?

GOLAUD. Nothing, nothing. . . . I have passed through a hedge of thorns.

MÉLISANDE. Bend down your head a little, my lord. . . . I will wipe your forehead. . . .

GOLAUD. [*Repulsing her.*] I will not that you touch me, do you understand? Go, go!—I am not speaking to you.—Where is my sword?—I came to seek my sword. . . .

MÉLISANDE. Here; on the praying-stool.

GOLAUD. Bring it. [*To* ARKËL.]—They have just found another peasant dead of hunger, along by the sea. You would say they all meant to die under our eyes.—[*To* MÉLISANDE.] Well, my sword?—Why do you tremble so?—I am not going to kill you. I would simply examine the blade. I do not employ the sword for these uses. Why do you examine me like a beggar?—I do not come to ask alms of you. You hope to see something in my eyes without my seeing anything in yours?—Do you think I may know something?—[*To* ARKËL.]—Do you see those great eyes?—It is as if they were proud of their richness. . . .

ARKËL. I see there only a great innocence. . . .

GOLAUD. A great innocence! . . . They are greater than innocence! . . . They are purer than the eyes of a lamb. . . . They would give God lessons in innocence! A great innocence! Listen: I am so near them I feel the freshness of their lashes when they wink; and yet I am less far away from the great secrets of the other world than from the smallest secret of those eyes! . . . A great innocence! . . . More than innocence! You would say the angels of heaven celebrated there an eternal baptism! . . . I know those eyes! I have seen them at their work! Close them! close them! or I shall close them for a long while! . . . —Do not put your right hand to your throat so; I am saying a very simple thing. . . . I have no under-thought. . . . If I had an under-thought, why should I not say it? Ah! ah!—do not attempt to flee!—Here!—Give me that hand!—Ah! your hands are too hot. . . . Go away! Your flesh disgusts me! . . . Here!—There is no more question of fleeing now!—[*He seizes her by the hair.*]—You shall follow me on your knees!—On your knees!—On your knees before me!—Ah! ah! your long hair serves some purpose at last! . . . Right, . . . left!—Left, . . . right! —Absalom! Absalom.—Forward! back! To the ground! to the ground! . . . You see, you see; I laugh already like an old man. . . .

ARKËL. [*Running up.*] Golaud! . . .

GOLAUD. [*Affecting a sudden calm.*] You will do as you may please, look you.—I attach no importance to that.—I am too old; and, besides, I am not a spy. I shall await chance; and then . . . Oh! then! . . . simply because it is the custom; simply because it is the custom. . . . [*Exit.*

ARKËL. What ails him?—He is drunk?

MÉLISANDE. [*In tears.*] No, no; he does not love me any more. . . . I am not happy! . . . I am not happy! . . .

ARKËL. If I were God, I would have pity on men's hearts. . . .

SCENE III.—*A terrace of the castle. Little* YNIOLD *discovered, trying to lift a bowlder.*

LITTLE YNIOLD. Oh, this stone is heavy! . . . It is heavier than I am. . . . It is heavier than everybody. . . . It is heavier than everything that ever happened. . . . I can see my golden ball between the rock and this naughty stone, and I cannot reach it. . . . My little arm is not long enough, . . . and this stone won't be lifted. . . . I can't lift it, . . . and nobody could lift it. . . . It is heavier than the whole house; . . . you would think it had roots in the earth. . . . [*The bleatings of a flock heard far away.*]—Oh! oh! I hear the sheep crying. . . . [*He goes to look, at the edge of the terrace.*] Why! there is no more sun. . . . They are coming . . . the little sheep . . . they are coming. . . . There is a lot of them! . . . There is a lot of them! . . . They are afraid of the dark. . . . They crowd together! they crowd together! . . . They can hardly walk any more. . . . They are crying! they are crying! and they go quick! . . . They go quick! . . . They are already at the great crossroads. Ah! ah! They don't know where they ought to go any more. . . . They don't cry any more. . . . They wait. . . . Some of them want to go to the right. . . . They all want to go to the right. . . . They cannot! . . . The shepherd is throwing earth at them. . . . Ah! ah! They are going to pass by here. . . . They obey! They obey! They are going to pass under the terrace. . . . They are going to pass under the rocks. . . . I am going to see them near by. . . . Oh! oh! what a lot of them! . . . What a lot of them! . . . The whole road is full of them. . . . They all keep still now. . . . Shepherd! shepherd! why don't they speak any more?

THE SHEPHERD. [*Who is out of sight.*] Because it is not longer the road to the stable. . . .

YNIOLD. Where are they going?—Shepherd! shepherd!—where are they going?—He doesn't hear me any more. They are too far away already. . . . They go quick. . . . They are not making a noise any more. . . . It is no longer the road to the stable. . . . Where are they going to sleep to-night?—Oh! oh!—It is too dark. . . . I am going to tell something to somebody. . . . [*Exit.*

SCENE IV.—*A fountain in the park.*

[*Enter* PÉLLÉAS.

PÉLLÉAS. It is the last evening . . . the last evening. It must all end. I have played like a child about a thing I did not guess. . . . I have played a-dream about the snares of fate. . . . Who has awakened me all at once? I shall flee, crying out for joy and woe like a blind man fleeing from his burning house. . . . I am going to tell her I shall flee. . . . My father is out of danger; and I have no more reason to lie to myself. . . . It is late; she does not come. . . . I should do better to go away without seeing her again. . . . I must look well at her this time. . . . There are some things that I no longer recall. . . . It seems at times as if I had not seen her for a hundred years. . . . And I have not yet looked upon her look. . . . There remains nought to me if I go away thus. And all those memories . . . it is as if I were to take away a little water in a muslin bag. . . . I must see her one last time, to the bottom of her heart. . . . I must tell her all that I have never told her.

[*Enter* MÉLISANDE.

MÉLISANDE. Pélléas!

PÉLLÉAS. Mélisande!—Is it thou, Mélisande?

MÉLISANDE. Yes.

PÉLLÉAS. Come hither; do not stay at the edge of the moonlight.—Come hither. We have so many things to tell each other. . . . Come hither in the shadow of the linden.

MÉLISANDE. Let me stay in the light. . . .

PÉLLÉAS. We might be seen from the windows of

the tower. Come hither; here, we have nothing to fear.—Take care; we might be seen. . . .

MÉLISANDE. I wish to be seen. . . .

PÉLLÉAS. Why, what doth ail thee?—Thou wert able to come out without being seen?

MÉLISANDE. Yes; your brother slept. . . .

PÉLLÉAS. It is late.—In an hour they will close the gates. We must be careful. Why art thou come so late?

MÉLISANDE. Your brother had a bad dream. And then my gown was caught on the nails of the gate. See, it is torn. I lost all this time, and ran. . . .

PÉLLÉAS. My poor Mélisande! . . . I should almost be afraid to touch thee. . . . Thou art still out of breath, like a hunted bird. . . . It is for me, for me, thou doest all that? . . . I hear thy heart beat as if it were mine. . . . Come hither . . . nearer, nearer me. . . .

MÉLISANDE. Why do you laugh?

PÉLLÉAS. I do not laugh;—or else I laugh for joy, unwittingly. . . . It were a weeping matter, rather. . . .

MÉLISANDE. We have come here before. . . . I recollect. . . .

PÉLLÉAS. Yes . . . yes. . . . Long months ago.—I knew not then. . . . Knowest thou why I asked thee to come here to-night?

MÉLISANDE. No.

PÉLLÉAS. It is perhaps the last time I shall see thee. . . . I must go away forever. . . .

MÉLISANDE. Why sayest thou always thou wilt go away? . . .

PÉLLÉAS. I must tell thee what thou knowest already?—Thou knowest not what I am going to tell thee?

MÉLISANDE. Why, no; why, no; I know nothing— . . .

PÉLLÉAS. Thou knowest not why I must go afar. . . . Thou knowest not it is because . . . [*He kisses her abruptly.*] I love thee. . . .

MÉLISANDE. [*In a low voice.*] I love thee too. . . .

PÉLLÉAS. Oh! oh! What saidst thou, Mélisande? . . . I hardly heard it! . . . Thou sayest that in a voice coming from the end of the world! . . . I hardly heard thee. . . . Thou lovest me?—Thou lovest me too? . . . Since when lovest thou me? . . .

MÉLISANDE. Since always. . . . Since I saw thee. . . .

PÉLLÉAS. Oh, how thou sayest that! . . . Thy voice seems to have blown across the sea in spring! . . . I have never heard it until now; . . . one would say it had rained on my heart! . . . Thou sayest that so frankly! . . . Like an angel questioned! . . . I cannot believe it, Mélisande! . . . Why shouldst thou love me? —Nay, why dost thou love me?—Is what thou sayest true?—Thou dost not mock me?—Thou dost not lie a little, to make me smile? . . .

MÉLISANDE. No; I never lie; I lie but to thy brother. . . .

PÉLLÉAS. Oh, how thou sayest that! . . . Thy voice! thy voice! . . . It is cooler and more frank than the water is! . . . It is like pure water on my lips! . . . It is like pure water on my hands. . . . Give me, give me thy hands! . . . Oh, how small thy hands are! . . . I did not know thou wert so beautiful! . . . I have never seen anything so beautiful before thee. . . . I was full of unrest; I sought throughout the house. . . . I sought throughout the country. . . . And I found not beauty. . . . And now I have found thee! . . . I have found thee! . . . I do not think there could be on the earth a fairer woman! . . . Where art thou?—I no longer hear thee breathe. . . .

MÉLISANDE. Because I look on thee. . . .

PÉLLÉAS. Why dost thou look so gravely on me?—We are already in the shadow.—It is too dark under this tree. Come into the light. We cannot see how happy we are. Come, come; so little time remains to us. . . .

MÉLISANDE. No, no; let us stay here. . . . I am nearer thee in the dark. . . .

PÉLLÉAS. Where are thine eyes?—Thou art not going to fly me?—Thou dost not think of me just now.

MÉLISANDE. Oh, yes; oh, yes; I only think of thee. . . .

PÉLLÉAS. Thou wert looking elsewhere. . . .

MÉLISANDE. I saw thee elsewhere. . . .

PÉLLÉAS. Thy soul is far away. . . . What ails thee, then?—Meseems thou art not happy. . . .

MÉLISANDE. Yes, yes; I am happy, but I am sad. . . .

PÉLLÉAS. One is sad often when one loves. . . .

MÉLISANDE. I weep always when I think of thee. . . .

PÉLLÉAS. I too. . . . I too, Mélisande. . . . I am quite near thee; I weep for joy, and yet . . . [*He kisses her again.*]—Thou art strange when I kiss thee so. . . . Thou art so beautiful that one would think thou wert about to die. . . .

MÉLISANDE. Thou too.

PÉLLÉAS. There, there. . . . We do not what we will. . . . I did not love thee the first time I saw thee. . . .

MÉLISANDE. Nor I . . . nor I. . . . I was afraid. . . .

PÉLLÉAS. I could not admit thine eyes. . . . I would have gone away at once . . . and then . . .

Mélisande. And I,—I would not have come. . . . I do not yet know why,—I was afraid to come. . . .

Pélléas. There are so many things one never knows. We are ever waiting; and then. . . . What is that noise? —They are closing the gates! . . .

Mélisande. Yes, they have closed the gates. . . .

Pélléas. We cannot go back now?—Hearest thou the bolts?—Listen! listen! . . . the great chains! . . . the great chains! . . . It is too late; it is too late! . . .

Mélisande. All the better! all the better! all the better! . . .

Pélléas. Thou— . . . ? Behold, behold! . . . It is no longer we who will it so! . . . All's lost, all's saved! all is saved to-night!—Come, come. . . . My heart beats like a madman,—up to my very throat. . . . [*They embrace.*] Listen! listen! my heart is almost strangling me. . . . Come! come! . . . Ah, how beautiful it is in the shadows! . . .

Mélisande. There is some one behind us! . . .

Pélléas. I see no one. . . .

Mélisande. I heard a noise. . . .

Pélléas. I hear only thy heart in the dark. . . .

Mélisande. I heard the crackling of dead leaves. . . .

Pélléas. Because the wind is silent all at once. . . . It fell as we were kissing. . . .

Mélisande. How long our shadows are to-night! . . .

Pélléas. They embrace to the very end of the garden. Oh, how they kiss far away from us! . . . Look! look! . . .

Mélisande. [*In a stifled voice.*] A-a-h!—He is behind a tree!

Pélléas. Who?

Mélisande. Golaud!

Pélléas. Golaud!—where?—I see nothing. . . .

MÉLISANDE. There . . . at the end of our shadows. . . .

PÉLLÉAS. Yes, yes; I saw him. . . . Let us not turn abruptly. . . .

MÉLISANDE. He has his sword. . . .

PÉLLÉAS. I have not mine. . . .

MÉLISANDE. He saw us kiss. . . .

PÉLLÉAS. He does not know we have seen him. . . . Do not stir; do not turn your head. . . . He would rush headlong on us. . . . He will remain there while he thinks we do not know. He watches us. . . . He is still motionless. . . . Go, go at once this way. . . . I will wait for him. . . . I will stop him. . . .

MÉLISANDE. No, no, no! . . .

PÉLLÉAS. Go! go! he has seen all! . . . He will kill us! . . .

MÉLISANDE. All the better! all the better! all the better! . . .

PÉLLÉAS. He comes! he comes! . . . Thy mouth! . . . Thy mouth! . . .

MÉLISANDE. Yes! . . . yes! yes! . . .

[*They kiss desperately.*

PÉLLÉAS. Oh! oh! All the stars are falling! . . .

MÉLISANDE. Upon me too! upon me too! . . .

PÉLLÉAS. Again! Again! . . . Give! give! . . .

MÉLISANDE. All! all! all! . . .

[GOLAUD *rushes upon them, sword in hand, and strikes* PÉLLÉAS, *who falls at the brink of the fountain.* MÉLISANDE *flees terrified.*

MÉLISANDE. [*Fleeing.*] Oh! oh! I have no courage! . . I have no courage! . . .

[GOLAUD *pursues her through the wood in silence.*

## ACT FIFTH

SCENE I.—*A lower hall in the castle. The women servants discovered, gathered together, while without children are playing before one of the ventilators of the hall.*

An Old Servant. You will see, you will see, my daughters; it will be to-night.—Some one will come to tell us by and by. . . .

Another Servant. They will not come to tell us. . . . They don't know what they are doing any longer. . . .

Third Servant. Let us wait here. . . .

Fourth Servant. We shall know well enough when we must go up. . . .

Fifth Servant. When the time is come, we shall go ourselves. . . .

Sixth Servant. There is no longer a sound heard in the house. . . .

Seventh Servant. We ought to make the children keep still, who are playing before the ventilator.

Eighth Servant. They will be still of themselves by and by.

Ninth Servant. The time has not yet come. . . .

[*Enter an old Servant.*

The Old Servant. No one can go in the room any longer. I have listened more than an hour. . . . You could hear the flies walk on the doors. . . . I heard nothing. . . .

First Servant. Has she been left alone in the room?

THE OLD SERVANT. No, no; I think the room is full of people.

FIRST SERVANT. They will come, they will come, by and by. . . .

THE OLD SERVANT. Lord! Lord! It is not happiness that has come into the house. . . . One may not speak, but if I could say what I know . . .

SECOND SERVANT. It was you who found them before the gate?

THE OLD SERVANT. Why, yes! why, yes! it was I who found them. The porter says it was he who saw them first; but it was I who waked them. He was sleeping on his face and would not get up.—And now he comes saying, "It was I who saw them first." Is that just?—See, I burned myself lighting a lamp to go down cellar.—Now what was I going to do down cellar?—I can't remember any more what I was going to do down cellar.—At any rate I got up very early; it was not yet very light; I said to myself, I will go across the courtyard, and then I will open the gate. Good; I go down the stairs on tiptoe, and I open the gate as if it were an ordinary gate. . . . My God! My God! What do I see? Divine a little what I see! . . .

FIRST SERVANT. They were before the gate?

THE OLD SERVANT. They were both stretched out before the gate! . . . Exactly like poor folk that are too hungry. . . . They were huddled together like little children who are afraid. . . . The little princess was nearly dead, and the great Golaud had still his sword in his side. . . . There was blood on the sill. . . .

SECOND SERVANT. We ought to make the children keep still. . . . They are screaming with all their might before the ventilator. . . .

THIRD SERVANT. You can't hear yourself speak. . . .

Fourth Servant. There is nothing to be done: I have tried already; they won't keep still. . . .

First Servant. It seems he is nearly cured?

The Old Servant. Who?

First Servant. The great Golaud.

Third Servant. Yes, yes; they have taken him to his wife's room. I met them just now, in the corridor. They were holding him up as if he were drunk. He cannot yet walk alone.

The Old Servant. He could not kill himself; he is too big. But she is hardly wounded, and it is she who is going to die. . . . Can you understand that?

First Servant. You have seen the wound?

The Old Servant. As I see you, my daughter.—I saw everything, you understand. . . . I saw it before all the others. . . . A tiny little wound under her little left breast,—a little wound that wouldn't kill a pigeon. Is it natural?

First Servant. Yes, yes; there is something underneath. . . .

Second Servant. Yes; but she was delivered of her babe three days ago. . . .

The Old Servant. Exactly! . . . She was delivered on her death-bed; is that a little sign?—And what a child! Have you seen it?—A wee little girl a beggar would not bring into the world. . . . A little wax figure that came much too soon; . . . a little wax figure that must live in lambs' wool. . . . Yes, yes; it is not happiness that has come into the house. . . .

First Servant. Yes, yes; it is the hand of God that has been stirring. . . .

Second Servant. Yes, yes; all that did not happen without reason. . . .

Third Servant. It is as good lord Pélléas . . . where is he?—No one knows. . . .

The Old Servant. Yes, yes; everybody knows. . . . But nobody dare speak of it. . . . One does not speak of this; . . . one does not speak of that; . . . one speaks no more of anything; . . . one no longer speaks truth. . . . But *I* know he was found at the bottom of Blind Man's Spring; . . . but no one, no one could see him. . . . Well, well, we shall only know all that at the last day. . . .

First Servant. I dare not sleep here any longer. . . .

The Old Servant. Yes, yes; once ill-fortune is in the house, one keeps silence in vain. . . .

Third Servant. Yes; it finds you all the same. . . .

The Old Servant. Yes, yes; but we do not go where we would. . . .

Fourth Servant. Yes, yes; we do not do what we would. . . .

First Servant. They are afraid of us now. . . .

Second Servant. They all keep silence. . . .

Third Servant. They cast down their eyes in the corridors.

Fourth Servant. They do not speak any more except in a low voice.

Fifth Servant. You would think they had all done it together.

Sixth Servant. One doesn't know what they have done. . . .

Seventh Servant. What is to be done when the masters are afraid? . . . [*A silence.*

First Servant. I no longer hear the children screaming.

Second Servant. They are sitting down before the ventilator.

Third Servant. They are huddled against each other.

THE OLD SERVANT. I no longer hear anything in the house. . . .

FIRST SERVANT. You no longer even hear the children breathe. . . .

THE OLD SERVANT. Come, come; it is time to go up. . . .

[*Exeunt, in silence.*

SCENE II.—*An apartment in the castle.* ARKËL, GOLAUD, *and the* PHYSICIAN *discovered in one corner of the room.* MÉLISANDE *is stretched upon her bed.*

THE PHYSICIAN. It cannot be of that little wound she is dying; a bird would not have died of it. . . . It is not you, then, who have killed her, good my lord; do not be so disconsolate. . . . She could not have lived. . . . She was born without reason . . . to die; and she dies without reason. . . . And then, it is not sure we shall not save her. . . .

ARKËL. No, no; it seems to me we keep too silent, in spite of ourselves, in her room. . . . It is not a good sign. . . . Look how she sleeps . . . slowly, slowly; . . . it is as if her soul was cold forever. . . .

GOLAUD. I have killed her without cause! I have killed her without cause! . . . Is it not enough to make the stones weep? . . . They had kissed like little children. . . . They had simply kissed. . . . They were brother and sister. . . . And I, and I at once! . . . I did it in spite of myself, look you. . . . I did it in spite of myself. . . .

THE PHYSICIAN. Stop; I think she is waking. . . .

MÉLISANDE. Open the window . . . open the window. . . .

ARKËL. Shall I open this one, Mélisande?

MÉLISANDE. No, no; the great window . . . the great window. . . . It is to see . . .

ARKËL. Is not the sea air too cold to-night?

THE PHYSICIAN. Do it; do it. . . .

MÉLISANDE. Thanks. . . . Is it sunset?

ARKËL. Yes; it is sunset on the sea; it is late.—How are you, Mélisande?

MÉLISANDE. Well, well.—Why do you ask that? I have never been better.—And yet it seems to me I know something. . . .

ARKËL. What sayest thou?—I do not understand thee. . . .

MÉLISANDE. Neither do I understand all I say, you see. . . . I do not know what I am saying. . . . I do not know what I know. . . . I no longer say what I would. . . .

ARKËL. Why, yes! why, yes! . . . I am quite happy to hear thee speak so; thou hast raved a little these last days, and one no longer understood thee. . . . But now all that is far away. . . .

MÉLISANDE. I do not know. . . . —Are you all alone in the room, grandfather?

ARKËL. No, there is the physician, besides, who cured thee. . . .

MÉLISANDE. Ah! . . .

ARKËL. And then there is still some one else. . . .

MÉLISANDE. Who is it?

ARKËL. It is . . . thou must not be frightened. . . . He does not wish thee the least harm, be sure. . . . If thou'rt afraid, he will go away. . . . He is very unhappy. . . .

MÉLISANDE. Who is it?

ARKËL. It is thy . . . thy husband. . . . It is Golaud. . . .

MÉLISANDE. Golaud is here? Why does he not come by me?

GOLAUD. [*Dragging himself toward the bed.*] Mélisande . . . Mélisande. . . .

MÉLISANDE. Is it you, Golaud? I should hardly recognize you any more. . . . It is the evening sunlight in my eyes. . . . Why look you on the walls? You have grown thin and old. . . . Is it a long while since we saw each other?

GOLAUD. [*To* ARKËL *and the* PHYSICIAN.] Will you withdraw a moment, if you please, if you please? . . . I will leave the door wide open. . . . One moment only. . . . I would say something to her; else I could not die. . . . Will you?—Go clear to the end of the corridor; you can come back at once, at once. . . . Do not refuse me this. . . . I am a wretch. . . . [*Exit* ARKËL *and the* PHYSICIAN.]—Mélisande, hast thou pity on me, as I have pity on thee? . . . Mélisande? . . . Dost thou forgive me, Mélisande? . . .

MÉLISANDE. Yes, yes, I do forgive thee. . . . What must I forgive? . . .

GOLAUD. I have wrought thee so much ill, Mélisande. . . . I cannot tell thee the ill I have wrought thee. . . . But I see it, I see it so clearly to-day . . . since the first day. . . . And all I did not know till now leaps in my eyes to-night. . . . And it is all my fault, all that has happened, all that will happen. . . . If I could tell it, thou wouldst see as I do! . . . I see all! I see all! . . . But I loved thee so! . . . I loved thee so! . . . But now there is some one dying. . . . It is I who am dying. . . . And I would know . . . I would ask thee. . . . Thou'lt bear me no ill-will . . . I would . . . The truth must be told to a dying man. . . . He must know the truth, or else he could not sleep. . . . Swearest thou to tell me the truth?

MÉLISANDE. Yes.

GOLAUD. Didst thou love Pélléas?

MÉLISANDE. Why, yes; I loved him.—Where is he?

GOLAUD. Thou dost not understand me?—Thou wilt not understand me?—It seems to me . . . it seems to me . . . Well, then, here: I ask thee if thou lovedst him with a forbidden love? . . . Wert thou . . . were you guilty? Say, say, yes, yes, yes! . . .

MÉLISANDE. No, no; we were not guilty.—Why do you ask that?

GOLAUD. Mélisande! . . . tell me the truth, for the love of God!

MÉLISANDE. Why have I not told the truth?

GOLAUD. Do not lie so any more, at the moment of death!

MÉLISANDE. Who is dying?—Is it I?

GOLAUD. Thou, thou! and I, I too, after thee! . . . And we must have the truth. . . . We must have the truth at last, dost thou understand? . . . Tell me all! Tell me all! I forgive thee all! . . .

MÉLISANDE. Why am I going to die?—I did not know it. . . .

GOLAUD. Thou knowest it now! . . . It is time! It is time! . . . Quick! quick! . . . The truth! the truth! . . .

MÉLISANDE. The truth . . . the truth . . .

GOLAUD. Where art thou?—Mélisande!—Where art thou?—It is not natural! Mélisande! Where art thou? —Where goest thou? [*Perceiving* ARKËL *and the* PHYSICIAN *at the door of the room.*]—Yes, yes; you may come in. . . . I know nothing; it is useless. . . . It is too late; she is already too far away from us. . . . I shall never know! . . . I shall die here like a blind man! . . .

ARKËL. What have you done? You will kill her. . . .

GOLAUD. I have already killed her. . . .

ARKËL. Mélisande. . . .

MÉLISANDE. Is it you, grandfather?

ARKËL. Yes, my daughter. . . . What would you have me do?

MÉLISANDE. Is it true that the winter is beginning? . . .

ARKËL. Why dost thou ask?

MÉLISANDE. Because it is cold, and there are no more leaves. . . .

ARKËL. Thou art cold?—Wilt thou have the windows closed?

MÉLISANDE. No, no, . . . not till the sun be at the bottom of the sea.—It sinks slowly; then it is the winter beginning?

ARKËL. Yes.—Thou dost not like the winter?

MÉLISANDE. Oh! no. I am afraid of the cold.—I am so afraid of the great cold. . . .

ARKËL. Dost thou feel better?

MÉLISANDE. Yes, yes; I have no longer all those qualms. . . .

ARKËL. Wouldst thou see thy child?

MÉLISANDE. What child?

ARKËL. Thy child.—Thou art a mother. . . . Thou hast brought a little daughter into the world. . . .

MÉLISANDE. Where is she?

ARKËL. Here. . . .

MÉLISANDE. It is strange. . . . I cannot lift my arms to take her. . . .

ARKËL. Because you are still very weak. . . . I will hold her myself; look. . . .

MÉLISANDE. She does not laugh. . . . She is little. . . . She is going to weep too. . . . I pity her. . . .

[*The room has been invaded, little by little, by*

*the women servants of the castle, who range themselves in silence along the walls and wait.*

GOLAUD. [*Rising abruptly.*] What is the matter?—What are all these women coming here for? . . .

THE PHYSICIAN. It is the servants. . . .

ARKËL. Who was it called them?

THE PHYSICIAN. It was not I. . . .

GOLAUD. Why do you come here?—No one has asked for you. . . . What come you here to do?—But what is it, then?—Answer me! . . .

[*The servants make no answer.*

ARKËL. Do not speak too loud. . . . She is going to sleep; she has closed her eyes. . . .

GOLAUD. It is not . . . ?

THE PHYSICIAN. No, no; see, she breathes. . . .

ARKËL. Her eyes are full of tears.—It is her soul weeping now. . . . Why does she stretch her arms out so?—What would she?

THE PHYSICIAN. It is toward the child, without doubt. . . . It is the struggle of motherhood against . . .

GOLAUD. At this moment?—At this moment?—You must say. Say! Say! . . .

THE PHYSICIAN. Perhaps.

GOLAUD. At once? . . . Oh! oh! I must tell her. . . . —Mélisande! Mélisande! . . . Leave me alone! leave me alone with her! . . .

ARKËL. No, no; do not come near. . . . Trouble her not. . . . Speak no more to her. . . . You know not what the soul is. . . .

GOLAUD. It is not my fault! . . . It is not my fault!

ARKËL. Hush! . . . Hush! . . . We must speak softly now.—She must not be disturbed. . . . The human soul is very silent. . . . The human soul likes to depart alone. . . . It suffers so timorously. . . . But the sadness, Golaud . . . the sadness of all we see! . . . Oh! oh! oh! . . .

[*At this moment, all the servants fall suddenly on their knees at the back of the chamber.*

ARKËL. [*Turning.*] What is the matter?

THE PHYSICIAN. [*Approaching the bed and feeling the body.*] They are right. . . . [*A long silence.*

ARKËL. I saw nothing.—Are you sure? . . .

THE PHYSICIAN. Yes, yes.

ARKËL. I heard nothing. . . . So quick, so quick! . . . All at once! . . . She goes without a word. . . .

GOLAUD. [*Sobbing.*] Oh! oh! oh!

ARKËL. Do not stay here, Golaud. . . . She must have silence now. . . . Come, come. . . . It is terrible, but it is not your fault. . . . 'Twas a little being, so quiet, so fearful, and so silent. . . . 'Twas a poor little mysterious being, like everybody. . . . She lies there as if she were the big sister of her child. . . . Come, come. . . . My God! My God! . . . I shall never understand it at all. . . . Let us not stay here.—Come; the child must not stay here in this room. . . . She must live now in her place. . . It is the poor little one's turn. . . .

[*They go out in silence.*

CURTAIN

# MAGDA

BY

HERMANN SUDERMANN

*Translated by* CHARLES EDWARD AMORY WINSLOW.

## Hermann Sudermann

b. 1857, Matzicken, East Prussia.
1875, entered University of Königsberg.
1877, studied in Berlin. Contributor to liberal journals.
1887, *Twilight Tales,* his first book.
1889, *Die Ehre* (*Honor*), his first play, at the Lessing Theater, Berlin.
d. 1928.

### Plays

1889 *Die Ehre* (translated as *Honor*).
1891 *Sodoms Ende* (*The Destruction of Sodom*).
1893 *Heimat* (translated as *Magda* and *Casa Paterna*).
1895 *Die Schmetterlingsschlacht* (translated as *The Battle of the Butterflies*).
1896 *Morituri* (cycle of one-act plays, translated under the same title).
*Teja* (also translated as *Teias*).
*Fritzchen* (translated under the same title).
*Das Ewig-Männliche* (translated as *The Eternal Masculine*).
1896 *Das Glück im Winkel* (translated as *The Vale of Content*).
1898 *Johannes* (translated under the same title, and as *John* and *John the Baptist*).
1899 *Die drei Reiherfedern* (a legend play, translated as *Three Heron Feathers*).
1900 *Johannisfeuer* (translated as *The Fires of St. John* and *St. John's Fire*).

1902 *Es lebe das Leben* (translated as *The Joy of Living*).
1903 *Der Sturmgeselle Sokrates* (*Storm-Brother Socrates*).
1905 *Stein unter Steinen* (*Stone Among Stones*).
1905 *Das Blumenboot* (adapted as *Scherzo*).
1907 *Rosen* (cycle of one-act plays, translated as *Roses*).
*Die Lichtbändern* (translated as *Streaks of Light*).
*Der letzte Besuch* (translated as *The Last Visit*).
*Margot* (translated under the same title).
*Die ferne Prinzessin* (translated as *The Far-Away Princess*).
1909 *Strandkinder* (*Children of the Strand*).
1911 *Der Bettler von Syrakus* (*The Beggar of Syracuse*).
1912 *Der gute Ruf* (translated as *A Good Reputation*).
1914 *Die Lobgesänge des Claudian* (*Claudian's Songs of Praise*).
1915 *Die entgötterte Welt* (cycle of plays, *The Godless World*).
*Die Freundin* (*The Woman Friend*).
*Die Gutgeschnittene Ecke* (*The Desirable Corner*).
*Das höhere Leben* (*The Higher Life*).
1916 *Der Katzensteg* (adapted from his novel of the same name, *The Cat-walk*).
1920 *Die Raschoffs* (*The Raschoffs*).
1921 *Der Hüter der Schwelle* (one-act play, *The Guardian of the Threshold*).
1921 *Das deutsche Schicksal* (a patriotic dramatic cycle, *German Destiny*).
*Heilige Zeit* (*Holy Time*).

*Opfer* (*Sacrifice*).
*Notruf* (*Cry of Need*).
1923 *Wie die Träumenden* (*Like Those Who Dream*).
1923 *Die Denkmalsweihe* (unpublished in German, but translated as *The Unveiling*).
1925 *Der Hasenfellhändler* (*The Rabbit Skin Dealer*).

### WRITING ABOUT THE DRAMA

*Verrohung der Theaterkritik*, 1902. *Die Sturmgesellen*, 1903.

## MAGDA

Sudermann broke the way in the German commercial theater for the *Junger Realismus,* elsewhere known as naturalism; and his *Heimat* (*Magda*) won world popularity as well. Bernhardt and Duse led the great actresses of the period in popularizing its tinselly heroine in all theatrical centers. Its lasting stageworthiness was shown in its recent New York revival (1926).

As a young radical from provincial East Prussia, Sudermann found in the contrast between life in Berlin and that of his then remote homeland, abundant material for stories, novels, and plays. To an instinct for construction he added a keen perceptiveness of colorful detail and atmosphere, which had become the mania of the naturalist school. He shared also their love for Zola, Ibsen, and the Russian novelists. He remained independent, however, refusing to become either partisan or theorist, and, unlike his fellows, he retained a hearty respect for the workmanship of the French problem play written in the "well-made" manner of Dumas, Augier, and Sardou. To this marked inclination, perhaps, he owed the gradual alienation in his own country and abroad of the more acute critics.

His first play, *Die Ehre* (*Honor*), produced an immense popular sensation in the very year (1889) in which the naturalist revolters, with Schlaf, Holz, and Hauptmann at their head, opened the Freie Bühne, which was to do for Germany what the Théâtre-Libre had done for France. (For a discussion of this movement see *European Plays,* I. of this series, pp. 229 f. and 301 ff.) In *Die Ehre* Sudermann contrasted with a sharpness peculiar to his genius the effect upon thought and character of life in Berlin with that of the narrow and restrictive standards of a provincial region like his own homeland. The freshly observed detail rather than the form or subject of the play made it appeal strongly to the young naturalists, who acclaimed it far beyond its deserts. It was even more loudly decried by the conventionally minded public. *Sodoms Ende*, his second, made a much closer approach to pure naturalism. The failure of this play to do more than arouse discussion perhaps explains the quick return in *Heimat* to a more theatrical manner. Reverting to the home-coming theme of *Die Ehre* with its possibilities of contrast, and building his play in Ibsen's fashion upon the results of antecedent action, he heightened his effects for the general public by an almost romantic exaggeration of characters and motives, indulging in *coups de théâtre* and improbabilities of situation like a pre-Ibsenite. He increased the effectiveness of the dual clash at the basis of the play, of daughter against father and of cosmopolitan ways against provincialism, by adding the fascination of a liberating artistic nature, which gave this work a universal appeal that no other play of Sudermann's has had. The fascination was the greater because the artist was an operatic star with infinite possibilities of robes and jewels. Principals as well as the minor characters hardly escape the suggestion of caricature. Sudermann's sure sense of the theater and his structural skill shown in the preparatory first act and brilliant scene climaxes, as well as his more admirable instinct for characterizing detail, are here displayed with more energy and theatrical vitality than in his later plays of superior literary value and greater artistic sincerity.

## PERSONS

SCHWARTZE, *Lieutenant-Colonel on half-pay.*

MAGDA, } *his children by his first wife.*
MARIE, }

AUGUSTA, *born* VON WENDLOWSKI, *his second wife.*

FRANZISKA VON WENDLOWSKI, *her sister.*

MAX VON WENDLOWSKI, *Lieutenant, their nephew.*

HEFFTERDINGT, *Pastor of St. Mary's.*

DR. VON KELLER, *Councillor.*

BECKMANN, *Professor Emeritus.*

VON KLEBS, *Major-General on half-pay.*

MRS. VON KLEBS.

MRS. JUSTICE ELLRICH.

MRS. SCHUMANN.

THERESA, *maidservant of the Schwartze family.*

*Place.* The principal city of a province.
*Time.* The present.

# MAGDA

## ACT FIRST

SCENE.—*Living-room in house of* LIEUTENANT-COLONEL SCHWARTZE, *furnished in simple and old-fashioned style. Left, at back, a glass door with white curtains through which the dining-room is seen. There is also a hall door, through which a staircase to the upper story is visible. Right, a corner window, with white curtains, surrounded by ivy. Left, a door to the* LIEUTENANT-COLONEL'S *room. Steel engravings of a religious and patriotic character, in tarnished gold frames, photographs of military groups, and cases of butterflies on the walls. Right, over the sofa, among other pictures, is the portrait of the first Mrs. Schwartze, young and charming, in the costume of the 'sixties. Behind the sofa, an old-fashioned desk. Before the window, a small table with work-box and hand sewing-machine. At the back, between the doors, an old-fashioned tall clock. In the left-hand corner, a stand with dried grasses; in front, a table with a small aquarium. Left, in front, a corner sofa with a small pipe-cupboard behind it. A stove with a stuffed bird on it; and behind, a bookcase with a bust of the old Emperor William.*

[MARIE *and* THERESA *discovered.* THERESA *at the door.* MARIE *is occupied with the sewing-machine.*

THERESA. Miss Marie!

MARIE. Well!

THERESA. Is your father still lying down?

MARIE. What's the matter? Has any one called?

THERESA. No, but—— There! Look at that! [*Producing a magnificent mass of flowers.*]

MARIE. Good Heavens! Take it to my room quickly, or papa—— But, Theresa, when the first came yesterday, weren't you told not to let any more be left?

THERESA. I'd have sent the florist's boy away if I could, but I was up on the ladder fixing the flag, and he laid it down and was gone before I could stop him. My, my, though, they're beautiful! and if I might make a guess, the Lieutenant——

MARIE. You may not make a guess.

THERESA. All right, all right. Oh, I know what I wanted to ask. Does the flag hang well? [MARIE *looks out, and nods assent.*] The whole town is full of flags and flowers, and the most expensive tapestries are hung out of the windows. One would think it was the King's birthday. And all this fuss is about a stupid Music Festival! What is this Music Festival, Miss Marie? Is it different from a choral festival?

MARIE. Yes, indeed.

THERESA. Is it better?

MARIE. Oh, much better!

THERESA. Oh, well, if it's better—— [*A knock.*]

MARIE. Come in!

[*Enter* MAX.

THERESA. Well, *now* I suppose I can leave the flowers. [*Exit* THERESA, *laughing.*

MARIE. You ought to be ashamed of yourself, Max.

MAX. What on earth do you mean?

MARIE. Aren't these flowers yours?

MAX. Good Heavens! I can afford a few pennies

for a bunch of violets once in a while, but this—— Oh, no!

MARIE. Nor yesterday's?

MAX. No, nor yesterday's. [MARIE *rings.*]

[*Enter* THERESA.

MARIE. Please throw these flowers away.

THERESA. What! Throw those beautiful flowers away?

MARIE. You are right. The pastor would say, "If God's gifts do not please us, we must at least take care that they give pleasure to others." Wouldn't he?

MAX. Probably he would.

MARIE. Then you had better take them back to the florist's. Did they come from Zimmerman's? [THERESA *nods.*] Well, we'll sell them if we can, and give the money to Pastor Heffterdingt for his hospital.

THERESA. Shall I go now?

MARIE. After you have made the coffee. I'll serve it myself. [*Exit* THERESA.] These flowers are an insult! I need not tell you, Max, that I have given no one the shadow of an excuse for such a thing.

MAX. I'm very sure of that.

MARIE. And papa was so angry. He simply stormed. And I was quiet because I suspected it was you. If he got hold of the poor fellow, it would go hard with him.

MAX. Do you think it would be any better if I got hold of him?

MARIE. What rights have you in the case?

MAX. Marie! [*Takes her hand.*]

MARIE. [*Gently disengaging herself.*] Oh, Max, please—not that. You know every corner of my heart. But we must think of the proprieties.

MAX. Proprieties! Oh, pshaw!

MARIE. Well, you know what a world we live in. Here, every one is afraid of every one else because each depends upon the good opinion of the other. If a few anonymous flowers can make me talked of, how much more——

MAX. Oh, yes, I know.

MARIE. [*Laying her hand on his shoulder.*] Max, you'll speak again to Aunt Frankie, won't you, about the guaranty[1] of your income?

MAX. I have already.

MARIE. Well?

MAX. [*Shrugging his shoulders.*] As long as she lives, not a penny.

MARIE. Then there's only one person who can help us.

MAX. Your father?

MARIE. No. For Heaven's sake, don't let him hear of it. He might forbid you the house.

MAX. What has he against me?

MARIE. You know how he has been since our misfortune. He feels that there is a blot to be wiped out; and especially now, when the whole town echoes with music—when everything recalls Magda.

MAX. What if she should come back, some day?

MARIE. After twelve years? She will never come. [*Weeps.*

MAX. Marie!

MARIE. You're right, you're right. I will put it away from me.

MAX. But who is the one person who can help us?

MARIE. Why, the pastor!

MAX. Yes, yes, he might.

MARIE. He can do everything. He stirs your very heart—as if—— And then he seems like a kind of relation. He should have been my brother-in-law.

MAX. Yes, but she wouldn't have it so.

[1] Without which officers in the German army might not marry.

MARIE. Don't speak angrily, Max. She must have made atonement. [*A ring.*] Oh, perhaps this is he.

MAX. No, no, I forgot to tell you. Councillor von Keller asked me to bring him here to-day.

MARIE. What does he want?

MAX. He wants to interest himself in the missions —no, it's in our home work particularly, I think. I don't know—— Well, at any rate he wants to come to the committee meeting to-morrow.

MARIE. I'll call father and mother. [*Enter* THERESA *with a card.*] Show him in. [*Exit* THERESA.] Entertain him until I come back. [*Gives him her hand.*] And we'll talk again about the pastor some other time?

MAX. In spite of the proprieties?

MARIE. Oh, Max, I've been too forward! Haven't I?

MAX. Marie!

MARIE. No, no—we won't speak of it. Good-bye.

[*Exit* MARIE.

[*Enter* VON KELLER.

MAX. You must content yourself with me for a few minutes, my dear Von Keller. [*They shake hands.*]

VON KELLER. With pleasure, my good sir, with pleasure. [*Sits.*] How our little town is changed by the festival! It really seems as if we were in the great world.

MAX. [*Laughing.*] I advise you not to say that aloud.

VON KELLER. What did I say? I assure you I did not mean anything. If such a misunderstanding got abroad——

MAX. You have nothing to fear from me!

VON KELLER. Oh, of course not. Ah, how much better it would be to know nothing of the outer world!

MAX. How long were you away?

VON KELLER. Five years, with examinations and being sent down to commissioners and all that. Well, now I am back again. I drink home-brewed beer; I patronize local tailors; I have even, with a noble fearlessness of death, eaten the deer-steak of the season; and this I call pleasure! Yes, youth, travel, and women are good things; but the world must be ruled, and sober men are needed. Your time will come some day. The years of honor are approaching. Yes, yes, especially when one joins the ecclesiastical courts.

MAX. Are you going to do that?

VON KELLER. I think of it. And to be at one with those of the cloth—I speak quite openly with you—it is worth my while, in short, to interest myself in religious questions. I have of late in my speeches, as perhaps you know, taken this position; and as for the connections which this household has—let me tell you I am proud of them.

MAX. You might have been proud long ago.

VON KELLER. Excuse me, am I over-sensitive? Or do I read a reproach in your words?

MAX. Not quite that, but—if you will pardon me, it has sometimes appeared—and not to me alone—as if you avoided the houses where my uncle's family were to be found.

VON KELLER. And my presence here now—does not that prove the contrary?

MAX. Exactly. And therefore I too will speak very frankly. You were the last person to meet my lost cousin, Magda.

VON KELLER. [*Confused.*] Who says——

MAX. You yourself have spoken of it, I am told. You met her with my friend Heydebrand when he was at the military academy.

VON KELLER. Yes, yes, it's true.

MAX. It was wrong of me not to ask you about her openly, but you will probably understand my reticence. I feel almost as if I belonged to this family and I feared to learn something which might disgrace it.

VON KELLER. Oh, not at all, not in the least. It was like this. When I was in Berlin for the State Examinations, I saw one day on Leipsic Street a familiar face—a home face, if I may say so. You know what that is when one is far away. Well, we spoke to each other. I learned that she was studying to sing in opera, and that for this purpose she had left her home.

MAX. Not exactly. She left home to be companion to an old lady. [*Hesitates.*] There was a difference with her father.

VON KELLER. A love affair?

MAX. In a way. Her father supported the suitor and told her to obey or leave his house.

VON KELLER. And she went away?

MAX. Yes. Then, a year later, when she wrote that she was going on the stage, it made the breach complete. But what else did you hear?

VON KELLER. That's all.

MAX. Nothing else?

VON KELLER. Well, well—I met her once or twice at the opera-house where she had a pass.

MAX. And you know absolutely nothing of her life?

VON KELLER. [*With a shrug.*] Have you heard nothing from her?

MAX. Nothing at all. Well, at any rate, I am grateful to you. I beg you, however, not to mention the meeting to my uncle, unless he asks you about it directly. He knows of it, of course, but the name of the lost daughter is never mentioned in this house.

VON KELLER. Oh, I have tact enough not to do that.

MAX. And what do you think has become of her?

VON KELLER. Oh, music is a lottery. Ten thousand blanks and one prize. A host of beginners and but one who makes a career. If one becomes a Patti or a Sembrich, or, to come down to our own Festival——

[*Enter* SCHWARTZE *and* MRS. SCHWARTZE.

SCHWARTZE. [*Shaking hands.*] Welcome to my house! Councillor von Keller, my wife.

MRS. SCHWARTZE. Pray sit down.

VON KELLER. I should not have dared, madam, to ask the honor of this introduction had I not wished so strongly to share in the good and useful work which centers here. My purpose may excuse my temerity.

SCHWARTZE. You're very kind; but you do us too much honor. If you seek the center of the whole movement, Pastor Heffterdingt is the man. He inspires all, he controls all; he——

MRS. SCHWARTZE. Do you know our pastor, sir?

VON KELLER. I have heard him speak many times, dear lady, and have admired equally the sincerity of his convictions and his naïve faith in human nature. But I cannot comprehend the influence he exerts.

MRS. SCHWARTZE. You will find it out. He is so plain and simple that one hardly realizes what a man he is. He brings every one round.

VON KELLER. I am almost converted already, dear lady.

SCHWARTZE. As for us here, all I can do is to give these weak and useless hands to help on the great work. It's only right that an old soldier should dedicate the little strength left him by the throne to the service of the altar. Those are the two causes to fight for.

VON KELLER. That's a great thought!

SCHWARTZE. Thanks, thanks, but no more of this. Ah, ten years ago, when they gave me my discharge, was a devil of a fellow. Max, doesn't my old battalion still tremble at my name?

MAX. That they do, uncle.

SCHWARTZE. Ah, that is one thing you escape in the civil service—being laid on the shelf without any fault of your own—without the shadow of a fault. Then there came a slight stroke of apoplexy. See how my hand trembles now! And what had I to look forward to? It was then that my young friend, Heffterdingt, showed me the way, through work and prayer, to a new youth. Without him I never should have found it.

MRS. SCHWARTZE. You mustn't believe all he says, Mr. von Keller. If he didn't always depreciate himself, he would be better thought of in the highest circles.

VON KELLER. High and low, madam, everywhere your husband is known and honored.

SCHWARTZE. [*Lighting up.*] Indeed? Ah, well, no vanity. No, no, that is the moth that corrupts.

MRS. SCHWARTZE. Is it really so wrong to wish for a little honor?

VON KELLER. Oh!

SCHWARTZE. What is honor? You would call it being led up the room by the governor, or being asked to tea at the castle when the royal family is here.

MRS. SCHWARTZE. You know very well that the latter honor has never fallen to my lot.

SCHWARTZE. Oh, yes, pardon me. I knew your weak spot. I should have avoided it.

MRS. SCHWARTZE. Yes, just think, Councillor, Mrs. Fanny Hirschfeld of the Children's Hospital was invited, and I was not.

VON KELLER. [*Deprecatingly.*] Oh!

SCHWARTZE. [*Laughing, and stroking her head.*] Ah, the moth that corrupts, the moth that corrupts! [*Enter* MARIE *with the coffee. She bows in a friendly way to* VON KELLER.] Herr von Keller, my daughter—my only daughter.

VON KELLER. I've already had the pleasure.

MARIE. I can't offer you a hand for welcome, Dr. Von Keller, but you may have a cup of coffee instead.

VON KELLER. [*Helping himself and looking at the others.*] I am very fortunate in being treated like an old acquaintance of the family.

SCHWARTZE. As far as we are concerned, you shall become not only an acquaintance but a friend. And that is no conventional politeness, Councillor; for I know you, and in these times, when all the ties of morality and authority seem strained to bursting, it is doubly necessary that those who stand for the good old patriarchal order should hold together.

VON KELLER. Very true, very true indeed. One doesn't hear such sentiments as that in the world in general, where modern ideas pass current for small change.

SCHWARTZE. Modern ideas! Oh, pshaw! I know them. But come into the quiet homes where are bred brave soldiers and virtuous wives. There you'll hear no talk about heredity, no arguments about individuality, no scandalous gossip. There modern ideas have no foothold, for it is there that the life and strength of the Fatherland abide. Look at this home! There is no luxury—hardly even what you call good taste—faded rugs, birchen chairs, old pictures; and yet when you see the beams of the western sun pour through the white curtains and lie with such a loving touch on the old room, does not something say to you, "Here dwells true happiness"? [VON KELLER *nods with conviction.*]

SCHWARTZE. [*Broodingly.*] And here it might have dwelt!

MARIE. [*Hurrying to him.*] Papa!

SCHWARTZE. Yes, yes, I know. Well, in this house rules old-fashioned paternal authority. And it shall rule as long as I live. And am I therefore a tyrant? Tell me. You ought to know.

MARIE. You're the best, the dearest——

MRS. SCHWARTZE. He is so excitable, you see, Councillor.

SCHWARTZE. Have you not been well brought up? And shall we not hold together, we three? But the age goes on planting rebellion in children's hearts, putting mistrust between man and wife, [*rises*] and it will never be satisfied till the last roof-tree smokes in ruins, and men wander about the streets, fearful and alone, like homeless curs. [*Sinks back exhausted.*]

MRS. SCHWARTZE. You ought not to get so wrought up, papa. You know it is bad for you. [MAX *makes a sign to* VON KELLER.]

VON KELLER. Shall I go? [MAX *nods.*] This is an interesting subject to develop, Colonel. I must say I think perhaps you are a little severe. But my time——

SCHWARTZE. Severe? Ah, well, don't think ill of an old man for speaking a little too hotly.

VON KELLER. Ah, sir, heat is the badge of youth. I believe I am a graybeard beside you.

SCHWARTZE. No, no. [*Presses his hand.*]

VON KELLER. Madam! Miss Marie! [*Exit.* MAX *follows him.*]

SCHWARTZE. Greet the battalion for me, my boy.

MAX. I will, dear uncle. [*Exit.*

MRS. SCHWARTZE. A very agreeable man.

MARIE. Almost too agreeable.

SCHWARTZE. You are speaking of our guest! [MRS. SCHWARTZE *makes* MARIE *a sign to be careful.*]

MARIE. Will you have your pipe, papa?

SCHWARTZE. Yes, dear.

MRS. SCHWARTZE. The gentlemen of the card-club will be here soon. How lucky that we didn't eat the haunch of venison Sunday! I've ordered some red wine for the General, too. I paid three marks; that's not too dear, is it?

SCHWARTZE. Not if it's good. Is your sister coming to-day?

MRS. SCHWARTZE. I think so.

SCHWARTZE. She was asked to the Governor's yesterday, wasn't she?

MRS. SCHWARTZE. [*Sighing.*] Yes.

SCHWARTZE. And we were not. Poor thing! She must look out for me to-day if she boasts. [*Aside.*] Old cat!

MARIE. [*Kneels before him, lighting his pipe.*] Be good, father dear. What harm does it do you?

SCHWARTZE. Yes, yes, darling. I'll be good. But my heart is sore. [*Bell rings.* MARIE *hurries out.*]

MRS. SCHWARTZE. Here they are.

[*Enter* MAJOR-GENERAL VON KLEBS, PROFESSOR BECKMANN, *and* MARIE.

VON KLEBS. My humblest respects to the ladies. Ah, my dear madam! [*Kisses her hand.*]

MRS. SCHWARTZE. Make yourselves at home, gentlemen.

VON KLEBS. Ha, my dear Colonel, hearty as ever? All ready for the fray, little one? Now we are all right. But we were almost too late. We were caught in the Music Festival crowd. Such a confusion! I was bringing the school-master along, and just as we passed by the German House, there was a great crush of people, gaping as if there were a princess at the least. And what do you suppose it was? A singer! These are really what one may call goings-on. All this fuss about a singer! What do they call the person?

BECKMANN. Ah, General, we seem to be in a strange land to-day.

VON KLEBS. We are under a curse, my dear madam. We are bearing a penance.

[*They sit at a card table.*

BECKMANN. But you must know dall' Orto, the great Italian Wagner singer. We are very fortunate in getting her for the festival. If she were not here—

VON KLEBS. Well, well, what if she were not? Eh? I hoped that our strictly moral circle, at least, would hold itself aloof from all this. But since the Governor gives receptions in the lady's honor! And, best of all, to cap the climax, who do you think was standing today among the enthusiasts, craning his neck like the rest? You'll never guess. It's too inconceivable. The pastor!

SCHWARTZE. The pastor?

VON KLEBS. Yes, our pastor.

SCHWARTZE. How extraordinary!

VON KLEBS. Now, I ask you, what did he want there? And what did the others want there? And what good is the whole festival?

BECKMANN. I should think that the cultivation of the faculty of the ideal among the people was an object—

VON KLEBS. The way to cultivate the faculty of the ideal is to found a Soldiers' Union.

SCHWARTZE. But, General, every one isn't so lucky as to be a soldier.

VON KLEBS. [*Sorting his cards.*] Well, we have been, Colonel. I know no one, I wish to know no one, who has not been a soldier. And all this so-called Art —what good does it do?

BECKMANN. Art raises the moral tone of the people.

VON KLEBS. There we have it, madam! I tell you Art is a mere invention of those who are afraid to be soldiers to gain an important position for themselves. I pass.

SCHWARTZE. I pass.

BECKMANN. And will you maintain that Art— I have the nine of spades.

[*Bell rings. Exit* MARIE. VON KLEBS *makes an impatient movement.* SCHWARTZE *quiets him. They begin to play. Enter* FRANZISKA, *followed by the* PASTOR.

VON KLEBS. Ah, Miss Franziska! [*Aside.*] That is the end of us!

SCHWARTZE. No, no, we'll send her into the garden.

FRANZISKA. [*Throwing herself into a chair.*] Oh, I am so hot! I must get my breath. Pray don't put yourself out, General.

BECKMANN. Nine of spades!

VON KLEBS. Hello, here's the pastor too!

HEFFTERDINGT. Good-day to you! [*He shakes hands with each.*]

VON KLEBS. How long have you been running after the singers, Pastor?

HEFFTERDINGT. What? Oh, yes. Yes, I am running after singers. That's my occupation now.

SCHWARTZE. You can play with our card-party though, can't you?

HEFFTERDINGT. Unfortunately, no. I must, on the contrary, ask for a few serious words with you, my dear sir.

VON KLEBS. Ah, but you'll put it off, won't you, Pastor?

FRANZISKA. Oh, for Heaven's sake! It's so important. There must be no delay.

SCHWARTZE. Is my sister-in-law in it too?

FRANZISKA. Very much so.

VON KLEBS. Oh, well, we can go away again.

MRS. SCHWARTZE. Oh, we shouldn't like that at all.

SCHWARTZE. If it were not you, dear pastor, who separated us!

MRS. SCHWARTZE. But perhaps, Marie, the gentlemen would be willing to take a turn with you in the garden.

VON KLEBS. Certainly! That's good! That's famous! That's what we'll do! Miss Marie, be so good as to lead the way.

BECKMANN. Shall we leave the cards as they lie?

VON KLEBS. Yes, you have the nine of spades. Come on. [*Exit* VON KLEBS, BECKMANN, *and* MARIE.

SCHWARTZE. Well?

FRANZISKA. Good Lord, don't you see how upset I am? You might at least give me a glass of water. [MRS. SCHWARTZE *brings it.*]

HEFFTERDINGT. Will you promise me, my dear sir, that whatever may happen you will preserve your calmness? You may believe me, much depends upon it.

SCHWARTZE. Yes, yes; but what—

HEFFTERDINGT. Miss Franziska will tell you better.

FRANZISKA. [*After drinking the water.*] This is a day indeed! Fate is avenging me. This man has for years outraged my holiest feelings, but to-day I can heap coals of fire on his head. [*Moved.*] Brother-in-law, give me your hand. Sister, yours.

HEFFTERDINGT. Pardon me, dear Miss Franziska, I think your news is so important that—

FRANZISKA. [*Melting.*] Don't be angry, don't be angry. I am so upset! Well, yesterday I was at the Governor's. Only the nobility and the most important people were asked. You weren't asked?

SCHWARTZE. [*Angrily.*] No.

FRANZISKA. I did not mean to offend you. Oh, I am so upset! [*Suppressing a sob at a sign from the* PASTOR.] Yes, yes, yes. I had on my yellow silk dress with the Brussels lace—you know I've had the train shortened. Well, as I stepped into the room—whom do you think I saw?

SCHWARTZE. Well, well, who?

FRANZISKA. [*Sobbing.*] Your child! Magdalene

[SCHWARTZE *staggers, and is supported by the* PASTOR. MRS. SCHWARTZE *cries out. A pause.*]

SCHWARTZE. Pastor?

HEFFTERDINGT. It is true.

SCHWARTZE. [*Standing up.*] Magdalene is no longer my child.

FRANZISKA. Ah, just wait. If you listen, you'll look at it in quite another light. Such a child you will welcome with open arms.

SCHWARTZE. Magdalene is no longer my child.

HEFFTERDINGT. But you may at least hear the circumstances.

SCHWARTZE. [*Dazed.*] Yes, I suppose so.

FRANZISKA. [*At a sign from* HEFFTERDINGT.] Well the great dining-hall was crammed. They were almost all strangers. Then I saw his Excellency coming down the room. And on his arm was a lady—

MRS. SCHWARTZE. On his Excellency's arm?

FRANZISKA. With dark hair, and very proud and tall—and around her a crowd of men just like the circle about royalty—and chatting and laughing. And any one to whom she spoke seemed as happy as if it were the Princess. And she wore half a dozen orders and an orange band with a medal about her neck. I was wondering what royal personage it could be—when she turned half around—and—I knew Magda's eyes!

SCHWARTZE. Impossible!

FRANZISKA. That is what I saw!

HEFFTERDINGT. My dear Colonel, it is true.

SCHWARTZE. If she—[*Clasping his hands.*] At least she has not fallen! She has not fallen! Father in Heaven, Thou hast kept her safely!

MRS. SCHWARTZE. And what is she, to have such honor—

HEFFTERDINGT. She has become a great singer, and calls herself, in Italian, Maddalene dall' Orto.

MRS. SCHWARTZE. Listen, listen, Leopold, the famous singer of whom the papers are so full is our child!

SCHWARTZE. Magda is no longer my child.

HEFFTERDINGT. Is that your fixed resolve?

FRANZISKA. What sort of heart have you? You ought to imitate me. She offended me as only she could—the little wretch! That is, then she was a little wretch. But now—well, she did not look at me; but if she had—

MRS. SCHWARTZE. Leopold, she was on his Excellency's arm!

SCHWARTZE. I tell you, and you—and you, too, Pastor—that I would rather have seen her lying in rags and tatters at my feet and begging for forgiveness. For then I should have known that she was still, at heart, my child. But why has she come back here? The world was large enough for her triumph. Why should she rob this humble provincial nest of ours? I know why. To show her miserable father how far one can rise in the world by treading filial duty into the dust—that is her intention. Pride and arrogance speak in her, and nothing else.

HEFFTERDINGT. My dear Colonel, I might ask, what speaks in you? A father's love? You could make no pretence to that. Your rights? I think rather it would be your right to rejoice in the good fortune of your child. Offended custom? I don't know— Your daughter has done so much through her own strength that even offended custom might at least condone it. It appears to me that pride and arrogance speak in you—and nothing else.

SCHWARTZE. [*Angrily.*] Pastor!

HEFFTERDINGT. Oh, don't be angry—there is no need of that. When I have something to say, I must say it, mustn't I? I might almost think that it displeased you that she has climbed so high in spite of you. Your pride demands something to forgive, and you are angry because there is nothing to be forgiven. And now, let me ask you, do you seriously wish that she had found her way home, lost and ruined? Do you dare answer for such a wish before the throne of God? [*A silence.*] No, my dear old friend. You have often, in jest, called me your good angel; let me be so once, in reality. Come with me—now—to-day.

FRANZISKA. If you'd only seen— [HEFFTERDINGT *stops her.*]

SCHWARTZE. Has she made the slightest effort to approach her parents? Has she thought of her home with one throb of love? Who will vouch for it that my outstretched hand will not be repulsed with scorn?

HEFFTERDINGT. I will vouch for it.

SCHWARTZE. You? You, above all, have had a proof of her untamable pride.

HEFFTERDINGT. [*With embarrassment.*] You should not have reminded me of that.

[*Enter* MARIE *with flowers, and* THERESA.

MARIE. Papa, papa, listen to what Theresa— Oh! am I interrupting?

SCHWARTZE. [*Pulling himself together.*] What is it?

MARIE. To-day I got some more flowers; and when I sent Theresa back to the florist's, she found out it was not a man, but a lady, who had ordered them. And she couldn't sell them again; so she brought them back. [*The others exchange glances.*]

HEFFTERDINGT. Tell me, Theresa, did they describe this lady to you?

THERESA. She was tall, with great dark eyes, and there was something very distinguished and foreign about her.

HEFFTERDINGT. [*Leads* MARIE *to the back of the stage, and lays his hand on* SCHWARTZE's *arm.*] You asked for a token of love!

SCHWARTZE. [*Staring at the flowers.*] From her!

MRS. SCHWARTZE. They must have cost a small fortune!

MARIE. Theresa has something else very wonderful to tell, too.

HEFFTERDINGT. What is it, Theresa? Quick!

THERESA. If the pastor wishes it. When I came back, the porter told me that last evening in the twilight a carriage stopped before the door; there was a lady inside. She didn't get out, but kept watching all the windows of our house where there were lights. And when he went out to ask what she wanted, she said something to her coachman, and they were gone! [*All show signs of astonishment.*]

HEFFTERDINGT. That's all, Theresa.

[*Exit* THERESA.

HEFFTERDINGT. Pardon us, dear Miss Marie, if we treat you once more like a child, and ask you to leave us alone for a moment.

MARIE. I am so frightened at all this, Pastor. [*Imploringly.*] Papa?

SCHWARTZE. What is it, child?

MARIE. Papa, papa, do you know who this lady is?

SCHWARTZE. I? No. I can only guess.

MARIE. [*Bursting out.*] Magdalene—Magda! Magda is here! [*Falling on her knees.*] Oh, you will forgive her?

SCHWARTZE. Get up, my child. Your sister is far above my poor forgiveness.

HEFFTERDINGT. She is not above your love.

MARIE. Magda is here! Magda herself is here! [*Throws her arms about her mother's neck, weeping.*]

FRANZISKA. Won't any one bring me a glass of water? I am so upset!

HEFFTERDINGT. Are you quite resolved? [SCHWARTZE *remains motionless.*] Will you let her go on her way without—

SCHWARTZE. That would be best.

HEFFTERDINGT. How will it be with you if in your death-hour a longing for your lost child comes upon you, and all you can say to yourself is, "She stood before my door and I would not open it"?

SCHWARTZE. [*Shaken and half convinced.*] What would you have me do? Must I abase myself before my runaway child?

HEFFTERDINGT. No, you shall not do that. I—I—will go to her.

SCHWARTZE. You? Pastor—you?

HEFFTERDINGT. This afternoon I waited before her hotel to see if Miss Franziska had not been mistaken. At a quarter to four she came out of the house and got into her carriage.

MARIE. You saw her?

MRS. SCHWARTZE. How did she look? What did she have on?

HEFFTERDINGT. The performance began at four, and must be almost over now. I will wait for her again at the hotel, and will tell her that she will find your arms open to her. May I?

MARIE. Yes, yes, papa, won't you let him?

MRS. SCHWARTZE. Just think with whom your daughter—

SCHWARTZE. Will you swear to me that no weak and personal motives are mixed with your intention—that you do what you do in the name of our Lord and Saviour?

HEFFTERDINGT. I swear it!

SCHWARTZE. Then God's will be done. [MARIE *gives a cry of joy.* HEFFTERDINGT *presses* SCHWARTZE'S *hand.*]

SCHWARTZE. [*Holding his hand, speaking softly.*] The way will be hard for you, I know. Your lost youth—your pride—

HEFFTERDINGT. Dear Colonel, I begin to think that pride is a very poor sort of thing. It really profits us little to have it always in our mouths. I am giving back a daughter to an old father. I am giving back a home to an erring soul. That, I think, is enough. [*Exit.* MARIE *throws herself on her father's breast, laughing and crying.*]

CURTAIN

## ACT II

SCENE *same as* ACT I. *It is evening; only a slight glow of sunset still shines through the windows.*

[MARIE *discovered at the window. Enter* THERESA, *bringing in a lighted lamp*

THERESA. Miss Marie! Miss Marie!—What is she staring at all the time? Miss Marie!

MARIE. [*Starting.*] What do you want?

THERESA. Shall I lay the supper?

MARIE. Not yet.

THERESA. It's half-past seven.

MARIE. And he left at half-past six. The performance must have been over long ago. She will not come.

THERESA. Who? Is any one coming to supper?

MARIE. No, no, no. [*As* THERESA *is going.*] Theresa! do you suppose you could pick a couple of bouquets in the garden?

THERESA. I might try, but I couldn't tell what I was getting. It's almost pitch dark.

MARIE. Yes, yes. You may go.

THERESA. Shall I try to pick the flowers, or—

MARIE. No—thank you, no.

THERESA. [*Aside.*] What is the matter with her? [*Exit.*

[*Enter* MRS. SCHWARTZE.

MRS. SCHWARTZE. Well, Marie, whatever happens I've put on my other cap—the one with the ribbons. Is it straight?

MARIE. Yes, mamma dear, very nice.

Mrs. Schwartze. Hasn't Aunt Frankie come up yet?

Marie. No.

Mrs. Schwartze. Heavens! I forgot the two gentlemen entirely. And papa has locked himself up, and will hear nothing and see nothing. Oh, if the General should be offended! It is our most aristocratic connection. That would be a misfortune indeed.

Marie. Oh, mamma dear, when he hears what is the matter!

Mrs. Schwartze. Yes, yes, I know. And the pastor has not come either. Marie, one minute. If she should ask you—

Marie. Who?

Mrs. Schwartze. Why, Magda.

Marie. Magda!

Mrs. Schwartze. What am I to you, Marie? They call it step-mother. I'm more than that, am I not?

Marie. Certainly, mamma dear.

Mrs. Schwartze. You see, *then* I could not get used to having two such big daughters. But it's all right now? [Marie *nods.*] And we do love each other?

Marie. Very much, mamma dear. [*She kisses her.*]

[*Enter* Franziska.

Franziska. [*Irritably.*] One's always disturbing these affecting tableaux!

Mrs. Schwartze. What did the General say?

Franziska. The General? H'm, he was angry enough. "To leave us alone for an hour and a half, that's nice courtesy," he said. And I think myself—

Mrs. Schwartze. [*To* Marie, *very sadly.*] There, what did I tell you?

Franziska. Well, this time I smoothed the thing

over, so that the gentlemen went away in a good humor.

MRS. SCHWARTZE. Really! Oh, I thank you, Frankie, a thousand times.

FRANZISKA. Yes, I'm good enough to run errands and play the scullery-maid; but when it comes to being one of the family, an old aunt with her heart full of love—

MARIE. Who has offended you, Aunt Frankie?

FRANZISKA. Yes, that's very fine. But a little while ago, when I was so upset, no one troubled himself about me one bit. To guarantee an income so that our little miss can be married, I am—

MARIE. Aunt Frankie!

FRANZISKA. But as long as I live—

MRS. SCHWARTZE. What are you talking about?

FRANZISKA. We know, we two. And to-day. Who brought back your daughter to you?

MRS. SCHWARTZE. But she hasn't yet—

FRANZISKA. I brought back your daughter to you. And who thanks me for it? And who recognizes that I have pardoned her? For I have pardoned her [*weeping*] everything!

[*Enter* THERESA, *in great excitement.*

MARIE. What is it, Theresa?

THERESA. I am so frightened—

MARIE. What's the matter?

THERESA. The carriage—

MARIE. What carriage?

THERESA. The same as last night.

MARIE. Is it there? Is it there? [*Runs to the window.*] Mamma, mamma, come, she's there—the carriage—

MRS. SCHWARTZE. Why, there *is* a carriage.

MARIE. [*Beating on the door at the left.*] Papa, papa! Come quickly, be merciful, come quickly!

[*Exit* THERESA *at a sign from* FRANZISKA.

[*Enter* SCHWARTZE.

SCHWARTZE. What's the matter?

MARIE. Magda—the carriage!

SCHWARTZE. Good God! [*Hurries to the window.*]

MARIE. Look—look! She's standing up! She's trying to look into the windows. [*Clapping her hands.*] Papa! papa!

SCHWARTZE. What is it you have to say?

MARIE. [*Frightened.*] I? Nothing.

SCHWARTZE. Perhaps you were going to say, "She stood before your door and you would not open it." Eh?

MARIE. Yes, yes.

SCHWARTZE. Do you hear, wife? She stands before our door. Shall we—in spite of our pride—shall we call her in?

MRS. SCHWARTZE. Oh, Leopold, since everybody thinks so much of her—

MARIE. Ah! She's driving away!

SCHWARTZE. No, no, she's not. Come, we will bring her to you.

FRANZISKA. Yes, yes, bring her to me, too.

[*Exit* SCHWARTZE *and* MRS. SCHWARTZE.

MARIE. She's sitting back again! If only the carriage doesn't— What a long time they are! They must have got downstairs. [*Frightened, almost beside herself.*] There—there—oh, don't go away! Magda! Magda!

FRANZISKA. Don't scream so! What's the matter?

MARIE. She's looking round. She's seen them. She's stopping. She's bursting open the door. She's jumped out! Now! Now! She's in father's arms!

[*Covers her face and sobs.*] Oh, Aunt Frankie! Aunt Frankie!

FRANZISKA. What else could a father do? Since I have forgiven her, he could not—he could not hold out—

MARIE. She's between father and mother. Oh, how grand she is! She's coming—she's coming. What a homely little thing I shall seem beside her! Oh, I am so frightened! [*Leans against the wall, left. A pause. Voices of* MAGDA *and her parents are heard outside.*]

[*Enter* MAGDA, *brilliantly dressed, with a large mantle, and a Spanish veil on her head. She embraces* MARIE.

MAGDA. My puss! My little one! How my little one has grown! My pet—my—[*kissing her passionately.*] But what's the matter? You're dizzy. Come, sit down. No, no, please sit down. Now. Yes, you must. [*Places* MARIE *in an arm-chair.*] Dear little hands, dear little hands! [*Kneels before her, kissing and stroking her hands.*] But they're rough and red, and my darling is pale. There are rings round her eyes.

SCHWARTZE. [*Lays his hand lightly on her shoulder.*] Magda, we are here too.

MAGDA. Yes, yes—I'm entirely—[*Standing up, affectionately.*] Dear old papa! How white you have become! Dear papa! [*Taking his hand.*] But what's the matter with your hand? It's trembling.

SCHWARTZE. Nothing, my child. Don't ask about it.

MAGDA. H'm—and you've grown handsomer with the years. I can't look at you enough. I shall be very proud with such a handsome papa. But she must get better [*indicating* MARIE.] She's as white as milk. Do you take iron? Eh? You must take iron? [*Tenderly.*] Just to think that I am at home! It seems like a fairy tale. It was a capital idea of yours to call me back without any explanations—*senza complimenti*—for we've outgrown those silly misunderstandings long ago.

SCHWARTZE. Misunderstandings!

MAGDA. I came near driving away. Would not that have been bad of me? But you must acknowledge, I have scratched at the door—very quietly, very modestly—like Lady when she had run away. Where is Lady? Her place is empty. [*Whistles.*]

MRS. SCHWARTZE. Why, she's been dead seven years!

MAGDA. Ah, *povera bestia*—yes, I forgot. And, mamma!—yes, mamma! I haven't looked at you yet. How pretty you've grown! You used to have an air of belated youth about you that was not becoming. But now you're a dear, old little mother. One wants to lay one's head quietly in your lap. I will, too. It'll do me good. Ah! what fine quarrels we used to have! I was a contrary little beast. And you held up your end. But now we'll smoke the pipe of peace, sha'n't we?

MRS. SCHWARTZE. You're joking with me, Magda.

MAGDA. Sha'n't I? Mayn't I? There, there—pure love, pure love. We will have nothing but love. We shall be the best of friends.

FRANZISKA. [*Who has for a long time tried to attract attention.*] And we also, eh, my dear Magda?

MAGDA. *Tiens, tiens!* [*Examines her critically through her lorgnette.*] Same as ever. Always active? Always, as of old, the center of the family?

FRANZISKA. Oh—

MAGDA. Well, give us your hand! There. I never could bear you, and shall never learn, I'm afraid. That runs in the blood, doesn't it?

FRANZISKA. I have already forgiven you.

MAGDA. Really! Such magnanimity! I hardly—Do you really forgive everything? From top to bottom? Even that you stirred up my mother against me before she ever came into the house? That you made my father—[*Puts her hand to her lips.*] *Meglio tacere! Meglio tacere!*

MARIE. [*Interrupting.*] For Heaven's sake, Magda!

MAGDA. Yes, my darling—nothing, not a word.

FRANZISKA. She has a fine presence!

MAGDA. And now let me look about me! Ah, everything's just the same. Not a speck of dust has moved.

MRS. SCHWARTZE. I hope, Magda, that you won't find any specks of dust.

MAGDA. I'm sure of that, *mammina.* That wasn't what I meant. Twelve years! Without a trace! Have I dreamed all that comes between?

SCHWARTZE. You will have a great deal to tell us, Magda.

MAGDA. [*Starting.*] What? Well, we will see, we will see. Now I should like— What would I like? I must sit still for a moment. It all comes over me so. When I think— From that door to the window, from this table to the old bureau—that was once my world.

SCHWARTZE. A world, my child, which one never outgrows, which one never should outgrow—you have always held to that?

MAGDA. What do you mean? And what a face you make over it! Yes, yes, though—that question came at the right time. I have been a fool! I have been a fool! My dear old papa, this happiness will be short.

MRS. SCHWARTZE. Why?

MAGDA. What do you think of me? Do you think I am as free as I appear? I'm a weary, worn-out drudge who is only fortunate when the lash is on her back.

SCHWARTZE. Whose drudge? What lash?

MAGDA. That I can't explain, dear father. You don't know my life. You probably wouldn't understand it, either. Every day, every hour has its work laid out. Ah, well, now I must go back to the hotel.

MARIE. No, Magda, no.

MAGDA. Yes, puss, yes. There have been six or seven men there for ever so long, waiting for an audience. But I tell you what, I must have you to-night. Can't you sleep with me?

SCHWARTZE. Of course. That is—what do you mean—sleep where?

MAGDA. At the hotel.

SCHWARTZE. What? You won't stay! You'll put such an affront on us?

MAGDA. What are you thinking of? I have a whole retinue with me.

SCHWARTZE. Your father's house is the place for this retinue.

MAGDA. I don't know. It is rather lively. First, there's Bobo, my parrot, a darling—he wouldn't be bad; then my pet maid, Giulietta, a little demon—I can't live without her; then my courier—he's a tyrant, and the terror of landlords; and then we mustn't forget my teacher.

FRANZISKA. He's a very old man, I hope.

MAGDA. No, he's a very young man.

SCHWARTZE. [*After a silence.*] Then you must have forgotten your—your *dame d'honneur.*

MAGDA. What *dame d'honneur?*

SCHWARTZE. You can't travel about from country to country with a young man without—

MAGDA. Ah! does that disquiet you? I can—be quite easy—I can. In my world we don't trouble ourselves about such things.

SCHWARTZE. What world is that?

MAGDA. The world I rule, father dear. I have no other. There, whatever I do is right because I do it.

SCHWARTZE. That is an enviable position. But you are still young. There must be cases when some direction—in short, whose advice do you follow in your transactions?

MAGDA. There is no one who has the right to advise me, papa dear.

SCHWARTZE. Well, my child, from this hour your old father claims that right. Theresa! [THERESA *answers from outside.*] Go to the German House and bring the baggage—

MAGDA. [*Entreatingly.*] Pardon, father dear, you forget that my orders are necessary.

SCHWARTZE. What?—Yes, yes, I forgot. Do what you will, my daughter.

MARIE. Magda—oh, Magda!

MAGDA. [*Taking her mantle.*] Be patient, darling. We'll have a talk soon all to our two selves. And you'll all come to breakfast with me, won't you? We can have a good chat and love each other!—so much!

MRS. SCHWARTZE. We—breakfast with you?

MAGDA. I want to have you all under my roof.

SCHWARTZE. The roof of a hotel?

MAGDA. Yes, papa dear, I have no other home.

SCHWARTZE. And this?

MARIE. Don't you see how you've hurt him?

[*Enter the* PASTOR. *He stops, and seems to control strong emotion.* MAGDA *examines him with her lorgnette.*

MAGDA. He too! Let me see.

MRS. SCHWARTZE. Just think. She is going away again!

HEFFTERDINGT. I don't know whether I am known to the lady.

MAGDA. [*Mockingly.*] You're too modest, Pastor.

And now since I have seen you all—[*Puts on her mantle.*]

SCHWARTZE. [*Quickly, aside.*] You must keep her.

HEFFTERDINGT. I? If you are powerless, how can I?

SCHWARTZE. Try!

HEFFTERDINGT. [*Constraining himself, with embarrassment.*] Pardon me, madam, it seems very officious of me—if I—will you give me a few moments' interview?

MAGDA. What have we two to say to each other, my dear Pastor?

MRS. SCHWARTZE. Oh, do, please! He knows best about everything.

MAGDA. [*Ironically.*] Indeed!

MARIE. I may never ask you for anything again, but do this one thing for my sake!

MAGDA. [*Patting her and looking from one to the other.*] Well, the child asks so prettily. Pastor, I am at your service. [MARIE *thanks her silently.*]

FRANZISKA. [*Aside to* MRS. SCHWARTZE.] Now he'll give her a lecture. Come.

SCHWARTZE. You were once the cause of my sending her from my home. To-day you must see to it that she remains. [HEFFTERDINGT *expresses doubt.*]

SCHWARTZE. Marie!

MARIE. Yes, papa.

[*Exit* SCHWARTZE, MRS. SCHWARTZE, FRANZISKA, *and* MARIE.

MAGDA. [*Sits down and examines him through her lorgnette.*] So this is the man who undertakes by a five minutes' interview entirely and absolutely to break my will. That they believe in your ability to do it shows me that you are a king in your own dominions.

I make obeisance. And now let me see you ply your arts.

HEFFTERDINGT. I understand no arts, madam, and would avail myself of none. If they put some trust in me here, it is because they know that I seek nothing for myself.

MAGDA. [*Ironically.*] That has always been the case?

HEFFTERDINGT. No, madam. I had, once in my life, a strong, an intense desire. It was to have you for my wife. I need only look at you to see that I was presumptuous. Since then I have put the wish away from me.

MAGDA. Ah, Pastor, I believe you're paying court to me now.

HEFFTERDINGT. Madam, if it were not discourteous—

MAGDA. Oh, then even a shepherd of souls may be discourteous!

HEFFTERDINGT. I should commiserate you on the atmosphere which has surrounded you.

MAGDA. [*With mocking superiority.*] Really? What do you know about my atmosphere?

HEFFTERDINGT. It seems to me that it has made you forget that serious men are to be taken seriously.

MAGDA. Ah! [*Rising.*] Well, then I will take you seriously; and I will tell you that you have always been unbearable to me, with your well-acted simplicity, your droning mildness, your— Since, however, you condescended to cast your eyes on my worthlessness and drove me from home with your suit—since then, I have hated you.

HEFFTERDINGT. It seems to me that according to this I was the foundation of your greatness.

MAGDA. You're right there. Here I was parched

and stifled. No, no, I don't hate you. Why should I hate you so much? It's all so far, so very far, behind me. If you only knew how far! You have sat here day after day in this heavy close air, reeking of lavender, tobacco, and cough mixture, while I have felt the storm breaking about my head. Pastor, if you had a suspicion of what life really is—of the trial of strength, of the taste of guilt, of conquest, and of pleasure—you would find yourself very comical with your clerical shop-talk. Ha, ha, ha! Pardon me, I don't believe such a laugh has rung through this respectable house for twelve years; for there's no one here who knows how to laugh. Is there, eh?

HEFFTERDINGT. No, I fear not.

MAGDA. Fear, you say. That sounds as though you deprecated it. But don't you hate laughter?

HEFFTERDINGT. Most of us cannot laugh, madam.

MAGDA. And to those who could, laughter is sin. You might laugh yourself. What have you to be solemn about? You need not look at the world with this funereal mien. Surely you have a little blond wife at home who knits industriously, and half a dozen curly heads around her, of course. It's always so in parsonages.

HEFFTERDINGT. I have remained single, madam.

MAGDA. Ah! [*Silence.*] Did I hurt you so much, then?

HEFFTERDINGT. Let that be, shall we not? It is so long ago.

MAGDA. [*Letting her mantle fall.*] And your work —does not that bring happiness enough?

HEFFTERDINGT. Thank God, it does. But if one takes it really in earnest, one cannot live only for one's self; at least, I cannot. One cannot exult in the fulness of one's personality, as you would call it. And then many hearts are opened to me— One sees too many wounds there, that one cannot heal, to be quite happy.

MAGDA. You're a remarkable man— I don't know —if I could only get rid of the idea that you're insincere.

HEFFTERDINGT. Will you let me ask you one question before you go?

MAGDA. Well!

HEFFTERDINGT. It is about an hour since you entered this house, your home—no, not so much. I could not have been waiting for you nearly as long as that.

MAGDA. For me? You? Where?

HEFFTERDINGT. In the corridor outside your room.

MAGDA. What did you want there?

HEFFTERDINGT. My errand was useless, for now you are here.

MAGDA. Do you mean to say that you came for me— you to whom I— If any one had an interest in keeping me away, it was you.

HEFFTERDINGT. Are you accustomed to regard everything which those about you do as the result of selfish interest?

MAGDA. Of course. It's so with me! [*Struck by a new thought.*] Or perhaps you— No, I'm not justified in that assumption. [*Sharply.*] Ah, such nonsense! it is only fit for fairy tales. Well, Pastor, I'll own that I like you now better, much better than of old when you—what shall I say?—made an honorable proposal.

HEFFTERDINGT. H'm!

MAGDA. If you could only end it all with a laugh— this stony visage of yours is so unfriendly—one is quite *sconcertata.* What do you say? *Je ne trouve pas le mot.*

Heffterdingt. Pardon me, may I ask the question now?

Magda. Good Lord, how inquisitive the holy man is! And you don't see that I was coquetting with you a little. For, to have been a man's fate—that flatters us women—we are grateful for it. You see I have acquired some art meanwhile. Well, out with your question!

Heffterdingt. Why—why did you come home?

Magda. Ah!

Heffterdingt. Was it not homesickness?

Magda. No. Well, perhaps a very little. I'll tell you. When I received the invitation to assist at this festival—why they did me the honor, I don't know—a very curious feeling began to seethe within me—half curiosity and half shyness, half melancholy and half defiance—which said: "Go home incognito. Go in the twilight and stand before the paternal house where for seventeen years you lived in bondage. There look upon what you were. But if they recognize you, show them that beyond their narrow virtues there may be something true and good."

Heffterdingt. Only defiance then?

Magda. At first, perhaps. Once on the way, though, my heart beat most wonderfully, as it used to do when I'd learnt my lesson badly. And I always did learn my lessons badly. When I stood before the hotel, the German House—just think, the German House, where the great officials and the great artists stayed—there I had again the abject reverence as of old, as if I were unworthy to step on the old threshold. I entirely forgot that I was now myself a so-called great artist. Since then, every evening I have stolen by the house—very quietly, very humbly—always almost in tears.

HEFFTERDINGT. And nevertheless you are going away.

MAGDA. I must.

HEFFTERDINGT. But—

MAGDA. Don't ask me why. I must.

HEFFTERDINGT. Has any one offended your pride? Has any one said a word of your needing forgiveness?

MAGDA. Not yet—or, yes, if you count the old cat.

HEFFTERDINGT. What is there in the world which draws you away again after an hour?

MAGDA. I will tell you. I felt it the first minute I came. The paternal authority already stretches its net over me again, and the yoke stands ready beneath which I must bow.

HEFFTERDINGT. But there is neither yoke nor net here. Do not fear shadows. Here are only wide-opened arms which wait to clasp the lost daughter to the empty breast.

MAGDA. Oh, I beg you, none of that. I do not intend to furnish a pendant to the prodigal son. If I came back as a daughter, as a lost daughter, I should not hold my head up before you as I do; I should grovel in the dust in full consciousness of all my sins. [*With growing excitement.*] And that I will not do—that I cannot do—for I am what I am, and I cannot be another. [*Sadly.*] And therefore I have no home—therefore I must go forth again—therefore—

[*Enter* MRS. SCHWARTZE.

HEFFTERDINGT. For Heaven's sake, hush!

MRS. SCHWARTZE. Excuse me, Pastor, I only wanted to know about supper. [*Imploringly to* MAGDA, *who sits turned away with her hands before her face.*] We happen to have a warm joint to-day. You know, Pastor, the gentlemen of the card-club were to be with us. Now, Magda, whether you're going away or not, can't you eat a mouthful in your father's house?

HEFFTERDINGT. Don't ask now, my dear madam.

MRS. SCHWARTZE. Oh, if I'm interrupting—I only thought—

HEFFTERDINGT. Later.

MARIE. [*Appearing in the doorway.*] Will she stay? [MAGDA *shrinks at the sound of the voice.*]

MRS. SCHWARTZE. 'Sh!

[*Exit* MRS. SCHWARTZE *and* MARIE.

HEFFTERDINGT. You have no home, Miss Magda? Did you hear the old mother beseeching and alluring with the best that she has, though it's only a poor dish? Did you hear Marie's voice trembling with tears in the fear that I should not prevail? They trust me too much; they think I only need to speak the word. They don't suspect how helpless I stand here before you. Look! Behind that door are three people in a fever of sorrow and love. If you cross this threshold, you rob each of them of so much life. And you have no home?

MAGDA. If I have one, it is not here.

HEFFTERDINGT. [*Embarrassed.*] Perhaps— Nevertheless you should not go. Only a few days—just not to take away the idea that you belong here. So much you owe to them!

MAGDA. [*Sadly.*] I owe nothing now to any one here.

HEFFTERDINGT. No? Really nothing? Then I must tell you about a certain day—eleven years ago now. I was called into this house in haste, for the Colonel was dying. When I came, he lay there stiff and motionless, his face drawn and white; one eye was already closed, in the other still flickered a little life. He tried to speak, but his lips only quivered and mumbled.

MAGDA. What had happened?

HEFFTERDINGT. What had happened? I will tell you. He had just received a letter in which his eldest daughter bade him farewell.

MAGDA. My God!

HEFFTERDINGT. It was a long time before he recovered from the apoplectic stroke. Only a trembling in the right arm, which you perhaps have noticed, now remains.

MAGDA. That is indeed a debt I owe.

HEFFTERDINGT. Ah, if that were all, Miss Magda! Pardon me, I call you by the name I used long ago. It springs to my lips.

MAGDA. Call me what you like. Go on.

HEFFTERDINGT. The necessary result followed. When he received his discharge—he will not believe in the cause, don't speak to him of it—then his mind broke down.

MAGDA. Yes, yes; that is my debt too.

HEFFTERDINGT. Then you see, Miss Magda, began my work. If I speak of it, you must not think I am pluming myself on it to you. What good would that do me? For a long, long time I nursed him, and by degrees I saw his mind revive again. First I let him collect slugs from the rose-bushes.

MAGDA. [*With a shudder.*] Ugh!

HEFFTERDINGT. Yes, so far had it gone; then I gave him charge of some money, and then I made him my assistant in the institutions with whose management I was intrusted. There is a hospital and a soup-kitchen and an infirmary, and it makes a great deal to be done. So he became a man once more. I have tried to influence your step-mother too; not because I was greedy for power. Perhaps you'll think that of me. In short, the old tension between her and Marie has been slowly smoothed away. Love and confidence have descended upon the house.

MAGDA. [*Staring at him.*] And why did you do all this?

HEFFTERDINGT. Well, first it is my calling. Then I did it for his sake, for I love the old man; and above all—for—your sake.

[MAGDA *starts, and points to herself interrogatively.*

HEFFTERDINGT. Yes, for your sake. For this weighed upon me: The day will come when she will turn homeward—perhaps as victor; but perhaps also as vanquished, broken and ruined in body and soul—Pardon me these thoughts, I had heard nothing of you—In either case she shall find a home ready for her. That was my work, the work of long years; and now I implore you not to destroy it.

MAGDA. [*In anguish.*] If you knew through what I have passed, you would not try to keep me.

HEFFTERDINGT. That is all shut out. This is home. Let it alone; forget it.

MAGDA. How can I forget it? How dare I?

HEFFTERDINGT. Why should you resist when all stretch their hands out to you in rejoicing? It's very easy. Let your heart speak when you see all around overflowing with love for you.

MAGDA. [*In tears.*] You make me a child again. [*A pause.*]

HEFFTERDINGT. Then you will stay?

MAGDA. [*Springing up.*] But they must not question me!

HEFFTERDINGT. Must not question you?

MAGDA. About my life outside there. They wouldn't understand—none of them; not even you.

HEFFTERDINGT. Well, then, they sha'n't.

MAGDA. And you will promise me, for yourself and for the others?

HEFFTERDINGT. Yes, I can promise it.

MAGDA. [*In a stifled voice.*] Call them, then.

HEFFTERDINGT. [*Opening the door on the left.*] She will stay.

[*Enter* MARIE; *then* MRS. SCHWARTZE, FRANZISKA, *and* SCHWARTZE. MARIE *throws herself joyfully into* MAGDA'S *arms.* MRS. SCHWARTZE *also embraces her.*

SCHWARTZE. It was your duty, my child.

MAGDA. Yes, father. [*She softly takes his right hand in both of hers, and carries it tenderly to her lips.*]

FRANZISKA. Thank Heaven! Now we can have supper at last! [*Opens the sliding door into the dining-room. The supper-table is seen, all set, and lighted brightly by a green-shaded hanging-lamp.*]

MAGDA. [*Gazing at it.*] Oh, look! The dear old lamp! [*The women go slowly out.*]

SCHWARTZE. [*Stretching out his hands.*] This is your greatest work, Pastor.

HEFFTERDINGT. Oh, don't, I beg you! And there's a condition attached.

SCHWARTZE. A condition?

HEFFTERDINGT. We must not ask about her life.

SCHWARTZE. [*Startled.*] What? What? I must not—

HEFFTERDINGT. No, no; you must not ask—you must not ask—or— [*Struck by a new thought.*] If you do not—yes—I am sure she will confess everything herself.

CURTAIN

## ACT III

SCENE: *the same. Morning. On the table at the left, coffee-service and flowers.*

[MRS. SCHWARTZE *and* FRANZISKA *discovered.*

MRS. SCHWARTZE. [*Excitedly.*] Thank Heaven, you've come. Such a time we've had this morning!

FRANZISKA. So?

MRS. SCHWARTZE. Just think, two people have come from the hotel—a gentleman who looks like a lord, and a young lady like a princess. They're her servants.

FRANZISKA. What extravagance!

MRS. SCHWARTZE. And they're calling and talking all over the house, and neither of them knows any German. And her ladyship ordered a warm bath, that was not warm enough; and a cold douche, which was not cold enough; and spirits, which she simply poured out of the window; and toilet vinegar, which we didn't have at all.

FRANZISKA. What demands! And where is your famous young lady?

MRS. SCHWARTZE. After her bath she has gone back to bed again.

FRANZISKA. I would not have such sloth in my house.

MRS. SCHWARTZE. I shall tell her so. For Leopold's sake— [*Enter* THERESA.] What do you want, Theresa?

THERESA. Councillor von Keller—he has sent his servant here to ask whether the Lieutenant has come yet, and what is the young lady's answer.

MRS. SCHWARTZE. What young lady?

THERESA. That's what I don't know.

MRS. SCHWARTZE. Then just give our regards, and say that the Lieutenant has not come yet.

FRANZISKA. He is on duty till twelve. After that he'll come.

[*Exit* THERESA. *As she opens the door, a great noise is heard in the hall,—a man's voice and a woman's disputing in Italian.*

MRS. SCHWARTZE. Listen to that! [*Speaking outside.*] Just you wait. Your Signora'll be here soon. [*Shuts the door.*] Ah! And now, breakfast. What do you think she drinks?

FRANZISKA. Why, coffee.

MRS. SCHWARTZE. No.

FRANZISKA. Tea, then?

MRS. SCHWARTZE. No.

FRANZISKA. Then it must be chocolate!

MRS. SCHWARTZE. No; coffee and chocolate mixed.

FRANZISKA. Horrible! But it must be good.

MRS. SCHWARTZE. And yesterday half a dozen trunks came from the hotel, and as many more are still there. Ah, what there is in them all! One whole trunk for hats! A peignoir of real point, and open-work stockings with gold embroidery, and [*in a whisper*] silk chemises—

FRANZISKA. What? Silk—

MRS. SCHWARTZE. Yes.

FRANZISKA. [*With a gesture of horror.*] It is simply sinful.

[*Enter* MAGDA, *in brilliant morning toilette, speaking outside as she opens the door.*

MAGDA. *Ma che cosa volete voi? Perché non aspettate, finché vi commando?* Ha?

MRS. SCHWARTZE. Now they are getting their share!

MAGDA. No, no; *è tempo!* [*Shutting the door.*]

*Va, bruto!* Good-morning, mamma. [*Kisses her.*] I'm a late sleeper, eh? Ah, good-morning, Aunt Frankie. In a good humor? So am I.

MRS. SCHWARTZE. What did the strange gentleman want, Magda?

MAGDA. Stupid beast! He wanted to know when I was going away, the idiot! How can I tell? [*Patting her.*] Eh, *mamma mia?* Oh, children, I slept like the dead. My ear on the pillow, and off! And the douche was so nice and cold. I feel so strong. *Allons, cousine!* Hop! [*Seizes* FRANZISKA *by the waist and jumps her into the air.*]

FRANZISKA. [*Furiously.*] What do you—

MAGDA. [*Haughtily.*] Eh?

FRANZISKA. [*Cringingly.*] You are so facetious.

MAGDA. Am I? [*Clapping her hands.*] Breakfast!

[*Enter* MARIE, *with a tray of coffee things.*

MARIE. Good-morning.

FRANZISKA. Good-morning, my child.

MAGDA. I'm dying of hunger. Ah! [*Pats her stomach.* MARIE *kisses* FRANZISKA'S *hand.*]

MAGDA. [*Taking off the cover, with unction.*] Delicious! One would know Giulietta was in the house.

FRANZISKA. She has made noise enough, at least.

MAGDA. Oh, she couldn't live without a good row. And when she gets too excited, she quietly throws a plate at your head. I'm accustomed to it. What is papa doing?

MRS. SCHWARTZE. He's making his excuses to the members of the Committee.

MAGDA. Is your life still half made up of excuses? What sort of committee is it?

MRS. SCHWARTZE. It's the Christian Aid Society. They should have had a meeting here this morning in our house. Now we thought it would not do. It would look as if we wanted to introduce you.

FRANZISKA. But, Augusta, now it will look as if your daughter were more important to you—

MAGDA. Well, I hope she is!

MRS. SCHWARTZE. Of course! But—oh dear, you don't know what sort of people they are. They are deserving of great respect. For instance, there's Mrs. General von Klebs. [*Proudly.*] We are friends of hers.

MAGDA. [*With sham respect.*] Really?

MRS. SCHWARTZE. Now, they'll probably come to-morrow. Then you'll meet, besides, some other pious and aristocratic ladies whose patronage gains us a great deal of influence. I'm curious to see how they'll like you.

MAGDA. How I shall like them, you should say.

MRS. SCHWARTZE. Yes—that is—but we're talking and talking—

MARIE. [*Jumping up.*] Oh, excuse me, mamma.

MAGDA. No, you must stay here.

MRS. SCHWARTZE. Yes, Magda; but about your trunks at the hotel—I am constantly on the rack for fear something should be left.

MAGDA. Send for them, then, children.

FRANZISKA. [*Aside to* MRS. SCHWARTZE.] Now I'll question her thoroughly, Augusta. Leave us alone.

[*Exit* MRS. SCHWARTZE.

FRANZISKA. [*Sitting down, with importance.*] And now, my dear Magda, you must tell your old aunt all about it.

MAGDA. Eh? Ah, look here, mamma needs help. Go on, quick! Make yourself useful.

FRANZISKA. [*Viciously.*] If you command it.

MAGDA. Oh, I have only to request.

FRANZISKA. [*Rising.*] It seems to me that your requests are somewhat forcible.

MAGDA. [*Laughing.*] Perhaps.

[*Exit* FRANZISKA *in a rage.*

MARIE. Oh, Magda!

MAGDA. Yes, sweet. That's the way to go through the world—bend or break; that is, I never bend. It's the only way.

MARIE. Oh, good Heavens!

MAGDA. Poor child! Yes, in this house one learns quite other views. I bent, myself, yesterday disgracefully. Ah, how nice our old mamma is! [*Earnestly, pointing to the mother's picture.*] And she up there! Do you remember her? [MARIE *shakes her head.*]

MAGDA. [*Thoughtfully.*] She died too soon! Where's papa? I want him. And yet I'm afraid of him too. Now, child, while I eat my breakfast, now you must make your confession.

MARIE. Oh, I can't.

MAGDA. Just show me the locket!

MARIE. There!

MAGDA. A lieutenant! Naturally. With us it's always a tenor.

MARIE. Oh, Magda, it's no joke. He is my fate.

MAGDA. What is the name of this fate?

MARIE. It's Cousin Max.

MAGDA. [*Whistles.*] Why don't you marry the good youth, then?

MARIE. Aunt Frankie wants a better match for him, and so she won't give him the guaranty he needs. It's abominable!

MAGDA. *Si! C'est bête, ça!* And how long have you loved each other?

MARIE. I don't remember when we did not.

MAGDA. And where does he meet you?

MARIE. Here.

MAGDA. I mean elsewhere—alone.

MARIE. We are never alone together. I think this precaution we owe to our own self-respect.

MAGDA. Come here—close—tell me the truth—has it never entered your mind to cast this whole network of precaution and respect away from you, and to go with the man you love out and away—anywhere—it doesn't matter much—and as you lie quietly on his breast, to hurl back a scornful laugh at the whole world which has sunk behind you?

MARIE. No, Magda, I never feel so.

MAGDA. But would you die for him?

MARIE. [*Standing up with a gesture of enthusiasm.*] I would die a thousand deaths for him!

MAGDA. My poor little darling! [*Aside.*] They bring everything to naught. The most terrible of all passions becomes in their hands a mere resigned defiance of death.

MARIE. Whom are you speaking of?

MAGDA. Nothing, nothing. See here, how large is this sum you need?

MARIE. Sixty thousand marks.

MAGDA. When can you be married? Must it be now, or will afternoon do?

MARIE. Don't mock me, Magda.

MAGDA. You must give me time to telegraph. One can't carry so much money about with one.

MARIE. [*Slowly taking it in, and then, with an outburst of joy, throwing herself at* MAGDA'S *feet.*] Magda!

MAGDA. [*After a silence.*] Be happy, love your husband. And if you hold your first-born on your arm, in the face of the world [*holding out her arms with angry emphasis*]—so, face to face, then think of one who— Ah! some one's coming.

[*Enter* HEFFTERDINGT *with a portfolio.*

MAGDA. [*Crossing to him.*] Oh, it's you. That's good. I wanted you.

HEFFTERDINGT. You wanted me? What for?

MAGDA. Only—I want to talk with you, holy man.

HEFFTERDINGT. Isn't it good, Miss Magda, to be at home again?

MAGDA. Oh, yes, except for the old aunt's sneaking about.

MARIE. [*Who is collecting the breakfast-things; laughing, but frightened.*] Oh, Heavens, Magda!

HEFFTERDINGT. Good-morning, Miss Marie.

MARIE. Good-morning, Pastor.

[*Exit, with the table.*

HEFFTERDINGT. Heavens, how she beams!

MAGDA. She has reason.

HEFFTERDINGT. Isn't your father here?

MAGDA. No.

HEFFTERDINGT. Isn't he well?

MAGDA. I think so. I haven't seen him yet. Yesterday we sat together till late. I told him what I could tell. But I think he was very unhappy; his eyes were always searching and probing. Oh, I fear your promise will be badly kept.

HEFFTERDINGT. That seems like a reproach. I hope you don't regret—

MAGDA. No, my friend, I don't regret it. But I feel very curiously. I seem to be in a tepid bath, I'm so weak and warm. What they call German sentiment is awaking again, and I have been so unused to it. My heart seems like a Christmas number of the "Gartenlaube,"—moonlight, betrothals, lieutenants, and I don't know what! But the best of it is, I know that I'm playing with myself. I can cast it all off as a child throws away its doll, and be my old self again.

HEFFTERDINGT. That would be bad for us.

MAGDA. Oh, don't be angry with me. I seem to be all torn and rooted up. And then I am so afraid—

HEFFTERDINGT. Of what?

MAGDA. I can't—I can't be quite one of you. I am an intruder. [*Aside, fearfully.*] If a specter from without were to appear, this whole idyl would go up in flames. [HEFFTERDINGT *suppresses a start of astonishment.*] And I'm confined, hemmed in. I begin to be a coward.

HEFFTERDINGT. I don't think one should be terrified at feeling filial love.

MAGDA. Filial love? I should like to take that snow white head in my lap and say, "You old child!" And nevertheless I must bend my will, I must bend my will. I am not accustomed to that. I must conquer; I must sing down opposition. I sing or I live—for both are one and the same—so that men must will as I do. I force them, I compel them to love and mourn and exult and lament as I do. And woe to him who resists! I sing them down—I sing and sing until they become slaves and playthings in my hands. I know I'm confused, but you understand what I mean.

HEFFTERDINGT. To work the impress of one's own personality—that's what you mean, isn't it?

MAGDA. *Si, si, si, si!* Oh, I could tell you everything. Your heart has tendrils which twine about other hearts and draw them out. And you don't do it selfishly. You don't know how mighty you are. The men outside there are beasts, whether in love or hate. But you are a man. And one feels like a man when one is near you. Just think, when you came in yesterday, you seemed to me so small; but something grows out from you and becomes always greater, almost too great for me.

HEFFTERDINGT. Good Heavens, what can it be?

MAGDA. What shall I call it—self-sacrifice, self-abnegation? It is something with self—or rather the reverse. That is what impresses me. And that is why you can do so much with me.

HEFFTERDINGT. How strange!

MAGDA. What?

HEFFTERDINGT. I must own it to you—it is—it is nonsense; but since I have seen you again, a sort of longing has awakened within me to be like you.

MAGDA. Ha, ha! You, model of men! Like me!

HEFFTERDINGT. I have had to stifle much in my nature. My peace is the peace of the dead. And as you stood before me yesterday in your freshness, your natural strength, your—your greatness, I said to myself, "That is what you might have been if at the right moment joy had entered into your life."

MAGDA. [*In a whisper.*] And one thing more, my friend—sin! We must sin if we wish to grow. To become greater than our sins is worth more than all the purity you preach.

HEFFTERDINGT. [*Impressed.*] That would be—— [*Voices outside.*]

MAGDA. [*Starting and listening.*] 'Sh!

HEFFTERDINGT. What's the matter?

MAGDA. Nothing, it's only my stupid nervousness; not on my own account, believe me, only out of pity for all these. We shall still be friends?

HEFFTERDINGT. As long as you need me.

MAGDA. And when I cease to need you?

HEFFTERDINGT. There will be no change in me, Miss

Magda. [*As he is going, he meets* SCHWARTZE *in the doorway.*]

[*Enter* SCHWARTZE.

SCHWARTZE. Good-morning, my dear pastor! Will you go out on the porch for a moment? I will follow you. [*Exit* HEFFTERDINGT.] Now, did you sleep well, my child? [*Kisses her on the forehead.*]

MAGDA. Finely. In my old room I found the old sleep of childhood.

SCHWARTZE. Had you lost it?

MAGDA. Haven't you?

SCHWARTZE. They say a good conscience—— Come to me, my child.

MAGDA. Gladly, papa! No, let me sit at your feet. There I can see your beautiful white beard. When I look at it, I always think of Christmas eve and a quiet snow-covered field.

SCHWARTZE. My child, you know how to say pretty things. When you speak, one seems to see pictures about one. Here we are not so clever; that is why we have nothing to conceal here.

MAGDA. We also—— But speak quietly, papa.

SCHWARTZE. Yes, I must. You know what agreement you made with the pastor.

MAGDA. Which you will keep?

SCHWARTZE. I am accustomed to keep to what I have promised. But you must see that the suspicion—whatever I may do, the suspicion weighs like a mountain——

MAGDA. What do you suspect?

SCHWARTZE. I don't know. You have appeared among us as wonderfully, as gloriously. But brilliance and worldly honor and all that don't blind a father's eyes. You seem to be warm at heart too. At least, one would think so to hear you speak. But there is something in your eyes which does not please me, and a scornful curl about your lips.

MAGDA. Dear, good old papa!

SCHWARTZE. You see! This tenderness is not that of a daughter towards her father. It is so that one pets a child, whether it be a young or an old one. And although I'm only a poor soldier, lame and disabled, I demand your respect, my child.

MAGDA. I have never withheld it. [*Rising.*]

SCHWARTZE. That is good, that is good, my daughter. Believe me, we are not so simple as we may appear to you. We have eyes to see, and ears to hear, that the spirit of moral revolt is abroad in the world. The seed which should take root in the heart, begins to decay. What were once sins easily become customs to you. My child, soon you will go away. When you return, you may find me in the grave.

MAGDA. Oh, no, papa!

SCHWARTZE. It's in God's hand. But I implore you—— Come here, my child—nearer—so—— [*He draws her down to him, and takes her head between his hands.*] I implore you—let me be happy in my dying hour. Tell me that you have remained pure in body and soul, and then go with my blessing on your way.

MAGDA. I have remained—true to myself, dear father.

SCHWARTZE. How? In good or in ill?

MAGDA. In what—for me—was good.

SCHWARTZE. [*Blankly.*] In what—for you—then?

MAGDA. [*Rising.*] And now don't worry any more. Let me enjoy these few days quietly. They will be over soon enough.

SCHWARTZE. [*Broodingly.*] I love you with my whole heart, because I have sorrowed for you—so long.

[*Threateningly, rising.*] But I must know who you are.

MAGDA. Father dear—— [*Bell rings.* MRS. SCHWARTZE *bursts in.*]

MRS. SCHWARTZE. Just think! the ladies of the Committee are here! They want to congratulate us in person. Do you think we ought to offer them coffee, Leopold?

SCHWARTZE. I will go into the garden, Augusta.

MRS. SCHWARTZE. For Heaven's sake—they're just coming—you must receive their congratulations.

SCHWARTZE. I can't—no—I can't do it! [*Exit, left.*

MRS. SCHWARTZE. What is the matter with your father?

[*Enter* MRS. GENERAL VON KLEBS, MRS. JUSTICE ELLRICH, MRS. SCHUMANN, *and* FRANZISKA.

FRANZISKA. [*As she opens the door.*] My dear, the ladies——

MRS. VON KLEBS. [*Giving her hand to* MRS. SCHWARTZE.] What a day for you, my dear! The whole town rejoices in the happy event.

MRS. SCHWARTZE. Permit me—my daughter—Mrs. General von Klebs, Mrs. Justice Ellrich, Mrs. Schumann.

MRS. SCHUMANN. I am only the wife of a simple merchant; but——

MRS. VON KLEBS. My husband will do himself the honor soon——

MRS. SCHWARTZE. Won't you sit down, ladies? [*They sit.*]

FRANZISKA. [*With aplomb.*] Yes, it is truly a joyful event for the whole family.

MRS. VON KLEBS. We have unfortunately not shared the pleasures of the festival, my dear young lady. I must therefore refrain from expressing that admiration to which you are so well accustomed.

MRS. SCHUMANN. If we had known, we should certainly have ordered tickets.

MRS. VON KLEBS. Do you expect to remain here for very long?

MAGDA. That I really cannot say, madam—or, pardon me—your ladyship?

MRS. VON KLEBS. I must beg you—no.

MAGDA. Oh, pardon me!

MRS. VON KLEBS. Oh, please!

MAGDA. We are such birds of passage, my dear madam, that we can really never plan for the future.

MRS. ELLRICH. But one must have one's real home.

MAGDA. Why? One must have a vocation. That seems to me enough.

FRANZISKA. It's all in the point of view, dear Magda.

MRS. VON KLEBS. Ah, we're so far removed from all these ideas, my dear young lady. Every now and then some person gives lectures here, but the good families have nothing to do with it.

MAGDA. [*Politely.*] Oh, I can quite understand that. The good families need nothing, as they have plenty to eat. [*A silence.*]

MRS. ELLRICH. But at least you must have some residence?

MAGDA. If you call it so—a place to sleep. Yes, I have a villa by the Lake of Como and an estate at Naples. [*Sensation.*]

MRS. SCHWARTZE. But you've said nothing to us about that.

MAGDA. I hardly ever make use of them, mamma dear.

MRS. ELLRICH. Art must be a very trying occupation?

MAGDA. [*In a friendly tone.*] It depends upon how one follows it, my dear madam.

MRS. ELLRICH. My daughter used to take singing-lessons, and it always taxed her very much.

MAGDA. [*Politely.*] Oh, I'm sorry for that.

MRS. ELLRICH. Naturally, you only do it for pleasure.

MAGDA. Oh, it's so much pleasure! [*Aside to* MRS. SCHWARTZE, *who sits near her.*] Get these women away, or I shall be rude!

MRS. VON KLEBS. Are you really engaged by a theater, my dear young lady?

MAGDA. [*Very sweetly.*] Sometimes, my dear madam.

MRS. VON KLEBS. Then you are out of an engagement at present?

MAGDA. [*Murmurs.*] Oh, come, come! [*Aloud.*] Yes, I'm a vagabond now. [*The ladies look at each other.*]

MRS. VON KLEBS. There are really not many daughters of good families on the stage, are there?

MAGDA. [*In a friendly tone.*] No, my dear madam; most of them are too stupid.

MRS. SCHWARTZE. Oh, Magda!

[*Enter* MAX.

MAGDA. Oh, that must be Max! [*Goes to him and shakes hands.*] Just think, I had quite forgotten your face. We were great friends, were we not?

MAX. Were we? [*Astonished.*]

MAGDA. Well, we can begin now.

MRS. ELLRICH. [*Aside.*] Do you understand this?

[MRS. VON KLEBS *shrugs her shoulder. The ladies rise and take their leave, shaking hands with* MRS. SCHWARTZE *and* FRANZISKA, *and bowing to* MAGDA.

MRS. SCHWARTZE. [*Confused.*] Must you go already, ladies? My husband will be so sorry——

MAGDA. [*Coolly.*] *Au revoir,* ladies, *au revoir!*

[*Exit the ladies in the order of their rank.*

MRS. SCHWARTZE. [*Turning back from the door.*] Mrs. von Klebs was offended, or she would have stayed. Magda, you certainly must have offended Mrs. von Klebs.

FRANZISKA. And the other ladies, too, were hurt.

MAGDA. Mamma dear, won't you see about my trunk?

MRS. SCHWARTZE. Yes, yes, I'll go to the hotel myself. Oh dear, oh dear, oh dear! [*Exit.*

FRANZISKA. Wait, I'm coming too. [*Spitefully.*] I must make myself useful, of course!

MAGDA. Oh, Aunt Frankie, a word with you.

FRANZISKA. Now?

MAGDA. We're going to celebrate a betrothal to-day.

FRANZISKA. What betrothal?

MAGDA. Between him and Marie.

MAX. [*Joyfully.*] Magda!

FRANZISKA. I think, as I occupy a mother's position towards him, that it is my right——

MAGDA. No; the giver alone has rights, my dear aunt. And now don't fail.

FRANZISKA. [*Furiously.*] I will make you——

[*Exit.*

MAX. How shall I thank you, my dear Miss——

MAGDA. Magda, my dear cousin, Magda!

MAX. Pardon me, it was my great respect——

MAGDA. Not so much respect, my boy—I don't like it; more weight, more individuality!

MAX. Ah, my dear cousin, should a young lieutenant with twenty-five marks' pay, not to speak of debts, have individuality? It would only be a hindrance to him.

MAGDA. Ah!

MAX. If I manage my men properly, and dance a correct figure at our regimental balls, and am not a coward, that is enough.

MAGDA. To make a wife happy, certainly. Go and find her. Go along!

MAX. [*Starts to go, and turns back.*] Oh, excuse me, in my happiness I entirely forgot the message I—— Early this morning—by-the-by, you can't think what a tumult the whole city is in about you—well, early this morning—I was still in bed—an acquaintance came in who is also an old acquaintance of yours, very pale from excitement, and he asked whether it were all true, and if he might come to see you.

MAGDA. Yes, let him come.

MAX. He wanted me to ask you first. He would then send in his card this morning.

MAGDA. What formalities the men go through here! Who is he?

MAX. Councillor von Keller.

MAGDA. [*Speaking with difficulty.*] He—what?—he?

MAX. [*Laughing.*] Pardon me, but you're as white now as he was.

MAGDA. [*Quietly.*] I? White?

[*Enter* THERESA *with a card.*

MAX. Here he is. Dr. von Keller.

MAGDA. Let him come up.

MAX. [*Smiling.*] I'll only say to you, my dear cousin, that he's a very important man, who has a great career before him, and promises to be a pillar of our religious circle.

MAGDA. Thank you!

[*Enter* VON KELLER *with a bouquet.*

MAX. [*Crossing to him.*] My dear Councillor, here

is my cousin, who is delighted to see you. You will excuse me.

[*Exit, with a bow to each.*

[VON KELLER *remains standing at the door.* MAGDA *moves about nervously. Silence.*]

MAGDA. [*Aside.*] Here is my specter! [*Indicates a seat at the table, left, and sits down opposite.*]

VON KELLER. First, you must allow me to express my warmest and most sincere good wishes. This is a surprise which you happily could not have expected. And as a sign of my interest, allow me, my dearest friend, to present you with these modest flowers.

MAGDA. Oh, how thoughtful! [*Takes the flowers with a laugh, and throws them on the table.*]

VON KELLER. [*In embarrassment.*] I—I see with sorrow that you resent this approach on my part. Have I in any way been wanting in the necessary delicacy? In these narrow circles a meeting could not have been avoided. I think it is better, my dearest friend, that we should come to an understanding—that we should know the relations——

MAGDA. [*Rising.*] You're right, my friend. I was not at the height of my own nature just now. Had I been, I might have played the deserted Marguerite to the end. The morals of home had infected me a little. But I am myself again. Give me your hand bravely. Don't be afraid, I won't harm you. So—tight—so!

VON KELLER. You make me happy.

MAGDA. I've painted this meeting to myself a thousand times, and have been prepared for it for years. Something warned me, too, when I undertook this journey home—though I must say I hardly expected just here to—— Yes, how is it that, after what has passed between us, you came into this house? It seems to me a little——

VON KELLER. I tried to avoid it until quite recently; but since we belong to the same circles, and since I agree with the views of this family—that is, at least in theory——

MAGDA. Yes, yes. Let me look at you, my poor friend. How you have changed!

VON KELLER. [*Laughing nervously.*] I seem to have the misfortune to make a rather absurd figure in your eyes.

MAGDA. No, oh, no! I can see it all. The effort to keep worthy of respect under such difficulties, with a bad conscience, is awkward. You look down from the height of your pure atmosphere on your sinful youth—for you are called a pillar, my dear friend.

VON KELLER. [*Looking at the door.*] Pardon me—I can hardly accustom myself again to the affectionate terms. And if any one should hear us—— Would it not be better——

MAGDA. [*Sadly.*] Let them hear us.

VON KELLER. [*At the door.*] Good Heavens! Well, [*sitting down again*] as I was saying, if you knew with what real longing I look back from this height at my gay, discarded youth——

MAGDA. [*Half to herself.*] So gay,—yes, so gay.

VON KELLER. Well, I felt myself called to higher things. I thought—— Why should I undervalue my position? I have become Councillor, and that comparatively young. An ordinary ambition might take satisfaction in that. But one sits and waits at home, while others are called to the ministry. And this environment, conventionality, and narrowness, all is so gray—gray! And the ladies here—for one who cares at all about elegance—I assure you something rejoiced within me when I read this morning that you were the famous singer—

you to whom I was tied by so many dear memories and——

MAGDA. And then you thought whether it might not be possible with the help of these dear memories to bring a little color into the gray background?

VON KELLER. [*Smiling.*] Oh, pray don't——

MAGDA. Well, between old friends——

VON KELLER. Really, are we that, really?

MAGDA. Certainly, *sans rancune.* Oh, if I took it from the other standpoint, I should have to range the whole gamut—liar, coward, traitor! But as I look at it, I owe you nothing but thanks, my friend.

VON KELLER. [*Pleased, but confused.*] This is a view which——

MAGDA. Which is very convenient for you. But why should I not make it convenient for you? In the manner in which we met, you had no obligations towards me. I had left my home; I was young and innocent, hot-blooded and careless, and I lived as I saw others live. I gave myself to you because I loved you. I might perhaps have loved any one who came in my way. That—that seemed to be all over. And we were so happy—weren't we?

VON KELLER. Ah, when I think of it, my heart seems to stop beating.

MAGDA. There in the old attic, five flights up, we three girls lived so merrily in our poverty. Two hired pianos, and in the evening bread and dripping. Emmy used to warm it herself over the oil-stove.

VON KELLER. And Katie with her verses! Good Lord! What has become of them?

MAGDA. *Chi lo sà?* Perhaps they're giving singing-lessons, perhaps they're on the stage. Yes, we were a merry set; and when the fun had lasted half a year, one day my lover vanished.

VON KELLER. An unlucky chance, I swear to you. My father was ill. I had to travel. I wrote everything to you.

MAGDA. H'm! I did not reproach you. And now I will tell you why I owe you thanks. I was a stupid, unsuspecting thing, enjoying freedom like a runaway monkey. Through you I became a woman. For whatever I have done in my art, for whatever I have become in myself, I have you to thank. My soul was like—yes, down below there, there used to be an Æolian harp which was left moldering because my father could not bear it. Such a silent harp was my soul; and through you it was given to the storm. And it sounded almost to breaking—the whole scale of passions which bring us women to maturity—love and hate and revenge and ambition, [*springing up*] and need, need, need—three times need—and the highest, the strongest, the holiest of all, the mother's love!—All I owe to you!

VON KELLER. What—what do you say?

MAGDA. Yes, my friend, you have asked after Emmy and Katie. But you haven't asked after your child.

VON KELLER. [*Jumping up and looking about anxiously.*] My child!

MAGDA. Your child? Who calls it so? Yours? Ha, ha! Dare to claim portion in him and I'll kill you with these hands. Who are you? You're a strange man who gratified his lust and passed on with a laugh. But I have a child—my son, my God, my all! For him I lived and starved and froze and walked the streets; for him I sang and danced in concert-halls—for my child who was crying for his bread! [*Breaks out in a convulsive laugh which changes to weeping, and throws herself on a seat, right.*]

VON KELLER. [*After a silence.*] I am confounded. If I could have suspected—yes, if I could have suspected—I will do everything; I will not shrink from any reparation. But now, I beg you to quiet yourself. They know that I am here. If they saw us so, I should be—[*correcting himself*] you would be lost.

MAGDA. Don't be afraid. I won't compromise you.

VON KELLER. Oh, I was not speaking for myself, not at all. But just think, if it were to come out, what the town and your father——

MAGDA. Poor old man! His peace is destroyed, at any rate.

VON KELLER. And think! the more brilliantly you are placed now, the more certain is your ruin.

MAGDA. [*Madly.*] And if I wish for ruin! If I——

VON KELLER. For Heaven's sake, hush! some one's coming.

MAGDA. [*Springing up.*] Let them come! Let them all come! I don't care, I don't care! To their faces I'll say what I think of you,—of you and your respectable society. Why should I be worse than you, that I must prolong my existence among you by a lie! Why should this gold upon my body, and the luster which surrounds my name, only increase my infamy? Have I not worked early and late for ten long years? Have I not woven this dress with sleepless nights? Have I not built up my career step by step, like thousands of my kind? Why should I blush before any one? I am myself, and through myself I have become what I am.

VON KELLER. Good! You may stand there proudly, but you might at least consider——

MAGDA. Whom? [*As he is silent.*] Whom? The pillar! Ha, ha! The pillar begins to totter! Be easy, my dear friend. I am not revengeful. But when I look at you in all your cowardly dignity—unwilling to take upon you the slightest consequence of your doings, and contrast you with myself, who sank through your love to be a pariah and an outcast—— Ah, I'm ashamed of you. Pah!

VON KELLER. For Heaven's sake! Your father! If he should see you like this!

MAGDA. [*In agony.*] My father! [*Escapes through the door of the dining-room, with her handkerchief to her face.*]

[*Enter* SCHWARTZE, *happy and excited, through the hall-door.*

SCHWARTZE. Ah, my dear Councillor—was that my daughter who just disappeared?

VON KELLER. [*In great embarrassment.*] Yes, it was——

SCHWARTZE. Why should she run away from me? Magda!

VON KELLER. [*Trying to block his path.*] Had you not better—— The young lady wished to be alone for a little!

SCHWARTZE. Now? Why? When one has visitors, one does not—— Why should she——

VON KELLER. She was a little—agitated.

SCHWARTZE. Agitated?

VON KELLER. Yes; that's all.

SCHWARTZE. Who has been here?

VON KELLER. No one. At least, as far as I know.

SCHWARTZE. Then, what agitating things could you two have to talk about?

VON KELLER. Nothing of importance—nothing at all, I assure you.

SCHWARTZE. What makes you look so, then? You can scarcely stand.

VON KELLER. I? Oh, you're mistaken, you're mistaken.

SCHWARTZE. One question, Councillor—— You and my daughter—— Please sit down.

VON KELLER. My time is unfortunately——

SCHWARTZE. [*Almost threatening.*] I beg you to sit down.

VON KELLER. [*Not daring to resist.*] Thank you. [*They sit.*]

SCHWARTZE. You met my daughter some years ago in Berlin?

VON KELLER. Yes.

SCHWARTZE. Councillor von Keller, I know you to be as discreet as you are sensible; but there are cases in which silence is a crime. I ask you—and your life-long relations with me give me the right to ask, as well as the mystery—which just now—— In short, I ask you, do you know anything discreditable about my daughter's life there?

VON KELLER. Oh, for Heaven's sake, how can you——

SCHWARTZE. Do you not know how and where she lived?

VON KELLER. No. I am absolutely——

SCHWARTZE. Have you never visited at her house?

VON KELLER. [*More and more confused.*] No, no, never, never.

SCHWARTZE. Not once?

VON KELLER. Well, I called on her once; but——

SCHWARTZE. Your relations were friendly?

VON KELLER. Oh, entirely friendly—of course, only friendly. [*A pause.*]

SCHWARTZE. [*Passes his hand over his forehead, looks earnestly at* VON KELLER; *then, speaking absently.*] So? Then, honestly—if it might be—if—if—— [*Gets up, goes to* VON KELLER, *and sits down again, trying to quiet himself.*] Dr. von Keller, we both live in a quiet world, where scandals are unknown. But I have grown old, very old. And therefore I can't—can't control my thoughts as I should. And I can't rid myself of an idea which has—suddenly—taken possession of me. I have just had a great joy which I don't want to be embittered. But, to quiet an old man, I beg you—give me your word of honor that——

VON KELLER. [*Rising.*] Pardon me, this seems almost like a cross-examination.

SCHWARTZE. You must know, then, what I——

VON KELLER. Pardon me, I wish to know nothing. I came here innocently to make a friendly visit, and you have taken me by surprise. I will not be taken by surprise. [*Takes his hat.*]

SCHWARTZE. Dr. von Keller, have you thought what this refusal means?

VON KELLER. Pardon me, if you wish to know anything, I beg you to ask your daughter. She will tell you what—what—— And now you must let me go. You know where I live. In case—— I am very sorry it has happened so: but—— Good-day, Colonel! [*Exit.*

SCHWARTZE. [*After brooding for a time.*] Magda!

MARIE. [*Running in anxiously.*] For Heaven's sake, what's the matter?

SCHWARTZE. [*Chokingly.*] Magda—I want Magda.

MARIE. [*Goes to the door and opens it.*] She's coming now—down the stairs.

SCHWARTZE. So! [*Pulls himself together with an effort.*]

MARIE. [*Clasping her hands.*] Don't hurt her! [*Pauses with the door open.* MAGDA *is seen descending the stairs. She enters in travelling-dress, hat in hand, very pale, but calm.*]

MAGDA. I heard you call, father.

SCHWARTZE. I have something to say to you.

MAGDA. And I to you.

SCHWARTZE. Go in—into my room.

MAGDA. Yes, father. [*She goes to the door, left.* SCHWARTZE *follows her.* MARIE, *who has drawn back frightened to the dining-room door, makes an unseen gesture of entreaty.*]

CURTAIN

## ACT IV

SCENE.—*The same.*

[MRS. SCHWARTZE *and* MARIE *discovered.* MRS. SCHWARTZE, *in hat and cloak, is knocking on the door at the left.*]

MRS. SCHWARTZE. Leopold! Oh, Heaven, I dare not go in.

MARIE. No, no, don't! Oh, if you'd only seen his face!

MRS. SCHWARTZE. And they've been in there half an hour, you say?

MARIE. Longer, longer!

MRS. SCHWARTZE. Now she's speaking! [*Listening, frightened.*] He's threatening her. Marie, Marie! Run into the garden. The pastor's there, in the arbor. Tell him everything—about Mr. von Keller's being here—and ask him to come in quickly.

MARIE. Yes, mamma. [*Hurries to the hall-door.*]

MRS. SCHWARTZE. Wait a minute, Marie. Has Theresa heard anything? If it should get about——

MARIE. I've already sent her away, mamma.

MRS. SCHWARTZE. That's right, that's right. [*Exit* MARIE. MRS. SCHWARTZE *knocks again.*] Leopold! listen to me, Leopold! [*Retreating.*] Oh, Heaven! he's coming! [*Enter* SCHWARTZE, *bent and tottering.*]

MRS. SCHWARTZE. How do you feel, Leopold?

SCHWARTZE. [*Sinking into a chair.*] Yes, yes,—just like the roses. The knife comes, and cuts the stem, and the wound can never be healed. What am I saying? What?

MRS. SCHWARTZE. He's out of his mind.

SCHWARTZE. No, no, I'm not out of my mind. I know quite well—— [MAGDA *appears at the door, left.*]

MRS. SCHWARTZE. What have you done to him?

SCHWARTZE. Yes, what have you—what have you? That is my daughter. What shall I do with my daughter now?

MAGDA. [*Humbly, almost beseechingly.*] Father, isn't it best, after what has happened, that you should let me go—that you should drive me into the streets? You must get free of me if this house is to be pure again.

SCHWARTZE. So, so, so! You think, then, you have only to go—to go away, out there, and all will be as before? And we? What will become of us? I—good God!—I—I have one foot in the grave—soon it will be over—but the mother, and your sister—your sister.

MAGDA. Marie has the husband she wants——

SCHWARTZE. No one will marry a sister of yours. [*With aversion.*] No, no. Don't think it!

MAGDA. [*Aside.*] My God!

SCHWARTZE. [*To* MRS. SCHWARTZE.] See, she's beginning now to realize what she has done.

MRS. SCHWARTZE. Yes; what——

MAGDA. [*In tender sympathy, but still with a tinge of superiority.*] My poor old father—listen to me—I can't change what has passed. I will give Marie half my fortune. I will make up a thousand times all that I have made you suffer to-day. But now, I implore you, let me go my way.

SCHWARTZE. Oho!

MAGDA. What do you want of me? What am I to you? Yesterday at this time you did not know even whether I still lived; and to-day—— It is madness to demand that I should think and feel again as you do; but I am afraid of you, father, I'm afraid of you all—ah, I am not myself—— [*Breaking out in torment.*] I cannot bear the sorrow.

SCHWARTZE. Ha, ha!

MAGDA. Father dear, I will humble myself before you willingly. I lament with my whole heart that I've brought sorrow to you to-day, for my flesh and blood still belong to you. But I must live out my own life. That I owe to myself—to myself and mine. Good-by!

SCHWARTZE. [*Stopping her.*] Where are you going?

MAGDA. Let me pass, father.

SCHWARTZE. I'll kill you first. [*Seizes her.*]

MRS. SCHWARTZE. Leopold! [*Enter* HEFFTERDINGT. *He throws himself between them with a cry of horror.* MAGDA, *freed by the old man, goes slowly back, with her eyes fixed on the* PASTOR, *to the seat, left, where she remains motionless.*]

HEFFTERDINGT. [*After a silence.*] In God's name!

SCHWARTZE. Yes, yes, yes, Pastor—it made a fine family group, eh? Look at her! She has soiled my name. Any scoundrel can break my sword. That is my daughter; that is——

HEFFTERDINGT. Dear Colonel, these are things which I do not understand, and which I do not care to understand. But it seems to me there must be something to do, instead of——

SCHWARTZE. Yes, to do—yes, yes—there's much to do here. I have much to do. I don't see why I'm standing here. The worst of it is—the worst of it is, he can say to me—this man—you are a cripple—with your shaking hand—with such a one I can't fight, even if I have had your daughter for a—— But I will show him—I will show him—— Where is my hat?

MRS. SCHWARTZE. Where are you going, Leopold? [MAGDA *rises.*]

SCHWARTZE. My hat!

MRS. SCHWARTZE. [*Gives him hat and stick.*] Here, here!

SCHWARTZE. So! [*To* MAGDA.] Learn to thank the God, in whom you disbelieve, that he has preserved your father until this hour, for he shall bring you back your honor!

MAGDA. [*Kneeling, and kissing his hand.*] Don't do it, father! I don't deserve this of you.

SCHWARTZE. [*Bends weeping over her head.*] My poor, poor child!

MAGDA. [*Calling after him.*] Father!

[*Exit* SCHWARTZE *quickly.*

MRS. SCHWARTZE. My child, whatever happens, we women—we must hold together.

MAGDA. Thanks, mamma. The play will soon be played out now.

HEFFTERDINGT. My dear Mrs. Schwartze, Marie is out there, full of sorrow. Go and say a kind word to her.

MRS. SCHWARTZE. What shall I say to comfort her, when all the happiness has gone out of her life? [MAGDA *jumps up in anguish.*] Oh, Pastor, Pastor!

[*Exit.*

MAGDA. [*After a silence.*] Oh, I am so tired!

HEFFTERDINGT. Miss Magda!

MAGDA. [*Brooding.*] I think I shall see those glaring bloodshot eyes before me always—wherever I go.

HEFFTERDINGT. Miss Magda!

MAGDA. How you must despise me!

HEFFTERDINGT. Ah, Miss Magda, I have long been a stranger to despite. We are all poor sinners——

MAGDA. [*With a bitter laugh.*] Truly we are——

Oh, I am so tired!—it is crushing me. There is that old man going out to let himself be shot dead for my sake, as if he could atone for all my sins with his single life! Oh, I am so tired!

HEFFTERDINGT. Miss Magda—I can only conjecture—what all this means—but you have given me the right to speak to you as a friend. And I feel that I am even more. I am your fellow-sinner, Miss Magda!

MAGDA. Good Heavens! Still harping on that!

HEFFTERDINGT. Do you feel the obligation, Miss Magda, to bring honor and peace back to this house?

MAGDA. [*Breaking out in anguish.*] You have lived through the sorrow, and ask whether I feel it?

HEFFTERDINGT. I think your father will obtain from that gentleman the declaration that he is ready for any sort of peaceable satisfaction.

MAGDA. Ha, ha! The noble soul! But what can I do?

HEFFTERDINGT. You can—not spurn the hand which he will offer you.

MAGDA. What? You don't mean—— This man—this strange man whom I despise—how, how could I——

HEFFTERDINGT. Dear Miss Magda, there comes an hour to almost every man when he collects the broken pieces of his life, to form them together into a new design. I have found it so with myself. And now it is your turn.

MAGDA. I will not do it—I will not do it.

HEFFTERDINGT. You will have to.

MAGDA. I would rather take my child in my arms and throw myself into the sea.

HEFFTERDINGT. [*Suppresses a violent start; continues after a silence, hoarsely.*] Of course, that is the simplest solution. And your father can follow you.

MAGDA. Oh, have pity on me! I must do whatever

you demand. I don't know how you have gained such power over me. Oh, man, if the slightest memory of what you once felt, if the least pity for your own youth, still lives within you, you cannot sacrifice me so!

HEFFTERDINGT. I do not sacrifice you alone, Miss Magda.

MAGDA. [*With awakening perception.*] Good God!

HEFFTERDINGT. There's no other way. I see none. You know yourself that the old man would not survive it. And what would become of your mother, and what would become of your poor sister? Miss Magda, it is as if with your own hand you set fire to the house and let everything burn that is within. And this house is still your home——

MAGDA. [*In growing agony.*] I will not, I will not. This house is not my home. My home is with my child!

HEFFTERDINGT. This child, too. He will grow up fatherless, and will be asked, "Where is your father?" He will come and ask you, "Where is my father?" What can you answer him? And, Miss Magda, he who has not peace in his heart from the beginning will never win it in the end.

MAGDA. All this is not true, and if it were true, have I not a heart too? Have I not a life to live also? Have I not a right to seek my own happiness?

HEFFTERDINGT. [*Harshly.*] No; no one has that. But do as you will. Ruin your home, ruin your father and sister and child, and then see what heart you have to seek your own happiness. [MAGDA *bows her head, sobbing. The* PASTOR *crosses to her, and leans over the table pityingly, with his hand on her hair.*] My poor——

MAGDA. [*Seizing his hand.*] Answer me one question. You have sacrificed your life for my sake. Do you think, to-day, in spite of what you know and what you do not know, do you think that I am worth this sacrifice?

HEFFTERDINGT. [*Constrained, as if making a confession.*] I have said already I am your fellow-sinner, Miss Magda.

MAGDA. [*After a pause.*] I will do what you demand.

HEFFTERDINGT. I thank you.

MAGDA. Good-by.

HEFFTERDINGT. Good-by. [*Exit. He is seen through the open door speaking to* MARIE *and sending her in.* MAGDA *remains motionless, with her face in her hands until he has gone.*

[*Enter* MARIE.

MARIE. What can I do, Magda?

MAGDA. Where has the pastor gone?

MARIE. Into the garden. Mamma is with him.

MAGDA. If father asks for me, say I shall wait there. [*Nods towards left.*]

MARIE. And haven't you a word for me, Magda?

MAGDA. Oh, yes. Fear nothing. [*Kisses her on the forehead.*] Everything will come out well, so well—no, no, no. [*In weary bitterness.*] Everything will come out quite well. [*Exit, left.* MARIE *goes into the dining-room.*]

[*Enter* SCHWARTZE. *He takes out a pistol-case and opens it. Takes a pistol, cocks it with difficulty, examines the barrel, and aims at a point on the wall. His arm trembles violently. He strikes it angrily, and lets the pistol sink. Enter* MAX.

SCHWARTZE. [*Without turning.*] Who's there?

MAX. It's I, uncle.

SCHWARTZE. Max? Ah, you may come in.

MAX. Uncle, Marie told me—— What are the pistols for, uncle?

SCHWARTZE. Ah, they used to be fine pistols—beautiful pistols. See, boy, with this I have hit the ace of hearts at twenty paces, or say fifteen. And fifteen would be enough. We ought to have been in the garden already, but—but [*helplessly touches his trembling arm, almost in tears*]—but I can nevermore——

MAX. [*Hurrying to him.*] Uncle? [*They embrace each other for a moment.*]

SCHWARTZE. It's all right,—it's all right.

MAX. Uncle, I need not say that I take your place, that I meet any man you point out; it is my right.

SCHWARTZE. Yours—why? In what capacity? Will you marry into a disgraced family?

MAX. Uncle!

SCHWARTZE. Are you prepared to strip off the uniform of our regiment? Yes, I might set up a gambling-house, and you could play the stool-pigeon for a living. There is no knowing what we might do. What! you, with your beautiful name, your noble name, propose this sacrifice—and I to profit by it! Ha, ha! No, my boy; even if you still were willing, I am not. This house and all within are marked for ruin. Go your way from it. With the name of Schwartze you have nothing more to do.

MAX. Uncle, I demand that you——

SCHWARTZE. Hush! Not now! [*Motions to the door.*] Soon I may need you as one needs a friend in such affairs, but not now—not now. First I must find the gentleman. He was not at home—the gentleman was not at home. But he shall not think he has escaped me. If he is out a second time, then, my son, your work begins. Until then, be patient—be patient.

[*Enter* THERESA *from hall.*

THERESA. Councillor von Keller. [SCHWARTZE *starts.*]

MAX. He here! How——

SCHWARTZE. Let him come in. [*Exit* THERESA.

MAX. Uncle! [*Points to himself in great excitement.* SCHWARTZE *shakes his head, and signs to* MAX *to leave the room. Enter* VON KELLER. *Exit* MAX. *They meet in the doorway.* VON KELLER *greets* MAX *courteously.* MAX *restrains himself from insulting him.*]

VON KELLER. Colonel, I am grieved at having missed you. When I returned from the Casino, where I am always to be found at noon—where, I say, I am always to be found—your card lay on the table; and as I imagine that there are matters of importance to be discussed between us, I made haste—as I say, I have made haste——

SCHWARTZE. Councillor, I do not know whether in this house there should be a chair for you, but since you have come here so quickly, you must be tired. I beg you to be seated.

VON KELLER. Thanks. [*Sits down, near the open pistol-case, starts as he sees it, watches the* COLONEL *apprehensively.*] H'm!

SCHWARTZE. Now, have you nothing to say to me?

VON KELLER. Allow me first one question: Did your daughter, after our conversation, say anything to you about me?

SCHWARTZE. Councillor, have you nothing to say to me?

VON KELLER. Oh, certainly, I have a great deal to say to you. I would gladly, for instance, express to you a wish, a request; but I don't quite know whether—— Won't you tell me, at least, has your daughter spoken of me at all favorably?

SCHWARTZE. [*Angrily.*] I must know, sir, how we stand, in what light I am to treat you.

VON KELLER. Oh, pardon me, now I understand—— [*Working himself up.*] Colonel, you see in me a man who takes life earnestly. The days of a light youth—— [SCHWARTZE *looks up angrily.*] Pardon me, I meant to say—since early this morning a holier and, if I may say so, a more auspicious resolution has arisen within me. Colonel, I am not a man of many words. I have already wandered from the point. As one man of honor to another, or—in short, Colonel, I have the honor to ask you for the hand of your daughter. [SCHWARTZE *sits motionless, breathing heavily.*] Pardon me, you do not answer—am I perhaps not worthy——

SCHWARTZE. [*Groping for his hand.*] No, no, no; not that—not that. I am an old man. These last hours have been a little too much for me. Don't mind me.

VON KELLER. H'm, h'm!

SCHWARTZE. [*Rising, and closing the lid of the pistol-case.*] Give me your hand, my young friend. You have brought heavy sorrow upon me—heavy sorrow. But you have promptly and bravely made it good. Give me the other hand. So, so! And now do you wish to speak to her also? You will have much to say. Eh?

VON KELLER. If I might be allowed.

SCHWARTZE. [*Opens the hall-door and speaks off, then opens the door, left.*] Magda!

[*Enter* MAGDA.

MAGDA. What is it, father?

SCHWARTZE. Magda, this gentleman asks for the honor—— [*As he sees the two together, he looks with sudden anger from one to the other.*]

MAGDA. [*Anxiously.*] Father?

SCHWARTZE. Now everything's arranged. Don't

make it too long! [*To* MAGDA.] Yes, everything's all right now. [*Exit.*

VON KELLER. Ah, my dearest Magda, who could have suspected it?

MAGDA. Then we are to be married.

VON KELLER. Above all, I don't want you to entertain the idea that any design of mine has been at the bottom of this development which I welcome so gladly, which I——

MAGDA. I haven't reproached you.

VON KELLER. No, you have no reason.

MAGDA. None whatever.

VON KELLER. Let me further say to you that it has always been my strongest wish that Providence might bring us together again.

MAGDA. Then you have really never ceased to love me?

VON KELLER. Well, as an honorable man and without exaggeration I can scarcely assert that. But since early this morning a holier and a more auspicious resolution has arisen within me——

MAGDA. Pardon me, would this holy and auspicious resolution have arisen within you just the same if I had come back to my home in poverty and shame?

VON KELLER. My dearest Magda, I am neither self-seeking nor a fortune-hunter, but I know what is due to myself and to my position. In other circumstances there would have been no social possibility of making legitimate our old relations——

MAGDA. I must consider myself, then, very happy in these ten long years to have worked up unconsciously towards such a high goal.

VON KELLER. I don't know whether I am too sensitive, but that sounds almost like irony. And I hardly think that——

MAGDA. That it is fitting from me?

VON KELLER. [*Deprecatingly.*] Oh!

MAGDA. I must ask for your indulgence. The rôle of a patient and forbearing wife is new to me. Let us speak, then, of the future [*sits and motions to him to do the same*]—of our future. What is your idea of what is to come?

VON KELLER. You know, my dearest Magda, I have great designs. This provincial town is no field for my statesmanship. Besides, it is my duty now to find a place which will be worthy of your social talents. For you will give up the stage and concert-hall—that goes without saying.

MAGDA. Oh, that goes without saying?

VON KELLER. Oh, I beseech you—you don't understand the conditions; it would be a fatal handicap for me. I might as well leave the service at once.

MAGDA. And if you did?

VON KELLER. Oh, you can't be in earnest. For a hard-working and ambitious man who sees a brilliant future before him to give up honor and position, and as his wife's husband to play the vagabond—to live merely as the husband of his wife? Shall I turn over your music, or take the tickets at the box-office? No, my dearest friend, you underestimate me, and the position I fill in society. But don't be uneasy. You will have nothing to repent of. I have every respect for your past triumphs, but [*pompously*] the highest reward to which your feminine ambition can aspire will be achieved in the drawing-room.

MAGDA. [*Aside.*] Good Heaven, this thing I'm doing is mere madness!

VON KELLER. What do you say? [MAGDA *shakes her head.*] And then the wife, the ideal wife, of modern times is the consort, the true, self-sacrificing helper of her husband. For instance, you, by your queenly personality and by the magic of your voice, will overcome my enemies, and knit even my friends more closely to me. And we will be largely hospitable. Our house shall be the center of the most distinguished society, who still keep to the severely gracious manners of our forefathers. Gracious and severe may seem contradictory terms, but they are not.

MAGDA. You forget that the child on whose account this union is to be consummated will keep the severely inclined away from us.

VON KELLER. Yes, I know, dear Magda, it will be painful for you; but this child must of course remain the deepest secret between us. No one must suspect——

MAGDA. [*Astounded and incredulous.*] What—what do you say?

VON KELLER. Why, it would ruin us. No, no, it is absurd to think of it. But we can make a little journey every year to wherever it is being educated. One can register under a false name; that is not unusual in foreign parts, and is hardly criminal. And when we are fifty years old, and other regular conditions have been fulfilled, [*laughing*] that can be arranged, can't it? Then we can, under some pretext, adopt it, can't we?

MAGDA. [*Breaks into a piercing laugh; then, with clasped hands and staring eyes.*] My sweet! My little one! *Mio bambino! Mio povero—bam*—you—you—I am to—ha, ha, ha! [*Tries to open the folding door.*] Go! go! [*Enter* SCHWARTZE.

SCHWARTZE. What——

MAGDA. Good, you're here! Free me from this man, take this man away from me.

SCHWARTZE. What?

MAGDA. I have done everything you demanded. I have humbled myself, I have surrendered my judgment,

I have let myself be carried like a lamb to the slaughter. But my child I will not leave. Give up my child to save *his* career!

[*Throws herself into a chair.*

SCHWARTZE. Mr. von Keller, will you please——

VON KELLER. I am inconsolable, Colonel. But it seems that the conditions which for the interest of both parties I had to propose, do not meet the approbation——

SCHWARTZE. My daughter is no longer in the position to choose the conditions under which she—— Dr. von Keller, I ask your pardon for the scene to which you have just been subjected. Wait for me at your home. I will myself bring you my daughter's consent. For that I pledge you my word of honor.

[*Sensation.* MAGDA *rises quickly.*

VON KELLER. Have you considered what——

SCHWARTZE. [*Holding out his hand.*] I thank you, Dr. von Keller.

VON KELLER. Not at all. I have only done my duty. [*Exit, with a bow.*

MAGDA. [*Stretching herself.*] So! Now I'm the old Magda again. [SCHWARTZE *locks the three doors silently.*] Do you think, father, that I shall become docile by being shut up?

SCHWARTZE. So! Now we are alone. No one sees us but He who sees us—there [*pointing upward*]. Quiet yourself, my child. We must talk together.

MAGDA. [*Sits down.*] Good! We can come to an understanding, then—my home and I.

SCHWARTZE. Do you see that I am now quite calm?

MAGDA. Certainly.

SCHWARTZE. Quite calm, am I not? Even my arm does not tremble. What has happened, has happened. But just now I gave your betrothed——

MAGDA. My betrothed?—— Father dear!

SCHWARTZE. I gave your betrothed my word of honor. And that must be kept, don't you see?

MAGDA. But if it is not in your power, my dear father.

SCHWARTZE. Then I must die—then I must simply die. One cannot live on when one—— You are an officer's daughter. Don't you understand that?

MAGDA. [*Compassionately.*] My God!

SCHWARTZE. But before I die, I must set my home in order, must I not? Every one has something which he holds sacred. What is sacred to your inmost soul?

MAGDA. My art.

SCHWARTZE. No, that is not enough. It must be more sacred.

MAGDA. My child.

SCHWARTZE. Good! Your child—your child—you love it? [MAGDA *nods.*] You wish to see it again? [*She nods.*] And—yes—if you made an oath upon its head, [*makes a motion as if he laid his hand upon a child's head*] then you would not perjure yourself? [MAGDA *shakes her head, smiling.*] That's well. [*Rising.*] Either you swear to me now, as upon his head, that you will become the honorable wife of his father, or—neither of us two shall go out of this room alive.

[*Sinks back on the seat.*

MAGDA. [*After a short silence.*] My poor, dear papa! Why do you torture yourself so? And do you think that I will let myself be constrained by locked doors? You cannot believe it.

SCHWARTZE. You will see.

MAGDA. [*In growing excitement.*] And what do you really want of me? Why do you trouble yourself about me? I had almost said, what have you all to do with me?

SCHWARTZE. That you will see.

MAGDA. You blame me for living out my life without asking you and the whole family for permission. And why should I not? Was I not without family? Did you not send me out into the world to earn my bread, and then disown me because the way in which I earned it was not to your taste? Whom did I harm? Against whom did I sin? Oh, if I had remained the daughter of the house, like Marie, who is nothing and does nothing without the sheltering roof of the home, who passes straight from the arms of her father into the arms of her husband; who receives from the family life, thought, character, everything—yes, then you would have been right. In such a one the slightest error would have ruined everything—conscience, honor, self-respect. But I? Look at me. I was alone. I was as shelterless as a man knocked about in the world, dependent on the work of my own hands. If you give us the right to hunger—and I have hungered—why do you deny us the right to love, as we can find it, and to happiness, as we can understand it?

SCHWARTZE. You think, my child, because you are free and a great artist, that you can set at naught——

MAGDA. Leave art out of the question. Consider me nothing more than the seamstress or the servant-maid who seeks, among strangers, the little food and the little love she needs. See how much the family with its morality demands from us! It throws us on our own resources, it gives us neither shelter nor happiness, and yet, in our loneliness, we must live according to the laws which it has planned for itself alone. We must still crouch in the corner, and there wait patiently until a respectful wooer happens to come. Yes, wait. And meanwhile the war for existence of body and soul is consuming us. Ahead we see nothing but sorrow and despair, and yet shall we not once dare to give what we have of youth and strength to the man for whom our whole being cries? Gag us, stupefy us, shut us up in harems or in cloisters—and that perhaps would be best. But if you give us our freedom, do not wonder if we take advantage of it.

SCHWARTZE. There, there! That is the spirit of rebellion abroad in the world. My child—my dear child—tell me that you were not in earnest—that you—that you—pity me—if—— [*Looking for the pistol-case.*] I don't know what may happen—child—have pity on me!

MAGDA. Father, father, be calm, I cannot bear that.

SCHWARTZE. I will not do it—I cannot do it—— [*Looking still for the pistol-case.*] Take it from me! Take it from me!

MAGDA. What, father?

SCHWARTZE. Nothing, nothing, nothing. I ask you for the last time.

MAGDA. Then you persist in it?

SCHWARTZE. My child, I warn you. You know I cannot do otherwise.

MAGDA. Yes, father, you leave me no other way. Well, then, are you sure that you ought to force me upon this man—[SCHWARTZE *listens*] that, according to your standards, I am altogether worthy of him? [*Hesitating, looking into space.*] I mean—that he was the only one in my life?

SCHWARTZE. [*Feels for the pistol-case and takes the pistol out.*] You jade! [*He advances upon her, trying to raise the weapon. At the same moment he falls back on the seat, where he remains motionless, with staring eyes, the pistol grasped in his hand, which hangs down by his side.*]

MAGDA. [*With a loud cry.*] Father! [*She flies*

*toward the stove for shelter from the weapon, then takes a few steps, with her hands before her face.]* Father!

[*She sinks, with her knees in a chair, her face on the back. Calling and knocking outside. The door is broken open.*

[*Enter* MAX, MARIE, HEFFTERDINGT, *and* MRS. SCHWARTZE.

MRS. SCHWARTZE. Leopold, what's the matter? Leopold! [*To the* PASTOR.] O my God, he's as he used to be!

MARIE. Papa dear! Speak, one word!

[*Throws herself down at his right.*

HEFFTERDINGT. Get the doctor, Max.

MAX. Is it a stroke?

HEFFTERDINGT. I think so. [*Exit* MAX. *Aside to* MAGDA.] Come to him. [*As she hesitates.*] Come; it is the end.

[*Leads her trembling to* SCHWARTZE'S *chair.*

MRS. SCHWARTZE. [*Who has tried to take the pistol.*] Let it go, Leopold; what do you want with it? See, he's holding the pistol and won't let it go.

HEFFTERDINGT. [*Aside.*] It is the convulsion. He cannot. My dear old friend, can you understand what I'm saying to you? [SCHWARTZE *bows his head a little.* MAGDA *sinks down at his left.*] God, the All-Merciful One, has called you from on high. You are not her judge. Have you no sign of forgiveness for her?

[SCHWARTZE *shakes his head slowly.*

MARIE. [*Sinking down by* MAGDA.] Papa, give her your blessing, dear papa!

[*A smile transfigures his face. The pistol escapes from his hand. He raises his hand slowly to place it on* MARIE'S *head. In the midst of this motion a spasm goes through his body. His arm falls back, his head sinks.*

MRS. SCHWARTZE. [*Crying out.*] Leopold!

HEFFTERDINGT. [*Taking her hand.*] He has gone home.

[*He folds his hands. Silent prayer, broken by the sobbing of the women.*

MAGDA. [*Springing up and spreading out her arms in agony.*] Oh, if I had only never come! [HEFFTERDINGT *makes a motion to beg her silence. She misunderstands.*] Are you going to drive me away? His life was the cost of my coming. May I not stay now?

HEFFTERDINGT. [*Simply and peacefully.*] No one will hinder you from praying upon his grave.

[*Curtain falls slowly.*]

# CYRANO DE BERGERAC

BY

EDMOND ROSTAND

*Translated from the French by* GERTRUDE HALL

## EDMOND ROSTAND

b. 1868, Marseilles, France.
Paris lycée and law school.
1888, His first play, *The Red Glove* (not produced).
1890, First volume of poems.
1894, *The Romancers,* the first of his plays to be produced at the Théâtre Français.
1895, *The Princess Faraway* played by Sarah Bernhardt.
1901, Made a member of the French Academy.
Retired to Cambo in the South of France because of ill health.
d. 1918.

### PLAYS

1888 *Le Gant Rouge* (*The Red Glove*).
1891 *Les Deux Pierrots* (translated as *Weeping Pierrot and Laughing Pierrot*).
1894 *Les Romanesques* (translated as *The Romancers, The Romantics,* and *The Fantasticks*).
1895 *La Princesse Lointaine* (translated as *The Princess Faraway* and *The Lady of Dreams*).
1897 *La Samaritaine* (translated as *The Woman of Samaria*).
1897 *Cyrano de Bergerac* (translated under the same title).
1900 *L'Aiglon* (translated as *L'Aiglon* and *The Eaglet*).
1910 *Chantecler* (translated under the same title).
1910 *Le Bois Sacré* (*The Sacred Wood*).
1921 *La Dernière Nuit de Don Juan* (translated as *The Last Night of Don Juan*).

## CYRANO DE BERGERAC

When Rostand was asked if his interest in Cyrano de Bergerac had begun in childhood, he replied: "Yes and no; I was for a long time pursued by that personage Cyrano; he haunted me at College and gradually, with some help from me, he became the center of a dramatic action." In this same conversation recently published by his intimate neighbor at Cambo, Paul Faure, Rostand traced the growth of this early interest towards the finished play. In school he had come greatly to admire a master "whose soul was as beautiful as his body was ugly." The final incentive to make a play on the theme came from Rostand's own assumption of the part in real life. He shared the love secrets of a dull and bashful schoolmate who had failed to make any progress with an evasive young lady. Rostand spurred him on and finally dictated love letters that won not only the girl but also the boy's father—who had artfully intercepted them—to a belief in the young rascal's genius. Even the duel, which to most readers no doubt passes as the good old stuff of footlights and laths, was for Rostand the vivid revival of another boyhood memory, that of a man who fought a duel while visiting Edmond's father and who allowed the young poet to play with the swords. The final composition of the play, as was true of all he wrote, was long delayed and painstakingly elaborated. For years he was "afraid to touch it," and the writing itself was "a kind of torture with constant change and rewriting and replanning." In later years ill health still further extended the time of writing.

That Cyrano stood in the same close relationship to

Rostand as Faust, Hamlet, and Alceste did to their dramatic authors accounts sufficiently for the immense superiority of this play to all others by the same poet; although in point of literary elaboration, *L'Aiglon* and *Chantecler* may even outdo it, *The Romancers, Princess Faraway,* and the *Woman of Samaria* seem by comparison pale and academic. Perhaps Clayton Hamilton is not greatly exaggerating when he says, "No other play in history, before or since, has attained a popular success so instantaneous and so enormous."

Certainly no other poet of comparable genius in the late nineteenth or in the twentieth century has given himself so painstakingly and with so little condescension to the business of stagecraft. At school he gave more attention to poetry than to law, and in summers spent at Luchon he and his pal, Henry de Gorsse, produced plays in Edmond's garden.

In 1890 Rostand was married and settled in Paris. He at once began work for the professional theater. His *Two Pierrots* is still unacted but *The Romancers* was chosen for production at the Théâtre Français. In this partly successful venture he made the friendship of the actor Constant Coquelin, who gave him the final inspiration in carrying out his plans for Cyrano and for whom also he wrote the rôles of Flambeau and Chantecler. Coquelin was also the poet's staunch defender in the dark period when only he and a forgotten Mme. Marni believed that *Cyrano de Bergerac* could possibly succeed.

"When from among our poor contemporary works," said Rostand, speaking at the great actor's funeral, "he had made a choice, he gave himself to it devotedly and with enthusiasm. He would allow no one to doubt its value; he carried it through with passionate zeal."

Similarly Mme. Sarah Bernhardt, who had produced with some success *The Woman of Samaria,* a play which without her interpretive genius stood little chance of success, inspired Rostand to write *L'Aiglon,* which, although inferior to *Cyrano,* easily takes rank as the next greatest verse play of our age. No dramatist has been more fortunate in his interpreters.

Although we inevitably think of Rostand's romantic verse dramas as a unique occurrence in an age when the naturalism of Ibsen, Strindberg, and Becque held sway in France as elsewhere, they were, in reality, part of a reactionary movement in the French theater, of which Jean Richepin was a distinguished leader. It marked a natural revulsion from the inundation of prose and even banality, but it had little new, except a tone of actuality in style, to make it more than a passing phenomenon without important results. The deeper and more fatal assaults on realism were yet to make themselves felt. It is at least significant that Rostand's later *Chantecler,* which failed in the elaborate representational production at the Porte Saint-Martin in 1910, could be produced successfully at the same theater in a futurist manner in 1928.

*Cyrano de Bergerac* is a romantic character study which owes its phenomenal popularity to a combination of favorable circumstances that few plays in the history of the world can boast: a colorful hero of romance as subject, whose inner and outer life were in sharp and dramatic contrast; a poet of genius devoting a life study to his play and to the theater; an actor endowed beyond all others of his age to speak its verse and to embody its conception, and a zeal for a fresh reactionary dramatic movement in which this play takes highest rank.

## Production

*Cyrano de Bergerac* was produced Dec. 28, 1897 by Constant Coquelin at the historic Théâtre Porte Saint-Martin, to which he had seceded from the Théâtre Français. Trained in the comedy technique of Molière's theater, Coquelin had gained a supremacy in speech, facial expression, and gesture such as no actor of our age has seriously challenged. His imagination put this skill finely in harmony with every character in his vast repertory. No one who did not see him can easily conceive the shades of expressiveness and the infinite variety of character suggestion that made his art pre-eminent. Artist and photographer have done much to assist, but they fail to reproduce the music of his voice and the expressive mobility of face and limb. The combination of poet and actor has rarely been more fortunate, each inspiring the other to the greatest achievement of their careers. The play was first given in New York, Oct. 3, 1898 by Richard Mansfield, who made it almost equally popular in English. It was not produced by any English actor until 1900, when Sir Charles Wyndham, who, in T. J. Grein's opinion, was, except in voice, better suited to the part than Coquelin himself. The phenomenal revival of the play in 1924 by Walter Hampden makes it almost as significant an event for our generation as it was for its own.

## DRAMATIS PERSONÆ

Cyrano de Bergerac.
Christian de Neuvillette.
Comte de Guiche.
Ragueneau.
Le Bret.
Captain Carbon de Castel-Jaloux.
Lignière.
De Valvert.
Montfleury.
Bellerose.
Jodelet.
Cuigy.
Brissaille.
A Bore.
A Mousquetaire.
Other Mousquetaires.
A Spanish Officer.
A Light-Cavalry Man.
A Doorkeeper.
A Burgher.
His Son.
A Pickpocket.
A Spectator.
A Watchman.
Bertrandou the Fifer.
A Capuchin.
Two Musicians.
Seven Cadets.
Three Marquises.
Poets.

PASTRYCOOKS.
ROXANE.
SISTER MARTHA.
LISE.
THE SWEETMEAT VENDER.
MOTHER MARGARET.
THE DUENNA.
SISTER CLAIRE.
AN ACTRESS.
A SOUBRETTE.
A FLOWER-GIRL.
PAGES.

*The crowd, bourgeois, marquises, mousquetaires, pick-pockets, pastrycooks, poets, Gascony Cadets, players, fiddlers, pages, children, Spanish soldiers, spectators, précieuses, actresses, bourgeoises, nuns, etc.*

# CYRANO DE BERGERAC

## ACT FIRST

### A PLAY AT THE HÔTEL DE BOURGOGNE

*The great hall of the Hôtel de Bourgogne, in 1640. A sort of tennis-court arranged and decorated for theatrical performances.*

*The hall is a long rectangle, seen obliquely, so that one side of it constitutes the background, which runs from the position of the front wing at the right, to the line of the furthest wing at the left, and forms an angle with the stage, which is equally seen obliquely.*

*This stage is furnished, on both sides, along the wings, with benches. The drop-curtain is composed of two tapestry hangings, which can be drawn apart. Above a Harlequin cloak, the royal escutcheon. Broad steps lead from the raised platform of the stage into the house. On either side of these steps, the musicians' seats. A row of candles fills the office of footlights.*

*Two galleries run along the side; the lower one is divided into boxes. No seats in the pit, which is the stage proper. At the back of the pit, that is to say, at the right, in the front, a few seats raised like steps, one above the other; and, under a stairway which leads to the upper seats, and of which the lower end only is visible, a stand decked with small candelabra, jars full of flowers, flagons and glasses, dishes heaped with sweetmeats, etc.*

*In the center of the background, under the box-tier, the entrance to the theater, large door which half opens to let in the spectators. On the panels of this door, and in several corners, and above the sweetmeat stand, red playbills announcing* LA CLORISE.

*At the rise of the curtain, the house is nearly dark, and still empty. The chandeliers are let down in the middle of the pit, until time to light them.*

*The audience, arriving gradually. Cavaliers, burghers, lackeys, pages, the fiddlers, etc.*

*A tumult of voices is heard beyond the door; enter brusquely a* CAVALIER.

DOORKEEPER. [*Running in after him.*] Not so fast! Your fifteen pence!

CAVALIER. I come in admission free!

DOORKEEPER. And why?

CAVALIER. I belong to the king's light cavalry!

DOORKEEPER. [*To another* CAVALIER *who has entered.*] You?

SECOND CAVALIER. I do not pay!

DOORKEEPER. But . . .

SECOND CAVALIER. I belong to the mousquetaires!

FIRST CAVALIER. [*To the* SECOND.] It does not begin before two. The floor is empty. Let us have a bout with foils. [*They fence with foils they have brought.*]

A LACKEY. [*Entering.*] Pst! . . . Flanquin!

OTHER LACKEY.. [*Arrived a moment before.*] Champagne? . . .

FIRST LACKEY. [*Taking a pack of cards from his doublet and showing it to* SECOND LACKEY.] Cards. Dice. [*Sits down on the floor.*] Let us have a game.

SECOND LACKEY. [*Sitting down likewise.*] You rascal, willingly!

FIRST LACKEY. [*Taking from his pocket a bit of candle which he lights and sticks on the floor.*] I prigged an eyeful of my master's light!

ONE OF THE WATCH. [*To a flower-girl, who comes forward.*] It is pleasant getting here before the lights.

[*Puts his arm around her waist.*

ONE OF THE FENCERS. [*Taking a thrust.*] Hit!

ONE OF THE GAMBLERS. Clubs!

THE WATCHMAN. [*Pursuing the girl.*] A kiss!

THE FLOWER-GIRL. [*Repulsing him.*] We shall be seen!

THE WATCHMAN. [*Drawing her into a dark corner.*] No, we shall not!

A MAN. [*Sitting down on the floor with others who have brought provisions.*] By coming early, you get a comfortable chance to eat.

A BURGHER. [*Leading his son.*] This should be a good place, my boy. Let us stay here.

ONE OF THE GAMBLERS. Ace wins!

A MAN. [*Taking a bottle from under his cloak and sitting down.*] A proper toper, toping Burgundy, [*drinks*] I say should tope it in Burgundy House!

THE BURGHER. [*To his son.*] Might one not suppose we had stumbled into some house of evil fame? [*Points with his cane at the drunkard.*] Guzzlers! . . . [*In breaking guard one of the fencers jostles him.*] Brawlers! . . . [*He falls between the gamblers.*] Gamesters! . . .

THE WATCHMAN. [*Behind him, still teasing the flower-girl.*] A kiss!

THE BURGHER. [*Dragging his son precipitately away.*] Bless my soul! . . . And to reflect that in this very house, my son, were given the plays of the great Rotrou!

THE YOUTH. And those of the great Corneille!

[*A band of* PAGES *holding hands rush in performing a farandole and singing.*

PAGES. Tra la la la la la la la! . . .

DOORKEEPER. [*Severely to the* PAGES.] Look, now! . . . you pages, you! none of your tricks!

FIRST PAGE. [*With wounded dignity.*] Sir! . . . this want of confidence . . . [*As soon as the doorkeeper has turned away, briskly to the* SECOND PAGE.] Have you a string about you?

SECOND PAGE. With a fish-hook at the end!

FIRST PAGE. We will sit up there and angle for wigs!

A PICKPOCKET. [*Surrounded by a number of individuals of dubious appearance.*] Come, now, my little hopefuls, and learn your A B C's of trade. Being as you're not used to hooking . . .

SECOND PAGE. [*Shouting to other* PAGES *who have already taken seats in the upper gallery.*] Ho! . . . Did you bring any pea-shooters?

THIRD PAGE. [*From above.*] Yes! . . . And peas! . . . [*Shoots down a volley of peas.*

THE YOUTH. [*To his father.*] What are we going to see?

THE BURGHER. Clorise.

THE YOUTH. By whom?

THE BURGHER. By Balthazar Baro. Ah, what a play it is! . . .

[*Goes toward the back on his son's arm.*

PICKPOCKET. [*To his disciples.*] Particularly the lace-ruffles at the knees, . . . you're to snip off carefully!

A SPECTATOR. [*To another, pointing toward an upper seat.*] Look! On the first night of the Cid, I was perched up there!

PICKPOCKET. [*With pantomimic suggestion of spiriting away.*] Watches . . .

THE BURGHER. [*Coming forward again with his son.*] The actors you are about to see, my son, are among the most illustrious . . .

PICKPOCKET. [*With show of abstracting with furtive little tugs.*] Pocket-handkerchiefs . . .

THE BURGHER. Montfleury . . .

SOMEBODY. [*Shouting from the upper gallery.*] Make haste, and light the chandeliers!

THE BURGHER. Bellerose, l'Épy, the Beaupré, Jodelet . . .

A PAGE. [*In the pit.*] Ah! . . . Here comes the goody-seller!

THE SWEETMEAT VENDER. [*Appearing behind the stand.*] Oranges . . . Milk . . . Raspberry cordial . . . citron-wine . . . [*Hubbub at the door.*

FALSETTO VOICE. [*Outside.*] Make room, ruffians!

ONE OF THE LACKEYS. [*Astonished.*] The marquises . . . in the pit!

OTHER LACKEY. Oh, for an instant only!

[ENTER *a band of foppish* YOUNG MARQUISES.

ONE OF THE MARQUISES. [*Looking around the half-empty house.*] What? . . . We happen in like so many linen-drapers? Without disturbing anybody? treading on any feet? . . . Too bad! too bad! too bad! [*He finds himself near several other gentlemen, come in a moment before.*] Cuigy, Brissaille!

[*Effusive embraces.*

CUIGY. We are of the faithful indeed. We are here before the lights.

THE MARQUIS. Ah, do not speak of it! . . . It has put me in such a humor!

OTHER MARQUIS. Be comforted, marquis . . . here comes the candle-lighter!

THE AUDIENCE. [*Greeting the arrival of the candle-lighter.*] Ah! . . .

[*Many gather around the chandeliers while they are being lighted. A few have taken seats in the galleries.* LIGNIÈRE *enters, arm in arm with* CHRISTIAN DE NEUVILLETTE. LIGNIÈRE, *in somewhat disordered apparel; appearance of gentlemanly drunkard.* CHRISTIAN, *becomingly dressed, but in clothes of a slightly obsolete elegance.*

CUIGY. Lignière!

BRISSAILLE. [*Laughing.*] Not tipsy yet?

LIGNIÈRE. [*Low to* CHRISTIAN.] Shall I present you? [CHRISTIAN *nods assent.*] Baron de Neuvillette . . . [*Exchange of bows.*

THE AUDIENCE. [*Cheering the ascent of the first lighted chandelier.*] Ah! . . .

CUIGY. [*To* BRISSAILLE, *looking at* CHRISTIAN.] A charming head . . . charming!

FIRST MARQUIS. [*Who has overheard.*] Pooh! . . .

LIGNIÈRE. [*Presenting* CHRISTIAN.] Messieurs de Cuigy . . . de Brissaille . . .

CHRISTIAN. [*Bowing.*] Delighted! . . .

FIRST MARQUIS. [*To* SECOND.] He is a pretty fellow enough, but is dressed in the fashion of some other year!

LIGNIÈRE. [*To* CUIGY.] Monsieur is lately arrived from Touraine.

CHRISTIAN. Yes, I have been in Paris not over twenty days. I enter the Guards to-morrow, the Cadets.

FIRST MARQUIS. [*Looking at those who appear in the boxes.*] There comes the présidente Aubry!

SWEETMEAT VENDER. Oranges! Milk!

THE FIDDLERS. [*Tuning.*] La . . . la . . .

CUIGY. [*To* CHRISTIAN, *indicating the house, which is filling.*] A good house! . . .

CHRISTIAN. Yes, crowded.

First Marquis. The whole of fashion!

[*They give the names of the women, as, very brilliantly attired, these enter the boxes. Exchange of bows and smiles.*

Second Marquis. Mesdames de Guéménée . . .

Cuigy. De Bois-Dauphin . . .

First Marquis. Whom . . . time was! . . . we loved! . . .

Brissaille. . . . de Chavigny . . .

Second Marquis. Who still plays havoc with our hearts!

Lignière. *Tiens!* Monsieur de Corneille has come back from Rouen!

The Youth. [*To his father.*] The Academy is present?

The Burgher. Yes . . . I perceive more than one member of it. Yonder are Boudu, Boissat, and Cureau . . . Porchères, Colomby, Bourzeys, Bourdon, Arbaut . . . All names of which not one will be forgotten. What a beautiful thought it is!

First Marquis. Attention! Our précieuses are coming into their seats . . . Barthénoide, Urimédonte, Cassandace, Félixérie . . .

Second Marquis. Ah, how exquisite are their surnames! . . . Marquis, can you tell them off, all of them?

First Marquis. I can tell them off, all of them, Marquis!

Lignière. [*Drawing* Christian *aside.*] Dear fellow, I came in here to be of use to you. The lady does not come. I revert to my vice!

Christian. [*Imploring.*] No! No! . . . You who turn into ditties Town and Court, stay by me: you will be able to tell me for whom it is I am dying of love!

The Leader of the Violins. [*Rapping on his desk with his bow.*] Gentlemen! . . .

[*He raises his bow.*

SWEETMEAT VENDER. Macaroons . . . Citronade . . .
[*The fiddles begin playing.*

CHRISTIAN. I fear . . . oh, I fear to find that she is fanciful and intricate! I dare not speak to her, for I am of a simple wit. The language written and spoken in these days bewilders and baffles me. I am a plain soldier . . . shy, to boot.—She is always at the right, there, the end: the empty box.

LIGNIÈRE. [*With show of leaving.*] I am going.

CHRISTIAN. [*Still attempting to detain him.*] Oh, no! . . . Stay, I beseech you!

LIGNIÈRE. I cannot. D'Assoucy is expecting me at the pot-house. Here is a mortal drought!

SWEETMEAT VENDER. [*Passing before him with a tray.*] Orangeade? . . .

LIGNIÈRE. Ugh!

SWEETMEAT VENDER. Milk? . . .

LIGNIÈRE. Pah! . . .

SWEETMEAT VENDER. Lacrima? . . .

LIGNIÈRE. Stop! [*To* CHRISTIAN.] I will tarry a bit. . . . Let us see this lacrima? [*Sits down at the sweetmeat stand. The* VENDER *pours him a glass of lacrima.*]

[*Shouts among the audience at the entrance of a little, merry-faced, roly-poly man.*

AUDIENCE. Ah, Ragueneau! . . .

LIGNIÈRE. [*To* CHRISTIAN.] Ragueneau, who keeps the great cook-shop.

RAGUENEAU. [*Attired like a pastrycook in his Sunday best, coming quickly toward* LIGNIÈRE.] Monsieur, have you seen Monsieur de Cyrano?

LIGNIÈRE. [*Presenting* RAGUENEAU *to* CHRISTIAN.] The pastrycook of poets and of players!

RAGUENEAU. [*Abashed.*] Too much honor. . . .

LIGNIÈRE. No modesty! . . . Mecænas! . . .

RAGUENEAU. It is true, those gentlemen are among my customers. . . .

LIGNIÈRE. Debitors! . . . A considerable poet himself. . . .

RAGUENEAU. It has been said! . . .

LIGNIÈRE. Daft on poetry! . . .

RAGUENEAU. It is true that for an ode. . . .

LIGNIÈRE. You are willing to give at any time a tart!

RAGUENEAU. . . . let. A tart-let.

LIGNIÈRE. Kind soul, he tries to cheapen his charitable acts! And for a triolet were you not known to give . . . ?

RAGUENEAU. Rolls. Just rolls.

LIGNIÈRE. [*Severely.*] Buttered! . . . And the play, you are fond of the play?

RAGUENEAU. It is with me a passion!

LIGNIÈRE. And you settle for your entrance fee with a pastry currency. Come now, among ourselves, what did you have to give to-day for admittance here?

RAGUENEAU. Four custards . . . eighteen ladyfingers. [*He looks all around.*] Monsieur de Cyrano is not here. I wonder at it.

LIGNIÈRE. And why?

RAGUENEAU. Montfleury is billed to play.

LIGNIÈRE. So it is, indeed. That ton of man will to-day entrance us in the part of Phœdo . . . Phœdo! . . . But what is that to Cyrano?

RAGUENEAU. Have you not heard? He interdicted Montfleury, whom he has taken in aversion, from appearing for one month upon the stage.

LIGNIÈRE. [*Who is at his fourth glass.*] Well?

RAGUENEAU. Montfleury is billed to play.

CUIGY. [*Who has drawn near with his companions.*] He cannot be prevented.

RAGUENEAU. He cannot? . . . Well, I am here to see!

FIRST MARQUIS. What is this Cyrano?

CUIGY. A crack-brain!

SECOND MARQUIS. Of quality?

CUIGY. Enough for daily uses. He is a cadet in the Guards. [*Pointing out a gentleman who is coming and going about the pit, as if in search of somebody.*] But his friend Le Bret can tell you. [*Calling.*] Le Bret! . . . [LE BRET *comes toward them.*] You are looking for Bergerac?

LE BRET. Yes. I am uneasy.

CUIGY. Is it not a fact that he is a most uncommon fellow?

LE BRET. [*Affectionately.*] The most exquisite being he is that walks beneath the moon!

RAGUENEAU. Poet!

CUIGY. Swordsman!

BRISSAILLE. Physicist!

LE BRET. Musician!

LIGNIÈRE. And what an extraordinary aspect he presents!

RAGUENEAU. I will not go so far as to say that I believe our grave Philippe de Champaigne will leave us a portrait of him; but, the bizarre, excessive, whimsical fellow that he is would certainly have furnished the late Jacques Callot with a type of madcap fighter for one of his masques. Hat with triple feather, doublet with twice-triple skirt, cloak which his interminable rapier lifts up behind, with pomp, like the insolent tail of a cock; prouder than all the Artabans that Gascony ever bred, he goes about in his stiff Punchinello ruff, airing a nose. . . . Ah, gentlemen, what a nose is that! One cannot look upon such a specimen of the nasigera without exclaiming, "No! truly, the man exaggerates,"

. . . After that, one smiles, one says: "He will take it off." . . . But Monsieur de Bergerac never takes it off at all.

LE BRET. [*Shaking his head.*] He wears it always . . . and cuts down whoever breathes a syllable in comment.

RAGUENEAU. [*Proudly.*] His blade is half the shears of Fate!

FIRST MARQUIS. [*Shrugging his shoulders.*] He will not come!

RAGUENEAU. He will. I wager you a chicken à la Ragueneau.

FIRST MARQUIS. [*Laughing.*] Very well!

> [*Murmur of admiration in the house.* ROXANE *has appeared in her box. She takes a seat in the front, her duenna at the back.* CHRISTIAN, *engaged in paying the sweetmeat vender, does not look.*

SECOND MARQUIS. [*Uttering a series of small squeals.*] Ah, gentlemen, she is horrifically enticing!

FIRST MARQUIS. A strawberry set in a peach, and smiling!

SECOND MARQUIS. So fresh, that being near her, one might catch cold in his heart!

CHRISTIAN. [*Looks up, sees* ROXANE, *and agitated, seizes* LIGNIÈRE *by the arm.*] That is she!

LIGNIÈRE. [*Looking.*] Ah, that is she! . . .

CHRISTIAN. Yes. Tell me at once. . . . Oh, I am afraid! . . .

LIGNIÈRE. [*Sipping his wine slowly.*] Magdeleine Robin, surnamed Roxane. Subtle. Euphuistic.

CHRISTIAN. Alack-a-day!

LIGNIÈRE. Unmarried. An orphan. A cousin of Cyrano's . . . the one of whom they were talking.

> [*While he is speaking, a richly dressed nobleman, wearing the order of the Holy Ghost on a*

*blue ribbon across his breast, enters* ROXANE'S *box, and, without taking a seat, talks with her a moment.*

CHRISTIAN. [*Starting.*] That man? . . .

LIGNIÈRE. [*Who is beginning to be tipsy, winking.*] Hé! Hé! Comte de Guiche. Enamored of her. But married to the niece of Armand de Richelieu. Wishes to manage a match between Roxane and a certain sorry lord, one Monsieur de Valvert, vicomte and . . . easy. She does not subscribe to his views, but De Guiche is powerful: he can persecute to some purpose a simple commoner. But I have duly set forth his shady machinations in a song which . . . Ho! he must bear me a grudge! The end was wicked . . . Listen! . . .

[*He rises, staggering, and lifting his glass, is about to sing.*

CHRISTIAN. No. Good-evening.

LIGNIÈRE. You are going? . . .

CHRISTIAN. To find Monsieur de Valvert.

LIGNIÈRE. Have a care. You are the one who will get killed. [*Indicating* ROXANE *by a glance.*] Stay. Some one is looking . . .

CHRISTIAN. It is true . . .

[*He remains absorbed in the contemplation of* ROXANE. *The pickpockets, seeing his abstracted air, draw nearer to him.*

LIGNIÈRE. Ah, you are going to stay. Well, I am going. I am thirsty! And I am looked for . . . at all the public-houses!

[*Exit unsteadily.*

LE BRET. [*Who has made the circuit of the house, returning toward* RAGUENEAU, *in a tone of relief.*] Cyrano is not here.

RAGUENEAU. And yet . . .

LE BRET. I will trust to Fortune he has not seen the announcement.

THE AUDIENCE. Begin! Begin!

ONE OF THE MARQUISES. [*Watching* DE GUICHE, *who comes from* ROXANE'S *box, and crosses the pit, surrounded by obsequious satellites, among whom the* VICOMTE DE VALVERT.] Always a court about him, De Guiche!

OTHER MARQUIS. Pf! . . . Another Gascon!

FIRST MARQUIS. A Gascon, of the cold and supple sort. That sort succeeds. Believe me, it will be best to offer him our duty.

[*They approach* DE GUICHE.

SECOND MARQUIS. These admirable ribbons! What color, Comte de Guiche? Should you call it Kiss-me-Sweet or . . . Expiring Fawn?

DE GUICHE. This shade is called Sick Spaniard.

FIRST MARQUIS. Appropriately called, for shortly, thanks to your valor, the Spaniard will be sick indeed, in Flanders!

DE GUICHE. I am going upon the stage. Are you coming? [*He walks toward the stage, followed by all the marquises and men of quality. He turns and calls.*] Valvert, come!

CHRISTIAN. [*Who has been listening and watching them, starts on hearing that name.*] The vicomte! . . . Ah, in his face . . . in his face I will fling my . . . [*He puts his hand to his pocket and finds the pick-pocket's hand. He turns.*] *Hein?*

PICKPOCKET. Aï!

CHRISTIAN. [*Without letting him go.*] I was looking for a glove.

PICKPOCKET. [*With an abject smile.*] And you found a hand. [*In a different tone, low and rapid.*] Let me go . . . I will tell you a secret.

CHRISTIAN. [*Without releasing him.*] Well?

PICKPOCKET. Lignière who has just left you . . .

CHRISTIAN. [*As above.*] Yes? . . .

PICKPOCKET. Has not an hour to live. A song he made annoyed one of the great, and a hundred men—I am one of them—will be posted to-night . . .

CHRISTIAN. A hundred? . . . By whom?

PICKPOCKET. Honor . . .

CHRISTIAN. [*Shrugging his shoulders.*] Oh! . . .

PICKPOCKET. [*With great dignity.*] Among rogues!

CHRISTIAN. Where will they be posted?

PICKPOCKET. At the Porte de Nesle, on his way home. Inform him.

CHRISTIAN. [*Letting him go.*] But where can I find him?

PICKPOCKET. Go to all the taverns: the Golden Vat, the Pine-Apple, the Belt and Bosom, the Twin Torches, the Three Funnels, and in each one leave a scrap of writing warning him.

CHRISTIAN. Yes. I will run! . . . Ah, the blackguards! A hundred against one! . . . [*Looks lovingly toward* ROXANE.] Leave her! . . . [*Furiously, looking toward* VALVERT.] And him! . . . But Lignière must be prevented. [*Exit running.*]

[DE GUICHE, *the* MARQUISES, *all the gentry have disappeared behind the curtain, to place themselves on the stage-seats. The pit is crowded. There is not an empty seat in the boxes or the gallery.*

THE AUDIENCE. Begin!

A BURGHER. [*Whose wig goes sailing off at the end of a string held by one of the pages in the upper gallery.*] My wig!

SCREAMS OF DELIGHT. He is bald! . . . The pages! . . . Well done! . . . Ha, ha, ha! . . .

THE BURGHER. [*Furious, shaking his fist.*] Imp of Satan! . . .

[*Laughter and screams, beginning very loud and decreasing suddenly. Dead silence.*

LE BRET. [*Astonished.*] This sudden hush? . . . [*One of the spectators whispers in his ear.*] Ah? . . .

THE SPECTATOR. I have it from a reliable quarter.

RUNNING MURMURS. Hush! . . . Has he come? No! . . . Yes, he has! . . . In the box with the grating. . . . The cardinal! . . . the cardinal! . . . the cardinal! . . .

ONE OF THE PAGES. What a shame! . . . Now we shall have to behave!

[*Knocking on the stage. Complete stillness. Pause.*

VOICE OF ONE OF THE MARQUISES. [*Breaking the deep silence, behind the curtain.*] Snuff that candle!

OTHER MARQUIS. [*Thrusting his head out between the curtains.*] A chair!

[*A chair is passed from hand to hand, above the heads. The marquis takes it and disappears, after kissing his hand repeatedly toward the boxes.*

A SPECTATOR. Silence!

[*Once more, the three knocks. The curtain opens. Tableau. The marquises seated at the sides, in attitudes of languid haughtiness. The stage-setting is the faint-colored bluish sort usual in a pastoral. Four small crystal candelabra light the stage. The violins play softly.*

LE BRET. [*To* RAGUENEAU, *under breath.*] Is Montfleury the first to appear?

RAGUENEAU. [*Likewise under breath.*] Yes. The opening lines are his.

LE BRET. Cyrano is not here.

RAGUENEAU. I have lost my wager.

LE BRET. Let us be thankful. Let us be thankful.

[*A bagpipe is heard.* MONTFLEURY *appears*

*upon the stage, enormous, in a conventional shepherd's costume, with a rose-wreathed hat set jauntily on the side of his head, breathing into a be-ribboned bagpipe.*

THE PIT. [*Applauding.*] Bravo, Montfleury! Montfleury!

MONTFLEURY. [*After bowing, proceeds to play the part of* PHŒDO.]

Happy the man who, freed from Fashion's fickle sway,
In exile self-prescribed whiles peaceful hours away;
Who when Zephyrus sighs amid the answering trees. . . .

A VOICE. [*From the middle of the pit.*] Rogue! Did I not forbid you for one month?

[*Consternation. Every one looks around. Murmurs.*

VARIOUS VOICES. *Hein?* What? What is the matter?

[*Many in the boxes rise to see.*

CUIGY. It is he!

LE BRET. [*Alarmed.*] Cyrano!

THE VOICE. King of the Obese! Incontinently vanish! . . .

THE WHOLE AUDIENCE. [*Indignant.*] Oh! . . .

MONTFLEURY. But . . .

THE VOICE. You stop to muse upon the matter?

SEVERAL VOICES. [*From the pit and the boxes.*] Hush! . . . Enough! . . . Proceed, Montfleury. . . . Fear nothing!

MONTFLEURY. [*In an unsteady voice.*] Happy the man who freed from Fashion's f—— . . .

THE VOICE. [*More threatening than before.*] How is this? Shall I be constrained, Man of the Monster Belly, to enforce my regulation . . . regularly?

[*An arm holding a cane leaps above the level of the heads.*

MONTFLEURY. [*In a voice growing fainter and fainter.*]

Happy the man. . .

[*The cane is wildly flourished.*

THE VOICE. Leave the stage!

THE PIT. Oh! . . .

MONTFLEURY. [*Choking.*]

Happy the man who freed . . .

CYRANO. [*Appears above the audience, standing upon a chair, his arms folded on his chest, his hat at a combative angle, his mustache on end, his nose terrifying.*] Ah! I shall lose my temper!

[*Sensation at sight of him.*

MONTFLEURY. [*To the* MARQUISES.] Messieurs, I appeal to you!

ONE OF THE MARQUISES. [*Languidly.*] But go ahead! . . . Play!

CYRANO. Fat man, if you attempt it, I will dust the paint off you with this!

THE MARQUIS. Enough!

CYRANO. Let every little lordling keep silence in his seat, or I will ruffle his ribbons with my cane!

ALL THE MARQUISES. [*Rising.*] This is too much! . . . Montfleury. . . .

CYRANO. Let Montfleury go home, or stay, and, having cut his ears off, I will disembowel him!

A VOICE. But . . .

CYRANO. Let him go home, I said!

OTHER VOICE. But after all . . .

CYRANO. It is not yet done? [*With show of turning up his sleeves.*] Very well, upon that stage, as on a platter trimmed with green, you shall see me carve that mount of brawn. . . .

MONTFLEURY. [*Calling up his whole dignity.*] Monsieur, you cast indignity, in my person, upon the Muse!

CYRANO. [*Very civilly.*] Monsieur, if that lady, with whom you have naught to do, had the pleasure of beholding you . . . just as you stand, there, like a decorated pot! . . . she could not live, I do protest, but she hurled her buskin at you!

THE PIT. Montfleury! . . . Montfleury! . . . Give us Baro's piece!

CYRANO. [*To those shouting around him.*] I beg you will show some regard for my scabbard: it is ready to give up the sword!

[*The space around him widens.*

THE CROWD. [*Backing away.*] Hey . . . softly, there!

CYRANO. [*To* MONTFLEURY.] Go off!

THE CROWD. [*Closing again, and grumbling.*] Oh! . . . Oh!

CYRANO. [*Turning suddenly.*] Has somebody objections?

[*The crowd again pushes away from him.*

A VOICE. [*At the back, singing.*]

Monsieur de Cyrano, one sees,
Inclines to be tyrannical;
In spite of that tyrannicle
We shall see La Clorise!

THE WHOLE AUDIENCE. [*Catching up the tune.*] La Clorise! La Clorise!

CYRANO. Let me hear that song again, and I will do you all to death with my stick!

A BURGHER. Samson come back! . . .

CYRANO. Lend me your jaw, good man!

A LADY. [*In one of the boxes.*] This is unheard of!

A MAN. It is scandalous!

A BURGHER. It is irritating, to say no more.

A PAGE. What fun it is!

THE PIT. Ksss! . . . Montfleury! . . . Cyrano! . . .

CYRANO. Be still! . . .

THE PIT. [*In uproar.*] Hee-haw! . . . Baaaaah! . . . Bow-wow! . . . Cockadoodledoooooo!

CYRANO. I will . . .

A PAGE. Meeeow!

CYRANO. I order you to hold your tongues! . . . I dare the floor collectively to utter another sound! . . . I challenge you, one and all! . . . I will take down your names . . . Step forward, budding heroes! Each in his turn. You shall be given numbers. Come, which one of you will open the joust with me? You, monsieur? No! You? No! The first that offers is promised all the mortuary honors due the brave. Let all who wish to die hold up their hands! [*Silence.*] It is modesty that makes you shrink from the sight of my naked sword? Not a name? Not a hand?—Very good. Then I proceed. [*Turning toward the stage where* MONTFLEURY *is waiting in terror.*] As I was saying, it is my wish to see the stage cured of this tumor. Otherwise . . . [*Claps hand to his sword.*] the lancet!

MONTFLEURY. I . . .

CYRANO. [*Gets down from his chair, and sits in the space that has become vacant around him, with the ease of one at home.*] Thrice will I clap my hands, O plenilune! At the third clap . . . eclipse!

THE PIT. [*Diverted.*] Ah! . . .

CYRANO. [*Clapping his hands.*] One! . . .

MONTFLEURY. I . . .

A VOICE. [*From one of the boxes.*] Do not go! . . .

THE PIT. He will stay! . . . He will go! . . .

MONTFLEURY. Messieurs, I feel . . .

CYRANO. Two! . . .

MONTFLEURY. I feel it will perhaps be wiser . . .

CYRANO. Three! . . .

[MONTFLEURY *disappears, as if through a trap-door. Storm of laughter, hissing, catcalls.*

THE HOUSE. Hoo! . . . Hoo! . . . Milksop! . . . Come back! . . .

CYRANO. [*Beaming, leans back in his chair and crosses his legs.*] Let him come back, if he dare!

A BURGHER. The spokesman of the company!

[BELLEROSE *comes forward on the stage and bows.*

THE BOXES. Ah, there comes Bellerose!

BELLEROSE. [*With elegant bearing and diction.*] Noble ladies and gentlemen . . .

THE PIT. No! No! Jodelet! . . . . We want Jodelet! . . .

JODELET. [*Comes forward, speaks through his nose.*] Pack of swine!

THE PIT. That is right! . . . Well said! . . . Bravo!

JODELET. Don't bravo me! . . . The portly tragedian, whose paunch is your delight, felt sick! . . .

THE PIT. He is a poltroon! . . .

JODELET. He was obliged to leave . . .

THE PIT. Let him come back!

SOME. No!

OTHERS. Yes! . . .

A YOUTH. [*To* CYRANO.] But, when all is said, monsieur, what good grounds have you for hating Montfleury?

CYRANO. [*Amiably, sitting as before.*] Young gosling, I have two, whereof each, singly, would be ample. Primo: He is an execrable actor, who bellows, and with grunts that would disgrace a water-carrier launches the verse that should go forth as if on pinions! . . . Secundo: is my secret.

THE OLD BURGHER. [*Behind* CYRANO.] But without compunction you deprive us of hearing La Clorise. I am determined . . .

CYRANO. [*Turning his chair around so as to face the old gentleman; respectfully.*] Venerable mule, old Baro's verses being what they are, I do it without compunction, as you say.

THE PRÉCIEUSES. [*In the boxes.*] Ha! . . . Ho! . . . Our own Baro! . . . My dear, did you hear that? How can such a thing be said? . . . Ha! . . . Ho! . . .

CYRANO. [*Turning his chair so as to face the boxes; gallantly.*] Beautiful creatures, do you bloom and shine, be ministers of dreams, your smiles our anodyne. Inspire poets, but poems . . . . spare to judge!

BELLEROSE. But the money which must be given back at the door!

CYRANO. [*Turning his chair to face the stage.*] Bellerose, you have said the only intelligent thing that has, as yet, been said! Far from me to wrong by so much as a fringe the worshipful mantle of Thespis. . . . [*He rises and flings a bag upon the stage.*] Catch! . . . and keep quiet!

THE HOUSE. [*Dazzled.*] Ah! . . . Oh! . . .

JODELET. [*Nimbly picking up the bag, weighing it with his hand.*] For such a price, you are authorized, monsieur, to come and stop the performance every day!

THE HOUSE. Hoo! . . . Hoo! . . .

JODELET. Should we be hooted in a body! . . .

BELLEROSE. The house must be evacuated!

JODELET. Evacuate it!

[*The audience begins to leave;* CYRANO *looking on with a satisfied air. The crowd, however, becoming interested in the following scene, the exodus is suspended. The women in the boxes who were already standing and had put on their wraps, stop to listen and end by resuming their seats.*

LE BRET. [*To* CYRANO.] What you have done . . . is mad!

A BORE. Montfleury! . . . the eminent actor! . . . What a scandal! . . . But the Duc de Candale is his patron! . . . Have you a patron, you?

CYRANO. No!

THE BORE. You have not?

CYRANO. No!

THE BORE. What? You are not protected by some great nobleman under the cover of whose name. . . .

CYRANO. [*Exasperated.*] No, I have told you twice. Must I say the same thing thrice? No, I have no protector . . . [*hand on sword*] but this will do.

THE BORE. Then, of course, you will leave town.

CYRANO. That will depend.

THE BORE. But the Duc de Candale has a long arm . . .

CYRANO. Not so long as mine . . . [*pointing to his sword*] pieced out with this!

THE BORE. But you cannot have the presumption . . .

CYRANO. I can, yes.

THE BORE. But . . .

CYRANO. And now, . . . face about!

THE BORE. But . . .

CYRANO. Face about, I say . . . or else, tell me why you are looking at my nose.

THE BORE. [*Bewildered.*] I . . .

CYRANO. [*Advancing upon him.*] In what is it unusual?

THE BORE. [*Backing.*] Your worship is mistaken.

CYRANO. [*Same business as above.*] Is it flabby and pendulous, like a proboscis?

THE BORE. I never said . . .

CYRANO. Or hooked like a hawk's beak?

THE BORE. I . . .

CYRANO. Do you discern a mole upon the tip?

THE BORE. But . . .

CYRANO. Or is a fly disporting himself thereon? What is there wonderful about it?

THE BORE. Oh . . .

CYRANO. Is it a freak of nature?

THE BORE. But I had refrained from casting so much as a glance at it!

CYRANO. And why, I pray, should you not look at it?

THE BORE. I had . . .

CYRANO. So it disgusts you?

THE BORE. Sir . . .

CYRANO. Its color strikes you as unwholesome?

THE BORE. Sir . . .

CYRANO. Its shape, unfortunate?

THE BORE. But far from it!

CYRANO. Then wherefore that depreciating air? . . . Perhaps monsieur thinks it a shade too large?

THE BORE. Indeed not. No, indeed. I think it small . . . small, I should have said, minute!

CYRANO. What? How? Charge me with such a ridiculous defect? Small, my nose? Ho! . . .

THE BORE. Heavens!

CYRANO. Enormous, my nose! . . . Contemptible stutterer, snub-nosed and flat-headed, be it known to you that I am proud, proud of such an appendage! inasmuch as a great nose is properly the index of an affable, kindly, courteous man, witty, liberal, brave, such as I am! and such as you are for evermore precluded from supposing yourself, deplorable rogue! For the inglorious surface my hand encounters above your ruff, is no less devoid—— [*Strikes him.*

THE BORE. Aï! aï! . . .

CYRANO. Of pride, alacrity, and sweep, of perception and of gift, of heavenly spark, of sumptuousness, to sum up all, of NOSE, than that [*turns him around by the shoulders and suits the action to the word*], which stops my boot below your spine!

THE BORE. [*Running off.*] Help! The watch! . . .

CYRANO. Warning to the idle who might find entertainment in my organ of smell. . . . And if the facetious fellow be of birth, my custom is, before I let him go, to chasten him, in front, and higher up, with steel, and not with hide!

DE GUICHE. [*Who has stepped down from the stage with the marquises.*] He is becoming tiresome!

VALVERT. [*Shrugging his shoulders.*] It is empty bluster!

DE GUICHE. Will no one take him up?

VALVERT. No one? . . . Wait! I will have one of those shots at him! [*He approaches* CYRANO *who is watching him, and stops in front of him, in an attitude of silly swagger.*] Your . . . your nose is . . . err . . . Your nose . . . is very large!

CYRANO. [*Gravely.*] Very.

VALVERT. [*Laughs.*] Ha! . . .

CYRANO. [*Imperturbable.*] Is that all?

VALVERT. But . . .

CYRANO. Ah, no, young man, that is not enough! You might have said, dear me, there are a thousand things . . . varying the tone . . . For instance . . . here you are:—Aggressive: "I, monsieur, if I had such a nose, nothing would serve but I must cut it off!" Amicable: "It must be in your way while drinking; you ought to have a special beaker made!" Descriptive: "It is a crag! . . . a peak! . . . a promontory! . . . A promontory, did I say? . . . It is a peninsula!" Inquisitive: "What may the office be of that oblong receptacle?

Is it an inkhorn or a scissor-case?" Mincing: "Do you so dote on birds, you have, fond as a father, been at pains to fit the little darlings with a roost?" Blunt: "Tell me, monsieur, you, when you smoke, is it possible you blow the vapor through your nose without a neighbor crying "The chimney is afire?" Anxious: "Go with caution, I beseech, lest your head, dragged over by that weight, should drag you over!" Tender: "Have a little sun-shade made for it! It might get freckled!" Learned: "None but the beast, monsieur, mentioned by Aristophanes, the hippocampelephantocamelos, can have borne beneath his forehead so much cartilage and bone!" Offhand: "What, comrade, is that sort of peg in style? Capital to hang one's hat upon!" Emphatic: "No wind can hope, O lordly nose, to give the whole of you a cold, but the Nor-Wester!" Dramatic: "It is the Red Sea when it bleeds!" Admiring: "What a sign for a perfumer's shop!" Lyrical: "Art thou a Triton, and is that thy conch?" Simple: "A monument! When is admission free?" Deferent: "Suffer, monsieur, that I should pay you my respects: that is what I call possessing a house of your own!" Rustic: "Hi, boys! Call that a nose? Ye don't gull me! It's either a prize carrot or else a stunted gourd!" Military: "Level against the cavalry!" Practical: "Will you put it up for raffle? Indubitably, sir, it will be the feature of the game!" And finally in parody of weeping Pyramus: "Behold, behold the nose that traitorously destroyed the beauty of its master! and is blushing for the same!"—That, my dear sir, or something not unlike, is what you would have said to me, had you the smallest leaven of letters or of wit; but of wit, O most pitiable of objects made by God, you never had a rudiment, and of letters, you have just those that are needed to spell "fool!"—But, had it been otherwise, and had you been possessed of the fertile fancy requisite to shower upon me, here, in this noble company, that volley of sprightly pleasantries, still should you not have delivered yourself of so much as a quarter of the tenth part of the beginning of the first. . . . For I let off these good things at myself, and with sufficient zest, but do not suffer another to let them off at me!

DE GUICHE. [*Attempting to lead away the amazed* VICOMTE.] Let be, Vicomte!

VALVERT. That insufferable haughty bearing! . . . A clodhopper without . . . without so much as gloves . . . who goes abroad without points . . . or bow-knots! . . .

CYRANO. My foppery is of the inner man. I do not trick myself out like a popinjay, but I am more fastidious, if I am not so showy. I would not sally forth, by any chance, not washed quite clean of an affront; my conscience foggy about the eye, my honor crumpled, my nicety black-rimmed. I walk with all upon me furbished bright. I plume myself with independence and straightforwardness. It is not a handsome figure, it is my soul, I hold erect as in a brace. I go decked with exploits in place of ribbon bows. I taper to a point my wit like a mustache. And at my passage through the crowd true sayings ring like spurs!

VALVERT. But, sir . . .

CYRANO. I am without gloves? . . . a mighty matter! I only had one left, of a very ancient pair, and even that became a burden to me . . . I left it in somebody's face.

VALVERT. Villain, clod-poll, flat-foot, refuse of the earth!

CYRANO. [*Taking off his hat and bowing as if the* VICOMTE *had been introducing himself.*] Ah! . . . And mine, Cyrano-Savinien-Hercule of Bergerac!

VALVERT. [*Exasperated.*] Buffoon!

CYRANO. [*Giving a sudden cry, as if seized with a cramp.*] Aï! . . .

VALVERT. [*Who had started toward the back, turning.*] What is he saying now?

CYRANO. [*Screwing his face as if in pain.*] It must have leave to stir . . . it has a cramp! It is bad for it to be kept still so long!

VALVERT. What is the matter?

CYRANO. My rapier prickles like a foot asleep!

VALVERT. [*Drawing.*] So be it!

CYRANO. I shall give you a charming little hurt!

VALVERT. [*Contemptuous.*] A poet!

CYRANO. Yes, a poet, . . . and to such an extent, that while we fence, I will, hop! extempore, compose you a ballade!

VALVERT. A ballade?

CYRANO. I fear you do not know what that is.

VALVERT. But . . .

CYRANO. [*As if saying a lesson.*] The ballade is composed of three stanzas of eight lines each. . . .

VALVERT. [*Stamps with his feet.*] Oh! . . .

CYRANO. [*Continuing.*] And an envoi of four.

VALVERT. You . . .

CYRANO. I will with the same breath fight you and compose one. And at the last line, I will hit you.

VALVERT. Indeed you will not!

CYRANO. No? . . . [*Declaiming.*]

Ballade of the duel which in Burgundy House
Monsieur de Bergerac fought with a jackanapes.

VALVERT. And what is that, if you please?

CYRANO. That is the title.

THE AUDIENCE. [*At the highest pitch of excitement.*]

Make room! . . . Good sport! . . . Stand aside! . . . Keep still! . . .

[*Tableau. A ring, in the pit, of the interested; the* MARQUISES *and* OFFICERS *scattered among the* BURGHERS *and* COMMON PEOPLE. *The* PAGES *have climbed on the shoulders of various ones, the better to see. All the women are standing in the boxes. At the right,* DE GUICHE *and his attendant gentlemen. At the left,* LE BRET, RAGUENEAU, CUIGY, *etc.*

CYRANO. [*Closing his eyes a second.*] Wait. I am settling upon the rhymes. There. I have them.

[*In declaiming, he suits the action to the word.*

Of my broad felt made lighter,
I cast my mantle broad,
And stand, poet and fighter,
To do and to record.
I bow, I draw my sword,
En garde! with steel and wit
I play you at first abord . . .
At the last line, I hit!

[*They begin fencing.*

You should have been politer;
Where had you best be gored?
The left side or the right—ah?
Or next your azure cord?
Or where the spleen is stored?
Or in the stomach pit?
Come we to quick accord . . .
At the last line, I hit!

You falter, you turn whiter?
You do so to afford

Your foe a rhyme in "iter"? . . .
You thrust at me—I ward—
And balance is restored.
Laridon! Look to your spit! . . .
No, you shall not be floored
Before my cue to hit!

[*He announces solemnly.*

ENVOI.

Prince, call upon the Lord! . . .
I skirmish . . . feint a bit . . .
I lunge! . . . I keep my word!

[*The* VICOMTE *staggers*; CYRANO *bows.*

At the last line, I hit!

[*Acclamations. Applause from the boxes. Flowers and handkerchiefs are thrown. The* OFFICERS *surround and congratulate* CYRANO. RAGUENEAU *dances with delight.* LE BRET *is is tearfully joyous and at the same time highly troubled. The friends of the* VICOMTE *support him off the stage.*

THE CROWD. [*In a long shout.*] Ah! . . .

A LIGHT-CAVALRY MAN. Superb!

A WOMAN. Sweet!

RAGUENEAU. Astounding!

A MARQUIS. Novel!

LE BRET. Insensate!

THE CROWD. [*Pressing around* CYRANO.] Congratulations! . . . Well done! . . . Bravo! . . .

A WOMAN'S VOICE. He is a hero!

A MOUSQUETAIRE. [*Striding swiftly toward* CYRANO, *with outstretched hand.*] Monsieur, will you allow me? It was quite, quite excellently done, and I think

I know whereof I speak. But, as a fact, I expressed my mind before, by making a huge noise. . . .

[*He retires.*

CYRANO. [*To* CUIGY.] Who may the gentleman be?

CUIGY. D'Artagnan.

LE BRET. [*To* CYRANO, *taking his arm.*] Come, I wish to talk with you.

CYRANO. Wait till the crowd has thinned. [*To* BELLEROSE.] I may remain?

BELLEROSE [*deferentially*]. Why, certainly! . . .

[*Shouts are heard outside.*

JODELET. [*After looking.*] They are hooting Montfleury.

BELLEROSE. [*Solemnly.*] *Sic transit!* . . . [*In a different tone, to the doorkeeper and the candle snuffer.*] Sweep and close. Leave the lights. We shall come back, after eating, to rehearse a new farce for to-morrow.

[*Exeunt* JODELET *and* BELLEROSE, *after bowing very low to* CYRANO.

THE DOORKEEPER. [*To* CYRANO.] Monsieur will not be going to dinner?

CYRANO. I? . . . No.

[*The doorkeeper withdraws.*

LE BRET. [*To* CYRANO.] And this, because? . . .

CYRANO. [*Proudly.*] Because. . . . [*In a different tone, having seen that the doorkeeper is too far to overhear.*] I have not a penny!

LE BRET. [*Making the motion of flinging a bag.*] How is this? The bag of crowns. . . .

CYRANO. Monthly remittance, thou lastedst but a day!

LE BRET. And to keep you the remainder of the month? . . .

CYRANO. Nothing is left!

LE BRET. But then, flinging that bag, what a child's prank!

CYRANO. But what a gesture! . . .

THE SWEETMEAT VENDER. [*Coughing behind her little counter.*] Hm! . . . [CYRANO *and* LE BRET *turn toward her. She comes timidly forward.*] Monsieur, to know you have not eaten . . . makes my heart ache. [*Pointing to the sweetmeat-stand.*] I have there all that is needed. . . . [*Impulsively.*] Help yourself!

CYRANO. [*Taking off his hat.*] Dear child, despite my Gascon pride, which forbids that I should profit at your hand by the most inconsiderable of dainties, I fear too much lest a denial should grieve you: I will accept therefore . . . [*He goes to the stand and selects.*] Oh, a trifle! . . . A grape off this. . . . [*She proffers the bunch, he takes a single grape.*] No . . . one! This glass of water . . . [*She starts to pour wine into it, he stops her.*] No . . . clear! And half a macaroon.

[*He breaks in two the macaroon, and returns half.*

LE BRET. This comes near being silly!

SWEETMEAT VENDER. Oh, you will take something more! . . .

CYRANO. Yes. Your hand to kiss.

[*He kisses the hand she holds out to him, as if it were that of a princess.*

SWEETMEAT VENDER. Monsieur, I thank you. [*Curtseys.*] Good evening! [*Exit.*

CYRANO. [*To* LE BRET.] I am listening. [*He establishes himself before the stand, sets the macaroon before him.*] Dinner! [*Does the same with the glass of water.*] Drink! [*And with the grape.*] Dessert! [*He sits down.*] La! let me begin! I was as hungry as a wolf! [*Eating.*] You were saying?

LE BRET. That if you listen to none but those great boobies and swashbucklers your judgment will become wholly perverted. Inquire, will you, of the sensible, concerning the effect produced to-day by your prowesses.

CYRANO. [*Finishing his macaroon.*] Enormous!

LE BRET. The cardinal . . .

CYRANO. [*Beaming.*] He was there, the cardinal?

LE BRET. Must have found what you did . . .

CYRANO. To a degree, original.

LE BRET. Still . . .

CYRANO. He is a poet. It cannot be distasteful to him wholly that one should deal confusion to a fellow-poet's play.

LE BRET. But, seriously, you make too many enemies!

CYRANO. [*Biting into the grape.*] How many, thereabouts, should you think I made to-night?

LE BRET. Eight and forty. Not mentioning the women.

CYRANO. Come, tell them over!

LE BRET. Montfleury, the old merchant, De Guiche, the Vicomte, Baro, the whole Academy . . .

CYRANO. Enough! You steep me in bliss!

LE BRET. But whither will the road you follow lead you? What can your object be?

CYRANO. I was wandering aimlessly; too many roads were open . . . too many resolves, too complex, allowed of being taken. I took . . .

LE BRET. Which?

CYRANO. By far the simplest of them all. I decided to be, in every matter, always, admirable!

LE BRET. [*Shrugging his shoulders.*] That will do. —But tell me, will you not, the motive—look, the true one!—of your dislike to Montfleury.

CYRANO. [*Rising.*] That old Silenus, who has not seen his knees this many a year, still believes himself a delicate desperate danger to the fair. And as he struts and burrs upon the stage, makes sheep's-eyes at them with his moist frog's-eyes. And I have hated him . . . oh, properly! . . . since the night he was so daring as to cast his glance on her . . . her, who—Oh, I thought I saw a slug crawl over a flower!

LE BRET. [*Amazed.*] Hey? What? Is it possible? . . .

CYRANO. [*With a bitter laugh.*] That I should love? [*In a different tone, seriously.*] I love.

LE BRET. And may one know? . . . You never told me. . . .

CYRANO. Whom I love? . . . Come, think a little. The dream of being beloved, even by the beautiless, is made, to me, an empty dream indeed by this good nose, my forerunner ever by a quarter of an hour. Hence, whom should I love? . . . It seems superfluous to tell you! . . . I love . . . it was inevitable! . . . the most beautiful that breathes!

LE BRET. The most beautiful? . . .

CYRANO. No less, in the whole world! And the most resplendent, and the most delicate of wit, and among the golden-haired . . . [*With overwhelming despair.*] Still the superlative!

LE BRET. Dear me, what is this fair one?

CYRANO. All unawares, a deadly snare, exquisite without concern to be so. A snare of nature's own, a musk-rose, in which ambush Love lies low. Who has seen her smile remembers the ineffable! There is not a thing so common but she turns it into prettiness; and in the merest nod or beck she can make manifest all the attributes of a goddess. No, Venus! you cannot step into your iridescent shell, nor, Dian, you, walk through the blossoming groves, as she steps into her chair and walks in Paris!

LE BRET. Sapristi! I understand! It is clear!

CYRANO. It is pellucid.

LE BRET. Magdeleine Robin, your cousin?

CYRANO. Yes, Roxane.

LE BRET. But, what could be better? You love her? Tell her so! You covered yourself with glory in her sight a moment since.

CYRANO. Look well at me, dear friend, and tell me how much hope you think can be justly entertained with this protuberance. Oh, I foster no illusions! . . . Sometimes, indeed, yes, in the violet dusk, I yield, even I! to a dreamy mood. I penetrate some garden that lies sweetening the hour. With my poor great devil of a nose I sniff the April . . . And as I follow with my eyes some woman passing with some cavalier, I think how dear would I hold having to walk beside me, linked like that, slowly, in the soft moonlight, such a one! I kindle—I forget—and then . . . then suddenly I see the shadow of my profile upon the garden-wall!

LE BRET. [*Touched.*] My friend . . .

CYRANO. Friend, I experience a bad half hour sometimes, in feeling so unsightly. . . and alone.

LE BRET. [*In quick sympathy, taking his hand.*] You weep?

CYRANO. Ah, God forbid! That? Never! No, that would be unsightly to excess! That a tear should course the whole length of this nose! Never, so long as I am accountable, shall the divine loveliness of tears be implicated with so much gross ugliness! Mark me well, nothing is so holy as are tears, nothing! and never shall it be that, rousing mirth through me, a single one of them shall seem ridiculous!

LE BRET. Come, do not despond! Love is a lottery.

CYRANO. [*Shaking his head.*] No! I love Cleopatra: do I resemble Cæsar? I worship Berenice: do I put you in mind of Titus?

LE BRET. But your courage . . . and your wit!—The little girl who but a moment ago bestowed on you that very modest meal, her eyes, you must have seen as much, did not exactly hate you!

CYRANO. [*Impressed.*] That is true!

LE BRET. You see? So, then!—But Roxane herself, in following your duel, went lily-pale.

CYRANO. Lily-pale? . . .

LE BRET. Her mind, her heart as well, are struck with wonder! Be bold, speak to her, in order that she may . . .

CYRANO. Laugh in my face! . . . No, there is but one thing upon earth I fear. . . . It is that.

THE DOORKEEPER. [*Admitting the* DUENNA *to* CYRANO.] Monsieur, you are inquired for.

CYRANO. [*Seeing the duenna.*] Ah, my God! . . . her duenna!

THE DUENNA. [*With a great curtsey.*] Somebody wishes to know of her valorous cousin where one may, in private, see him.

CYRANO. [*Upset.*] See me?

THE DUENNA. [*With curtsey.*] See you. There are things for your ear.

CYRANO. There are . . . ?

THE DUENNA. [*Another curtsey.*] Things.

CYRANO. [*Staggering.*] Ah, my God! . . .

THE DUENNA. Somebody intends, tomorrow, at the earliest roses of the dawn, to hear Mass at Saint Roch.

CYRANO. [*Upholds himself by leaning on* LE BRET.] Ah, my God!

THE DUENNA. That over, where might one step in a moment . . . have a little talk?

CYRANO. [*Losing his senses.*] Where? . . . I . . . But . . . Ah, my God!

THE DUENNA. Expedition, if you please.

CYRANO. I am casting about . . .

THE DUENNA. Where?

CYRANO. At . . . at . . . at Ragueneau's . . . the pastrycook's.

THE DUENNA. He lodges?

CYRANO. In . . . In Rue . . . Ah, my God! my God! . . . St. Honoré.

THE DUENNA. [*Retiring.*] We will be there. Do not fail. At seven.

CYRANO. I will not fail. [*Exit* DUENNA.

CYRANO. [*Falling on* LE BRET'S *neck.*] To me . . . from her . . . a meeting!

LE BRET. Well, your gloom is dispelled?

CYRANO. Oh, to whatever end it may be, she is aware of my existence!

LE BRET. And now you will be calm?

CYRANO. [*Beside himself.*] Now, I shall be fulminating and frenetical! I want an army all complete to put to rout! I have ten hearts and twenty arms . . . I cannot now be suited with felling dwarfs to earth. . . [*At the top of his lungs.*] Giants are what I want!

[*During the last lines, on the stage at the back, shadowy shapes of players have been moving about. The rehearsal has begun; the fiddlers have resumed their places.*

A VOICE. [*From the stage.*] Hey! Psst! Over there! A little lower. We are trying to rehearse!

CYRANO. [*Laughing.*] We are going.

[*He goes toward the back.*

[*Through the street door, enter* CUIGY, BRISSAILLE, *several* OFFICERS *supporting* LIGNIÈRE *in a state of complete intoxication.*

CUIGY. Cyrano!

CYRANO. What is this?

CUIGY. A drunken sot we are bringing you.

CYRANO. [*Recognizing him.*] Lignière! Hey, what has happened to you?

CUIGY. He is looking for you.

BRISSAILLE. He cannot go home.

CYRANO. Why?

LIGNIÈRE. [*In a thick voice, showing him a bit of crumpled paper.*] This note bids me beware . . . A hundred men against me . . . on account of lampoon. . . . Grave danger threatening me. . . . Porte de Nesle . . . must pass it to get home. Let me come and sleep under your roof.

CYRANO. A hundred, did you say?—You shall sleep at home!

LIGNIÈRE. [*Frightened.*] But . . .

CYRANO. [*In a terrible voice, pointing to the lighted lantern which the* DOORKEEPER *stands swinging as he listens to this scene.*] Take that lantern [LIGNIÈRE *hurriedly takes it*] and walk! . . . I swear to tuck you in your bed to-night myself. [*To the* OFFICERS.] You, follow at a distance. You may look on!

CUIGY. But a hundred men . . .

CYRANO. Are not one man too many for my mood to-night!

[*The players, in their several costumes, have stepped down from the stage and come nearer.*

LE BRET. But why take under your especial care . . .

CYRANO. Still Le Bret is not satisfied!

LE BRET. That most commonplace of sots?

CYRANO. [*Slapping* LIGNIÈRE *on the shoulder.*] Because this sot, this cask of muscatel, this hogshead of rosolio, did once upon a time a wholly pretty thing. On leaving Mass, having seen her whom he loved take holy-water, as the rite prescribes, he, whom the sight of water puts to flight, ran to the holy-water bowl, and stooping over, drank it dry. . . .

AN ACTRESS. [*In the costume of soubrette.*] *Tiens,* that was nice!

CYRANO. Was it not, soubrette?

THE SOUBRETTE. [*To the others.*] But why are they, a hundred, all against one poor poet?

CYRANO. Let us start! [*To the* OFFICERS.] And you, gentlemen, when you see me attack, whatever you may suppose to be my danger, do not stir to second me!

ANOTHER OF THE ACTRESSES. [*Jumping from the stage.*] Oh, I will not miss seeing this!

CYRANO. Come!

ANOTHER ACTRESS. [*Likewise jumping from the stage, to an elderly actor.*] Cassandre, will you not come?

CYRANO. Come, all of you! the Doctor, Isabel, Leander, all! and you shall lend, charming fantastic swarm, an air of Italian farce to the Spanish drama in view. Yes, you shall be a tinkling heard above a roar, like bells about a tambourine!

ALL THE WOMEN. [*In great glee.*] Bravo! . . . Hurry! . . . A mantle! . . . A hood!

JODELET. Let us go!

CYRANO. [*To the fiddlers.*] You will favor us with a tune, messieurs the violinists!

[*The fiddlers fall into the train. The lighted candles which furnished the footlights are seized and distributed. The procession becomes a torchlight procession.*

CYRANO. Bravo! Officers, beauty in fancy dress, and, twenty steps ahead . . . [*He takes the position he describes.*] I, by myself, under the feather stuck, with her own hand, by Glory, in my hat! Proud as a Scipio trebly Nasica!*—It is understood? Formal interdiction to interfere with me!—We are ready? One! Two! Three! Doorkeeper, open the door!

[*The* DOORKEEPER *opens wide the folding door. A picturesque corner of Old Paris appears, bathed in moonlight.*

CYRANO. Ah! . . . Paris floats in dim nocturnal mist. . . . The sloping bluish roofs are washed with moonlight. . . . A setting, exquisite indeed, offers itself for the scene about to be enacted. . . . Yonder, under silvery vapor wreaths, like a mysterious magic mirror, glimmers the Seine. . . . And you shall see what you shall see!

ALL. To the Porte de Nesle!

CYRANO. [*Standing on the threshold.*] To the Porte de Nesle! [*Before crossing it, he turns to the* SOUBRETTE.] Were you not asking, mademoiselle, why upon that solitary rhymster a hundred men were set? [*He draws his sword, and tranquilly.*] Because it was well known he is a friend of mine!

[*Exit.*

[*To the sound of the violins, by the flickering light of the candles, the procession*—LIGNIÈRE *staggering at the head, the* ACTRESSES *arm in arm with the* OFFICERS, *the players capering behind,—follows out into the night.*

CURTAIN

* Scipio Nasica was the leader of a successful revolt in Rome against the supporters of Tiberius Gracchus, B.C. 133.

## ACT SECOND

### THE COOKSHOP OF POETS

RAGUENEAU'S *shop, vast kitchen at the corner of Rue St. Honoré and Rue de l'Arbre-Sec, which can be seen at the back, through the glass door, gray in the early dawn.*

*At the left, in front, a counter overhung by a wrought-iron canopy from which geese, ducks, white peacocks are hanging. In large china jars, tall nosegays composed of the simpler flowers, mainly sunflowers. On the same side, in the middle distance, an enormous fireplace, in front of which, between huge andirons, each of which supports a small iron pot, roasting meats drip into appropriate pans.*

*At the right, door in the front wing. In the middle distance, a staircase leading to a loft, the interior of which is seen through open shutters; a spread table, lighted by a small Flemish candelabrum, shows it to be an eating-room. A wooden gallery continuing the stairway suggests other similar rooms to which it may lead.*

*In the center of the shop, an iron hoop—which can be lowered by means of a rope,—to which large roasts are hooked.*

*In the shadow, under the stairway, ovens are glowing. Copper molds and saucepans are shining; spits turning, hams swinging, pastry pyramids showing fair. It is the early beginning of the workday. Bustling of hurried scullions, portly cooks, and young cook's-assistants; swarming of caps decorated with hen feathers and guinea-fowl wings. Wicker crates and broad sheets of tin are brought in loaded with brioches and tarts.*

*There are tables covered with meats and cakes; others, surrounded by chairs, await customers. In a corner, a smaller table, littered with papers. At the rise of the curtain,* RAGUENEAU *is discovered seated at this table, writing with an inspired air, and counting upon his fingers.*

FIRST PASTRYCOOK. [*Bringing in a tall molded pudding.*] Nougat of fruit!

SECOND PASTRYCOOK. [*Bringing in the dish he names.*] Custard!

THIRD PASTRYCOOK. [*Bringing in a fowl roasted in its feathers.*] Peacock!

FOURTH PASTRYCOOK. [*Bringing in a tray of cakes.*] Mince-pies!

FIFTH PASTRYCOOK. [*Bringing in a deep earthen dish.*] Beef stew!

RAGUENEAU. [*Laying down his pen, and looking up.*] Daybreak already plates with silver the copper pans! Time, Ragueneau, to smother within thee the singing divinity! The hour of the lute will come anon—now is that of the ladle! [*He rises; speaking to one of the cooks.*] You, sir, be so good as to lengthen this gravy, —it is too thick!

THE COOK. How much?

RAGUENEAU. Three feet. [*Goes further.*

THE COOK. What does he mean?

FIRST PASTRYCOOK. Let me have the tart!

SECOND PASTRYCOOK. The dumpling!

RAGUENEAU. [*Standing before the fireplace.*] Spread thy wings, Muse, and fly further, that thy lovely eyes may not be reddened at the sordid kitchen fire! [*To one of the cooks, pointing at some small loaves of bread.*] You have improperly placed the cleft in those loaves; the cæsura belongs in the middle,—between the hemistichs! [*To another of the* COOKS, *pointing at an unfinished pastry.*] This pastry palace requires a roof! [*To a young cook's-apprentice, who, seated upon the floor, is putting fowls on a spit.*] And you, on that long spit, arrange, my son, in pleasing alternation, the modest pullet and the splendid turkey-cock,—even as our wise Malherbe alternated of old the greater with the lesser lines, and so with roasted fowls compose a poem!

ANOTHER APPRENTICE. [*Coming forward with a platter covered by a napkin.*] Master, in your honor, see what I have baked. . . . I hope you are pleased with it!

RAGUENEAU. [*Ecstatic.*] A lyre!

THE APPRENTICE. Of pie-crust!

RAGUENEAU. [*Touched.*] With candied fruits!

THE APPRENTICE. And the strings, see,—of spun sugar!

RAGUENEAU. [*Giving him money.*] Go, drink my health! [*Catching sight of* LISE *who is entering.*] Hush! My wife! . . . Move on, and hide that money. [*To* LISE, *showing her the lyre, with a constrained air.*] Fine, is it not?

LISE. Ridiculous!

[*She sets a pile of wrapping-paper on the counter.*

RAGUENEAU. Paper bags? Good. Thanks. [*He examines them.*] Heavens! My beloved books! The masterpieces of my friends,—dismembered,—torn!—to fashion paper bags for penny pies!—Ah, the abominable case is reënacted of Orpheus and the Mænads!*

* Orpheus was torn to pieces by Mænads, female attendants upon Dionysus, for neglect of women.

LISE. [*Drily.*] And have I not an unquestionable right to make what use I can of the sole payment ever got from your paltry scribblers of uneven lines?

RAGUENEAU. Pismire! Forbear to insult those divine, melodious crickets!

LISE. Before frequenting that low crew, my friend, you did not use to call me a Mænad,—no, nor yet a pismire!

RAGUENEAU. Put poems to such a use!

LISE. To that use and no other!

RAGUENEAU. If with poems you do this, I should like to know, Madame, what you do with prose!

[*Two children have come into the shop.*

RAGUENEAU. What can I do for you, little ones?

FIRST CHILD. Three patties.

RAGUENEAU. [*Waiting on them.*] There you are! Beautifully browned, and piping hot.

SECOND CHILD. Please, will you wrap them for us?

RAGUENEAU. [*Starting, aside.*] There goes one of my bags! [*To the children.*] You want them wrapped, do you? [*He takes one of the paper bags, and as he is about to put in the patties, reads.*] "*No otherwise, Ulysses from Penelope departing. . . .*" Not this one! [*He lays it aside and takes another. At the moment of putting in the patties, he reads.*] "*Phœbus of the aureate locks. . . .*" Not that one!

[*Same business.*

LISE. [*Out of patience.*] Well, what are you waiting for?

RAGUENEAU. Here we are. Here we are. Here we are. [*He takes a third bag and resigns himself.*] The sonnet to Phyllis! . . . It is hard, all the same.

LISE. It is lucky you made up your mind. [*Shrugging her shoulders.*] Nicodemus!

[*She climbs on a chair and arranges dishes on the sideboard.*

RAGUENEAU. [*Taking advantage of her back being turned, calls back the children who had already reached the door.*] Psst! . . . Children! Give me back the sonnet to Phyllis, and you shall have six patties instead of three! [*The children give back the paper-bag, joyfully take the patties and exeunt.* RAGUENEAU *smoothes out the crumpled paper and reads declaiming.*] "*Phyllis!*" . . . Upon that charming name, a grease-spot! . . . "*Phyllis!*" . . .

[*Enter brusquely* CYRANO.

CYRANO. What time is it?

RAGUENEAU. [*Bowing with eager deference.*] Six o'clock.

CYRANO. [*With emotion.*] In an hour!

[*He comes and goes in the shop.*

RAGUENEAU. [*Following him.*] Bravo! I too was witness. . . .

CYRANO. Of what?

RAGUENEAU. Your fight.

CYRANO. Which?

RAGUENEAU. At the Hôtel de Bourgogne.

CYRANO. [*With disdain.*] Ah, the duel!

RAGUENEAU. [*Admiringly.*] Yes,—the duel in rhyme.

LISE. He can talk of nothing else.

CYRANO. Let him! . . . It does no harm.

RAGUENEAU. [*Thrusting with a spit he has seized.*] "*At the last line, I hit!*" "*At the last line I hit!*"—How fine that is! [*With growing enthusiasm.*] "*At the last line, I ——*"

CYRANO. What time, Ragueneau?

RAGUENEAU. [*Remaining fixed in the attitude of thrusting, while he looks at the clock.*] Five minutes past six.—"*I hit!*" [*He recovers from his duelling posture.*] Oh, to be able to make a ballade!

LISE. [*To* CYRANO, *who in passing her counter has absentmindedly shaken hands with her.*] What ails your hand?

CYRANO. Nothing. A scratch.

RAGUENEAU. You have been exposed to some danger?

CYRANO. None whatever.

LISE. [*Shaking her finger at him.*] I fear that is a fib!

CYRANO. From the swelling of my nose? The fib in that case must have been good-sized. . . . [*In a different tone.*] I am expecting some one. You will leave us alone in here.

RAGUENEAU. But how can I contrive it? My poets shortly will be coming . . .

LISE. [*Ironically.*] For breakfast!

CYRANO. When I sign to you, you will clear the place of them.—What time is it?

RAGUENEAU. It is ten minutes past six.

CYRANO. [*Seating himself nervously at* RAGUENEAU'S *table and helping himself to paper.*] A pen?

RAGUENEAU. [*Taking one from behind his ear, and offering it.*] A swan's quill.

A MOUSQUETAIRE. [*With enormous moustachios, enters; in a stentorian voice.*] Good-morning!

[LISE *goes hurriedly to him, toward the back.*

CYRANO. [*Turning.*] What is it?

RAGUENEAU. A friend of my wife's,—a warrior,—terrible, from his own report.

CYRANO. [*Taking up the pen again, and waving* RAGUENEAU *away.*] Hush! . . . [*To himself.*] Write to her, . . . fold the letter, . . . hand it to her, . . . and make my escape. . . . [*Throwing down the pen.*] Coward! . . . But may I perish if I have the courage to speak to her, . . . to say a single word. . . . [*To* RAGUENEAU.] What time is it?

RAGUENEAU. A quarter past six.

CYRANO. [*Beating his breast.*] A single word of all I carry here! . . . Whereas in writing. . . . [*He takes up the pen again.*] Come, let us write it then, in very deed, the love-letter I have written in thought so many times, I have but to lay my soul beside my paper, and copy!

[*He writes.*

[*Beyond the glass-door, shadowy, lank, hesitating, shabby forms are seen moving. Enter the poets, clad in black, with hanging hose, sadly mudsplashed.*

LISE. [*Coming forward, to* RAGUENEAU.] Here they come, your scarecrows!

FIRST POET. [*Entering, to* RAGUENEAU.] Brother in art! . . .

SECOND POET. [*Shaking both* RAGUENEAU'S *hands.*] Dear fellow-bard. . . .

THIRD POET. Eagle of pastrycooks, [*sniffs the air*] your eyrie smells divine!

FOURTH POET. Phœbus turned baker!

FIFTH POET. Apollo master-cook!

RAGUENEAU. [*Surrounded, embraced, shaken by the hand.*] How at his ease a man feels at once with them!

FIRST POET. The reason we are late is the crowd at the Porte de Nesle!

SECOND POET. Eight ugly ruffians, ripped open with the sword, lie weltering on the pavement.

CYRANO. [*Raising his head a second.*] Eight? I thought there were only seven.

[*Goes on with his letter.*

RAGUENEAU. [*To* CYRANO.] Do you happen to know who is the hero of this event?

CYRANO. [*Negligently.*] I? . . . No.

LISE. [*To the* MOUSQUETAIRE.] Do you?

THE MOUSQUETAIRE. [*Turning up the ends of his mustache.*] Possibly!

CYRANO. [*Writing, from time to time he is heard murmuring a word or two.*] . . . "I love you . . ."

FIRST POET. A single man, we were told, put a whole gang to flight!

SECOND POET. Oh, it was a rare sight! The ground was littered with pikes, and cudgels. . . .

CYRANO. [*Writing.*] . . . "Your eyes . . ."

THIRD POET. Hats were strewn as far as the Goldsmiths' square!

FIRST POET. Sapristi! He must have been a madman of mettle. . . .

CYRANO. [*As above.*] ". . . your lips . . ."

FIRST POET. An infuriate giant, the doer of that deed!

CYRANO. [*Same business.*] ". . . but when I see you, I come near to swooning with a tender dread . . ."

SECOND POET. [*Snapping up a tart.*] What have you lately written, Ragueneau?

CYRANO. [*Same business.*] ". . . who loves you devotedly . . ." [*In the act of signing the letter, he stops, rises, and tucks it inside his doublet.*] No need to sign it. I deliver it myself.

RAGUENEAU. [*To* SECOND POET.] I have rhymed a recipe.

THIRD POET. [*Establishing himself beside a tray of cream puffs.*] Let us hear this recipe!

FOURTH POET. [*Examining a brioche of which he has possessed himself.*] It should not wear its cap so saucily on one side . . . it scarcely looks well! . . .

[*Bites off the top.*

First Poet. See, the spice-cake there, ogling a susceptible poet with eyes of almond under citron brows! . . .
[*He takes the spice cake.*

Second Poet. We are listening!

Third Poet. [*Slightly squeezing a cream puff between his fingers.*] This puff creams at the mouth. . . . I water!

Second Poet. [*Taking a bite out of the large pastry lyre.*] For once the Lyre will have filled my stomach!

Ragueneau. [*Who has made ready to recite, has coughed, adjusted his cap, struck an attitude.*] A recipe in rhyme!

Second Poet. [*To* First Poet, *nudging him.*] Is it breakfast, with you?

First Poet. [*To* Second Poet.] And with you, is it dinner?

Ragueneau. *How Almond Cheese-Cakes should be made.*

Briskly beat to lightness due,
Eggs, a few;
With the eggs so beaten, beat—
Nicely strained for this same use,—
Lemon-juice,
Adding milk of almonds, sweet.

With fine pastry dough, rolled flat,
After that,
Line each little scalloped mold;
Round the sides, light-fingered, spread
Marmalade;
Pour the liquid eggy gold,
Into each delicious pit;
Prison it
In the oven,—and, bye and bye,

Almond cheesecakes will in gay
Blond array
Bless your nostril and your eye!

THE POETS. [*Their mouths full.*] Exquisite! . . . Delicious!

ONE OF THE POETS. [*Choking.*] Humph!

[*They go toward the back, eating.* CYRANO, *who has been watching them, approaches* RAGUENEAU.

CYRANO. While you recite your works to them, have you a notion how they stuff?

RAGUENEAU. [*Low, with a smile.*] Yes, I see them . . . without looking, lest they should be abashed. I get a double pleasure thus from saying my verses over: I satisfy a harmless weakness of which I stand convicted, at the same time giving those who have not fed a needed chance to feed!

CYRANO. [*Slapping him on the shoulder.*] You, . . . I like you! [RAGUENEAU *joins his friends.* CYRANO *looks after him; then, somewhat sharply.*] Hey, Lise! [LISE, *absorbed in tender conversation with the* MOUSQUETAIRE, *starts and comes forward toward* CYRANO.] Is that captain . . . laying siege to you?

LISE. [*Offended.*] My eyes, sir, have ever with a glance been able to frown down those who meant hurt to my character. . . .

CYRANO. For eyes so resolute . . . I thought yours looked a little languishing!

LISE. [*Choking with anger.*] But . . .

CYRANO. [*Bluntly.*] I like your husband. Wherefore, Madame Lise, I say he shall not be sc . . . horned!

LISE. But . . .

CYRANO. [*Raising his voice so as to be heard by the* MOUSQUETAIRE.] A word to the wise!

[*He bows to the* MOUSQUETAIRE, *and after looking at the clock, goes to the door at the back and stands on watch.*

LISE. [*To the* MOUSQUETAIRE, *who has simply returned* CYRANO'S *bow.*] Really . . . I am astonished at you. . . . Defy him . . . to his face!

THE MOUSQUETAIRE. To his face, indeed! . . . to his face! . . .

[*He quickly moves off.* LISE *follows him.*

CYRANO. [*From the door at the back, signalling to* RAGUENEAU *that he should clear the room.*] Pst! . . .

RAGUENEAU. [*Urging the* POETS *toward the door at the right.*] We shall be much more comfortable in there. . . .

CYRANO. [*Impatiently.*] Pst! . . . Pst! . . .

RAGUENEAU. [*Driving along the* POETS.] I want to read you a little thing of mine. . . .

FIRST POET. [*Despairingly, his mouth full.*] But the provisions. . . .

SECOND POET. Shall not be parted from us!

[*They follow* RAGUENEAU *in procession, after making a raid on the eatables.*

CYRANO. If I feel that there is so much as a glimmer of hope . . . I will out with my letter! . . .

[ROXANE, *masked, appears behind the glass door followed by the* DUENNA.

CYRANO. [*Instantly opening the door.*] Welcome! [*Approaching the* DUENNA.] Madame, a word with you!

THE DUENNA. A dozen.

CYRANO. Are you fond of sweets?

THE DUENNA. To the point of indigestion!

CYRANO. [*Snatching some paper bags off the counter.*] Good. Here are two sonnets of Benserade's. . . .

THE DUENNA. Pooh!

CYRANO. Which I fill for you with grated almond drops.

THE DUENNA. [*With a different expression.*] Ha!

CYRANO. Do you look with favor upon the cate they call a trifle?

THE DUENNA. I affect it out of measure, when it has whipped cream inside.

CYRANO. Six shall be yours, thrown in with a poem by Saint-Amant. And in these verses of Chapelain I place this wedge of fruit-cake, light by the side of them. . . . Oh! And do you like tarts . . . little jam ones . . . fresh?

THE DUENNA. I dream of them at night!

CYRANO. [*Loading her arms with crammed paper bags.*] Do me the favor to go and eat these in the street.

THE DUENNA. But . . .

CYRANO. [*Pushing her out.*] And do not come back till you have finished! [*He closes the door upon her, comes forward toward* ROXANE, *and stands, bareheaded, at a respectful distance.*] Blessed forevermore among all hours the hour in which, remembering that so lowly a being still draws breath, you were so gracious as to come to tell me . . . to tell me? . . .

ROXANE. [*Who has removed her mask.*] First of all, that I thank you. For that churl, that coxcomb yesterday, whom you taught manners with your sword, is the one whom a great nobleman, who fancies himself in love with me. . . .

CYRANO. De Guiche?

ROXANE. [*Dropping her eyes.*] Has tried to force upon me as a husband.

CYRANO. Honorary? [*Bowing.*] It appears, then,

that I fought, and I am glad of it, not for my graceless nose, but your thrice-beautiful eyes.

Roxane. Further than that . . . I wished . . . But, before I can make the confession I have in mind to make, I must find in you once more the . . . almost brother, with whom as a child I used to play, in the park—do you remember?—by the lake!

Cyrano. I have not forgotten. Yes . . . you came every summer to Bergerac.

Roxane. You used to fashion lances out of reeds. . . .

Cyrano. The silk of the tasselled corn furnished hair for your doll . . .

Roxane. It was the time of long delightful games. . . .

Cyrano. And somewhat sour berries . . .

Roxane. The time when you did everything I bade you!

Cyrano. Roxane, wearing short frocks, was known as Magdeleine.

Roxane. Was I pretty in those days?

Cyrano. You were not ill-looking.

Roxane. Sometimes, in your venturesome climbings you used to hurt yourself. You would come running to me, your hand bleeding. And, playing at being your mamma, I would harden my voice and say . . . [*She takes his hand.*] "Will you never keep out of mischief?" [*She stops short, amazed.*] Oh, it is too much! Here you have done it again! [Cyrano *tries to draw back his hand.*] No! Let me look at it! . . . Aren't you ashamed! A great boy like you! . . . How did this happen, and where?

Cyrano. Oh, fun . . . near the Porte de Nesle.

Roxane. [*Sitting down at a table and dipping her handkerchief into a glass of water.*] Let me have it.

CYRANO. [*Sitting down too.*] So prettily, so cheeringly maternal!

ROXANE. And tell me, while I wash this naughty blood away . . . with how many were you fighting?

CYRANO. Oh, not quite a hundred.

ROXANE. Tell me about it.

CYRANO. No. What does it matter? You tell me, you . . . what you were going to tell me before, and did not dare . . .

ROXANE. [*Without releasing his hand.*] I do dare, now. I have breathed in courage with the perfume of the past. Oh, yes, now I dare. Here it is. There is someone whom I love.

CYRANO. Ah! . . .

ROXANE. Oh, he does not know it.

CYRANO. Ah! . . .

ROXANE. As yet. . . .

CYRANO. Ah! . . .

ROXANE. But if he does not know it, he soon will.

CYRANO. Ah! . . .

ROXANE. A poor boy who until now has loved me timidly, from a distance, without daring to speak. . . .

CYRANO. Ah! . . .

ROXANE. No, leave me your hand. It is hot, this will cool it. . . . But I have read his heart in his face.

CYRANO. Ah! . . .

ROXANE. [*Completing the bandaging of his hand with her small pocket-handkerchief.*] And, cousin, is it not a strange coincidence—that he should serve exactly in your regiment!

CYRANO. Ah! . . .

ROXANE. [*Laughing.*] Yes. He is a cadet, in the same company!

CYRANO. Ah! . . .

ROXANE. He bears plain on his forehead the stamp

of wit, of genius! He is proud, noble, young, brave, handsome. . . .

CYRANO. [*Rising, pale.*] Handsome! . . .

ROXANE. What . . . what is the matter?

CYRANO. With me? . . . Nothing! . . . It is . . . it is . . . [*Showing his hand, smiling.*] You know! . . . It smarts a little . . .

ROXANE. In short, I love him. I must tell you, however, that I have never seen him save at the play.

CYRANO. Then you have never spoken to each other?

ROXANE. Only with our eyes.

CYRANO. But, then . . . how can you know? . . .

ROXANE. Oh, under the lindens of Place Royale, people will talk. A trustworthy gossip told me many things!

CYRANO. A cadet, did you say?

ROXANE. A cadet, in your company.

CYRANO. His name?

ROXANE. Baron Christian de Neuvillette.

CYRANO. What? He is not in the cadets.

ROXANE. He is! He certainly is, since morning. Captain Carbon de Castel-Jaloux.

CYRANO. And quickly, quickly, she throws away her heart! . . . But my poor little girl . . .

THE DUENNA. [*Opening the door at the back.*] Monsieur de Bergerac, I have eaten them, every one!

CYRANO. Now read the poetry printed upon the bags! [*The* DUENNA *disappears.*] My poor child, you who can endure none but the choicest language, who savor eloquence and wit, . . . if he should be a barbarian!

ROXANE. No! no! . . . He has hair like one of D'Urfé's heroes!

CYRANO. If he had on proof as homely a wit as he has pretty hair!

ROXANE. No! No! . . . I can see at a single glance, his utterances are fine, pointed . . .

CYRANO. Ah, yes! A man's utterances are invariably like his mustache! . . . Still, if he *were* a ninny? . . .

ROXANE. [*Stamping with her foot.*] I should die, there!

CYRANO. [*After a time.*] You bade me come here that you might tell me this? I scarcely see the appropriateness, Madame.

ROXANE. Ah, it was because someone yesterday let death into my soul by telling me that in your company you are all Gascons, . . . all!

CYRANO. And that we pick a quarrel with every impudent fledgling, not Gascon, admitted by favor to our thoroughbred Gascon ranks? That is what you heard?

ROXANE. Yes, and you can imagine how distracted I am for him!

CYRANO. [*In his teeth.*] You well may be!

ROXANE. But I thought, yesterday, when you towered up, great and invincible, giving his due to that miscreant, standing your ground against those caitiffs, I thought "Were he but willing, he of whom all are in awe . . ."

CYRANO. Very well, I will protect your little baron.

ROXANE. Ah, you will . . . you will protect him for me? . . . I have always felt for you the tenderest regard!

CYRANO. Yes, yes.

ROXANE. You will be his friend?

CYRANO. I will!

ROXANE. And never shall he have to fight a duel?

CYRANO. I swear it.

ROXANE. Oh, I quite love you! . . . Now I must go. [*She hurriedly resumes her mask, throws a veil over her head; says absentmindedly.*] But you have not yet told me about last night's encounter. It must have been amazing! . . . Tell him to write to me. [*She kisses her hand to him.*] I love you dearly!

CYRANO. Yes, yes.

ROXANE. A hundred men against you? . . . Well, adieu. We are fast friends.

CYRANO. Yes, yes.

ROXANE. Tell him to write me! . . . A hundred men! you shall tell me another time. I must not linger now . . . A hundred men! What a heroic thing to do!

CYRANO. [*Bowing.*] Oh, I have done better since!

[*Exit* ROXANE. CYRANO *stands motionless, staring at the ground. Silence. The door at the right opens.* RAGUENEAU *thrusts in his head.*

RAGUENEAU. May we come back?

CYRANO. [*Without moving.*] Yes . . .

[RAGUENEAU *beckons, his friends come in again. At the same time, in the doorway at the back, appears* CARBON DE CASTEL-JALOUX, *costume of a Captain of the Guards. On seeing* CYRANO, *he gesticulates exaggeratedly by way of signal to someone out of sight.*

CARBON DE CASTEL-JALOUX. He is here!

CYRANO. [*Looking up.*] Captain!

CARBON DE CASTEL-JALOUX. [*Exultant.*] Hero! We know all! . . . About thirty of my cadets are out there! . . .

CYRANO. [*Drawing back.*] But . . .

CARBON DE CASTEL-JALOUX. [*Trying to lead him off.*] Come! . . . You are in request!

CYRANO. No!

CARBON DE CASTEL-JALOUX. They are drinking across the way, at the Cross of the Hilt.

CYRANO. I . . .

CARBON DE CASTEL-JALOUX. [*Going to the door and shouting toward the street corner, in a voice of thunder.*] The hero refuses. He is not in the humor!

A VOICE. [*Outside.*] Ah, *sandious!* . . .

[*Tumult outside, noise of clanking swords and of boots drawing nearer.*

CARBON DE CASTEL-JALOUX. [*Rubbing his hands.*] Here they come, across the street. . . .

THE CADETS. [*Entering the cookshop.*] *Mille dious!* . . . *Capdedious!* . . . *Mordious!* . . . *Pocapdedious!** . . .

RAGUENEAU. [*Backing in alarm.*] Messieurs, are you all natives of Gascony?

THE CADETS. All!

ONE OF THE CADETS. [*To* CYRANO.] Bravo!

CYRANO. Baron.

OTHER CADET. [*Shaking both* CYRANO'S *hands.*] Vivat!

CYRANO. Baron!

THIRD CADET. Let me hug you to my heart!

CYRANO. Baron!

SEVERAL GASCONS. Let us hug him!

CYRANO. [*Not knowing which one to answer.*] Baron! . . . baron! . . . your pardon!

RAGUENEAU. Messieurs, are you all barons?

THE CADETS. All!

RAGUENEAU. Are they truly?

FIRST CADET. Our coats of arms piled up would dwindle in the clouds!

LE BRET. [*Entering, running to* CYRANO.] They are loking for you! A crowd, gone mad as March, led by those who were with you last night.

CYRANO. [*Alarmed.*] You never told them where to find me? . . .

LE BRET. [*Rubbing his hands.*] I did.

* Oaths in the Gascon dialect.

A BURGHER. [*Entering, followed by a number of others.*] Monsieur, the Marais is coming in a body!

[*The street outside has filled with people. Sedan-chairs, coaches stop before the door.*

LE BRET. [*Smiling, low to* CYRANO.] And Roxane?

CYRANO. [*Quickly.*] Be quiet!

THE CROWD. [*Outside.*] Cyrano!

[*A rabble bursts into the cookshop. Confusion. Shouting.*

RAGUENEAU. [*Standing upon a table.*] My shop is invaded! They are breaking everything! It is glorious!

PEOPLE. [*Pressing round* CYRANO.] My friend . . . my friend. . . .

CYRANO. I had not so many friends . . . yesterday!

LE BRET. This is success!

A YOUNG MARQUIS. [*Running toward* CYRANO, *with outstretched hands.*] If you knew, my dear fellow . . .

CYRANO. Dear? . . . Fellow? . . . Where was it we stood sentinel together?

OTHER MARQUIS. I wish to present you, sir, to several ladies, who are outside in my coach. . . .

CYRANO. [*Coldly.*] But you, to me, by whom will you first be presented?

LE BRET. [*Astonished.*] But what is the matter with you?

CYRANO. Be still!

A MAN OF LETTERS. [*With an inkhorn.*] Will you kindly favor me with the details of . . .

CYRANO. No.

LE BRET. [*Nudging him.*] That is Theophrastus Renaudot, the inventor of the gazette.

CYRANO. Enough!

LE BRET. A sheet close packed with various information! It is an idea, they say, likely to take firm root and flourish!

A POET. [*Coming forward.*] Monsieur . . .

CYRANO. Another!

THE POET. I am anxious to make a pentacrostic on your name.

SOMEBODY ELSE. [*Likewise approaching* CYRANO.] Monsieur . . .

CYRANO. Enough, I say!

[*At the gesture of impatience which* CYRANO *cannot repress, the crowd draws away.* DE GUICHE *appears, escorted by officers; among them* CUIGY, BRISSAILLE, *those who followed* CYRANO *at the end of the first act.* CUIGY *hurries toward* CYRANO.

CUIGY. [*To* CYRANO.] Monsieur de Guiche! [*Murmurs. Every one draws back.*] He comes at the request of the Marshal de Gaussion.

DE GUICHE. [*Bowing to* CYRANO.] Who wishes to express his admiration for your latest exploit, the fame of which has reached him.

THE CROWD. Bravo!

CYRANO. [*Bowing.*] The Marshal is qualified to judge of courage.

DE GUICHE. He would scarcely have believed the report, had these gentlemen not been able to swear they had seen the deed performed.

CUIGY. With our own eyes!

LE BRET. [*Low to* CYRANO, *who wears an abstracted air.*] But . . .

CYRANO. Be silent!

LE BRET. You appear to be suffering . . .

CYRANO. [*Starting, and straightening himself.*] Before these people? . . . [*His mustache bristles; he expands his chest.*] I . . . suffering? . . . You shall see!

DE GUICHE. [*In whose ear* CUIGY *has been whis-*

*pering.*] But this is by no means the first gallant achievement marking your career. You serve in the madcap Gascon company, do you not?

CYRANO. In the cadets, yes.

ONE OF THE CADETS. [*In a great voice.*] Among his countrymen!

DE GUICHE. [*Considering the* GASCONS, *in line behind* CYRANO.] Ah, ha!—All these gentlemen then of the formidable aspect, are the famous . . .

CARBON DE CASTEL-JALOUX. Cyrano!

CYRANO. Captain? . . .

CARBON DE CASTEL-JALOUX. My company, I believe, is here in total. Be so obliging as to present it to the Count.

CYRANO. [*Taking a step toward* DE GUICHE, *and pointing at the* CADETS.]

They are the Gascony Cadets
Of Carbon de Castel-Jaloux;
Famed fighters, liars, desperates,
They are the Gascony Cadets!
All, better-born than pickpockets,
Talk couchant, rampant, . . . pendent, too!
They are the Gascony Cadets
Of Carbon de Castel-Jaloux!

Cat-whiskered, eyed like falconets,
Wolf-toothed and heron-legged, they hew
The rabble down that snarls and threats . . .
Cat-whiskered, eyed like falconets!
Great pomp of plume hides and offsets
Holes in those hats they wear askew . . .
Cat-whiskered, eyed like falconets,
They drive the snarling mob, and hew!

The mildest of their sobriquets
Are Crack-my-crown and Run-me-through;
Mad drunk on glory Gascon gets!
These boasters of soft sobriquets
Wherever rapier rapier whets
Are met in punctual rendezvous. . . .
The mildest of their sobriquets
Are Crack-my-crown and Run-me-through!

They are the Gascony Cadets
That give the jealous spouse his due!
Lean forth, adorable coquettes,
They are the Gascony Cadets,
With plumes and scarfs and aigulets!
The husband gray may well look blue. . . .
They are the Gascony Cadets
That give the jealous spouse his due!

De Guiche. [*Nonchalantly seated in an armchair which* Ragueneau *has hurriedly brought for him.*] A gentleman provides himself to-day, by way of luxury, with a poet. May I look upon you as mine?

Cyrano. No, your lordship, as nobody's.

De Guiche. My uncle Richelieu yesterday found your spontaneity diverting. I shall be pleased to be of use to you with him.

Le Bret. [*Dazzled.*] Great God!

De Guiche. I cannot think I am wrong in supposing that you have rhymed a tragedy?

Le Bret. [*Whispering to* Cyrano.] My boy, your Agrippina will be played!

De Guiche. Take it to him. . . .

Cyrano. [*Tempted and pleased.*] Really . . .

De Guiche. He has taste in such matters. He will

no more than, here and there, alter a word, recast a passage. . . .

CYRANO. [*Whose face has instantly darkened.*] Not to be considered, monsieur! My blood runs cold at the thought of a single comma added or suppressed.

DE GUICHE. On the other hand, my dear sir, when a verse finds favor with him, he pays for it handsomely.

CYRANO. He scarcely can pay me as I pay myself, when I have achieved a verse to my liking, by singing it over to myself!

DE GUICHE. You are proud.

CYRANO. You have observed it?

ONE OF THE CADETS. [*Coming in with a number of disreputable, draggled tattered hats threaded on his sword.*] Look, Cyrano! at the remarkable feathered game we secured this morning near the Porte de Nesle! The hats of the fugitives!

CARBON DE CASTEL-JALOUX. *Spolia opima!*

ALL. [*Laughing.*] Ha! Ha! Ha! . . .

CUIGY. The one who planned that military action, my word! must be proud of it to-day!

BRISSAILLE. Is it known who did it?

DE GUICHE. I!— [*The laughter stops short.*] They had instructions to chastise—a matter one does not attend to in person,—a drunken scribbler.

[*Constrained silence.*

THE CADET. [*Under breath, to* CYRANO, *indicating the hats.*] What can we do with them? They are oily. . . . Make them into a hotch pot?

CYRANO. [*Taking the sword with the hats, and bowing, as he shakes them off at* DE GUICHE'S *feet.*] Monsieur, if you should care to return them to your friends? . . .

DE GUICHE. [*Rises, and in a curt tone.*] My chair

and bearers, at once. [*To* CYRANO, *violently*.] As for you, sir . . .

A VOICE. [*In the street, shouting.*] The chairmen of Monseigneur the Comte de Guiche!

DE GUICHE. [*Who has recovered control over himself, with a smile.*] Have you read Don Quixote?

CYRANO. I have. And at the name of that divine madman, I uncover . . .

DE GUICHE. My advice to you is to ponder. . . .

A CHAIRMAN. [*Appearing at the back.*] The chair is at the door!

DE GUICHE. The chapter of the wind mills.

CYRANO. [*Bowing.*] Chapter thirteen.

DE GUICHE. For when a man attacks them, it often happens. . . .

CYRANO. I have attacked, am I to infer, a thing that veers with every wind?

DE GUICHE. That one of their far-reaching canvas arms pitches him down into the mud!

CYRANO. Or up among the stars!

[*Exit* DE GUICHE. *He is seen getting into his chair. The gentlemen withdraw whispering.* LE BRET *goes to the door with them. The crowd leaves. The* CADETS *remain seated at the right and left at tables where food and drink is brought to them.*

CYRANO. [*Bowing with a derisive air to those who leave without daring to take leave of him.*] Gentlemen . . . gentlemen . . . gentlemen. . . .

LE BRET. [*Coming forward, greatly distressed, lifting his hands to Heaven.*] Oh, in what a pretty pair of shoes. . . .

CYRANO. Oh, you! . . . I expect you to grumble!

LE BRET. But yourself, you will agree with me that

invariably to cut the throat of opportunity becomes an exaggeration! . . .

CYRANO. Yes. I agree. I do exaggerate.

LE BRET. [*Triumphant.*] You see, you admit it! . . .

CYRANO. But for the sake of principle, and of example, as well, I think it a good thing to exaggerate as I do!

LE BRET. Could you but leave apart, once in a while, your mousquetaire of a soul, fortune, undoubtedly, fame. . . .

CYRANO. And what should a man do? Seek some grandee, take him for patron, and like the obscure creeper clasping a tree-trunk, and licking the bark of that which props it up, attain to height by craft instead of strength? No, I thank you. Dedicate, as they all do, poems to financiers? Wear motley in the humble hope of seeing the lips of a minister distend for once in a smile not ominous of ill? No, I thank you. Eat every day a toad? Be threadbare at the belly with groveling? Have his skin dirty soonest at the knees? Practice feats of dorsal elasticity? No, I thank you. With one hand stroke the goat while with the other he waters the cabbage? Make gifts of senna that counter-gifts of rhubarb may accrue, and indefatigably swing his censer in some beard? No, I thank you. Push himself from lap to lap, become a little great man in a great little circle, propel his ship with madrigals for oars and in his sails the sighs of the elderly ladies? No, I thank you. Get the good editor Sercy to print his verses at proper expense? No, I thank you. Contrive to be nominated Pope in conclaves held by imbeciles in wine-shops? No, I thank you. Work to construct a name upon the basis of a sonnet, instead of constructing other sonnets? No, I thank you. Discover talent in tyros, and in them alone? Stand in terror of what gazettes may please to say, and say to himself "At whatever cost, may I figure in the Paris Mercury!" No, I thank you. Calculate, cringe, peak, prefer making a call to a poem,—petition, solicit, apply? No, I thank you! No, I thank you! No, I thank you! But . . . sing, dream, laugh, loaf, be single, be free, have eyes that look squarely, a voice with a ring; wear, if he chooses, his hat hindside afore; for a yes, for a no, fight a duel or turn a ditty! . . . Work, without concern of fortune or of glory, to accomplish the heart's-desired journey to the moon! Put forth nothing that has not its spring in the very heart, yet, modest, say to himself, "Old man, be satisfied with blossoms, fruits, yea, leaves alone, so they be gathered in your garden and not another man's!" Then, if it happen that to some small extent he triumph, be obliged to render of the glory, to Cæsar not one jot, but honestly appropriate it all. In short, scorning to be the parasite, the creeper, if even failing to be the oak, rise, not perchance to a great height, . . . but rise alone!

Le Bret. Alone? Good! but not one against all! How the devil did you contract the mania that possesses you for making enemies, always, everywhere?

Cyrano. By seeing you make friends, and smile to those same flocks of friends with a mouth that takes for model an old purse! I wish not to be troubled to return bows in the street, and I exclaim with glee "An enemy the more!"

Le Bret. This is mental aberration!

Cyrano. I do not dispute it. I am so framed. To displease is my pleasure. I love that one should hate me. Dear friend, if you but knew how much better a man walks under the exciting fire of hostile eyes, and how amused he may become over the spots on his doublet, spattered by Envy and Cowardice! . . . You, the facile friendship wherewith you surround yourself, resembles those wide Italian collars, loose and easy, with a perforated pattern, in which the neck looks like a woman's. They are more comfortable, but of less high effect; for the brow not held in proud position by any constraint from them, falls to nodding this way and that. . . . But for me every day Hatred starches and flutes the ruff whose stiffness holds the head well in place. Every new enemy is another plait in it, adding compulsion, but adding, as well, a ray: for, similar in every point to the Spanish ruff, Hatred is a bondage, . . . but is a halo, too!

LE BRET. [*After a pause, slipping his arm through* CYRANO'S.] To the hearing of all be proud and bitter, . . . but to me, below breath, say simply that she does not love you!

CYRANO. [*Sharply.*] Not a word!

[CHRISTIAN *has come in and mingled with the cadets; they ignore him; he has finally gone to a little table by himself, where* LISE *waits on him.*

ONE OF THE CADETS. [*Seated at a table at the back, glass in hand.*] Hey, Cyrano! [CYRANO *turns toward him.*] Your story!

CYRANO. Presently!

[*He goes toward the back on* LE BRET'S *arm. They talk low.*

THE CADET. [*Rising and coming toward the front.*] The account of your fight! It will be the best lesson [*stopping in front of the table at which* CHRISTIAN *is sitting*] for this timorous novice!

CHRISTIAN. [*Looking up.*] . . . Novice?

OTHER CADET. Yes, sickly product of the North!

CHRISTIAN. Sickly?

FIRST CADET. [*Impressively.*] Monsieur de Neuvillette, it is a good deed to warn you that there is a thing no more to be mentioned in our company than rope in the house of the hanged!

CHRISTIAN. And what is it?

OTHER CADET. [*In a terrifying voice.*] Look at me! [*Three times, darkly, he places his finger upon his nose.*] You have understood?

CHRISTIAN. Ah, it is the . . .

OTHER CADET. Silence! . . . Never must you so much as breathe that word, or . . . [*He points toward* CYRANO *at the back talking with* LE BRET.] You will have him, over there, to deal with!

OTHER CADET. [*Who while* CHRISTIAN *was turned toward the first, has noiselessly seated himself on the table behind him.*] Two persons were lately cut off in their pride by him for talking through their noses. He thought it personal.

OTHER CADET. [*In a cavernous voice, as he rises from under the table where he had slipped on all fours.*] Not the remotest allusion, ever, to the fatal cartilage, . . . unless you fancy an early grave!

OTHER CADET. A word will do the business! What did I say? . . . A word? . . . A simple gesture! Make use of your pocket-handerchief, you will shortly have use for your shroud!

[*Silence. All around* CHRISTIAN *watch him, with folded arms. He rises and goes to* CARBON DE CASTEL-JALOUX, *who, in conversation with an officer, affects to notice nothing.*

CHRISTIAN. Captain!

CARBON. [*Turning and looking him rather contemptuously up and down.*] Monsieur?

CHRISTIAN. What is the proper course for a man when he finds gentlemen of the South too boastful?

CARBON DE CASTEL-JALOUX. He must prove to them that one can be of the North, yet brave.

[*He turns his back upon him.*

CHRISTIAN. I am much obliged.

FIRST CADET. [*To* CYRANO.] And now, the tale of your adventure!

ALL. Yes, yes, now let us hear!

CYRANO. [*Coming forward among them.*] My adventure? [*All draw their stools nearer, and sit around him, with craned necks.* CHRISTIAN *sits astride a chair.*] Well, then, I was marching to meet them. The moon up in the skies was shining like a silver watch, when suddenly I know not what careful watch-maker having wrapped it in a cottony cloud, there occurred the blackest imaginable night; and, the streets being nowise lighted,—*mordious!*—you could see no further than . . .

CHRISTIAN. Your nose.

[*Silence. Everyone slowly gets up; all look with terror at* CYRANO. *He has stopped short, amazed. Pause.*

CYRANO. Who is that man?

ONE OF THE CADETS. [*Low.*] He joined this morning.

CYRANO. [*Taking a step toward* CHRISTIAN.] This morning?

CARBON DE CASTEL-JALOUX. [*Low.*] His name is Baron de Neuvill. . . .

CYRANO. [*Stopping short.*] Ah, very well. . . . [*He turns pale, then red, gives evidence of another impulse to throw himself upon* CHRISTIAN.] I . . . [*He conquers it, and says in a stifled voice.*] Very well. [*He takes up his tale.*] As I was saying . . . [*with a burst of rage.*] *Mordious!* . . . [*He continues in a natural tone*] one could not see in the very least. [*Consternation. All resume their seats, staring at one an-*

*other.*] And I was walking along, reflecting that for a very insignificant rogue I was probably about to offend some great prince who would bear me a lasting grudge, that, in brief, I was about to thrust my . . .

CHRISTIAN. Nose . . .

[*All get up.* CHRISTIAN *has tilted his chair and is rocking on the hind legs.*

CYRANO. [*Choking.*] Finger . . . between the tree and the bark;* for the aforesaid prince might be of sufficient power to trip me and throw me . . .

CHRISTIAN. On my nose . . .

CYRANO. [*Wipes the sweat from his brow.*] But, said I, "Gascony forward! Never falter when duty prompts! Forward, Cyrano!" and, saying this, I advance—when suddenly, in the darkness, I barely avoid a blow . . .

CHRISTIAN. Upon the nose . . .

CYRANO. I ward it. . . . and thereupon find myself . . .

CHRISTIAN. Nose to nose . . .

CYRANO. [*Springing toward him.*] *Ventre-Saint-Gris!* . . . [*All the* GASCONS *rush forward, to see;* CYRANO, *on reaching* CHRISTIAN, *controls himself and proceeds*] . . . with a hundred drunken brawlers, smelling . . .

CHRISTIAN. To the nose's limit . . .

CYRANO. [*Deathly pale, and smiling.*] . . . Of garlic and of grease. I leap forward, head lowered . . .

CHRISTIAN. Nose to the wind! . . .

CYRANO. And I charge them. I knock two breathless and run a third through the body. One lets off at me: Paf! and I retort . . .

CHRISTIAN. Pif!

* *Entre l'arbre et l'écorce il ne faut pas mettre le doigt* is the French proverb.

CYRANO. [*Exploding.*] Death and damnation! Go —all of you!

[*All the* CADETS *make for the door.*

FIRST CADET. The tiger is roused at last!

CYRANO. All! and leave me with this man.

SECOND CADET. *Bigre!* When we see him again, it will be in the shape of mince-meat!

RAGUENEAU. Mince-meat? . . .

OTHER CADET. In one of your pies.

RAGUENEAU. I feel myself grow white and flabby as a table-napkin!

CARBON DE CASTEL-JALOUX. Let us go!

OTHER CADET. Not a smudge of him will be left!

OTHER CADET. What these walls are about to behold gives me gooseflesh to think upon!

OTHER CADET. [*Closing the door at the right.*] Ghastly! . . . Ghastly!

[*All have left, by the back or the sides, a few up the stairway.* CYRANO *and* CHRISTIAN *remain face to face, and look at each other a moment.*

CYRANO. Embrace me!

CHRISTIAN. Monsieur . . .

CYRANO. Brave fellow.

CHRISTIAN. But what does this . . .

CYRANO. Very brave fellow. I wish you to.

CHRISTIAN. Will you tell me? . . .

CYRANO. Embrace me, I am her brother.

CHRISTIAN. Whose?

CYRANO. Hers!

CHRISTIAN. What do you mean?

CYRANO. Roxane's!

CHRISTIAN. [*Running to him.*] Heavens! You, her brother?

CYRANO. Or the same thing: her first cousin.

CHRISTIAN. And she has . . .

CYRANO. Told me everything!

CHRISTIAN. Does she love me?

CYRANO. Perhaps!

CHRISTIAN. [*Seizing his hands.*] How happy I am, monsieur, to make your acquaintance! . . .

CYRANO. That is what I call a sudden sentiment!

CHRISTIAN. Forgive me! . . .

CYRANO. [*Looking at him, laying his hand upon his shoulder.*] It is true that he is handsome, the rascal!

CHRISTIAN. If you but knew, Monsieur, how greatly I admire you! . . .

CYRANO. But all those noses which you . . .

CHRISTIAN. I take them back!

CYRANO. Roxane expects a letter to-night . . .

CHRISTIAN. Alas!

CYRANO. What is the matter?

CHRISTIAN. I am lost if I cease to be dumb!

CYRANO. How is that?

CHRISTIAN. Alas! I am such a dunce that I could kill myself for shame!

CYRANO. But, no . . . no. . . . You are surely not a dunce, if you believe you are! Besides, you scarcely attacked me like a dunce.

CHRISTIAN. Oh, it is easy to find words in mounting to the assault! Indeed, I own to a certain cheap military readiness, but when I am before women, I have not a word to say. . . . Yet their eyes, when I pass by, express a kindness toward me. . . .

CYRANO. And do their hearts not express the same when you stop beside them?

CHRISTIAN. No! . . . for I am of those—I recognize it, and am dismayed!—who do not know how to talk of love.

CYRANO. *Tiens!* . . . It seems to me that if Nature

had taken more pains with my shape, I should have been of those who do know how to talk of it.

CHRISTIAN. Oh, to be able to express things gracefully!

CYRANO. Oh, to be a graceful little figure of a passing mousquetaire!

CHRISTIAN. Roxane is a précieuse, . . . there is no chance but that I shall be a disillusion to Roxane!

CYRANO. [*Looking at* CHRISTIAN.] If I had to express my soul, such an interpreter! . . .

CHRISTIAN. [*Desperately.*] I ought to have eloquence! . . .

CYRANO. [*Abruptly.*] Eloquence I will lend you! . . . And you, to me, shall lend all-conquering physical charm . . . and between us we will compose a hero of romance!

CHRISTIAN. What?

CYRANO. Should you be able to say as your own, things which I day by day would teach you?

CHRISTIAN. You are suggesting? . . .

CYRANO. Roxane shall not have disillusions! Tell me, shall we win her heart, we two as one? will you submit to feel, transmitted from my leather doublet into your doublet stitched with silk, the soul I wish to share?

CHRISTIAN. But Cyrano! . . .

CYRANO. Christian, will you?

CHRISTIAN. You frighten me!

CYRANO. Since you fear, left to yourself, to chill her heart, will you consent,—and soon it will take fire, I vouch for it!—to contribute your lips to my phrases?

CHRISTIAN. Your eyes shine! . . .

CYRANO. Will you?

CHRISTIAN. What, would it please you so much?

CYRANO. [*With rapture.*] It would . . . [*Remembering, and confining himself to expressing an artistic pleasure*] . . . amuse me! It is an experiment fit surely to tempt a poet. Will you complete me, and let me in exchange complete you? We will walk side by side: you in full light, I in your shadow. . . . I will be wit to you . . . you, to me, shall be good looks!

CHRISTIAN. But the letter, which should be sent to her without delay? . . . Never shall I be able . . .

CYRANO. [*Taking from his doublet the letter written in the first part of the act.*] The letter? Here it is!

CHRISTIAN. How? . . .

CYRANO. It only wants the address.

CHRISTIAN. I . . .

CYRANO. You can send it without uneasiness. It is a good letter.

CHRISTIAN. You had? . . .

CYRANO. You shall never find us—poets!—without epistles in our pockets to the Chlorises . . . of our imagining! For we are those same that have for mistress a dream blown into the bubble of a name! Take, —you shall convert this feigning into earnest; I was sending forth at random these confessions and laments: you shall make the wandering birds to settle . . . Take it! You shall see . . . I was as eloquent as if I had been sincere! Take, and have done!

CHRISTIAN. But will it not need to be altered in any part? . . . Written without object, will it fit Roxane?

CYRANO. Like a glove!

CHRISTIAN. But . . .

CYRANO. Trust to the blindness of love . . . and vanity! Roxane will never question that it was written for her.

CHRISTIAN. Ah, my friend!

[*He throws himself into* CYRANO'S *arms. They stand embraced.*

ONE OF THE CADETS. [*Opening the door a very*

*little.*] Nothing more. . . . The stillness of death. . . . I dare not look . . . [*He thrusts in his head.*] What is this?

ALL THE CADETS. [*Entering and seeing* CYRANO *and* CHRISTIAN *locked in each other's arms.*] Ah! . . . Oh! . . .

ONE OF THE CADETS. This passes bounds!

[*Consternation.*

THE MOUSQUETAIRE. [*Impudent.*] *Ouais?*

CARBON DE CASTEL-JALOUX. Our demon is waxen mild as an apostle; smitten upon one nostril, he turns the other also!

THE MOUSQUETAIRE. It is in order now to speak of his nose, is it? [*Calling* LISE, *with a swaggering air.*] Hey, Lise! now listen and look. [*Pointedly sniffing the air.*] Oh, . . . oh, . . . it is surprising! . . . what an odor! [*Going to* CYRANO.] But monsieur must have smelled it, too? Can you tell me what it is, so plain in the air?

CYRANO. [*Beating him.*] Why, sundry blows!

[*Joyful antics of the* CADETS *in beholding* CYRANO *himself again.*

CURTAIN

## ACT THIRD

### ROXANE'S KISS

*A small square in the old Marais. Old-fashioned houses. Narrow streets seen in perspective. At the right,* ROXANE'S *house and the wall of her garden, above which spreading tree-tops. Over the house-door, a balcony and window. A bench beside the door-step.*

*The wall is overclambered by ivy, the balcony wreathed with jasmine.*

*By means of the bench and projecting stones in the wall, the balcony can easily be scaled.*

*On the opposite side, old house in the same style of architecture, brick and stone, with entrance-door. The door-knocker is swaddled in linen.*

*At the rise of the curtain, the* DUENNA *is seated on the bench. The window on* ROXANE'S *balcony is wide open.*

RAGUENEAU, *in a sort of livery, stands near the* DUENNA; *he is finishing the tale of his misfortunes, drying his eyes.*

RAGUENEAU. And then, she eloped with a mousquetaire! Ruined, forsaken, I was hanging myself. I had already taken leave of earth, when Monsieur de Bergerac happening along, unhanged me, and proposed me to his cousin as her steward. . . .

THE DUENNA. But how did you fall into such disaster?

RAGUENEAU. Lise was fond of soldiers, I, of poets!

Mars ate up all left over by Apollo. Under those circumstances, you conceive, the pantry soon was bare.

THE DUENNA. [*Rising and calling toward the open window.*] Roxane, are you ready? . . . They are waiting for us! . . .

ROXANE'S VOICE. [*Through the window.*] I am putting on my mantle!

THE DUENNA. [*To* RAGUENEAU, *pointing at the door opposite.*] It is over there, opposite, we are expected. At Clomire's. She holds a meeting in her little place. A disquisition upon the Softer Sentiments is to be read.

RAGUENEAU. Upon the Softer Sentiments.

THE DUENNA. [*Coyly.*] Yes! . . . [*Calling toward the window.*] Roxane, you must make haste, or we shall miss the disquisition upon the Softer Sentiments!

ROXANE'S VOICE. I am coming!

[*A sound of string-instruments is heard, drawing nearer.*

CYRANO'S VOICE. [*Singing in the wings.*] La! la! la! la! la! . . .

THE DUENNA. [*Surprised.*] We are to have music?

CYRANO. [*Enters followed by two* PAGES *with theorbos.**] I tell you it is a demi-semi-quaver! . . . you demi-semi-noddle!

FIRST PAGE. [*Ironically.*] Monsieur knows then about quavers, semi and demi?

CYRANO. I know music, as do all Gassendi's disciples!

THE PAGE. [*Playing and singing.*] La! la!

CYRANO. [*Snatching the theorbo from him and continuing the musical phrase.*] I can carry on the melody. . . . La, la, la, la, . . .

ROXANE. [*Appearing on the balcony.*] It is you?

CYRANO. [*Singing upon the tune he is continuing.*] I,

* A theorbo is a bass lute.

indeed, who salute your lilies and present my respects to your ro-o-oses! . . .

ROXANE. I am coming down!

[*She leaves the balcony.*

THE DUENNA. [*Pointing at the* PAGES.] What is the meaning of these two virtuosi?

CYRANO. A wager I won, from D'Assoucy. We were disputing upon a question of grammar. Yes! No! Yes! No! Suddenly pointing at these two tall knaves, expert at clawing strings, by whom he constantly goes attended, he said, "I wager a day long of music!" He lost. Until therefore the next rise of the sun, I shall have dangling after me these archlute players, harmonious witnesses of all I do! . . . At first I liked it very well, but now it palls a little. [*To the musicians.*] Hey! . . . Go, from me, to Montfleury, and play him a pavane!* . . . [*The* PAGES *go toward the back. To the* DUENNA.] I have come to inquire of Roxane, as I do every evening. . . . [*To the* PAGES *who are leaving.*] Play a long time . . . and out of tune! [*To the* DUENNA]. . . . whether in the friend of her soul she can still detect no fault?

ROXANE. [*Coming out of the house.*] Ah, how beautiful he is, what wit he has, how deeply I love him!

CYRANO. [*Smiling.*] Christian has so much wit? . . .

ROXANE. Cousin, more than yourself!

CYRANO. I grant you.

ROXANE. There is not one alive, I truly believe, more apt at turning those pretty nothings which yet are everything. . . . Sometimes he is of an absent mood, his muse is wool-gathering, then, suddenly, he will say the most enchanting things!

CYRANO. [*Incredulous.*] Come! . . .

ROXANE. Oh, it is too bad! Men are all alike, nar-

* A dance with a slow, stately measure.

row, narrow: because he is handsome, he cannot possibly be witty!

CYRANO. So he talks of the heart in acceptable fashion?

ROXANE. Talks, cousin, is feeble. . . . He dissertates!

CYRANO. And writes? . . .

ROXANE. Still better! Listen now to this. . . . [*Declaiming.*] *"The more of my heart you steal from me, the more heart I have!"* [*Triumphantly to* CYRANO.] Well? . . .

CYRANO. Pooh!

ROXANE. And to this: *"Since you have stolen my heart, and since I must suffer, to suffer with, send me your own!"*

CYRANO. Now he has too much heart, now he has not enough, . . . just what does he want, in the matter of quantity?

ROXANE. You vex me! You are eaten up with jealousy. . . .

CYRANO. [*Starting.*] *Hein?*

ROXANE. Author's jealousy! And this, could anything be more exquisitely tender? *"Believe it, my heart cries out to you, and if kisses could be sent in writing, Love, you should read my letter with your lips. . . ."*

CYRANO. [*In spite of himself smiling with satisfaction.*] Ha! Ha! Those particular lines seem to me . . . ho! . . . ho! . . . [*Remembering himself, disdainfully*] . . . puny, pretty . . .

ROXANE. This, then . . .

CYRANO. [*Delighted.*] You know his letters by heart?

ROXANE. All!

CYRANO. It is flattering, one cannot deny.

ROXANE. In this art of expressing love he is a master!

CYRANO. [*Modest.*] Oh, . . . a master!

ROXANE. [*Peremptory.*] A master!

CYRANO. As you please, then . . . a master!

THE DUENNA. [*Who had gone toward the back, coming quickly forward.*] Monsieur de Guiche! [*To* CYRANO, *pushing him toward the house.*] Go in! It is perhaps better that he should not see you here! it might put him on the scent . . .

ROXANE. [*To* CYRANO.] Yes, of my dear secret! He loves me, he is powerful, . . . he must not find out! He might cut in sunder our loves . . . with an axe!

CYRANO. [*Going into the house.*] Very well, very well. [DE GUICHE *appears.*

ROXANE. [*To* DE GUICHE, *with a curtsey.*] I was leaving the house.

DE GUICHE. I have come to bid you farewell.

ROXANE. You are going away?

DE GUICHE. To war.

ROXANE. Ah!

DE GUICHE. I have my orders. Arras is besieged.

ROXANE. Ah! . . . it is besieged?

DE GUICHE. Yes. . . . I see that my departure does not greatly affect you.

ROXANE. Oh! . . .

DE GUICHE. As for me, I own it wrings my heart. Shall I see you again? . . When? . . . You know that I am made commander-in-general?

ROXANE. [*Uninterested.*] I congratulate you.

DE GUICHE. Of the Guards.

ROXANE. [*Starting.*] Ah, . . . of the Guards?

DE GUICHE. Among whom your cousin serves, . . . the man of the boasts and tirades. I shall have opportunity in plenty to retaliate upon him down there.

ROXANE. [*Suffocating.*] What? The Guards are going down there?

DE GUICHE. Surely. It is my regiment.

ROXANE. [*Falls sitting upon the bench; aside.*] Christian!

DE GUICHE. What is it troubles you?

ROXANE. [*Greatly moved.*] This departure . . . grieves me mortally. When one cares for a person . . . to know him away at the war!

DE GUICHE. [*Surprised and charmed.*] For the first time you utter a kind and feeling word, when I am leaving!

ROXANE. [*In a different tone, fanning herself.*] So . . . you are thinking of revenge upon my cousin?

DE GUICHE. [*Smiling.*] You side with him?

ROXANE. No . . . against him.

DE GUICHE. Do you see much of him?

ROXANE. Very little.

DE GUICHE. He is everywhere to be met with one of the cadets . . . [*trying to remember*] that Neu . . . villen . . . viller . . .

ROXANE. A tall man?

DE GUICHE. Light haired.

ROXANE. Red haired.

DE GUICHE. Good looking.

ROXANE. Pooh!

DE GUICHE. But a fool!

ROXANE. He looks like one. [*In a different tone.*] Your vengeance upon Cyrano is then to place him within reach of shot, which is the thing of all he loves! . . . A miserable vengeance! . . . I know, I do, what would more seriously concern him!

DE GUICHE. And that is?

ROXANE. Why . . . that the regiment should march, and leave him behind, with his beloved cadets, arms folded, the whole war through, in Paris! That is the only way to cast down a man like him. You wish to punish him? Deprive him of danger.

DE GUICHE. A woman! A woman! None but a woman could devise a vengeance of the sort!

ROXANE. His friends will gnaw their fists, and he his very soul, with chagrin at not being under fire; and you will be abundantly avenged!

DE GUICHE. [*Coming nearer.*] Then you do love me a little? [ROXANE *smiles.*] I wish to see in this fact of your espousing my grudge a proof of affection, Roxane . . .

ROXANE. . . . You may!

DE GUICHE. [*Showing several folded papers.*] I have here upon me the orders to be transmitted at once to each of the companies . . . except . . . [*He takes one from among the others.*] This one! . . . the company of the cadets . . . [*He puts it in his pocket.*] This, I will keep. [*Laughing.*] Ah, ah, ah! Cyrano! his belligerent humor! . . . So you sometimes play tricks upon people, you? . . .

ROXANE. Sometimes.

DE GUICHE. [*Very near her.*] I love you to distraction! This evening . . . listen, . . . it is true that I must be gone. But to go when I feel that it is a matter for your caring! Listen! . . . There is, not far from here, in Rue Orléans, a convent founded by the Capuchins. Father Athanasius. A layman may not enter. But the good fathers . . . I fear no difficulty with them! They will hide me up their sleeve . . . their sleeve is wide. They are the Capuchins that serve Richelieu at home. Fearing the uncle, they proportionately fear the nephew. I shall be thought to have left. I will come to you masked. Let me delay by a single day, wayward enchantress!

ROXANE. But if it should transpire . . . your fame . . .

DE GUICHE. Bah!

ROXANE. But . . . the siege . . . Arras! . . .

DE GUICHE. Must wait! Allow me, I beg . . .

ROXANE. No!

DE GUICHE. I beseech!

ROXANE. [*Tenderly.*] No! Love itself bids me forbid you!

DE GUICHE. Ah!

ROXANE. You must go! [*Aside.*] Christian will stay! [*Aloud.*] For my sake, be heroic . . . Antony!

DE GUICHE. Ah, heavenly word upon your lips! . . . Then you love the one who . . .

ROXANE. Who shall have made me tremble for his sake . . .

DE GUICHE. [*In a transport of joy.*] Ah, I will go! [*He kisses her hand.*] Are you satisfied with me?

ROXANE. My friend, I am.

[*Exit* DE GUICHE.

THE DUENNA. [*Dropping a mocking curtsey toward his back.*] My friend, we are!

ROXANE. [*To the* DUENNA.] Not a word of what I have done: Cyrano would never forgive me for defrauding him of his war! [*She calls toward the house.*] Cousin! [CYRANO *comes out.*] We are going to Clomire's. [*She indicates the house opposite.*] Alcandre has engaged to speak, and so has Lysimon.

THE DUENNA. [*Putting her little finger to her ear.*] Yes, but my little finger tells me that we shall be too late to hear them!

CYRANO. [*To* ROXANE.] Of all things do not miss the trained monkeys.

[*They have reached Clomire's door.*

THE DUENNA. See! . . . See! they have muffled the doorknocker! [*To the doorknocker.*] You have been gagged, that your voice should not disturb the beautiful lecture, . . . little brutal disturber!

[*She lifts it with infinite care and knocks softly.*

ROXANE. [*Seeing the door open.*] Come! [*From the threshold to* CYRANO.] If Christian should come, as probably he will, say he must wait!

CYRANO. [*Hurriedly, as she is about to disappear.*] Ah! [*She turns.*] Upon what shall you, according to your custom, question him to-day?

ROXANE. Upon . . .

CYRANO. [*Eagerly.*] Upon? . . .

ROXANE. But you will be silent . . .

CYRANO. As that wall!

ROXANE. Upon nothing! I will say! Forward! Free rein! No curb! Improvise! Talk of love! Be magnificent!

CYRANO. [*Smiling.*] Good.

ROXANE. Hush!

CYRANO. Hush!

ROXANE. Not a word!

[*She goes in and closes the door.*

CYRANO. [*Bowing, when the door is closed.*] A thousand thanks!

[*The door opens again and* ROXANE *looks out.*

ROXANE. He might prepare his speeches . . .

CYRANO. Ah, no! . . . the devil, no!

BOTH. [*Together.*] Hush! . . .

[*The door closes.*

CYRANO. [*Calling.*] Christian! [*Enter* CHRISTIAN.] I know all that we need to. Now make ready your memory. This is your chance to cover yourself with glory. Let us lose no time. Do not look sullen, like that. Quick! Let us go to your lodging and I will rehearse you . . .

CHRISTIAN. No!

CYRANO. What?

CHRISTIAN. No, I will await Roxane here.

CYRANO. What insanity possesses you? Come quickly and learn . . .

CHRISTIAN. No, I tell you! I am weary of borrowing my letters, my words . . . of playing a part, and living in constant fear. . . . It was very well at first, but now I feel that she loves me. I thank you heartily. I am no longer afraid. I will speak for myself . . .

CYRANO. *Ouais?* . . .

CHRISTIAN. And what tells you that I shall not know how? I am not such an utter blockhead, after all! You shall see! Your lessons have not been altogether wasted. I can shift to speak without your aid! And, that failing, by Heaven! I shall still know enough to take her in my arms! [*Catching sight of* ROXANE *who is coming out from Clomire's.*] She is coming! Cyrano, no, do not leave me! . . .

CYRANO. [*Bowing to him.*] I will not meddle, Monsieur.

[*He disappears behind the garden wall.*

ROXANE. [*Coming from Clomire's house with a number of people from whom she is taking leave. Curtseys and farewells.*] Barthénoide! . . . Alcandre! . . . Grémione! . . .

THE DUENNA. [*Comically desperate.*] We missed the disquisition upon the Softer Sentiments!

[*She goes into* ROXANE'S *house.*

ROXANE. [*Still taking leave of this one and that.*] Urimédonte! . . . Good-bye!

[*All bow to* ROXANE, *to one another, separate*

*and go off by the various streets.* ROXANE *sees* CHRISTIAN.

ROXANE. You are here! [*She goes to him.*] Evening is closing round. . . . Wait! . . . They have all gone. . . . The air is so mild. . . . Not a passer in sight. . . . Let us sit here. . . . Talk! . . . I will listen.

CHRISTIAN. [*Sits beside her, on the bench. Silence.*] I love you.

ROXANE. [*Closing her eyes.*] Yes. Talk to me of love.

CHRISTIAN. I love you.

ROXANE. Yes. That is the theme. Play variations upon it.

CHRISTIAN. I love . . .

ROXANE. Variations!

CHRISTIAN. I love you so much . . .

ROXANE. I do not doubt it. What further? . . .

CHRISTIAN. And further . . . I should be so happy if you loved me! Tell me, Roxane, that you love me . . .

ROXANE. [*Pouting.*] You proffer cider to me when I was hoping for champagne! . . . Now tell me a little *how* you love me?

CHRISTIAN. Why . . . very, very much.

ROXANE. Oh! . . . unravel, disentangle your sentiments!

CHRISTIAN. Your throat! . . . I want to kiss it! . . .

ROXANE. Christian!

CHRISTIAN. I love you! . . .

ROXANE. [*Attempting to rise.*] Again! . . .

CHRISTIAN. [*Hastily, holding her back.*] No, I do not love you! . . .

ROXANE. [*Sitting down again.*] That is fortunate!

CHRISTIAN. I adore you!

ROXANE. [*Rising and moving away.*] Oh! . . .

CHRISTIAN. Yes, . . . love makes me into a fool!

ROXANE. [*Drily.*] And I am displeased at it! as I should be displeased at your no longer being handsome.

CHRISTIAN. But . . .

ROXANE. Go, and rally your routed eloquence!

CHRISTIAN. I . . .

ROXANE. You love me. I have heard it. Good-evening.

[*She goes toward the house.*

CHRISTIAN. No, no, not yet! . . . I wish to tell you . . .

ROXANE. [*Pushing open the door to go in.*] That you adore me. Yes, I know. No! No! Go away! . . . Go! . . . Go! . . .

CHRISTIAN. But I . . .

[*She closes the door in his face.*

CYRANO. [*Who has been on the scene a moment, unnoticed.*] Unmistakably a success.

CHRISTIAN. Help me!

CYRANO. No, sir, no.

CHRISTIAN. I will go kill myself if I am not taken back into favor at once . . . at once!

CYRANO. And how can I . . . how, the devil? . . . make you learn on the spot . . .

CHRISTIAN. [*Seizing him by the arm.*] Oh, there! . . . Look! . . . See!

[*Light has appeared in the balcony window.*

CYRANO. [*With emotion.*] Her window!

CHRISTIAN. Oh, I shall die!

CYRANO. Not so loud!

CHRISTIAN. [*In a whisper.*] I shall die!

CYRANO. It is a dark night. . . .

CHRISTIAN. Well?

CYRANO. All may be mended. But you do not deserve. . . . There! stand there, miserable boy! . . . in front of the balcony! I will stand under it and prompt you.

CHRISTIAN. But . . .

CYRANO. Do as I bid you!

THE PAGES. [*Reappearing at the back, to* CYRANO.] Hey!

CYRANO. Hush!

[*He signs to them to lower their voices.*

FIRST PAGE. [*In a lower voice.*] We have finished serenading Montfleury!

CYRANO. [*Low, quickly.*] Go and stand out of sight. One at this street corner, the other at that; and if any one comes near, play! . . .

SECOND PAGE. What sort of tune, Monsieur the Gassendist?

CYRANO. Merry if it be a woman, mournful if it be a man. [*The pages disappear, one at each street corner. To* CHRISTIAN.] Call her!

CHRISTIAN. Roxane!

CYRANO. [*Picking up pebbles and throwing them at the window-pane.*] Wait! A few pebbles . . .

ROXANE. [*Opening the window.*] Who is calling me?

CHRISTIAN. It is I . . .

ROXANE. Who is . . . I?

CHRISTIAN. Christian!

ROXANE. [*Disdainfully.*] Oh, you!

CHRISTIAN. I wish to speak with you.

CYRANO. [*Under the balcony, to* CHRISTIAN.] Speak low! . . .

ROXANE. No, your conversation is too common. You may go home!

CHRISTIAN. In mercy! . . .

ROXANE. No . . . you do not love me any more!

CHRISTIAN. [*Whom* CYRANO *is prompting.*] You

accuse me . . . just Heaven! of loving you no more . . . when I can love you no more!

ROXANE. [*Who was about to close her window, stopping.*] Ah, that is a little better!

CHRISTIAN. [*Same business.*] To what a . . . size has Love grown in my . . . sigh-rocked soul which the . . . cruel cherub has chosen for his cradle!

ROXANE. [*Stepping nearer to the edge of the balcony.*] That is distinctly better! . . . But, since he is so cruel, this Cupid, you were unwise not to smother him in his cradle!

CHRISTIAN. [*Same business.*] I tried to, but, Madame, the . . . attempt was futile. This . . . new-born Love is . . . a little Hercules . . .

ROXANE. Much, much better!

CHRISTIAN. [*Same business.*] . . . Who found it merest baby-play to . . . strangle the serpents . . . twain, Pride and . . . Mistrust.

ROXANE. [*Leaning her elbows on the balcony-rail.*] Ah, that is very good indeed! . . . But why do you speak so slowly and stintedly? Has your imagination gout in its wings?

CYRANO. [*Drawing* CHRISTIAN *under the balcony, and taking his place.*] Hush! It is becoming too difficult!

ROXANE. To-night your words come falteringly. . . . Why is it?

CYRANO. [*Talking low like* CHRISTIAN.] Because of the dark. They have to grope to find your ear.

ROXANE. My words do not find the same difficulty.

CYRANO. They reach their point at once? Of course they do! That is because I catch them with my heart. My heart, you see, is very large, your ear particularly small. . . . Besides, your words drop . . . that goes quickly; mine have to climb . . . and that takes longer!

ROXANE. They have been climbing more nimbly, however, in the last few minutes.

CYRANO. They are becoming used to this gymnastic feat!

ROXANE. It is true that I am talking with you from a very mountain top!

CYRANO. It is sure that a hard word dropped from such a height upon my heart would shatter it!

ROXANE. [*With the motion of leaving.*] I will come down.

CYRANO. [*Quickly.*] Do not!

ROXANE. [*Pointing at the bench at the foot of the balcony.*] Then do you get up on the seat! . . .

CYRANO. [*Drawing away in terror.*] No!

ROXANE. How do you mean . . . no?

CYRANO. [*With ever-increasing emotion.*] Let us profit a little by this chance of talking softly together without seeing each other . . .

ROXANE. Without seeing each other? . . .

CYRANO. Yes, to my mind, delectable! Each guesses at the other, and no more. You discern but the trailing blackness of a mantle, and I a dawn-gray glimmer which is a summer gown. I am a shadow merely, a pearly phantom are you! You can never know what these moments are to me! If ever I was eloquent . . .

ROXANE. You were!

CYRANO. My words never till now surged from my very heart . . .

ROXANE. And why?

CYRANO. Because, till now, they must strain to reach you through . . .

ROXANE. What?

CYRANO. Why, the bewildering emotion a man feels who sees you, and whom you look upon! . . . But this evening, it seems to me that I am speaking to you for the first time!

ROXANE. It is true that your voice is altogether different.

CYRANO. [*Coming nearer, feverishly.*] Yes, altogether different, because, protected by the dark, I dare at last to be myself. I dare . . . [*He stops, and distractedly.*] What was I saying? . . . I do not know. . . . All this . . . forgive my incoherence! . . . is so delicious . . . is so new to me!

ROXANE. So new? . . .

CYRANO. [*In extreme confusion, still trying to mend his expressions.*] So new . . . yes, new, to be sincere; the fear of being mocked always constrains my heart . . .

ROXANE. Mocked . . . for what?

CYRANO. Why, . . . for its impulses, its flights! . . . Yes, my heart always cowers behind the defense of my wit. I set forth to capture a star . . . and then, for dread of laughter, I stop and pick a flower . . . of rhetoric!

ROXANE. That sort of flower has its pleasing points . . .

CYRANO. But yet, to-night, let us scorn it!

ROXANE. Never before had you spoken as you are speaking! . . .

CYRANO. Ah, if far from Cupid-darts and quivers, we might seek a place of somewhat fresher things! If instead of drinking, flat sip by sip, from a chiseled golden thimble, drops distilled and dulcified, we might try the sensation of quenching the thirst of our souls by stooping to the level of the great river, and setting our lips to the stream!

ROXANE. But yet, wit . . . fancy . . . delicate conceits. . . .

CYRANO. I gave my fancy leave to frame conceits,

before, to make you linger, . . . but now it would be an affront to this balm-breathing night, to Nature and the hour, to talk like characters in a pastoral performed at Court! . . . Let us give Heaven leave, looking at us with all its earnest stars, to strip us of disguise and artifice: I fear, . . . oh, fear! . . . lest in our mistaken alchemy sentiment should be subtilized to evaporation; lest the life of the heart should waste in these empty pastimes, and the final refinement of the fine be the undoing of the refined!

ROXANE. But yet, wit, . . . aptness . . . ingenuity . . .

CYRANO. I hate them in love! Criminal, when one loves, to prolong overmuch that paltry thrust and parry! The moment, however, comes inevitably,—and I pity those for whom it never comes!—in which, we apprehending the noble depth of the love we harbor, a shallow word hurts us to utter!

ROXANE. If . . . if, then, that moment has come for us two, what words will you say to me?

CYRANO. All those, all those, all those that come to me! Not in formal nosegay order, . . . I will throw them you in a wild sheaf! I love you, choke with love, I love you, dear. . . . My brain reels, I can bear no more, it is too much. . . . Your name is in my heart the golden clapper in a bell; and as I know no rest, Roxane, always the heart is shaken, and ever rings your name! . . . Of you, I remember all, all have I loved! Last year, one day, the twelfth of May, in going out at morning you changed the fashion of your hair. . . . I have taken the light of your hair for my light, and as having stared too long at the sun, on everything one sees a scarlet wheel, on everything when I come from my chosen light, my dazzled eye sets swimming golden blots! . . .

ROXANE. [*In a voice unsteady with emotion.*] Yes . . . this is love . . .

CYRANO. Ah, verily! The feeling which invades me, terrible and jealous, is love . . . with all its mournful frenzy! It is love, yet self-forgetting more than the wont of love! Ah, for your happiness how readily would I give mine, though you should never know it, might I but, from a distance, sometimes, hear the happy laughter bought by my sacrifice! Every glance of yours breeds in me new strength, new valor! Are you beginning to understand? Tell me, do you grasp my love's measure? Does some little part of my soul make itself felt of you there in the darkness? . . . Oh, what is happening to me this evening is too sweet, too deeply dear! I tell you all these things, and you listen to me, you! Not in my least modest hoping did I ever hope so much! I have now only to die! It is because of words of mine that she is trembling among the dusky branches! For you are trembling, like a flower among leaves! Yes, you tremble, . . . for whether you will or no, I have felt the worshiped trembling of your hand all along this thrilled and blissful jasmin-bough!

[*He madly kisses the end of a pendent bough.*

ROXANE. Yes, I tremble . . . and weep . . . and love you . . . and am yours! . . . For you have carried me away . . . away! . . .

CYRANO. Then, let death come! I have moved you, I! . . . There is but one thing more I ask . . .

CHRISTIAN. [*Under the balcony.*] A kiss!

ROXANE. [*Drawing hastily back.*] What?

CYRANO. Oh!

ROXANE. You ask? . . .

CYRANO. Yes . . . I . . . [*To* CHRISTIAN.] You are in too great haste!

CHRISTIAN. Since she is so moved, I must take advantage of it!

CYRANO. [*To* ROXANE.] I . . . Yes, it is true I asked . . . but, merciful heavens! . . . I knew at once that I had been too bold.

ROXANE. [*A shade disappointed.*] You insist no more than so?

CYRANO. Indeed, I insist . . . without insisting! Yes! yes! but your modesty shrinks! . . . I insist, but yet . . . the kiss I begged . . . refuse it me!

CHRISTIAN. [*To* CYRANO, *pulling at his mantle.*] Why?

CYRANO. Hush, Christian!

ROXANE. [*Bending over the balcony-rail.*] What are you whispering?

CYRANO. Reproaches to myself for having gone too far; I was saying "Hush, Christian!" [*The theorbos are heard playing.*] Your pardon! . . . a second! . . . Someone is coming!

[ROXANE *closes the window.* CYRANO *listens to the theorbos, one of which plays a lively, and the other a lugubrious tune.*

CYRANO. A dance? . . . A dirge? . . . What do they mean? Is it a man or a woman? . . . Ah, it is a monk!

[*Enter a* CAPUCHIN MONK, *who goes from house to house, with a lantern, examining the doors.*

CYRANO. [*To* THE CAPUCHIN.] What are you looking for, Diogenes?

THE CAPUCHIN. I am looking for the house of Madame . . .

CHRISTIAN. He is in the way!

THE CAPUCHIN. Magdeleine Robin . . .

CYRANO. [*Pointing up one of the streets.*] This way! . . . Straight ahead . . . go straight ahead . . .

THE CAPUCHIN. I thank you. I will say ten Aves for your peace. [*Exit.*

CYRANO. My good wishes speed your cowl!

[*He comes forward toward* CHRISTIAN.

CHRISTIAN. Insist upon the kiss! . . .

CYRANO. No, I will not!

CHRISTIAN. Sooner or later . . .

CYRANO. It is true! It must come, the moment of inebriation when your lips shall imperiously be impelled toward each other, because the one is fledged with youthful gold and the other is so soft a pink! . . . [*To himself.*] I had rather it should be because . . .

[*Sound of the window reopening;* CHRISTIAN *hides under the balcony.*

ROXANE. [*Stepping forward on the balcony.*] Are you there? We were speaking of . . . of . . . of a . . .

CYRANO. Kiss. The word is sweet. Why does your fair lip stop at it? If the mere word burns it, what will be of the thing itself? Do not make it into a fearful matter, and then fear! Did you not a moment ago insensibly leave playfulness behind and slip without trepidation from a smile to a sigh, from a sigh to a tear? Slip but a little further in the same blessed direction: from a tear to a kiss there is scarcely a dividing shiver!

ROXANE. Say no more!

CYRANO. A kiss! When all is said, what is a kiss? An oath of allegiance taken in closer proximity, a promise more precise, a seal on a confession, a rose-red dot upon the letter i in loving; a secret which elects the mouth for ear; an instant of eternity murmuring like a bee; balmy communion with a flavor of flowers; a fashion of inhaling each other's heart, and of tasting, on the brink of the lips, each other's soul!

ROXANE. Say no more . . . no more!

CYRANO. A kiss, Madame, is a thing so noble that the Queen of France, on the most fortunate of lords, bestowed one, did the queen herself!

ROXANE. If that be so . . .

CYRANO. [*With increasing fervor.*] Like Buckingham I have suffered in long silence, like him I worship a queen, like him I am sorrowful and unchanging . . .

ROXANE. Like him you enthrall through the eyes of the heart that follows you!

CYRANO. [*To himself, sobered.*] True, I am handsome . . . I had forgotten!

ROXANE. Come then and gather it, the supreme flower . . .

CYRANO. [*Pushing* CHRISTIAN *toward the balcony.*] Go!

ROXANE. . . . tasting of the heart.

CYRANO. Go! . . .

ROXANE. . . . murmuring like a bee . . .

CYRANO. Go!

CHRISTIAN. [*Hesitating.*] But now I feel as if I ought not!

ROXANE. . . . making Eternity an instant . . .

CYRANO. [*Pushing* CHRISTIAN.] Scale the balcony, you donkey!

[CHRISTIAN *springs toward the balcony, and climbs by means of the bench, the vine, the posts and balusters.*

CHRISTIAN. Ah, Roxane!

[*He clasps her to him, and bends over her lips.*

CYRANO. Ha! . . . What a turn of the screw to my heart! . . . Kiss, banquet of Love at which I am Lazarus, a crumb drops from your table even to me, here in the shade. . . . Yes, in my outstretched heart a little falls, as I feel that upon the lip pressing her lip Roxane kisses the words spoken by me! . . . [*The theorbos are heard.*] A merry tune . . . a mournful one . . . The monk! [*He goes through the pretense of arriving on the spot at a run, as if from a distance; calling.*] Ho, there!

ROXANE. What is it?

CYRANO. It is I. I was passing this way. Is Christian there?

CHRISTIAN. [*Astonished.*] Cyrano!

ROXANE. Good-evening, cousin!

CYRANO. Cousin, good-evening!

ROXANE. I will come down.

[ROXANE *disappears in the house.* THE CAPUCHIN *re-enters at the back.*

CHRISTIAN. [*Seeing him.*] Oh, again!

[*He follows* ROXANE.

THE CAPUCHIN. It is here she lives, I am certain . . . Magdeleine Robin.

CYRANO. You said Ro-lin.

THE CAPUCHIN. No, bin, . . . b, i, n, bin!

ROXANE. [*Appearing upon the threshold, followed by* RAGUENEAU, *carrying a lantern, and* CHRISTIAN.] What is it?

THE CAPUCHIN. A letter.

CHRISTIAN. What?

THE CAPUCHIN. [*To* ROXANE.] Oh, the contents can be only of a sacred character! It is from a worthy nobleman who . . .

ROXANE. [*To* CHRISTIAN.] It is from De Guiche!

CHRISTIAN. He dares to . . . ?

ROXANE. Oh, he will not trouble me much longer! [*Opening the letter.*] I love you, and if . . . [*By the light of* RAGUENEAU'S *lantern she reads, aside, low.*] Mademoiselle: The drums are beating. My regiment is buckling on its corselet. It is about to leave. I am thought to have left already, but lag behind. I am disobeying you. I am in the convent here. I am coming to you, and send you word by a friar, silly as a sheep, who has no suspicion of the import of this letter. You smiled too sweetly upon me an hour ago: I must see you smile again. Provide to be alone, and deign graciously to receive the audacious worshipper, forgiven already, I can but hope, who signs himself your—etc. . . . [*To* THE CAPUCHIN.] Father, this is what the letter tells me . . . Listen: [*All draw nearer; she reads aloud.*] Mademoiselle: The wishes of the cardinal may not be disregarded, however hard compliance with them prove. I have therefore chosen as bearer of this letter a most reverend, holy, and sagacious Capuchin; it is our wish that he should at once, in your own dwelling, pronounce the nuptial blessing over you. Christian must secretly become your husband. I send him to you. You dislike him. Bow to Heaven's will in resignation, and be sure that it will bless your zeal, and sure, likewise, Mademoiselle, of the respect of him who is and will be ever your most humble and . . . etc.

THE CAPUCHIN. [*Beaming.*] The worthy gentleman! . . . I knew it! You remember that I said so: the contents of that letter can be only of a sacred character!

ROXANE. [*Low, to* CHRISTIAN.] I am a fluent reader, am I not?

CHRISTIAN. Hm!

ROXANE. [*With feigned despair.*] Ah . . . it is horrible!

THE CAPUCHIN. [*Who has turned the light of his lantern upon* CYRANO.] You are the one?

CHRISTIAN. No, I am.

THE CAPUCHIN. [*Turning the light upon him, and as if his good looks aroused suspicion.*] But . . .

ROXANE. [*Quickly.*] Postscript: You will bestow upon the convent two hundred and fifty crowns.

THE CAPUCHIN. The worthy, worthy gentleman! [*To* ROXANE.] Be reconciled!

ROXANE [*With the expression of a martyr.*] I will endeavor! [*While* RAGUENEAU *opens the door for* THE CAPUCHIN, *whom* CHRISTIAN *is showing into the house,* ROXANE *says low to* CYRANO.] De Guiche is coming! . . . Keep him here! Do not let him enter until . . .

CYRANO. I understand! [*To* THE CAPUCHIN.] How long will it take to marry them?

THE CAPUCHIN. A quarter of an hour.

CYRANO. [*Pushing all toward the house.*] Go in! I shall be here!

ROXANE. [*To* CHRISTIAN.] Come!

[*They go in.*

CYRANO. How can I detain De Guiche for a quarter of an hour? [*He jumps upon the bench, climbs the wall toward the balcony-rail.*] So! . . . I climb up here! . . . I know what I will do! . . . [*The theorbos play a melancholy tune.*] Ho, it is a man! [*The tune quavers lugubriously.* ] Ho, ho, this time there is no mistake! [*He is on the balcony; he pulls the brim of his hat over his eyes, takes off his sword, wraps his cloak about him, and bends over the balcony-rail.*] No, it is not too far! [*He climbs over the balcony-rail, and reaching for a long bough that projects beyond the garden wall, holds on to it with both hands, ready to let himself drop.*] I shall make a slight commotion in the atmosphere!

DE GUICHE. [*Enters masked, groping in the dark.*] What can that thrice-damned Capuchin be about?

CYRANO. The devil! if he should recognize my voice? [*Letting go with one hand, he makes show of turning a key.*] Cric! crac! [*Solemnly.*] Cyrano, resume the accent of Bergerac!

DE GUICHE. [*Looking at* ROXANE'S *house.*] Yes, that is it. I can scarcely see. This mask bothers my eyes!

[*He is about to enter* ROXANE'S *house;* CYRANO *swings from the balcony, holding on to the bough, which bends and lets him down between the door and* DE GUICHE. *He intentionally drops very heavily, to give the effect of dropping from a great height, and lies flattened upon the ground, motionless, as if stunned.*

DE GUICHE. What is it? [*When he looks up, the bough has swung into place; he sees nothing but the sky.*] Where did this man drop from?

CYRANO. [*Rising to a sitting posture.*] From the moon!

DE GUICHE. From the . . . ?

CYRANO. [*In a dreamy voice.*] What time is it?

DE GUICHE. Is he mad?

CYRANO. What time? What country? What day? What season?

DE GUICHE. But . . .

CYRANO. I am dazed!

DE GUICHE. Monsieur . . .

CYRANO. I have dropped from the moon like a bomb!

DE GUICHE. [*Impatiently.*] What are you babbling about?

CYRANO. [*Rising, in a terrible voice.*] I tell you I have dropped from the moon!

DE GUICHE. [*Backing a step.*] Very well. You have dropped from the moon! . . . He is perhaps a lunatic!

CYRANO. [*Walking up close to him.*] Not metaphorically, mind that!

DE GUICHE. But . . .

CYRANO. A hundred years ago, or else a minute, —for I have no conception how long I have been falling,—I was up there, in that saffron-colored ball!

DE GUICHE. [*Shrugging his shoulders.*] You were. Now, let me pass!

CYRANO. [*Standing in his way.*] Where am I? Be frank with me! Keep nothing from me! In what region, among what people, have I been shot like an aerolite?

DE GUICHE. I wish to pass!

CYRANO. While falling I could not choose my way, and have no notion where I have fallen! Is it upon a moon, or is it upon an earth, I have been dragged by my posterior weight?

DE GUICHE. I tell you, sir . . .

CYRANO. [*With a scream of terror at which* DE GUICHE *starts backward a step.*] Great God! . . . In this country men's faces are soot-black!

DE GUICHE. [*Lifting his hand to his face.*] What does he mean?

CYRANO. [*Still terrified.*] Am I in Algeria? Are you a native? . . .

DE GUICHE. [*Who has felt his mask.*] Ah, my mask!

CYRANO. [*Pretending to be easier.*] So I am in Venice! . . . Or am I in Genoa?

DE GUICHE. [*Attempting to pass.*] A lady is expecting me!

CYRANO. [*Completely reassured.*] Ah, then I am in Paris.

DE GUICHE. [*Smiling in spite of himself.*] The rogue is not far from amusing!

CYRANO. Ah, you are laughing!

DE GUICHE. I laugh . . . but intend to pass!

CYRANO. [*Beaming.*] To think I should strike Paris! [*Quite at his ease, laughing, brushing himself, bowing.*] I arrived—pray, pardon my appearance!—by the last whirlwind. I am rather unpresentable—Travel, you know! My eyes are still full of star-dust. My spurs are clogged with bristles off a planet. [*Appearing to pick something off his sleeve.*] See, on my sleeve, a comet's hair!

[*He makes a feint of blowing it away.*

DE GUICHE. [*Beside himself.*] Sir . . .

CYRANO. [*As* DE GUICHE *is about to pass, stretching out his leg as if to show something on it, thereby stopping him.*] Embedded in my calf, I have brought back one of the Great Bear's teeth . . . and as, falling too near the Trident, I strained aside to clear one of its prongs, I landed sitting in Libra, . . . yes, one of the scales! . . . and now my weight is registered up there! [*Quickly preventing* DE GUICHE *from passing, and taking hold of a button on his doublet.*] And if, Monsieur, you should take my nose between your fingers and compress it . . . milk would result!

DE GUICHE. What are you saying? Milk? . . .

CYRANO. Of the Milky Way.

DE GUICHE. Go to the devil!

CYRANO. No! I am sent from Heaven, literally. [*Folding his arms.*] Will you believe—I discovered it in passing—that Sirius at night puts on a night-cap? [*Confidentially.*] The lesser Bear is too little yet to bite. . . . [*Laughing.*] I tumbled plump through Lyra, and snapped a string! . . . [*Magnificent.*] But I intend setting all this down in a book,* and the golden stars I have brought back caught in my shaggy mantle,

* This reference and those that follow are to the *Histoires comiques des états et empires de la lune et du soleil*, the best known of Bergerac's works.

when the book is printed, will be seen serving as asterisks!

De Guiche. I have stood this long enough! I want . . .

Cyrano. I know perfectly what you want!

De Guiche. Man . . .

Cyrano. You want to know, from me, at first hand, what the moon is made of, and whether that monumental pumpkin is inhabited?

De Guiche. [*Shouting.*] Not in the very least! I want . . .

Cyrano. To know how I got there? I got there by a method of my own invention.

De Guiche. [*Discouraged.*] He is mad! . . . stark!

Cyrano. [*Disdainfully.*] Do not imagine that I resorted to anything so absurd as Regiomontanus's eagle, or anything so lacking in enterprise as Archytas's pigeon!* . . .

De Guiche. The madman is erudite . . .

Cyrano. I drew up nothing that had ever been thought of before! [De Guiche *has succeeded in getting past* Cyrano, *and is nearing* Roxane's *door;* Cyrano *follows him, ready to buttonhole him.*] I invented no less than six ways of storming the blue fort of Heaven!

De Guiche. [*Turning around.*] Six, did you say?

Cyrano. [*Volubly.*] One way was to stand naked in the sunshine, in a harness thickly studded with glass phials, each filled with morning dew. The sun in draw-

* Regiomontanus, a German astronomer of the fifteenth century, A. D., and Archytas, a Greek philosopher of the fifth century, B. C., constructed flying machines of the shapes here mentioned.

ing up the dew, you see, could not have helped drawing me up too!

DE GUICHE. [*Surprised, taking a step toward* CYRANO.] True. That is one!

CYRANO. [*Taking a step backward, with a view of drawing* DE GUICHE *away from the door.*] Or else, I could have let the wind into a cedar coffer, then rarified the imprisoned element by means of cunningly adjusted burning-glasses, and soared up with it!

DE GUICHE. [*Taking another step toward* CYRANO.] Two!

CYRANO. [*Backing.*] Or else, mechanic as well as artificer, I could have fashioned a giant grasshopper, with steel joints, which, impelled by successive explosions of saltpeter, would have hopped with me to the azure meadows where graze the starry flocks!

DE GUICHE. [*Unconsciously following* CYRANO, *and counting on his fingers.*] That makes three!

CYRANO. Since smoke by its nature ascends, I could have blown into an appropriate globe a sufficient quantity to ascend with me!

DE GUICHE. [*As above, more and more astonished.*] Four!

CYRANO. Since Phœbe, the moon-goddess, when she is at wane, is greedy, O beeves! of your marrow, . . . with that marrow I could have besmeared myself!

DE GUICHE. [*Amazed.*] Five!

CYRANO. [*Who while talking has backed, followed by* DE GUICHE, *to the further side of the square, near a bench.*] Or else, I could have placed myself upon an iron plate, have taken a magnet of suitable size, and thrown it in the air! That way is a very good one! The magnet flies upward, the iron instantly after; the magnet no sooner overtaken than you fling it up again. . . . The rest is clear! You can go upward indefinitely.

DE GUICHE. Six! . . . But here are six excellent methods! Which of the six, my dear sir, did you select?

CYRANO. A seventh!

DE GUICHE. Did you, indeed? And what was that?

CYRANO. I give you a hundred guesses!

DE GUICHE. I must confess that I should like to know!

CYRANO. [*Imitating the noise of the surf, and making great mysterious gestures.*] Hoo-ish! hoo-ish!

DE GUICHE. Well! What is that?

CYRANO. Cannot you guess?

DE GUICHE. No!

CYRANO. The tide! . . . At the hour in which the moon attracts the deep, I lay down upon the sands, after a sea-bath . . . and, my head being drawn up first,—the reason of this, you see, that the hair will hold a quantity of water in its mop!—I rose in the air, straight, beautifully straight, like an angel. I rose . . . I rose softly . . . without an effort . . . when, suddenly, I felt a shock. Then . . .

DE GUICHE. [*Lured on by curiosity, taking a seat on the bench.*] Well, . . . then?

CYRANO. Then . . . [*resuming his natural voice.*] The time is up, Monsieur, and I release you. They are married.

DE GUICHE. [*Getting to his feet with a leap.*] I am dreaming or drunk! That voice? [*The door of* ROXANE'S *house opens; lackeys appear carrying lighted candelabra.* CYRANO *removes his hat.*] And that nose! . . . Cyrano!

CYRANO. [*Bowing.*] Cyrano. They have exchanged rings within the quarter of the hour.

DE GUICHE. Who have? [*He turns round. Tableau. Behind the lackey stand* ROXANE *and* CHRISTIAN *holding hands.* THE CAPUCHIN *follows them smiling.*

RAGUENEAU *holds high a flambeau.* THE DUENNA *closes the procession, bewildered, in her bedgown.*] Heavens! [*To* ROXANE.] You! [*Recognizing* CHRISTIAN *with amazement.*] He? [*Bowing to* ROXANE.] Your astuteness compels my admiration! [*To* CYRANO.] My compliments to you, ingenious inventor of flying machines. Your experiences would have beguiled a saint on the threshold of Paradise! Make a note of them. . . . They can be used again, with profit, in a book!

CYRANO. [*Bowing.*] I will confidently follow your advice.

THE CAPUCHIN. [*To* DE GUICHE, *pointing at the lovers, and wagging his great white beard with satisfaction.*] A beautiful couple, my son, brought together by you!

DE GUICHE. [*Eyeing him frigidly.*] As you say! [*To* ROXANE.] And now proceed, Madame, to take leave of your husband.

ROXANE. What?

DE GUICHE. [*To* CHRISTIAN.] The regiment is on the point of starting. You are to join it!

ROXANE. To go to war?

DE GUICHE. Of course!

ROXANE. But the cadets are not going!

DE GUICHE. They are! [*Taking out the paper which he had put in his pocket.*] Here is the order. [*To* CHRISTIAN.] I beg you will take it to the Captain, baron, yourself.

ROXANE. [*Throwing herself in* CHRISTIAN'S *arms.*] Christian!

DE GUICHE. [*To* CYRANO, *with a malignant laugh.*] The wedding night is somewhat far as yet!

CYRANO. [*Aside.*] He thinks that he is giving me great pain!

CHRISTIAN. [*To* ROXANE.] Oh, once more, dear! . . . Once more!

CYRANO. Be reasonable . . . Come! . . . Enough!

CHRISTIAN. [*Still clasping* ROXANE.] Oh, it is hard to leave her. . . . You cannot know. . . .

CYRANO. [*Trying to draw him away.*] I know.

[*Drums are heard in the distance sounding a march.*

DE GUICHE. [*At the back.*] The regiment is on its way!

ROXANE. [*To* CYRANO, *while she clings to* CHRISTIAN *whom he is trying to draw away.*] Oh! . . . I entrust him to your care! Promise that under no circumstance shall his life be placed in danger!

CYRANO. I will endeavor . . . but obviously cannot promise . . .

ROXANE. [*Same business.*] Promise that he will be careful of himself!

CYRANO. I will do my best, but . . .

ROXANE. [*As above.*] That during this terrible siege he shall not take harm from the cold!

CYRANO. I will try, but . . .

ROXANE. [*As above.*] That he will be true to me!

CYRANO. Of course, but yet, you see . . .

ROXANE. [*As above.*] That he will write to me often!

CYRANO. [*Stopping.*] Ah, that . . . I promise freely!

CURTAIN

# ACT FOURTH

## THE GASCONY CADETS

*The post occupied at the siege of Arras by the company of* CARBON DE CASTEL-JALOUX. *At the back, across the whole stage, sloping earthwork. Beyond this is seen a plain stretching to the horizon; the country is covered with constructions relating to the siege. In the distance, against the sky, the outlines of the walls and roofs of Arras. Tents; scattered arms; drums, etc. It is shortly before sunrise. The East is yellow. Sentinels at even intervals. Camp-fires. The* GASCONY CADETS *lie asleep, rolled in their cloaks.* CARBON DE CASTEL-JALOUX *and* LE BRET *are watching. All are very pale and gaunt.* CHRISTIAN *lies sleeping among the others, in his military cape, in the foreground, his face lighted by one of the camp-fires. Silence.*

LE BRET. It is dreadful!

CARBON. Yes. Nothing left.

LE BRET. *Mordious!*

CARBON. [*Warning him by a gesture to speak lower.*] Curse in a whisper! You will wake them! . . . [*To the* CADETS.] Hush! Go to sleep! [*To* LE BRET.] Who sleeps dines.

LE BRET. Who lies awake misses two good things . . . What a situation!

[*A few shots are heard in the distance.*

CARBON. The devil take their popping! They will

wake my young ones! . . . [*To the* CADETS *who lift their heads.*] Go to sleep!

[*The* CADETS *lie down again. Other shots are heard, nearer.*

ONE OF THE CADETS. [*Stirring.*] The devil! Again?

CARBON. It is nothing. It is Cyrano getting home.

[*The heads which had started up, go down again.*

A SENTINEL. [*Outside.*] *Ventrebieu!* Who goes there?

CYRANO'S VOICE. Bergerac!

THE SENTINEL. [*Upon the embankment.*] *Ventrebieu!* Who goes there?

CYRANO. [*Appearing at the top of the embankment.*] Bergerac, blockhead!

[*He comes down.* LE BRET *goes to him, uneasy.*

LE BRET. Ah, thank God!

CYRANO. [*Warning him by a sign to wake no one.*] Hush!

LE BRET. Wounded?

CYRANO. Do you not know that it has become a habit with them to miss me?

LE BRET. To me, it seems a little excessive that you should, every morning, for the sake of taking a letter, risk . . .

CYRANO. [*Stopping in front of* CHRISTIAN.] I promised that he would write often. [*He looks at* CHRISTIAN.] He sleeps. He has grown pale. If the poor little girl could know that he is starving. . . . But handsome as ever!

LE BRET. Go at once and sleep.

CYRANO. Le Bret, do not grumble! Learn this: I nightly cross the Spanish lines at a point where I know beforehand every one will be drunk.

LE BRET. You ought some time to bring us back some victuals!

CYRANO. I must be lightly burdened to flit through! . . . But I know that there will be events before the evening. The French, unless I am much mistaken, will eat or die.

LE BRET. Oh, tell us!

CYRANO. No, I am not certain . . . You will see!

CARBON. What a shameful reversal of the order of things, that the besieger should be starved!

LE BRET. Alas! never was more complicated siege than this of Arras: We besiege Arras, and, caught in a trap, are ourselves besieged by the Cardinal-prince of Spain. . . .

CYRANO. Someone now ought to come and besiege him.

LE BRET. I am not joking!

CYRANO. Oh, oh!

LE BRET. To think, ungrateful boy, that every day you risk a life precious as yours, solely to carry . . . [CYRANO *goes toward one of the tents.*] Where are you going?

CYRANO. I am going to write another.

[*He lifts the canvas flap, and disappears in the tent.*

[*Daybreak has brightened. Rosy flush. The city of Arras at the horizon catches a golden light. The report of a cannon is heard, followed at once by a drum-call, very far away, at the left. Other drums beat, nearer. The drum-calls answer one another, come nearer, come very near, and go off, decreasing, dying in the distance, toward the right, having made the circuit of the camp. Noise of general awakening. Voices of officers in the distance.*

CARBON. [*With a sigh.*] The reveille. . . . Ah, me! . . . [*The* CADETS *stir in their cloaks, stretch.*] An end to the succulent slumbers! I know but too well what their first word will be!

ONE OF THE CADETS. [*Sitting up.*] I am famished!

OTHER CADET. I believe I am dying!

ALL. Oh! . . .

CARBON. Get up!

THIRD CADET. I cannot go a step!

FOURTH CADET. I have not strength to stir!

FIRST CADET. [*Looking at himself in a bit of armor.*] My tongue is coated: it must be the weather that is indigestible!

OTHER CADET. Any one who wants them, can have all my titles of nobility for a Chester cheese . . . or part of one!

OTHER CADET. If my stomach does not have something put into it to take up the attention of my gastric juice, I shall retire into my tent before long . . . like Achilles!

OTHER CADET. Yes, they ought to provide us with bread!

CARBON. [*Going to the tent into which* CYRANO *has retired; low.*] Cyrano!

OTHER CADETS. We cannot stand this much longer!

CARBON. [*As above, at the door of the tent.*] To the rescue, Cyrano! You who succeed so well always in cheering them, come and make them pluck up spirits!

SECOND CADET. [*Falling upon* FIRST CADET *who is chewing something.*] What are you chewing, man?

FIRST CADET. A bit of gun-tow fried in axle-grease . . . using a burganet as frying pan. The suburbs of Arras are not precisely rich in game. . . .

OTHER CADET. [*Entering.*] I have been hunting!

OTHER CADET. [*The same.*] I have been fishing!

ALL. [*Rising and falling upon the newcomers.*] What?—what did you catch?—A pheasant?—A carp? —Quick! quick! . . . Let us see!

THE HUNTSMAN. A sparrow!

THE ANGLER. A gudgeon!

ALL. [*Exasperated.*] Enough of this! Let us revolt!

CARBON. To the rescue, Cyrano!

[*It is now broad daylight.*

CYRANO. [*Coming out of the tent, tranquil, a pen behind his ear, a book in his hand.*] What is the matter? [*Silence. To* FIRST CADET.] Why do you go off like that, with that slouching gait?

THE CADET. I have something away down in my heels which inconveniences me.

CYRANO. And what is that?

THE CADET. My stomach.

CYRANO. That is where mine is, too.

THE CADET. Then you too must be inconvenienced.

CYRANO. No. The size of the hollow within me merely increases my sense of my size.

SECOND CADET. I happen to have teeth, long ones!

CYRANO. The better will you bite . . . in good time!

THIRD CADET. I reverberate like a drum!

CYRANO. You will be of use . . . to sound the charge!

OTHER CADET. I have a buzzing in my ears!

CYRANO. A mistake. Empty belly, no ears. You hear no buzzing.

OTHER CADET. Ah, a trifling article to eat . . . and a little oil upon it!

CYRANO. [*Taking off the* CADET'S *morion and placing it in his hand.*] That is seasoned.

OTHER CADET. What is there we could devour?

CYRANO. [*Tossing him the book he has been holding.*] Try the Iliad!

OTHER CADET. The minister, in Paris, makes his four meals a day!

CYRANO. You feel it remiss in him not to send you a bit of partridge?

THE SAME. Why should he not? And some wine!

CYRANO. Richelieu, some Burgundy, if you please?

THE SAME. He might, by one of his Capuchins!

CYRANO. By his Eminence, perhaps, in sober gray?

OTHER CADET. No ogre was ever so hungry!

CYRANO. You may have your fill yet of humble-pie!

FIRST CADET. [*Shrugging his shoulders.*] Forever jests! . . . puns! . . . *mots!*

CYRANO. *Le mot* forever, indeed! And I would wish to die, on a fine evening, under a rose-flushed sky, delivering myself of a good *mot* in a good cause! . . . Ah, yes, the best were indeed, far from fever-bed and potion, pierced with the only noble weapon, by an adversary worthy of oneself, to fall upon a glorious field, the point of a sword through his heart, the point of a jest on his lips! . . .

ALL. [*In a wail.*] I am hungry!

CYRANO. [*Folding his arms.*] God have mercy! can you think of nothing but eating? . . . Come here, Bertrandou the fifer, once the shepherd! Take from the double case one of your fifes: breathe into it, play to this pack of guzzlers and of gluttons our homely melodies, of haunting rhythm, every note of which appeals like a little sister, through whose every strain are heard strains of beloved voices . . . mild melodies whose slowness brings to mind the slowness of the smoke upcurling from our native hamlet hearths . . . melodies that seem to speak to a man in his native dialect! . . . [*The old fifer sits down and makes ready his fife.*]

To-day let the fife, martial unwillingly, be reminded, while your fingers upon its slender stem flutter like birds in a delicate minuet, that before being ebony it was reed; surprise itself by what you make it sing, . . . let it feel restored to it the soul of its youth, rustic and peaceable! [*The old man begins playing Languedoc tunes.*] Listen, Gascons! It is no more, beneath his fingers, the shrill fife of the camp, but the soft flute of the woodland! It is no more, between his lips, the whistling note of battle, but the lowly lay of goatherds leading their flocks to feed! . . . Hark! . . . It sings of the valley, the heath, the forest! . . . of the little shepherd, sunburned under his crimson cap! . . . the green delight of evening on the river! . . . Hark, Gascons all! It sings of Gascony!

[*Every head has drooped; all eyes have grown dreamy; tears are furtively brushed away with a sleeve, the hem of a cloak.*

CARBON. [*To* CYRANO, *low.*] You are making them weep!

CYRANO. With homesickness! . . . a nobler pain than hunger . . . not physical: mental! I am glad the seat of their suffering should have removed . . . that the gripe should now afflict their hearts!

CARBON. But you weaken them, making them weep!

CYRANO. [*Beckoning to a drummer.*] Never fear! The hero in their veins is quickly roused. It is enough to . . .

[*He signs to the drummer who begins drumming.*

ALL. [*Starting to their feet and snatching up their arms.*] *Hein?* . . . What? . . . What is it?

CYRANO. [*Smiling.*] You see? . . . The sound of the drum was enough! Farewell dreams, regrets, old homestead, love. . . . What comes with the fife with the drum may go . . .

ONE OF THE CADETS. [*Looking off at the back.*] Ah! ah! . . . Here comes Monsieur de Guiche!

ALL THE CADETS. [*Grumbling.*] Hoo . . .

CYRANO. [*Smiling.*] Flattering murmur . . .

ONE OF THE CADETS. He bores us! . . .

OTHER CADET. Showing himself off, with his broad point collar on top of his armor! . . .

OTHER CADET. As if lace were worn with steel!

FIRST CADET. Convenient, if you have a boil on your neck to cover . . .

SECOND CADET. There is another courtier for you!

OTHER CADET. His uncle's own nephew!

CARBON. He is a Gascon, nevertheless!

FIRST CADET. Not genuine! . . . Never trust him. For a Gascon, look you, must be something of a madman: nothing is so deadly to deal with as a Gascon who is completely rational!

LE BRET. He is pale!

OTHER CADET. He is hungry, as hungry as any poor devil of us! But his corselet being freely embellished with gilt studs, his stomach-ache is radiant in the sun!

CYRANO. [*Eagerly.*] Let us not appear to suffer, either! You, your cards, your pipes, your dice . . . [*All briskly set themselves to playing with cards and dice, on the heads of drums, on stools, on cloaks spread over the ground. They light long tobacco pipes.*] And I will be reading Descartes. . . .

[*He walks to and fro, forward and backward, reading a small book which he has taken from his pocket. Tableau. Enter* DE GUICHE. *Every one appears absorbed and satisfied.* DE GUICHE *is very pale. He goes toward* CARBON.

De Guiche. [*To* Carbon.] Ah, good-morning. [*They look at each other attentively. Aside, with satisfaction.*] He is pale as plaster.

Carbon. [*Same business.*] His eyes are all that is left of him.

De Guiche. [*Looking at the* Cadets.] So here are the wrongheaded rascals? . . . Yes, gentlemen, it is reported to me on every side that I am your scoff and derision; that the cadets, highland nobility, Béarn clodhoppers, Périgord baronets, cannot express sufficient contempt for their colonel; call me intriguer, courtier, find it irksome to their taste that I should wear, with my cuirass, a collar of Genoese point, and never cease to air their wondering indignation that a man should be a Gascon without being a vagabond! [*Silence. The* Cadets *continue smoking and playing.*] Shall I have you punished by your captain? . . . I do not like to.

Carbon. Did you otherwise, however, . . . I am free, and punish only . . .

De Guiche. Ah? . . .

Carbon. My company is paid by myself, belongs to me. I obey no orders but such as relate to war.

De Guiche. Ah, is it so? Enough, then. I will treat your taunts with simple scorn. My fashion of deporting myself under fire is well known. You are not unaware of the manner in which yesterday, at Bapaume, I forced back the columns of the Comte de Bucquoi; gathering my men together to plunge forward like an avalanche, three times I charged him. . . .

Cyrano. [*Without lifting his nose from his book.*] And your white scarf?

De Guiche. [*Surprised and self-satisfied.*] You heard of that circumstance? . . . In fact, it happened that as I was wheeling about to collect my men for the third charge, I was caught in a stream of fugitives which bore me onward to the edge of the enemy. I was in danger of being captured and cut off with an arquebuse, when I had the presence of mind to untie and let slip to the ground the white scarf which proclaimed my military grade. Thus was I enabled, undistinguished, to withdraw from among the Spaniards, and thereupon returning with my reinspirited men, to defeat them. Well? . . . What do you say to the incident?

[*The* CADETS *have appeared not to be listening; at this point, however, hands with cards and dice-boxes remain suspended in the air; no pipe-smoke is ejected; all expresses expectation.*

CYRANO. That never would Henry the Fourth, however great the number of his opponents, have consented to diminish his presence by the size of his white plume.

[*Silent joy. Cards fall, dice rattle, smoke upwreathes.*

DE GUICHE. The trick was successful, however!

[*As before, expectation suspends gambling and smoking.*

CYRANO. Very likely. But one should not resign the honor of being a target. [*Cards, dice, smoke, fall, rattle, and upwreathe, as before, in expression of increasing glee.*] Had I been at hand when you allowed your scarf to drop—the quality of our courage, monsieur, shows different in this,—I would have picked it up and worn it. . . .

DE GUICHE. Ah, yes,—more of your Gascon bragging! . . .

CYRANO. Bragging? . . . Lend me the scarf. I engage to mount, ahead of all, to the assault, wearing it crosswise upon my breast!

DE GUICHE. A Gascon's offer, that too! You know

that the scarf was left in the enemy's camp, by the banks of the Scarpe, where bullets since then have hailed . . . whence no one can bring it back!

CYRANO. [*Taking a white scarf from his pocket and handing it to* DE GUICHE.] Here it is.

[*Silence. The* CADETS *smother their laughter behind cards and in dice-boxes.* DE GUICHE *turns around, looks at them; instantly they become grave; one of them, with an air of unconcern, whistles the tune played earlier by the fifer.*

DE GUICHE. [*Taking the scarf.*] I thank you. I shall be able with this shred of white to make a signal . . . which I was hesitating to make. . . .

[*He goes to the top of the bank and waves the scarf.*

ALL. What now? . . . What is this?

THE SENTINEL. [*At the top of the bank.*] A man . . . over there . . . running off . . .

DE GUICHE. [*Coming forward again.*] It is a supposed Spanish spy. He is very useful to us. The information he carries to the enemy is that which I give him,—so that their decisions are influenced by us.

CYRANO. He is a scoundrel!

DE GUICHE. [*Coolly tying on his scarf.*] He is a convenience. We were saying? . . . Ah, I was about to tell you. Last night, having resolved upon a desperate stroke to obtain supplies, the Marshal secretly set out for Dourlens. The royal sutlers are encamped there. He expects to join them by way of the tilled fields; but, to provide against interference, he took with him troops in such number that, certainly, if we were now attacked, the enemy would find easy work. Half of the army is absent from the camp.

CARBON. If the Spaniards knew that, it might be serious. But they do not know.

DE GUICHE. They do. And are going to attack us.

CARBON. Ah!

DE GUICHE. My pretended spy came to warn me of their intention. He said, moreover: I can direct the attack. At what point shall it be? I will lead them to suppose it the least strong, and they will center their efforts against it. I answered: Very well. Go from the camp. Look down the line. Let them attack at the point I signal from.

CARBON. [*To the* CADETS.] Gentlemen, get ready!

[*All get up. Noise of swords and belts being buckled on.*

DE GUICHE. They will be here in an hour.

FIRST CADET. Oh! . . . if there is a whole hour! . . .

[*All sit down again, and go on with their games.*

DE GUICHE. [*To* CARBON.] The main object is to gain time. The Marshal is on his way back.

CARBON. And to gain time?

DE GUICHE. You will be so obliging as to keep them busy killing you.

CYRANO. Ah, this is your revenge!

DE GUICHE. I will not pretend that if I had been fond of you, I would have thus singled out you and yours; but, as your bravery is unquestionably beyond that of others, I am serving my King at the same time as my inclination.

CYRANO. Suffer me, Monsieur, to express my gratitude.

DE GUICHE. I know that you affect fighting one against a hundred. You will not complain of lacking opportunity.

[*He goes toward the back with* CARBON.

CYRANO. [*To the* CADETS.] We shall now be able, gentlemen, to add to the Gascon escutcheon, which bears, as it is, six chevrons, or and azure, the chevron that was wanting to complete it,—blood-red!

[DE GUICHE *at the back speaks low with* CARBON. *Orders are given. All is made ready to repel an attack.* CYRANO *goes toward* CHRISTIAN, *who stands motionless, with folded arms.*

CYRANO. [*Laying his hand on* CHRISTIAN'S *shoulder.*] Christian?

CHRISTIAN. [*Shaking his head.*] Roxane!

CYRANO. Ah me!

CHRISTIAN. I wish I might at least put my whole heart's last blessing in a beautiful letter!

CYRANO. I mistrusted that it would come to-day . . . [*he takes a letter from his doublet*] and I have written your farewells.

CHRISTIAN. Let me see!

CYRANO. You wish to see it? . . .

CHRISTIAN. [*Taking the letter.*] Yes! [*He opens the letter, begins to read, stops short.*] Ah? . . .

CYRANO. What?

CHRISTIAN. That little round blister?

CYRANO. [*Hurriedly taking back the letter, and looking at it with an artless air.*] A blister?

CHRISTIAN. It is a tear!

CYRANO. It looks like one, does it not? . . . A poet, you see, is sometimes caught in his own snare,—that is what constitutes the interest, the charm! . . . This letter, you must know, is very touching. In writing it I apparently made myself shed tears.

CHRISTIAN. Shed tears? . . .

CYRANO. Yes, because . . . well, to die is not terrible at all . . . but never to see her again, . . . never! . . . that, you know, is horrible beyond all thinking.

. . . And, things having taken the turn they have, I shall not see her. . . . [CHRISTIAN *looks at him.*] We shall not see her. . . . [*Hastily.*] You will not see her. . . .

CHRISTIAN. [*Snatching the letter from him.*] Give me the letter!

[*Noise in the distance.*

VOICE OF A SENTINEL. *Ventrebieu,* who goes there?

[*Shots. Noise of voices, tinkling of bells.*

CARBON. What is it?

THE SENTINEL. [*On the top of the bank.*] A coach!

[*All run to see.*

THE CADETS. [*Noisy exclamations.*] What?—In the camp?—It is driving into the camp!—It comes from the direction of the enemy! The devil! Fire upon it!—No! the coachman is shouting something!—What does he say?—He shouts: Service of the King!

DE GUICHE. What? Service of the King?

[*All come down from the bank and fall into order.*

CARBON. Hats off, all!

DE GUICHE. [*At the corner.*] Service of the King! Stand back, low rabble, and give it room to turn around with a handsome sweep!

[*The coach comes in at a trot. It is covered with mud and dust. The curtains are drawn. Two lackeys behind. It comes to a standstill.*

CARBON. [*Shouting.*] Salute!

[*Drums roll. All the* CADETS *uncover.*

DE GUICHE. Let down the steps!

[*Two men hurry forward. The coach door opens.*

ROXANE. [*Stepping from the carriage.*] Good-morning!

[*At the sound of a feminine voice, all the men,*

*in the act of bowing low, straighten themselves. Consternation.*

DE GUICHE. Service of the King! You?

ROXANE. Of the only King! . . . of Love!

CYRANO. Ah, great God!

CHRISTIAN. [*Rushing to her.*] You? Why are you here?

ROXANE. The siege lasted too long!

CHRISTIAN. Why have you come?

ROXANE. I will tell you!

CYRANO. [*Who at the sound of her voice has started, then stood motionless without venturing to look her way.*] God! . . . can I trust myself to look at her?

DE GUICHE. You cannot remain here.

ROXANE. But I can,—I can, indeed! Will you favor me with a drum? [*She seats herself upon a drum brought forward for her.*] There! I thank you! [*She laughs.*] They fired upon my carriage. [*Proudly.*] A patrol!—It does look rather as if it were made out of a pumpkin, does it not? like Cinderella's coach! and the footmen made out of rats! [*Blowing a kiss to* CHRISTIAN.] How do you do? [*Looking at them all.*] You do not look overjoyed! . . . Arras is a long way from Paris, do you know it? [*Catching sight of* CYRANO.] Cousin, delighted!

CYRANO. [*Coming toward her*]. But how did you . . . ?

ROXANE. How did I find the army? Dear me, cousin, that was simple: I followed straight along the line of devastation. . . . Ah, I should never have believed in such horrors had I not seen them! Gentlemen, if that is the service of your King, I like mine better!

CYRANO. But this is mad! . . . By what way did you come?

ROXANE. Way? . . . I drove through the Spaniards' camp.

FIRST CADET. Ah, what will keep lovely woman from her way!

DE GUICHE. But how did you contrive to get through their lines?

LE BRET. That must have been difficult . . .

ROXANE. No, not very. I simply drove through them, in my coach, at a trot. If a hidalgo, with arrogant front, showed likely to stop us, I put my face at the window, wearing my sweetest smile, and, those gentlemen being—let the French not grudge my saying so! —the most gallant in the world, . . . I passed!

CARBON. Such a smile is a passport, certainly! . . . But you must have been not unfrequently bidden to stand and deliver where you were going?

ROXANE. Not unfrequently, you are right. Whereupon I would say, "I am going to see my lover!" At once, the fiercest-looking Spaniard of them all would gravely close my carriage door; and, with a gesture the King might emulate, motion aside the musket-barrels leveled at me; and, superb at once for grace and haughtiness, bringing his spurs together, and lifting his plumed hat, bow low and say, "Pass, señorita, pass!"

CHRISTIAN. But, Roxane . . .

ROXANE. I said, "My lover!" yes, forgive me!—You see, if I had said, "My husband!" they would never have let me by!

CHRISTIAN. But . . .

ROXANE. What troubles you?

DE GUICHE. You must leave at once.

ROXANE. I?

CYRANO. At once!

LE BRET. As fast as you can.

CHRISTIAN. Yes, you must.

ROXANE. But why?

CHRISTIAN. [*Embarrassed.*] Because . . .

CYRANO. [*Embarrassed too.*] In three-quarters of an hour . . .

DE GUICHE. [*The same.*] Or an hour . . .

CARBON. [*The same.*] You had much better . . .

LE BRET. [*The same.*] You might . . .

ROXANE. I shall remain. You are going to fight.

ALL. Oh, no! . . . No!

ROXANE. He is my husband! [*She throws herself in* CHRISTIAN'S *arms.*] Let me be killed with you!

CHRISTIAN. How your eyes shine!

ROXANE. I will tell you why they shine!

DE GUICHE. [*Desperately.*] It is a post of horrible probabilities!

ROXANE. [*Turning toward him.*] What—of horrible . . . ?

CYRANO. In proof of which he appointed us to it! . . .

ROXANE. Ah, you wish me made a widow?

DE GUICHE. I swear to you . . .

ROXANE. No! Now I have lost all regard. . . . Now I will surely not go. . . . Besides, I think it fun!

CYRANO. What? The précieuse contained a heroine?

ROXANE. Monsieur de Bergerac, I am a cousin of yours!

ONE OF THE CADETS. Never think but that we will take good care of you!

ROXANE. [*More and more excited.*] I am sure you will, my friends!

OTHER CADET. The whole camp smells of iris!

ROXANE. By good fortune I put on a hat that will look well in battle! [*Glancing toward* DE GUICHE.]

But perhaps it is time the Count should go.—The battle might begin.

DE GUICHE. Ah, it is intolerable!—I am going to inspect my guns, and coming back.—You still have time: think better of it!

ROXANE. Never! [*Exit* DE GUICHE.

CHRISTIAN. [*Imploring.*] Roxane!

ROXANE. No!

FIRST CADET. She is going to stay!

ALL. [*Hurrying about, pushing one another, snatching things from one another.*] A comb!—Soap!—My jacket is torn, a needle!—A ribbon!—Lend me your pocket-mirror!—My cuffs!—Curling-irons!—A razor!

ROXANE. [*To* CYRANO, *who is still pleading with her.*] No! Nothing shall prevail upon me to stir from this spot!

CARBON. [*After having, like the others, tightened his belt, dusted himself, brushed his hat, straightened his feather, pulled down his cuffs, approaches* ROXANE, *and ceremoniously.*] It is, perhaps, proper, since you are going to stay, that I should present to you a few of the gentlemen about to have the honor of dying in your presence . . . [ROXANE *bows, and stands waiting, with her arm through* CHRISTIAN'S.] Baron Peyrescous de Colignac!

THE CADET. [*Bowing.*] Madame!

CARBON. [*Continuing to present the* CADETS.] Baron de Casterac de Cahuzac,—Vidame de Malgouyre Estressac Lesbas d'Escarabiot,—Chevalier d'Antignac-Juzet,—Baron Hillot de Blagnac-Saléchan de Castel Crabioules . . .

ROXANE. But how many names have you apiece?

BARON HILLOT. Innumerable!

CARBON. [*To* ROXANE.] Open your hand with the handkerchief!

ROXANE. [*Opens her hand; the handkerchief drops.*] Why?

[*The whole company starts forward to pick it up.*

CARBON. [*Instantly catching it.*] My company had no flag! Now, my word, it will have the prettiest one in the army!

ROXANE. [*Smiling.*] It is rather small!

CARBON. [*Fastening the handkerchief on the staff of his captain's spear.*] But it is lace!

ONE OF THE CADETS. [*To the others.*] I could die without a murmur, having looked upon that beautiful face, if I had so much as a walnut inside me! . . .

CARBON. [*Who has overheard, indignant.*] Shame! . . . to talk of food when an exquisite woman . . .

ROXANE. But the air of the camp is searching, and I myself am hungry: Patties, jellied meat, light wine . . . are what I should like best! Will you kindly bring me some? [*Consternation.*

ONE OF THE CADETS. Bring you some?

OTHER CADET. And where, great God, shall we get them?

ROXANE. [*Quietly.*] In my coach.

ALL. What?

ROXANE. But there is much to be done, carving and boning and serving. Look more closely at my coachman, gentlemen, and you will recognize a precious individual: the sauces, if we wish, can be warmed over . . .

THE CADETS. [*Springing toward the coach.*] It is Ragueneau! [*Cheers.*] Oh! Oh!

ROXANE. [*Watching them.*] Poor fellows!

CYRANO. [*Kissing her hand.*] Kind fairy!

RAGUENEAU. [*Standing upon the box-seat like a vendor at a public fair.*] Gentlemen!

[*Enthusiasm.*

THE CADETS. Bravo! Bravo!

RAGUENEAU. How should the Spaniards, when so much beauty passed, suspect the repast?

[*Applause.*

CYRANO. [*Low to* CHRISTIAN.] Hm! Hm! Christian!

RAGUENEAU. Absorbed in gallantry, no heed took they . . . [*he takes a dish from the box-seat*] . . . of galantine!

[*Applause. The galantine is passed from hand to hand.*

CYRANO. [*Low to* CHRISTIAN.] A word with you . . .

RAGUENEAU. Venus kept their eyes fixed upon herself, while Diana slipped past with the . . . [*he brandishes a joint*] . . . game!

[*Enthusiasm. The joint is seized by twenty hands at once.*

CYRANO. [*Low to* CHRISTIAN.] I must speak with you.

ROXANE. [*To the* CADETS *who come forward, their arms full of provisions.*] Spread it all upon the ground!

[*Assisted by the two imperturbable footmen who were on the back of the coach, she arranges everything on the grass.*

ROXANE. [*To* CHRISTIAN, *whom* CYRANO *is trying to draw aside.*] Make yourself useful, sir!

[CHRISTIAN *comes and helps her.* CYRANO *gives evidence of uneasiness.*

RAGUENEAU. A truffled peacock!

FIRST CADET. [*Radiant, comes forward cutting off a large slice of ham.*] Praise the pigs, we shall not go to our last fight with nothing in our b . . . [*correcting himself at sight of* ROXANE] . . . hm . . . stomachs!

RAGUENEAU. [*Flinging the carriage cushions.*] The cushions are stuffed with snipe!

[*Tumult. The cushions are ripped open. Laughter. Joy.*

RAGUENEAU. [*Flinging bottles of red wine.*] Molten ruby! [*Bottles of white wine.*] Fluid topaz!

ROXANE. [*Throwing a folded tablecloth to* CYRANO.] Unfold the cloth: Hey! . . . be nimble!

RAGUENEAU. [*Waving one of the coach lanterns.*] Each lantern is a little larder!

CYRANO. [*Low to* CHRISTIAN, *while together they spread the cloth.*] I must speak with you before you speak with her . . .

RAGUENEAU. The handle of my whip, behold, is a sausage!

ROXANE. [*Pouring wine, dispensing it.*] Since we are the ones to be killed, *morbleu,* we will not fret ourselves about the rest of the army! Everything for the Gascons! . . . And if De Guiche comes, nobody must invite him! [*Going from one to the other.*] Gently! You have time. . . . You must not eat so fast! There, drink. What are you crying about?

FIRST CADET. It is too good!

ROXANE. Hush! White wine or red?—Bread for Monsieur de Carbon!—A knife!—Pass your plate!—You prefer crust?—A little more?—Let me help you.—Champagne?—A wing? ——

CYRANO. [*Following* ROXANE, *his hands full of dishes, helping her.*] I adore her!

ROXANE. [*Going to* CHRISTIAN.] What will you take?

CHRISTIAN. Nothing!

ROXANE. Oh, but you must take something! This biscuit—in a little Muscatel—just a little?

CHRISTIAN. [*Trying to keep her from going.*] Tell me what made you come?

ROXANE. I owe myself to those poor fellows. . . . Be patient. . . . By and by . . .

LE BRET. [*Who had gone toward the back to pass a loaf of bread on the end of a pike to the* SENTINEL *upon the earthwork.*] De Guiche!

CYRANO. Presto! Vanish basket, flagon, platter and pan! Hurry! Let us look as if nothing were! [*To* RAGUENEAU.] Take a flying leap on to your box!—Is everything hidden?

[*In a wink, all the eatables have been pushed into the tents, or hidden under clothes, cloaks, hats. Enter* DE GUICHE, *hurriedly; he stops short, sniffing the air. Silence.*

DE GUICHE. What a good smell!

ONE OF THE CADETS. [*Singing, with effect of mental abstraction.*] To lo lo lo. . . .

DE GUICHE. [*Stopping and looking at him closely.*] What is the matter with you—you, there? You are red as a crab.

THE CADET. I? Nothing. . . . It is just my blood. . . . We are going to fight: it tells . . .

OTHER CADET. Poom . . . poom . . . poom . . .

DE GUICHE. [*Turning.*] What is this?

THE CADET. [*Slightly intoxicated.*] Nothing. . . . A song . . . just a little song.

DE GUICHE. You look in good spirits, my boy!

THE CADET. Danger affects me that way!

DE GUICHE. [*Calling* CARBON DE CASTEL-JALOUX *to give an order.*] Captain, I . . . [*He stops at sight of his face.*] *Peste!* You look in good spirits, too.

CARBON. [*Flushed, holding a bottle behind him; with an evasive gesture.*] Oh! . . .

DE GUICHE. I had a cannon left over, which I have

ordered them to place [*he points in the wing*] there, in that corner, and which your men can use, if necessary . . .

ONE OF THE CADETS. [*Swaying from one foot to the other.*] Charming attention!

OTHER CADET. [*Smiling sugarily.*] Our thanks for your gracious thoughtfulness!

DE GUICHE. Have they gone mad? . . . [*Drily.*] As you are not accustomed to handling a cannon, look out for its kicking . . .

FIRST CADET. Ah, pfft! . . .

DE GUICHE. [*Going toward him, furious.*] But . . .

THE CADET. A cannon knows better than to kick a Gascon!

DE GUICHE. [*Seizing him by the arm and shaking him.*] You are all tipsy: on what?

THE CADET. [*Magnificently.*] The smell of powder!

DE GUICHE. [*Shrugs his shoulders, pushes aside the* CADET, *and goes rapidly toward* ROXANE.] Quick, Madame! what have you condescended to decide?

ROXANE. I remain.

DE GUICHE. Retire, I beseech you!

ROXANE. No.

DE GUICHE. If you are determined, then. . . . Let me have a musket!

CARBON. What do you mean?

DE GUICHE. I, too, will remain.

CYRANO. At last, Monsieur, an instance of pure and simple bravery!

FIRST CADET. Might you be a Gascon, lace collar notwithstanding?

DE GUICHE. I do not leave a woman in danger.

SECOND CADET. [*To* FIRST CADET.] Look here! I think he might be given something to eat!

[*All the food reappears, as if by magic.*

DE GUICHE. [*His eyes brightening.*] Provisions?

THIRD CADET. Under every waistcoat!

DE GUICHE. [*Mastering himself haughtily.*] Do you imagine that I will eat your leavings?

CYRANO. [*Bowing.*] You are improving!

DE GUICHE. [*Proudly, falling at the last of the sentence into a slightly* GASCON *accent.*] I will fight before I eat!

FIRST CADET. [*Exultant.*] Fight! Eat! . . . He spoke with an accent!

DE GUICHE. [*Laughing.*] I did?

THE CADET. He is one of us!

[*All fall to dancing.*

CARBON. [*Who a moment before disappeared behind the earthworks, reappearing at the top.*] I have placed my pikemen. They are a determined troop . . .

[*He points at a line of pikes projecting above the bank.*

DE GUICHE. [*To* ROXANE, *bowing.*] Will you accept my hand and pass them in review?

[*She takes his hand; they go toward the bank. Every one uncovers and follows.*

CHRISTIAN. [*Going to* CYRANO, *quickly.*] Speak! Be quick!

[*As* ROXANE *appears at the top of the bank, the pikes disappear, lowered in a salute, and a cheer goes up;* ROXANE *bows.*

PIKEMEN. [*Outside.*] Vivat!

CHRISTIAN. What did you want to tell me?

CYRANO. In case Roxane . . .

CHRISTIAN. Well?

CYRANO. Should speak to you of the letters . . .

CHRISTIAN. Yes, the letters. I know!

CYRANO. Do not commit the blunder of appearing surprised . . .

CHRISTIAN. At what?

CYRANO. I must tell you! . . . It is quite simple, and merely comes into my mind to-day because I see her. You have . . .

CHRISTIAN. Hurry!

CYRANO. You . . . you have written to her oftener than you suppose . . .

CHRISTIAN. Oh, have I?

CYRANO. Yes. It was my business, you see. I had undertaken to interpret your passion, and sometimes I wrote without having told you I should write.

CHRISTIAN. Ah?

CYRANO. It is very simple.

CHRISTIAN. But how did you succeed since we have been so closely surrounded, in . . . ?

CYRANO. Oh, before daybreak I could cross the lines . . .

CHRISTIAN. [*Folding his arms.*] Ah, that is very simple, too? . . . And how many times a week have I been writing? Twice? Three times? Four? . . .

CYRANO. More.

CHRISTIAN. Every day?

CYRANO. Yes, every day . . . twice.

CHRISTIAN. [*Violently.*] And you cared so much about it that you were willing to brave death. . . .

CYRANO. [*Seeing* ROXANE *who returns.*] Be still. . . . Not before her!

[*He goes quickly into his tent.*

[CADETS *come and go at the back.* CARBON *and* DE GUICHE *give orders.*

ROXANE. [*Running to* CHRISTIAN.] And now, Christian . . .

CHRISTIAN. [*Taking her hands.*] And now, you shall tell me why, over these fearful roads, through these ranks of rough soldiery, you risked your dear self to join me?

ROXANE. Because of the letters!

CHRISTIAN. The . . . ? What did you say?

ROXANE. It is through your fault that I have been exposed to such and so many dangers. It is your letters that have gone to my head! Ah, think how many you have written me in a month, each one more beautiful. . . .

CHRISTIAN. What? . . . Because of a few little love letters . . .

ROXANE. Say nothing! You cannot understand! Listen: The truth is that I took to idolizing you one evening, when, below my window, in a voice I did not know before, your soul began to reveal itself. . . . Think then what the effect should be of your letters, which have been like your voice heard constantly for one month, your voice of that evening, so tender, caressing . . . You must bear it as you can, I have come to you! Prudent Penelope would not have stayed at home with her eternal tapestry, if Ulysses, her lord, had written as you write . . . but, impulsive as Helen, would have tossed aside her yarns, and flown to join him!

CHRISTIAN. But . . .

ROXANE. I read them, I re-read them, in reading I grew faint . . . I became your own indeed! Each fluttering leaf was like a petal of your soul wafted to me . . . In every word of those letters, love is felt as a flame would be felt,—love, compelling, sincere, profound . . .

CHRISTIAN. Ah, sincere, profound? . . . You say that it can be felt, Roxane?

ROXANE. He asks me!

CHRISTIAN. And so you came?

ROXANE. I came—oh Christian, my own, my master!

If I were to kneel at your feet you would lift me, I know. It is my soul therefore which kneels, and never can you lift it from that posture!—I came to implore your pardon—as it is fitting, for we are both perhaps about to die!—your pardon for having done you the wrong, at first, in my shallowness, of loving you . . . for mere looking!

CHRISTIAN. [*In alarm.*] Ah, Roxane! . . .

ROXANE. Later, dear one, grown less shallow—similar to a bird which flutters before it can fly,—your gallant exterior appealing to me still, but your soul appealing equally, I loved you for both! . . .

CHRISTIAN. And now?

ROXANE. Now at last yourself are vanquished by yourself: I love you for your soul alone. . . .

CHRISTIAN. [*Drawing away.*] Ah, Roxane!

ROXANE. Rejoice! For to be loved for that wherewith we are clothed so fleetingly must put a noble heart to torture. . . . Your dear thought at last casts your dear face in shadow: the harmonious lineaments whereby at first you pleased me, I do not see them, now my eyes are open!

CHRISTIAN. Oh!

ROXANE. You question your own triumph?

CHRISTIAN. [*Sorrowfully.*] Roxane!

ROXANE. I understand, you cannot conceive of such a love in me?

CHRISTIAN. I do not wish to be loved like that! I wish to be loved quite simply . . .

ROXANE. For that which other women till now have loved in you? Ah, let yourself be loved in a better way.

CHRISTIAN. No . . . I was happier before! . . .

ROXANE. Ah, you do not understand! It is now that

I love you most, that I truly love you. It is that which makes you, you—can you not grasp it?—that I worship . . . And did you no longer walk our earth like a young martial Apollo . . .

CHRISTIAN. Say no more!

ROXANE. Still would I love you! . . . Yes, though a blight should have fallen upon your face and form . . .

CHRISTIAN. Do not say it!

ROXANE. But I do say it, . . . I do!

CHRISTIAN. What? If I were ugly, distinctly, offensively?

ROXANE. If you were ugly, dear, I swear it!

CHRISTIAN. God!

ROXANE. And you are glad, profoundly glad?

CHRISTIAN. [*In a smothered voice.*] Yes . . .

ROXANE. What is it?

CHRISTIAN. [*Pushing her gently away.*] Nothing. I have a word or two to say to some one: your leave, for a second . . .

ROXANE. But . . .

CHRISTIAN. [*Pointing at a group of* CADETS *at the back.*] In my selfish love, I have kept you from those poor brothers. . . . Go, smile on them a little, before they die, dear . . . go!

ROXANE. [*Moved.*] Dear Christian!

[*She goes toward the* GASCONS *at the back; they respectfully gather around her.*

CHRISTIAN. [*Calling toward* CYRANO'S *tent.*] Cyrano!

CYRANO. [*Appears, armed for battle.*] What is it? . . . How pale you are!

CHRISTIAN. She does not love me any more!

CYRANO. What do you mean?

CHRISTIAN. She loves you.

CYRANO. No!

CHRISTIAN. She only loves my soul!

CYRANO. No!

CHRISTIAN. Yes! Therefore it is you she loves . . . and you love her . . .

CYRANO. I . . .

CHRISTIAN. I know it!

CYRANO. It is true.

CHRISTIAN. To madness!

CYRANO. More.

CHRISTIAN. Tell her then.

CYRANO. No!

CHRISTIAN. Why not?

CYRANO. Look at me!

CHRISTIAN. She would love me grown ugly.

CYRANO. She told you so?

CHRISTIAN. With the utmost frankness!

CYRANO. Ah! I am glad she should have told you that! But, believe me, believe me, place no faith in such a mad avowal! Dear God, I am glad such a thought should have come to her, and that she should have spoken it,—but believe me, do not take her at her word. Never cease to be the handsome fellow you are. . . . She would not forgive me!

CHRISTIAN. That is what I wish to discover.

CYRANO. No! no!

CHRISTIAN. Let her choose between us! You shall tell her everything.

CYRANO. No . . . No . . . I refuse the ordeal!

CHRISTIAN. Shall I stand in the way of your happiness because my outside is not so much amiss?

CYRANO. And I? Shall I destroy yours, because thanks to the hazard that sets us upon earth, I have the gift of expressing . . . what you perhaps feel?

CHRISTIAN. You shall tell her everything!

CYRANO. He persists in tempting me . . . It is a mistake . . . and cruel!

CHRISTIAN. I am weary of carrying about, in my own self, a rival!

CYRANO. Christian!

CHRISTIAN. Our marriage . . . contracted without witnesses . . . can be annulled . . . if we survive!

CYRANO. He persists! . . .

CHRISTIAN. Yes. I will be loved for my sole self, or not at all!—I am going to see what they are about. Look! I will walk to the end of the line and back . . . Tell her, and let her pronounce between us.

CYRANO. She will pronounce for you.

CHRISTIAN. I can but hope she will! [*Calling.*] Roxane!

CYRANO. No! No!

ROXANE. [*Coming forward.*] What is it?

CHRISTIAN. Cyrano has something to tell you . . . something important!

[ROXANE *goes hurriedly to* CYRANO. *Exit* CHRISTIAN.

ROXANE. Something important?

CYRANO. [*Distracted.*] He is gone! . . . [*To* ROXANE.] Nothing whatever! He attaches—but you must know him of old!—he attaches importance to trifles . . .

ROXANE. [*Quickly.*] He did not believe what I told him a moment ago? . . . I saw that he did not believe . . .

CYRANO. [*Taking her hand.*] But did you tell him all the truth?

ROXANE. Yes. Yes. I should love him even . . .

[*She hesitates a second.*

CYRANO. [*Smiling sadly.*] You do not like to say it before me?

ROXANE. But . . .

CYRANO. I shall not mind! . . . Even if he were ugly?

ROXANE. Yes . . . Ugly. [*Musket shots outside.*] They are firing!

CYRANO. [*Ardently.*] Dreadfully ugly?

ROXANE. Dreadfully.

CYRANO. Disfigured?

ROXANE. Disfigured!

CYRANO. Grotesque?

ROXANE. Nothing could make him grotesque . . . to me.

CYRANO. You would love him still?

ROXANE. I believe that I should love him more . . . if that were possible!

CYRANO. [*Losing his head, aside.*] My God, perhaps she means it . . . perhaps it is true . . . and that way is happiness! [*To* ROXANE.] I . . . Roxane . . . listen!

LE BRET. [*Comes in hurriedly; calls softly.*] Cyrano!

CYRANO. [*Turning.*] *Hein?*

LE BRET. Hush!

[*He whispers a few words to* CYRANO.

CYRANO. [*Letting* ROXANE's *hand drop, with a cry.*] Ah! . . .

ROXANE. What ails you?

CYRANO. [*To himself, in consternation.*] It is finished!

[*Musket reports.*

ROXANE. What is it? What is happening? Who is firing?

[*She goes to the back to look off.*

CYRANO. It is finished. . . . My lips are sealed for evermore!

[CADETS *come in, attempting to conceal some-*

*thing they carry among them; they surround it, preventing* Roxane's *seeing it.*

Roxane. What has happened?

Cyrano. [*Quickly stopping her as she starts toward them.*] Nothing!

Roxane. These men? . . .

Cyrano. [*Drawing her away.*] Pay no attention to them!

Roxane. But what were you about to say to me before?

Cyrano. What was I about to say? . . . Oh, nothing! . . . Nothing whatever, I assure you. [*Solemnly.*] I swear that Christian's spirit, that his soul, were . . . [*in terror, correcting himself*] are the greatest that . . .

Roxane. Were? . . . [*With a great cry.*] Ah! . . .

[*Runs to the group of* Cadets, *and thrusts them aside.*

Cyrano. It is finished!

Roxane. [*Seeing* Christian *stretched out in his cloak.*] Christian!

Le Bret. [*To* Cyrano.] At the enemy's first shot!

[Roxane *throws herself on* Christian's *body. Musket reports. Clashing of swords. Tramping. Drums.*

Carbon. [*Sword in hand.*] The attack! To your muskets!

[*Followed by the* Cadets *he goes to the further side of the earthworks.*

Roxane. Christian!

Carbon's Voice. [*Beyond the earthworks.*] Make haste!

Roxane. Christian!

Carbon. Fall into line!

ROXANE. Christian!

CARBON. Measure . . . match!

[RAGUENEAU *has come running in with water in a steel cap.*

CHRISTIAN. [*In a dying voice.*] Roxane!

CYRANO. [*Quick, low in* CHRISTIAN'S *ear, while* ROXANE, *distracted, dips into the water a fragment of linen torn from her breast to bind his wound.*] I have told her everything! . . . You are still the one she loves!

[CHRISTIAN *closes his eyes.*

ROXANE. What, dear love?

CARBON. Muzzle . . . high!

ROXANE. [*To* CYRANO.] He is not dead? . . .

CARBON. Open charge . . . with teeth!

ROXANE. I feel his cheek grow cold against my own!

CARBON. Take aim!

ROXANE. A letter on his breast. . . . [*She opens it.*] To me!

CYRANO. [*Aside.*] My letter!

CARBON. Fire!

[*Musket shots. Cries. Roar of battle.*

CYRANO. [*Trying to free his hand which* ROXANE *clasps kneeling.*] But, Roxane, they are fighting.

ROXANE. [*Clinging.*] No! . . . Stay with me a little! . . . He is dead. You are the only one that truly knew him. . . . [*She cries subduedly.*] Was he not an exquisite being, . . . an exceptional, marvelous being? . . .

CYRANO. [*Standing bareheaded.*] Yes, Roxane.

ROXANE. A poet without his peer, . . . one verily to reverence?

CYRANO. Yes, Roxane.

ROXANE. A sublime spirit?

CYRANO. Yes, Roxane.

ROXANE. A profound heart, such as the profane could never have understood . . . a soul as noble as it was charming? . . .

CYRANO. [*Firmly.*] Yes, Roxane.

ROXANE. [*Throwing herself on* CHRISTIAN'S *body.*] And he is dead!

CYRANO. [*Aside, drawing his sword.*] And I have now only to die, since, without knowing it, she mourns my death in his!

[*Trumpets in the distance.*

DE GUICHE. [*Reappears on the top of the bank, bareheaded, his forehead bloody; in a thundering voice.*] The signal they promised! The flourish of trumpets! . . . The French are entering the camp with supplies! . . . Stand fast a little longer!

ROXANE. Upon his letter . . . blood, . . . tears!

A VOICE. [*Outside, shouting.*] Surrender!

VOICES OF THE CADETS. No!

RAGUENEAU. [*Who from the top of the coach is watching the battle beyond the bank.*] The conflict rages hotter! . . .

CYRANO. [*To* DE GUICHE *pointing at* ROXANE.] Take her away! . . . I am going to charge.

ROXANE. [*Kissing the letter, in a dying voice.*] His blood! . . . his tears!

RAGUENEAU. [*Leaping from the coach and running to* ROXANE.] She is fainting!

DE GUICHE. [*At the top of the bank, to the* CADETS, *madly.*] Stand fast!

VOICE. [*Outside.*] Surrender!

VOICES OF THE CADETS. No!

CYRANO. [*To* DE GUICHE.] Your courage none will question . . . [*Pointing at* ROXANE.] Fly for the sake of saving her!

DE GUICHE. [*Runs to* ROXANE *and lifts her in his*

*arms.*] So be it! But we shall win the day if you can hold out a little longer . . .

CYRANO. We can. [*To* ROXANE, *whom* DE GUICHE, *helped by* RAGUENEAU, *is carrying off insensible.*] Good-bye, Roxane!

[*Tumult. Cries.* CADETS *reappear wounded, and fall upon the stage.* CYRANO *dashing forward to join the combatants is stopped on the crest of the bank by* CARBON *covered with blood.*

CARBON. We are losing ground . . . have got two halberd wounds . . .

CYRANO. [*Yelling to the* GASCONS.] Steadfast! . . . Never give them an inch! . . . Brave boys! [*To* CARBON.] Fear nothing! I have various deaths to avenge: Christian's and all my hopes'! [*They come down.* CYRANO *brandishes the spear at the head of which* ROXANE'S *handkerchief is fastened.*] Float free, little cobweb flag, embroidered with her initials! [*He drives the spear-staff into the earth; shouts to the* CADETS.] Fall on them, boys! . . . Crush them! [*To the fifer.*] Fifer, play!

[*The fifer plays. Some of the wounded get to their feet again. Some of the* CADETS, *coming down the bank, group themselves around* CYRANO *and the little flag. The coach, filled and covered with men, bristles with muskets and becomes a redoubt.*

ONE OF THE CADETS. [*Appears upon the top of the bank backing while he fights; he cries.*] They are coming up the slope!

[*Falls dead.*

CYRANO. We will welcome them!

[*Above the bank suddenly rises a formidable*

*array of enemies. The great banners of the Imperial Army appear.*

CYRANO. Fire!

[*General discharge.*

CRY. [*Among the hostile ranks.*] Fire!

[*Shots returned.* CADETS *drop on every side.*

A SPANISH OFFICER. [*Taking off his hat.*] What are these men, so determined all to be killed?

CYRANO. [*Declaiming, as he stands in the midst of flying bullets.*]

They are the Gascony Cadets
Of Carbon de Castel-Jaloux;
Famed fighters, liars, desperates . . .

[*He leaps forward, followed by a handful of survivors.*

They are the Gascony Cadets! . . .

[*The rest is lost in the confusion of battle.*

CURTAIN

# ACT FIFTH

## CYRANO'S GAZETTE

*Fifteen years later, 1655. The park belonging to the convent of the Sisters of the Cross, in Paris.*

*Superb shade-trees. At the left, the house; several doors opening on to a broad terrace with steps. In the center of the stage, huge trees standing alone in a clear oval space. At the right, first wing, a semicircular stone seat, surrounded by large box-trees.*

*All along the back of the stage, an avenue of chestnut-trees, which leads, at the right, fourth wing, to the door of a chapel seen through trees. Through the double row of trees overarching the avenue are seen lawns, other avenues, clumps of trees, the further recesses of the park, the sky.*

*The chapel opens by a small side-door into a colonnade, overrun by a scarlet creeper; the colonnade comes forward and is lost to sight behind the box-trees at the right.*

*It is autumn. The leaves are turning, above the still fresh grass. Dark patches of evergreens, box and yew. Under each tree a mat of yellow leaves. Fallen leaves litter the whole stage, crackle underfoot, lie thick on the terrace and the seats.*

*Between the seat at the right and the tree in the center, a large embroidery frame, in front of which a small chair. Baskets full of wools, in skeins and balls. On the frame, a piece of tapestry, partly done.*

*At the rise of the curtain, nuns come and go in the park; a few are seated on the stone seat around an older nun; leaves are falling.*

SISTER MARTHA. [*To* MOTHER MARGARET.] Sister Claire, after putting on her cap, went back to the mirror, to see herself again.

MOTHER MARGARET. [*To* SISTER CLAIRE.] It was unbecoming, my child.

SISTER CLAIRE. But Sister Martha, to-day, after finishing her portion, went back to the tart for a plum. I saw her!

MOTHER MARGARET. [*To* SISTER MARTHA.] My child, it was ill done.

SISTER CLAIRE. I merely glanced! . . .

SISTER MARTHA. The plum was about so big! . . .

MOTHER MARGARET. This evening, when Monsieur Cyrano comes, I will tell him.

SISTER CLAIRE. [*Alarmed.*] No! He will laugh at us!

SISTER MARTHA. He will say that nuns are very vain!

SISTER CLAIRE. And very greedy!

MOTHER MARGARET. And really very good.

SISTER CLAIRE. Mother Margaret, is it not true that he has come here every Saturday in the last ten years?

MOTHER MARGARET. Longer! Ever since his cousin brought among our linen coifs her coif of crape, the worldly symbol of her mourning, which settled like a sable bird amidst our flock of white some fourteen years ago.

SISTER MARTHA. He alone, since she took her abode in our cloister, has art to dispel her never-lessening sorrow.

ALL THE NUNS. He is so droll!—It is merry when

he comes!—He teases us!—He is delightful!—We are greatly attached to him!—We are making Angelica paste to offer him!

SISTER MARTHA. He is not, however, a very good Catholic!

SISTER CLAIRE. We will convert him.

THE NUNS. We will! We will!

MOTHER MARGARET. I forbid your renewing that attempt, my children. Do not trouble him: he might not come so often!

SISTER MARTHA. But . . . God!

MOTHER MARGARET. Set your hearts at rest: God must know him of old!

SISTER MARTHA. But every Saturday, when he comes, he says to me as soon as he sees me, "Sister, I ate meat, yesterday!"

MOTHER MARGARET. Ah, that is what he says? . . . Well, when he last said it, he had eaten nothing for two days.

SISTER MARTHA. Mother!

MOTHER MARGARET. He is poor.

SISTER MARTHA. Who told you?

MOTHER MARGARET. Monsieur Le Bret.

SISTER MARTHA. Does no one offer him assistance?

MOTHER MARGARET. No, he would take offense.

> [*In one of the avenues at the back, appears* ROXANE, *in black, wearing a widow's coif and long mourning veil;* DE GUICHE *markedly older, magnificently dressed, walks beside her. They go very slowly.* MOTHER MARGARET *gets up.*

MOTHER MARGARET. Come, we must go within. Madame Magdeleine is walking in the park with a visitor.

SISTER MARTHA. [*Low to* SISTER CLAIRE.] Is not that the Marshal-duke de Grammont?

SISTER CLAIRE. [*Looking.*] I think it is!

SISTER MARTHA. He has not been to see her in many months!

THE NUNS. He is much engaged!—The Court!—The Camp!—

SISTER CLAIRE. Cares of this world!

[*Exeunt.* DE GUICHE *and* ROXANE *come forward silently, and stop near the embroidery frame. A pause.*

DE GUICHE. And so you live here, uselessly fair, always in mourning?

ROXANE. Always.

DE GUICHE. As faithful as of old?

ROXANE. As faithful.

DE GUICHE. [*After a time.*] Have you forgiven me?

ROXANE. Since I am here.

[*Another silence.*

DE GUICHE. And he was really such a rare being?

ROXANE. To understand, one must have known him!

DE GUICHE. Ah, one must have known him! . . . Perhaps I did not know him well enough. And his last letter, still and always, against your heart?

ROXANE. I wear it on this velvet, as a more holy scapular.

DE GUICHE. Even dead, you love him?

ROXANE. It seems to me sometimes he is but half dead, that our hearts have not been severed, that his love still wraps me round, no less than ever living!

DE GUICHE. [*After another silence.*] Does Cyrano come here to see you?

ROXANE. Yes, often. That faithful friend fulfils for me the office of gazette. His visits are regular. He comes: when the weather is fine, his armchair is brought out under the trees. I wait for him here with my work; the hour strikes; on the last stroke, I hear—I do not even turn to see who comes!—his cane upon the steps; he takes his seat; he rallies me upon my never-ending tapestry; he tells off the events of the week, and . . . [LE BRET *appears on the steps.*] Ah, Le Bret! [LE BRET *comes down the steps.*] How does your friend?

LE BRET. Ill.

DE GUICHE. Oh!

ROXANE. He exaggerates! . . .

LE BRET. All is come to pass as I foretold: neglect! poverty! his writings ever breeding him new enemies! Fraud he attacks in every embodiment: usurpers, pious pretenders, plagiarists, asses in lions' skins . . . all! He attacks all!

ROXANE. No one, however, but stands in profound respect of his sword. They will never succeed in silencing him.

DE GUICHE. [*Shaking his head.*] Who knows?

LE BRET. What I fear is not the aggression of man; what I fear is loneliness and want and winter creeping upon him like stealthy wolves in his miserable attic; they are the insidious foes that will have him by the throat at last! . . . Every day he tightens his belt by an eyelet; his poor great nose is pinched, and turned the sallow of old ivory; the worn black serge you see him in is the only coat he has!

DE GUICHE. Ah, there is one who did not succeed! . . . Nevertheless, do not pity him too much.

LE BRET. [*With a bitter smile.*] Marshal! . . .

DE GUICHE. Do not pity him too much: he signed no bonds with the world; he has lived free in his thoughts as in his actions.

LE BRET. [*As above.*] Duke . . .

DE GUICHE. [*Haughtily.*] I know, yes: I have

everything, he has nothing. . . . But I should like to shake hands with him. [*Bowing to* ROXANE.] Good-bye.

ROXANE. I will go with you to the door.

[DE GUICHE *bows to* LE BRET *and goes with* ROXANE *toward the terrace steps.*

DE GUICHE. [*Stopping, while she goes up the steps.*] Yes, sometimes I envy him. You see, when a man has succeeded too well in life, he is not unlikely to feel—dear me! without having committed any very serious wrong!—a multitudinous disgust at himself, the sum of which does not constitute a real remorse, but an obscure uneasiness; and a ducal mantle, while it sweeps up the stairs of greatness, may trail in its furry lining a rustling of sere illusions and regrets, as, when you slowly climb toward those doors, your black gown trails the withered leaves.

ROXANE. [*Ironical.*] Are you not unusually pensive? . . .

DE GUICHE. Ah, yes! [*As he is about to leave, abruptly.*] Monsieur Le Bret! [*To* ROXANE.] Will you allow me? A word. [*He goes to* LE BRET, *and lowering his voice.*] It is true that no one will dare overtly to attack your friend, but many have him in particular disrelish; and some one was saying to me yesterday, at the Queen's, "It seems not unlikely that this Cyrano will meet with an accident."

LE BRET. Ah? . . .

DE GUICHE. Yes. Let him keep indoors. Let him be cautious.

LE BRET. [*Lifting his arms toward Heaven.*] Cautious! . . . He is coming here. I will warn him. Warn him! . . . Yes, but . . .

ROXANE. [*Who has been standing at the head of the steps, to a nun who comes toward her.*] What is it?

THE NUN. Ragueneau begs to see you, Madame.

ROXANE. Let him come in. [*To* DE GUICHE *and* LE BRET.] He comes to plead distress. Having determined one day to be an author, he became in turn precentor . . .

LE BRET. Bath-house keeper . . .

ROXANE. Actor . . .

LE BRET. Beadle . . .

ROXANE. Barber . . .

LE BRET. Arch-lute teacher . . .

ROXANE. I wonder what he is now!

RAGUENEAU. [*Entering precipitately.*] Ah, Madame! [*He sees* LE BRET.] Monsieur!

ROXANE. [*Smiling.*] Begin telling your misfortunes to Le Bret. I am coming back.

RAGUENEAU. But, Madame . . .

[ROXANE *leaves without listening, with the* DUKE. RAGUENEAU *goes to* LE BRET.

RAGUENEAU. It is better so. Since you are here, I had liefer not tell her! Less than half an hour ago, I was going to see your friend. I was not thirty feet from his door, when I saw him come out. I hurried to catch up with him. He was about to turn the corner. I started to run, when from a window below which he was passing—was it pure mischance? It may have been!—a lackey drops a block of wood . . .

LE BRET. Ah, the cowards! . . . Cyrano!

RAGUENEAU. I reach the spot, and find him . . .

LE BRET. Horrible!

RAGUENEAU. Our friend, Monsieur, our poet, stretched upon the ground, with a great hole in his head!

LE BRET. He is dead?

RAGUENEAU. No, but . . . God have mercy! I carried him to his lodging . . . . Ah, his lodging! You should see that lodging of his!

LE BRET. Is he in pain?

RAGUENEAU. No, Monsieur, he is unconscious.

LE BRET. Has a doctor seen him?

RAGUENEAU. One came . . . out of good nature.

LE BRET. My poor, poor Cyrano! . . . We must not tell Roxane outright. And the doctor? . . .

RAGUENEAU. He talked . . . I hardly grasped . . . of fever . . . cerebral inflammation! Ah, if you should see him, with his head done up in cloths! . . . Let us hurry . . . No one is there to tend him . . . And he might die if he attempted to get up!

LE BRET. [*Dragging* RAGUENEAU *off at the right.*] This way. Come, it is shorter through the chapel.

ROXANE. [*Appearing at the head of the steps, catching sight of* LE BRET *hurrying off through the colonnade which leads to the chapel side-door.*] Monsieur Le Bret! [LE BRET *and* RAGUENEAU *make their escape without answering.*] Le Bret not turning back when he is called? . . . Poor Ragueneau must be in some new trouble! [*She comes down the steps.*] How beautiful . . . how beautiful, this golden-hazy waning day of September at its wane! My sorrowful mood, which the exuberant gladness of April offends, Autumn, the dreamy and subdued, lures on to smile . . . [*She sits down at her embroidery frame. Two* NUNS *come from the house bringing a large armchair which they place under the tree.*] Ah, here comes the classic armchair in which my old friend always sits!

SISTER MARTHA. The best in the convent parlor!

ROXANE. I thank you, sister. [*The nuns withdraw.*] He will be here in a moment. [*She adjusts the embroidery frame before her.*] There! The clock is striking . . . My wools! . . . The clock has struck?

. . . I wonder at this! . . . Is it possible that for the first time he is late? . . . It must be that the sister who keeps the door . . . my thimble? ah, here it is! . . . is detaining him to exhort him to repentance . . . [*A pause.*] She exhorts him at some length! . . . He cannot be much longer . . . A withered leaf! [*She brushes away the dead leaf which has dropped on the embroidery.*] Surely nothing could keep . . . my scissors? . . . in my workbag! . . . could keep him from coming!

A NUN. [*Appearing at the head of the steps.*] Monsieur de Bergerac!

ROXANE. [*Without turning round.*] What was I saying? . . . [*She begins to embroider.* CYRANO *appears, exceedingly pale, his hat drawn down over his eyes. The* NUN *who has shown him into the garden withdraws. He comes down the steps very slowly, with evident difficulty to keep on his feet, leaning heavily on his cane.* ROXANE *proceeds with her sewing.*] Ah, these dull soft shades! . . . How shall I match them? [*To* CYRANO, *in a tone of friendly chiding.*] After fourteen years, for the first time you are late!

CYRANO. [*Who has reached the armchair and seated himself, in a jolly voice which contrasts with his face.*] Yes, it seems incredible! I am savage at it. I was detained, spite of all I could do! . . .

ROXANE. By . . . ?

CYRANO. A somewhat inopportune call.

ROXANE. [*Absent-minded, sewing.*] Ah, yes . . . some troublesome fellow!

CYRANO. Cousin, it was a troublesome Madame.

ROXANE. You excused yourself?

CYRANO. Yes. I said, "Your pardon, but this is Saturday, on which day I am due in a certain dwelling. On no account do I ever fail. Come back in an hour!"

ROXANE. [*Lightly.*] Well, she will have to wait some time to see you. I shall not let you go before evening.

CYRANO. Perhaps . . . I shall have to go a little earlier.

[*He closes his eyes and is silent a moment.* [SISTER MARTHA *is seen crossing the park from the chapel to the terrace.* ROXANE *sees her and beckons to her by a slight motion of her head.*

ROXANE. [*To* CYRANO.] Are you not going to tease Sister Martha to-day?

CYRANO. [*Quickly, opening his eyes.*] I am indeed! [*In a comically gruff voice.*] Sister Martha, come nearer! [*The* NUN *demurely comes toward him.*] Ha! ha! ha! Beautiful eyes, ever studying the ground!

SISTER MARTHA. [*Lifting her eyes and smiling.*] But . . . [*She sees his face and makes a gesture of surprise.*] Oh!

CYRANO. [*Low, pointing at* ROXANE.] Hush! . . . It is nothing! [*In a swaggering voice, aloud.*] Yesterday, I ate meat!

SISTER MARTHA. I am sure you did! [*Aside.*] That is why he is so pale! [*Quickly, low.*] Come to the refectory presently. I shall have ready for you there a good bowl of broth . . . You will come!

CYRANO. Yes, yes, yes.

SISTER MARTHA. Ah, you are more reasonable to-day!

ROXANE. [*Hearing them whisper.*] She is trying to convert you?

SISTER MARTHA. Indeed I am not!

CYRANO. It is true, you, usually almost discursive in the holy cause, are reading me no sermon! You amaze me! [*With comical fury.*] I will amaze you, too! Listen, you are authorized . . . [*With the air of casting about in his mind, and finding the jest he wants.*]

Ah, now I shall amaze you! to . . . pray for me, this evening . . . in the chapel.

ROXANE. Oh! oh!

CYRANO. [*Laughing.*] Sister Martha . . . lost in amazement!

SISTER MARTHA. [*Gently.*] I did not wait for your authorization. [*She goes in.*

CYRANO. [*Turning to* ROXANE, *who is bending over her embroidery.*] The devil, tapestry . . . the devil, if I hope to live to see the end of you!

ROXANE. I was waiting for that jest.

[*A slight gust of wind makes the leaves fall.*

CYRANO. The leaves!

ROXANE. [*Looking up from her work and gazing off toward the avenues.*] They are the russet gold of a Venetian beauty's hair . . . Watch them fall!

CYRANO. How consummately they do it! In that brief fluttering from bough to ground, how they contrive still to put on beauty! And though foredoomed to moulder upon the earth that draws them, they wish their fall invested with the grace of a free bird's flight!

ROXANE. Serious, you?

CYRANO. [*Remembering himself.*] Not at all, Roxane!

ROXANE. Come, never mind the falling leaves! Tell me the news, instead . . . Where is my budget?

CYRANO. Here it is!

ROXANE. Ah!

CYRANO. [*Growing paler and paler, and struggling with pain.*] Saturday, the nineteenth: The king having filled his dish eight times with Cette preserves, and emptied it, was taken with a fever; his distemper, for high treason, was condemned to be let blood, and now the royal pulse is rid of febriculosity! On Sunday: at the Queen's great ball, were burned seven hundred and sixty-three wax candles; our troops, it is said, defeated Austrian John; four sorcerers were hanged; Madame Athis's little dog had a distressing turn, the case called for a . . .

ROXANE. Monsieur de Bergerac, leave out the little dog!

CYRANO. Monday, . . . nothing, or next to it: Lygdamire took a fresh lover.

ROXANE. Oh!

CYRANO. [*Over whose face is coming a change more and more marked.*] Tuesday: the whole Court assembled at Fontainebleau. Wednesday, the fair Monglat said to Count Fiesco "No!" Thursday, Mancini, Queen of France, . . . or little less. Twenty-fifth, the fair Monglat said to Count Fiesco "Yes!" And Saturday, the twenty-sixth . . .

[*He closes his eyes. His head drops on his breast. Silence.*

ROXANE. [*Surprised at hearing nothing further, turns, looks at him and starts to her feet in alarm.*] Has he fainted? [*She runs to him, calling.*] Cyrano!

CYRANO. [*Opening his eyes, in a faint voice.*] What is it? . . . What is the matter? [*He sees* ROXANE *bending over him, hurriedly readjusts his hat, pulling it more closely over his head, and shrinks back in his armchair in terror.*] No! no! I assure you, it is nothing! . . . Do not mind me!

ROXANE. But surely . . .

CYRANO. It is merely the wound I received at Arras . . . Sometimes . . . you know . . . even now . . .

ROXANE. Poor friend!

CYRANO. But it is nothing . . . It will pass . . . [*He smiles with effort.*] It has passed.

ROXANE. Each one of us has his wound. I too

have mine. It is here, never to heal, that ancient wound . . . [*She places her hand on her breast.*] It is here beneath the yellowing letter on which are still faintly visible tear-drops and drops of blood!

[*The light is beginning to grow less.*

CYRANO. His letter? . . . Did you not once say that some day . . . you might show it to me?

ROXANE. Ah! . . . Do you wish? . . . His letter?

CYRANO. Yes . . . to-day . . . I wish to . . .

ROXANE. [*Handing him the little bag from her neck.*] Here!

CYRANO. I may open it?

ROXANE. Open it . . . read!

[*She goes back to her embroidery frame, folds it up, orders her wools.*

CYRANO. "Good-bye, Roxane! I am going to die!"

ROXANE. [*Stopping in astonishment.*] You are reading it aloud?

CYRANO. [*Reading.*] "It is fated to come this evening, beloved, I believe! My soul is heavy, oppressed with love it had not time to utter . . . and now Time is at end! Never again, never again shall my worshiping eyes . . ."

ROXANE. How strangely you read his letter!

CYRANO. [*Continuing.*] ". . . whose passionate revel it was, kiss in its fleeting grace your every gesture. One, usual to you, of tucking back a little curl, comes to my mind . . . and I cannot refrain from crying out . . ."

ROXANE. How strangely you read his letter! . . .

[*The darkness gradually increases.*

CYRANO. "and I cry out: Good-bye!"

ROXANE. You read it . . .

CYRANO. "my dearest, my darling, . . . my treasure . . ."

ROXANE. . . . in a voice . . .

CYRANO. ". . . my love! . . ."

ROXANE. . . . in a voice . . . a voice which I am not hearing for the first time!

[ROXANE *comes quietly nearer to him, without his seeing it; she steps behind his armchair, bends noiselessly over his shoulder, looks at the letter. The darkness deepens.*

CYRANO. ". . . My heart never desisted for a second from your side . . . and I am and shall be in the world that has no end, the one who loved you without measure, the one . . ."

ROXANE. [*Laying her hand on his shoulder.*] How can you go on reading? It is dark. [CYRANO *starts, and turns round; sees her close to him, makes a gesture of dismay and hangs his head. Then, in the darkness which has completely closed round them, she says slowly, clasping her hands:*] And he, for fourteen years, has played the part of the comical old friend who came to cheer me!

CYRANO. Roxane!

ROXANE. So it was you.

CYRANO. No, no, Roxane!

ROXANE. I ought to have divined it, if only by the way in which he speaks my name!

CYRANO. No, it was not I!

ROXANE. So it was you!

CYRANO. I swear to you . . .

ROXANE. Ah, I detect at last the whole generous imposture. The letters . . . were yours!

CYRANO. No!

ROXANE. The tender fancy, the dear folly, . . . yours!

CYRANO. No!

ROXANE. The voice in the night, was yours!

CYRANO. I swear to you that it was not!

ROXANE. The soul . . . was yours! .

CYRANO. I did not love you, no!

ROXANE. And you loved me!

CYRANO. Not I . . . it was the other!

ROXANE. You loved me!

CYRANO. No!

ROXANE. Already your denial comes more faintly!

CYRANO. No, no, my darling love, I did not love you!

ROXANE. Ah, how many things within the hour have died . . . how many have been born! Why, why have you been silent these long years, when on this letter, in which he had no part, the tears were yours?

CYRANO. [*Handing her the letter.*] Because . . . the blood was his.

ROXANE. Then why let the sublime bond of this silence be loosed to-day?

CYRANO. Why?

[LE BRET *and* RAGUENEAU *enter running.*

LE BRET. Madness! Monstrous madness! . . . Ah, I was sure of it! There he is!

CYRANO. [*Smiling and straightening himself.*] *Tiens!* Where else?

LE BRET. Madame, he is likely to have got his death by getting out of bed!

ROXANE. Merciful God! A moment ago, then . . . that faintness . . . that . . .?

CYRANO. It is true. I had not finished telling you the news. And on Saturday, the twenty-sixth, an hour after sundown, Monsieur de Bergerac died of murder done upon him.

[*He takes off his hat; his head is seen wrapped in bandages.*

ROXANE. What is he saying? . . . Cyrano? . . . Those bandages about his head? . . . Ah, what have they done to you? . . . Why? . . .

CYRANO. "Happy who falls, cut off by a hero, with

an honest sword through his heart!" I am quoting from myself! . . . Fate will have his laugh at us! . . . Here am I killed, in a trap, from behind, by a lackey, with a log! Nothing could be completer! In my whole life I shall have not had anything I wanted . . . not even a decent death!

RAGUENEAU. Ah, Monsieur! . . .

CYRANO. Ragueneau, do not sob like that! [*Holding out his hand to him.*] And what is the news with you, these latter days, fellow-poet?

RAGUENEAU. [*Through his tears.*] I am candle-snuffer at Molière's theater.

CYRANO. Molière!

RAGUENEAU. But I intend to leave no later than to-morrow. Yes, I am indignant! Yesterday, they were giving Scapin, and I saw that he has appropriated a scene of yours.

LE BRET. A whole scene?

RAGUENEAU. Yes, Monsieur. The one in which occurs the famous "What the devil was he doing in . . ."*

LE BRET. Molière has taken that from you!

CYRANO. Hush! hush! He did well to take it! [*To* RAGUENEAU.] The scene was very effective, was it not?

RAGUENEAU. Ah, Monsieur, the public laughed . . . laughed!

CYRANO. Yes, to the end, I shall have been the one who prompted . . . and was forgotten! [*To* ROXANE.] Do you remember that evening on which Christian spoke to you from below the balcony? There was the epitome of my life: while I have stood below in darkness, others have climbed to gather the kiss and glory! It is well done, and on the brink of my grave I approve it: Molière has genius . . . Christian was a fine fellow!

* *Que diable allait il faire daus cette galère?* was the phrase that Molière rendered proverbial in this play.

[*At this moment, the chapel bell having rung, the* NUNS *are seen passing at the back, along the avenue, on their way to service.*] Let them hasten to their prayers . . . the bell is summoning them . . .

ROXANE. [*Rising and calling.*] Sister! Sister!

CYRANO. [*Holding her back.*] No! No! do not leave me to fetch anybody! When you came back I might not be here to rejoice . . . [*The* NUNS *have gone into the chapel; the organ is heard.*] I longed for a little music . . . it comes in time!

ROXANE. I love you . . . you shall live!

CYRANO. No! for it is only in the fairy-tale that the shy and awkward prince when he hears the beloved say "I love you!" feels his ungainliness melt and drop from him in the sunshine of those words! . . . But you would always know full well, dear Heart, that there had taken place in your poor slave no beautifying change!

ROXANE. I have hurt you . . . I have wrecked your life, I! . . . I!

CYRANO. You? . . . The reverse! Woman's sweetness I had never known. My mother . . . thought me unflattering. I had no sister. Later, I shunned Love's cross-road in fear of mocking eyes. To you I owe having had, at least, among the gentle and fair, a friend. Thanks to you there has passed across my life the rustle of a woman's gown.

LE BRET. [*Calling his attention to the moonlight peering through the branches.*] Your other friend, among the gentle and fair, is there . . . she comes to see you!

CYRANO. [*Smiling to the moon.*] I see her!

ROXANE. I never loved but one . . . and twice I lose him!

CYRANO. Le Bret, I shall ascend into the opalescent moon, without need this time of a flying-machine!

ROXANE. What are you saying?

CYRANO. Yes, it is there, you may be sure, I shall be sent for my Paradise. More than one soul of those I have loved must be apportioned there . . . There I shall find Socrates and Galileo!

LE BRET. [*In revolt.*] No! No! It is too senseless, too cruel, too unfair! So true a poet! So great a heart! To die . . . like this! To die! . . .

CYRANO. As ever . . . Le Bret is grumbling!

LE BRET. [*Bursting into tears.*] My friend! My friend!

CYRANO. [*Lifting himself, his eyes wild.*] They are the Gascony Cadets! . . . Man in the gross . . . Eh, yes! . . . the weakness of the weakest point . . .

LE BRET. Learned . . . even in his delirium! . . .

CYRANO. Copernicus said . . .

ROXANE. Oh!

CYRANO. But what the devil was he doing . . . and what the devil was he doing in that galley?

Philosopher and physicist,
Musician, rhymester, duellist,
Explorer of the upper blue,
Retorter apt with point and point,
Lover as well,—not for his peace!
Here lies Hercule Savinien
De Cyrano de Bergerac,
Who was everything . . . but of account!

But, your pardons, I must go . . . I wish to keep no one waiting . . . See, a moonbeam, come to take me home! [*He has dropped in his chair;* ROXANE's *weeping calls him back to reality; he looks at her and gently stroking her mourning veil.*] I do not wish . . . indeed, I do not wish . . . that you should sorrow less for Christian, the comely and the kind! Only I wish that when the everlasting cold shall have seized upon my fibers, this funereal veil should have a twofold meaning, and the mourning you wear for him be worn for me too . . . a little!

ROXANE. I promise . . .

CYRANO. [*Seized with a great shivering, starts to his feet.*] Not there! No! Not in an elbow-chair! [*All draw nearer to help him.*] Let no one stay me! No one. [*He goes and stands against the tree.*] Nothing but this tree! [*Silence.*] She comes. Mors, the indiscriminate Madame! . . . Already I am booted with marble . . . gauntleted with lead! [*He stiffens himself.*] Ah, since she is on her way, I will await her standing . . . [*He draws his sword.*] Sword in hand!

LE BRET. Cyrano!

ROXANE. [*Swooning.*] Cyrano!

[*All start back, terrified.*

CYRANO. I believe she is looking at me . . . that she dares to look at my nose, the bony baggage who has none! [*He raises his sword.*] What are you saying? That it is no use? . . . I know it! But one does not fight because there is hope of winning! No! . . . no! . . . it is much finer to fight when it is no use! . . . What are all those? You are a thousand strong? . . . Ah, I know you now . . . all my ancient enemies! . . . Hypocrisy? . . . [*He beats with his sword, in the vacancy.*] Take this! and this! Ha! Ha! Compromises? . . . and Prejudices? and dastardly Expedients? [*He strikes.*] That I should come to terms, I? . . . Never! Never! . . . Ah, you are there too, you bloated and pompous Silliness! I know full well that you will lay me low at last . . . No matter: whilst I have breath, I will fight you, I will fight you, I will fight you! [*He waves his sword in great sweeping circles, and stops, panting.*] Yes, you have wrested from me everything, laurel as well as rose . . . Work your wills! . . . Spite of your worst, something will still be left me to take whither I go . . . and to-night when I enter God's house, in saluting, broadly will I sweep the azure threshold with what despite of all I carry forth unblemished and unbent . . . [*he starts forward, with lifted sword*] . . . and that is . . .

[*The sword falls from his hands, he staggers, drops in the arms of* LE BRET *and* RAGUENEAU.

ROXANE. [*Bending over him and kissing his forehead.*] That is? . . .

CYRANO. [*Opens his eyes again, recognizes her and says with a smile:*] . . . My plume!

CURTAIN

# UNCLE VANYA

## SCENES FROM COUNTRY LIFE

BY

ANTON P. CHEKHOV

*Translated by* MARIAN FELL.

## Anton Pavlovich Chekhov

b. 1860, Taganrog, Russia.
M. D., University of Moscow, 1884.
1886, First volume of short stories published.
1888, Awarded Pushkin prize.
1898, Begins association with the Moscow Art Theatre.
1904, Dies of tuberculosis.
Journalist and short-story writer.

### Plays

1884 *On the High Road* (one act, also translated as *On the Highway*).
1887 *Ivanov.*
1888 *The Tragedian in Spite of Himself* (one act, also translated as *An Unwilling Martyr*).
1888 *The Bear* (one act, also translated as *The Boor*).
1889 *The Wood Demon.*
1889 *That Worthless Fellow Platonov* (unfinished).
1889 *Tatyana Riepin* (one act, continuation of A. S. Suvorin's play of same name).
1889 *The Swan Song* (one act).
1889 *The Proposal* (one act, also translated as *A Marriage Proposal*).
1896 *The Sea Gull.*
1897 *Uncle Vanya* (revision of *The Wood Demon*).
1900 *The Three Sisters.*
1903 *The Jubilee* (one act, also translated as *The Anniversary*).
1903 *The Wedding* (one act).
1904 *The Cherry Orchard* (also translated as *The Cherry Garden*).

## UNCLE VANYA

Chekhov's feeling toward the theater and playwriting was curious. He seems always to have felt distrust of them, in relation at least to his own work. Though he began writing plays as early as he began to write at all, he usually destroyed his work. As late as September, 1887, he writes, "I will not write any play. I have absolutely no interest in the theatre, nor in humanity." But, persuaded by his friends, and by the opportunity for making money, he wrote *Ivanov,* his first full-length play, in two weeks during October, 1887. Then he had fits of nervousness lest the play should be inadequately mounted and acted. He could only with difficulty be persuaded that in performance it had been a marked success. These fears, the counterpart, no doubt, of the highest hopes, became habitual with him in regard to all his plays. By his short stories he had early won reputation, and he regarded his work in that form with more confidence, but he said, "The novel is a lawful wife, but the stage is a noisy, flashy, and insolent mistress."

*Uncle Vanya,* in its original form, was Chekhov's second full-length play. Planned by him in collaboration with A. S. Suvorin, who withdrew, it was entitled *The Wood Demon,* and occupied Chekhov from October, 1888, to October, 1889. He seems at first to have thought well of it, but when it was not favorably received on performance, to have become quite discouraged. *The Wood Demon* was therefore not printed during his lifetime. But he seems to have kept the manuscript by him, and to have worked over it from time to time, so that in 1897, when an edition of his plays was being published, he decided to include with the already produced *Sea Gull* and *Ivanov* what he called "the universally unknown *Uncle Vanya.*" By means of this publication the play became known, and was frequently played in the provincial theaters of Russia during 1898, and by the Moscow Art Theatre in 1899.

The steps in the development of *Uncle Vanya* from synopsis through *The Wood Demon* to the form in which we now have it may be fairly easily traced, by reference to Chekhov's letters and the still extant early play. Through them it may be seen how consistently Chekhov moved toward economy and force: by elimination of unnecessary characters, by tautening emotion, by subtilizing action, by giving the whole an allegorical value. The early play has thirteen speaking characters, the revision only nine; in *The Wood Demon* the quarrel between the professor and his brother-in-law is broken into by the entrance of extraneous people, in *Uncle Vanya* it continues with rising tensity to the attempted murder; and in *The Wood Demon* there is no parallel to the beautiful speech of Sonia which closes *Uncle Vanya.*

The outstanding production of *Uncle Vanya* in America took place in 1930 under the direction of Jed Harris, with Lillian Gish as Helena and Osgood Perkins as Astroff.

For further discussion of Chekhov's work, see the prefaces to *The Sea Gull* and *The Cherry Orchard,* in *Contemporary Drama, European Plays, III* and *IV.*

## CHARACTERS

ALEXANDER SEREBRAKOFF, *a retired professor.*
HELENA, *his wife, twenty-seven years old.*
SONIA, *his daughter by a former marriage.*
MME. VOITSKAYA, *widow of a privy councilor, and mother of Serebrakoff's first wife.*
IVAN (VANYA) VOITSKI, *her son.*
MICHAEL ASTROFF, *a doctor.*
ILIA (WAFFLES) TELEGIN, *an impoverished landowner.*
MARINA, *an old nurse.*
A WORKMAN.

*The scene is laid on* SEREBRAKOFF'S *country place.*

# UNCLE VANYA

## ACT FIRST

*A country house on a terrace. In front of it a garden. In an avenue of trees, under an old poplar, stands a table set for tea, with a samovar, etc. Some benches and chairs stand near the table. On one of them is lying a guitar. A hammock is swung near the table. It is three o'clock in the afternoon of a cloudy day.*

MARINA, *a quiet, gray-haired, little old woman, is sitting at the table knitting a stocking.* ASTROFF *is walking up and down near her.*

MARINA. [*Pouring some tea into a glass.*] Take a little tea, my son.

ASTROFF. [*Takes the glass from her unwillingly.*] Somehow, I don't seem to want any.

MARINA. Then will you have a little vodka instead?

ASTROFF. No, I don't drink vodka every day, and besides, it is too hot now. [*A pause.*] Tell me, nurse, how long have we known each other?

MARINA. [*Thoughtfully.*] Let me see, how long is it? Lord—help me to remember. You first came here, into our parts—let me think—when was it? Sonia's mother was still alive—it was two winters before she died; that was eleven years ago—[*thoughtfully*] perhaps more.

ASTROFF. Have I changed much since then?

MARINA. Oh, yes. You were handsome and young then, and now you are an old man and not handsome any more. You drink, too.

ASTROFF. Yes, ten years have made me another man. And why? Because I am overworked. Nurse, I am on my feet from dawn till dusk. I know no rest; at night I tremble under my blankets for fear of being dragged out to visit some one who is sick; I have toiled without repose or a day's freedom since I have known you; could I help growing old? And then, existence is tedious, anyway; it is a senseless, dirty business, this life, and goes heavily. Every one about here is silly, and after living with them for two or three years one grows silly oneself. It is inevitable. [*Twisting his mustache.*] See what a long mustache I have grown. A foolish, long mustache. Yes, I am as silly as the rest, nurse, but not as stupid; no, I have not grown stupid. Thank God, my brain is not addled yet, though my feelings have grown numb. I ask nothing, I need nothing, I love no one, unless it is yourself alone. [*He kisses her head.*] I had a nurse just like you when I was a child.

MARINA. Don't you want a bite of something to eat?

ASTROFF. No. During the third week of Lent I went to the epidemic at Malitskoi. It was eruptive typhoid. The peasants were all lying side by side in their huts, and the calves and pigs were running about the floor among the sick. Such dirt there was, and smoke! Unspeakable! I slaved among those people all day, not a crumb passed my lips, but when I got home there was still no rest for me; a switchman was carried in from the railroad; I laid him on the operating table and he went and died in my arms under chloroform, and then my feelings that should have been deadened awoke again, my conscience tortured me as if I had killed the man. I sat down and closed my eyes—like this—and thought: will our descendants two hundred years from now, for whom we are breaking the road, remember to give us a kind word? No, nurse, they will forget.

MARINA. Man is forgetful, but God remembers.

ASTROFF. Thank you for that. You have spoken the truth.

[*Enter* VOITSKI *from the house. He has been asleep after dinner and looks rather disheveled. He sits down on the bench and straightens his collar.*

VOITSKI. H'm. Yes. [*A pause.*] Yes.

ASTROFF. Have you been asleep?

VOITSKI. Yes, very much so. [*He yawns.*] Ever since the Professor and his wife have come, our daily life seems to have jumped the track. I sleep at the wrong time, drink wine, and eat all sorts of messes for luncheon and dinner. It isn't wholesome. Sonia and I used to work together and never had an idle moment, but now Sonia works alone and I only eat and drink and sleep. Something is wrong.

MARINA. [*Shaking her head.*] Such a confusion in the house! The Professor gets up at twelve, the samovar is kept boiling all the morning, and everything has to wait for him. Before they came we used to have dinner at one o'clock, like everybody else, but now we have it at seven. The Professor sits up all night writing and reading, and suddenly, at two o'clock, there goes the bell! Heavens, what is that? The Professor wants some tea! Wake the servants, light the samovar! Lord, what disorder!

ASTROFF. Will they be here long?

VOITSKI. A hundred years! The Professor has decided to make his home here.

MARINA. Look at this now! The samovar has been on the table for two hours, and they are all out walking!

VOITSKI. All right, don't get excited; here they come.

[*Voices are heard approaching.* SEREBRAKOFF, HELENA, SONIA, *and* TELEGIN *come in from the depths of the garden, returning from their walk.*

SEREBRAKOFF. Superb! Superb! What beautiful views!

TELEGIN. They are wonderful, your Excellency.

SONIA. To-morrow we shall go into the woods, shall we, papa?

VOITSKI. Ladies and gentlemen, tea is ready.

SEREBRAKOFF. Won't you please be good enough to send my tea into the library? I still have some work to finish.

SONIA. I am sure you will love the woods.

[HELENA, SEREBRAKOFF, *and* SONIA *go into the house.* TELEGIN *sits down at the table beside* MARINA.

VOITSKI. There goes our learned scholar on a hot, sultry day like this, in his overcoat and goloshes and carrying an umbrella!

ASTROFF. He is trying to take good care of his health.

VOITSKI. How lovely she is! How lovely! I have never in my life seen a more beautiful woman.

TELEGIN. Do you know, Marina, that as I walk in the fields or in the shady garden, as I look at this table here, my heart swells with unbounded happiness. The weather is enchanting, the birds are singing, we are all living in peace and contentment—what more could the soul desire? [*Takes a glass of tea.*

VOITSKI. [*Dreaming.*] Such eyes—a glorious woman!

ASTROFF. Come, Ivan, tell us something.

VOITSKI. [*Indolently.*] What shall I tell you?

ASTROFF. Haven't you any news for us?

VOITSKI. No, it is all stale. I am just the same as usual, or perhaps worse, because I have become lazy. I don't do anything now but croak like an old raven. My mother, the old magpie, is still chattering about the emancipation of woman, with one eye on her grave and the other on her learned books, in which she is always looking for the dawn of a new life.

ASTROFF. And the Professor?

VOITSKI. The Professor sits in his library from morning till night, as usual—

> "Straining the mind, wrinkling the brow,
> We write, write, write,
> Without respite
> Or hope of praise in the future or now."

Poor paper! He ought to write his autobiography; he would make a really splendid subject for a book! Imagine it, the life of a retired professor, as stale as a piece of hardtack, tortured by gout, headaches, and rheumatism, his liver bursting with jealousy and envy, living on the estate of his first wife, although he hates it, because he can't afford to live in town. He is everlastingly whining about his hard lot, though, as a matter of fact, he is extraordinarily lucky. He is the son of a common deacon and has attained the professor's chair, become the son-in-law of a senator, is called "your Excellency," and so on. But I'll tell you something; the man has been writing on art for twenty-five years, and he doesn't know the very first thing about it. For twenty-five years he has been chewing on other men's thoughts about realism, naturalism, and all such foolishness; for twenty-five years he has been reading and writings things that clever men have long known and stupid ones are not interested in; for twenty-five years he has been making his imaginary mountains out of molehills. And just think of the man's self-conceit and presumption all this time! For twenty-five years he has been masquerading in false clothes and has now retired, absolutely unknown to any living soul; and yet see him! stalking across the earth like a demi-god!

ASTROFF. I believe you envy him.

VOITSKI. Yes, I do. Look at the success he has had with women! Don Juan himself was not more favored. His first wife, who was my sister, was a beautiful, gentle being, as pure as the blue heaven there above us, noble, great-hearted, with more admirers than he has pupils, and she loved him as only beings of angelic purity can love those who are as pure and beautiful as themselves. His mother-in-law, my mother, adores him to this day, and he still inspires a sort of worshipful awe in her. His second wife is, as you see, a brilliant beauty; she married him in his old age and has surrendered all the glory of her beauty and freedom to him. Why? What for?

ASTROFF. Is she faithful to him?

VOITSKI. Yes, unfortunately she is.

ASTROFF. Why "unfortunately"?

VOITSKI. Because such fidelity is false and unnatural, root and branch. It sounds well, but there is no logic in it. It is thought immoral for a woman to deceive an old husband whom she hates, but quite moral for her to strangle her poor youth in her breast and banish every vital desire from her heart.

TELEGIN. [*In a tearful voice.*] Vanya, I don't like to hear you talk so. Listen, Vanya; every one who betrays husband or wife is faithless, and could also betray his country.

VOITSKI. [*Crossly.*] Turn off the tap, Waffles.

TELEGIN. No, allow me, Vanya. My wife ran away with a lover on the day after our wedding, because my exterior was unprepossessing. I have never failed in my duty since then. I love her and am true to her to this day. I help her all I can and have given my fortune to educate the daughter of herself and her lover. I have forfeited my happiness, but I have kept my pride. And she? Her youth has fled, her beauty has faded according to the laws of nature, and her lover is dead. What has she kept?

[HELENA *and* SONIA *come in; after them comes* MME. VOITSKAYA *carrying a book. She sits down and begins to read. Some one hands her a glass of tea which she drinks without looking up.*

SONIA. [*Hurriedly, to the nurse.*] There are some peasants waiting out there. Go and see what they want. I shall pour the tea.

[*Pours out some glasses of tea.*

[MARINA *goes out.* HELENA *takes a glass and sits drinking in the hammock.*

ASTROFF. I have come to see your husband. You wrote me that he had rheumatism and I know not what else, and that he was very ill, but he appears to be as lively as a cricket.

HELENA. He had a fit of the blues yesterday evening and complained of pains in his legs, but he seems all right again to-day.

ASTROFF. And I galloped over here twenty miles at breakneck speed! No matter, though, it is not the first time. Once here, however, I am going to stay until to-morrow, and at any rate sleep *quantum satis*.

SONIA. Oh, splendid! You so seldom spend the night with us. Have you had dinner yet?

ASTROFF. No.

SONIA. Good. So you will have it with us. We

dine at seven now. [*Drinks her tea.*] This tea is cold!

TELEGIN. Yes, the samovar has grown cold.

HELENA. Don't mind, Monsieur Ivan, we will drink cold tea, then.

TELEGIN. I beg your pardon, my name is not Ivan, but Ilia, ma'am—Ilia Telegin, or Waffles, as I am sometimes called on account of my pock-marked face. I am Sonia's godfather, and his Excellency, your husband, knows me very well. I now live with you, ma'am, on this estate, and perhaps you will be so good as to notice that I dine with you every day.

SONIA. He is our great help, our right-hand man. [*Tenderly.*] Dear godfather, let me pour you some tea.

MME. VOITSKAYA. Oh! Oh!

SONIA. What is it, grandmother?

MME. VOITSKAYA. I forgot to tell Alexander—I have lost my memory—I received a letter to-day from Paul Alexevitch in Kharkoff. He has sent me a new pamphlet.

ASTROFF. Is it interesting?

MME. VOITSKAYA. Yes, but strange. He refutes the very theories which he defended seven years ago. It is appalling!

VOITSKI. There is nothing appalling about it. Drink your tea, mamma.

MME. VOITSKAYA. It seems you never want to listen to what I have to say. Pardon me, Jean, but you have changed so in the last year that I hardly know you. You used to be a man of settled convictions and had an illuminating personality——

VOITSKI. Oh, yes. I had an illuminating personality, which illuminated no one. [*A pause.*] I had an illuminating personality! You couldn't say anything more biting. I am forty-seven years old. Until last year I endeavored, as you do now, to blind my eyes by your pedantry to the truths of life. But now—— Oh, if you only knew! If you knew how I lie awake at night, heartsick and angry, to think how stupidly I have wasted my time when I might have been winning from life everything which my old age now forbids.

SONIA. Uncle Vanya, how dreary!

MME. VOITSKAYA. [*To her son.*] You speak as if your former convictions were somehow to blame, but you yourself, not they, were at fault. You have forgotten that a conviction, in itself, is nothing but a dead letter. You should have done something.

VOITSKI. Done something! Not every man is capable of being a writer *perpetuum mobile* like your Herr Professor.

MME. VOITSKAYA. What do you mean by that?

SONIA. [*Imploringly.*] Mother! Uncle Vanya! I entreat you!

VOITSKI. I am silent. I apologize and am silent.

[*A pause.*

HELENA. What a fine day! Not too hot. [*A pause.*

VOITSKI. A fine day to hang oneself.

[TELEGIN *tunes the guitar.* MARINA *appears near the house, calling the chickens.*

MARINA. Chick, chick, chick!

SONIA. What did the peasants want, nurse?

MARINA. The same old thing, the same old nonsense. Chick, chick, chick!

SONIA. Why are you calling the chickens?

MARINA. The speckled hen has disappeared with her chicks. I am afraid the crows have got her.

[TELEGIN *plays a polka. All listen in silence. Enter* WORKMAN.

WORKMAN. Is the doctor here? [*To* ASTROFF.] Excuse me, sir, but I have been sent to fetch you.

ASTROFF. Where are you from?

WORKMAN. The factory.

ASTROFF. [*Annoyed.*] Thank you. There is nothing for it, then, but to go. [*Looking around him for his cap.*] Damn it, this is annoying!

SONIA. Yes, it is too bad, really. You must come back to dinner from the factory.

ASTROFF. No, I won't be able to do that. It will be too late. Now where, where—— [*To the* WORKMAN.] Look here, my man, get me a glass of vodka, will you? [*The* WORKMAN *goes out.*] Where—where—— [*Finds his cap.*] One of the characters in Ostroff's plays is a man with a long mustache and short wits, like me. However, let me bid you good-bye, ladies and gentlemen. [*To* HELENA.] I should be really delighted if you would come to see me some day with Miss Sonia. My estate is small, but if you are interested in such things I should like to show you a nursery and seed-bed whose like you will not find within a thousand miles of here. My place is surrounded by government forests. The forester is old and always ailing, so I superintend almost all the work myself.

HELENA. I have always heard that you were very fond of the woods. Of course one can do a great deal of good by helping to preserve them, but does not that work interfere with your real calling?

ASTROFF. God alone knows what a man's real calling is.

HELENA. And do you find it interesting?

ASTROFF. Yes, very.

VOITSKI. [*Sarcastically.*] Oh, extremely!

HELENA. You are still young, not over thirty-six or seven, I should say, and I suspect that the woods do not interest you as much as you say they do. I should think you would find them monotonous.

SONIA. No, the work is thrilling. Dr. Astroff watches over the old woods and sets out new plantations every year, and he has already received a diploma and a bronze medal. If you will listen to what he can tell you, you will agree with him entirely. He says that forests are the ornaments of the earth, that they teach mankind to understand beauty and attune his mind to lofty sentiments. Forests temper a stern climate, and in countries where the climate is milder, less strength is wasted in the battle with nature, and the people are kind and gentle. The inhabitants of such countries are handsome, tractable, sensitive, graceful in speech and gesture. Their philosophy is joyous, art and science blossom among them, their treatment of women is full of exquisite nobility——

VOITSKI. [*Laughing.*] Bravo! Bravo! All that is very pretty, but it is also unconvincing. So, my friend [*to* ASTROFF], you must let me go on burning firewood in my stoves and building my sheds of planks.

ASTROFF. You can burn peat in your stoves and build your sheds of stone. Oh, I don't object, of course, to cutting wood from necessity, but why destroy the forests? The woods of Russia are trembling under the blows of the axe. Millions of trees have perished. The homes of the wild animals and birds have been desolated; the rivers are shrinking, and many beautiful landscapes are gone forever. And why? Because men are too lazy and stupid to stoop down and pick up their fuel from the ground. [*To* HELENA.] Am I not right, Madame? Who but a stupid barbarian could burn so much beauty in his stove and destroy that which he cannot make? Man is endowed with reason and the power to create, so that he may increase that which has been given him, but until now he has not created, but demolished. The forests are disappearing, the rivers are running dry, the game is exterminated, the climate is spoiled, and the earth becomes poorer and uglier every day. [*To* VOITSKI.] I read irony in your eye; you do not take what I am saying seriously, and—and—after all, it may very well be nonsense. But when I pass peasant-forests that I have preserved from the axe, or hear the rustling of the young plantations set out with my own hands, I feel as if I had had some small share in improving the climate, and that if mankind is happy a thousand years from now I will have been a little bit responsible for their happiness. When I plant a little birch tree and then see it budding into young green and swaying in the wind, my heart swells with pride and I—— [*Sees the* WORKMAN, *who is bringing him a glass of vodka on a tray.*] However—[*he drinks*] I must be off. Probably it is all nonsense, anyway. Good-bye.

[*He goes toward the house.* SONIA *takes his arm and goes with him.*

SONIA. When are you coming to see us again?

ASTROFF. I can't say.

SONIA. In a month?

[ASTROFF *and* SONIA *go into the house.* HELENA *and* VOITSKI *walk over to the terrace.*

HELENA. You have behaved shockingly again. Ivan, what sense was there in teasing your mother and talking about *perpetuum mobile*? And at breakfast you quarreled with Alexander again. Really, your behavior is too petty.

VOITSKI. But if I hate him?

HELENA. You hate Alexander without reason; he is like every one else, and no worse than you are.

VOITSKI. If you could only see your face, your gestures! Oh, how tedious your life must be.

HELENA. It is tedious, yes, and dreary! You all abuse my husband and look on me with compassion; you think, "Poor woman, she is married to an old man."

How well I understand your compassion! As Astroff said just now, see how you thoughtlessly destroy the forests, so that there will soon be none left. So you also destroy mankind, and soon fidelity and purity and self-sacrifice will have vanished with the woods. Why cannot you look calmly at a woman unless she is yours? Because, the doctor was right, you are all possessed by a devil of destruction; you have no mercy on the woods or the birds or on women or on one another.

VOITSKI. I don't like your philosophy.

HELENA. That doctor has a sensitive, weary face—an interesting face. Sonia evidently likes him, and she is in love with him, and I can understand it. This is the third time he has been here since I have come, and I have not had a real talk with him yet or made much of him. He thinks I am disagreeable. Do you know, Ivan, the reason you and I are such friends? I think it is because we are both lonely and unfortunate. Yes, unfortunate. Don't look at me in that way, I don't like it.

VOITSKI. How can I look at you otherwise when I love you? You are my joy, my life, and my youth. I know that my chances of being loved in return are infinitely small, do not exist, but I ask nothing of you. Only let me look at you, listen to your voice——

HELENA. Hush, some one will overhear you.

[*They go toward the house.*

VOITSKI. [*Following her.*] Let me speak to you of my love, do not drive me away, and this alone will be my greatest happiness!

HELENA. Ah! This is agony!

[TELEGIN *strikes the strings of his guitar and plays a polka.* MME. VOITSKAYA *writes something on the leaves of her pamphlet.*

[*The curtain falls.*]

## ACT SECOND

*The dining-room of* SEREBRAKOFF'S *house. It is night. The tapping of the* WATCHMAN'S *rattle is heard in the garden.* SEREBRAKOFF *is dozing in an arm-chair by an open window and* HELENA *is sitting beside him, also half asleep.*

SEREBRAKOFF. [*Rousing himself.*] Who is here? Is it you, Sonia?

HELENA. It is I.

SEREBRAKOFF. Oh, it is you, Nelly. This pain is intolerable.

HELENA. Your shawl has slipped down. [*She wraps up his legs in the shawl.*] Let me shut the window.

SEREBRAKOFF. No, leave it open; I am suffocating. I dreamt just now that my left leg belonged to some one else, and it hurt so that I woke. I don't believe this is gout, it is more like rheumatism. What time is it?

HELENA. Half-past twelve. [*A pause.*

SEREBRAKOFF. I want you to look for Batushka's works in the library to-morrow. I think we have him.

HELENA. What is that?

SEREBRAKOFF. Look for Batushka to-morrow morning; we used to have him, I remember. Why do I find it so hard to breathe?

HELENA. You are tired; this is the second night you have had no sleep.

SEREBRAKOFF. They say that Turgenieff got angina of the heart from gout. I am afraid I am getting angina too. Oh, damn this horrible, accursed old age! Ever since I have been old I have been hateful to myself, and I am sure, hateful to you all as well.

HELENA. You speak as if we were to blame for your being old.

SEREBRAKOFF. I am more hateful to you than to any one.

[HELENA *gets up and walks away from him, sitting down at a distance.*

SEREBRAKOFF. You are quite right, of course. I am not an idiot; I can understand you. You are young and healthy and beautiful, and longing for life, and I am an old dotard, almost a dead man already. Don't I know it? Of course I see that it is foolish for me to live so long, but wait! I shall soon set you all free. My life cannot drag on much longer.

HELENA. You are overtaxing my powers of endurance. Be quiet, for God's sake!

SEREBRAKOFF. It appears that, thanks to me, everybody's power of endurance is being overtaxed; everybody is miserable, only I am blissfully triumphant. Oh, yes, of course!

HELENA. Be quiet! You are torturing me.

SEREBRAKOFF. I torture everybody. Of course.

HELENA. [*Weeping.*] This is unbearable! Tell me, what is it you want me to do?

SEREBRAKOFF. Nothing.

HELENA. Then be quiet, please.

SEREBRAKOFF. It is funny that everybody listens to Ivan and his old idiot of a mother, but the moment I open my lips you all begin to feel ill-treated. You can't even stand the sound of my voice. Even if I am hateful, even if I am a selfish tyrant, haven't I the right to be one at my age? Haven't I deserved it? Haven't I, I ask you, the right to be respected, now that I am old?

HELENA. No one is disputing your rights. [*The window slams in the wind.*] The wind is rising, I must shut the window. [*She shuts it.*] We shall have rain in a moment. Your rights have never been questioned by anybody.

[*The* WATCHMAN *in the garden sounds his rattle.*

SEREBRAKOFF. I have spent my life working in the interests of learning. I am used to my library and the lecture hall and to the esteem and admiration of my colleagues. Now I suddenly find myself plunged in this wilderness, condemned to see the same stupid people from morning till night and listen to their futile conversation. I want to live; I long for success and fame and the stir of the world, and here I am in exile! Oh, it is dreadful to spend every moment grieving for the lost past, to see the success of others and sit here with nothing to do but to fear death. I cannot stand it! It is more than I can bear. And you will not even forgive me for being old!

HELENA. Wait, have patience; I shall be old myself in four or five years.

[SONIA *comes in.*

SONIA. Father, you sent for Dr. Astroff, and now when he comes you refuse to see him. It is not nice to give a man so much trouble for nothing.

SEREBRAKOFF. What do I care about your Astroff? He understands medicine about as well as I understand astronomy.

SONIA. We can't send for the whole medical faculty, can we, to treat your gout?

SEREBRAKOFF. I won't talk to that madman!

SONIA. Do as you please. It's all the same to me.

[*She sits down.*

SEREBRAKOFF. What time is it?

HELENA. One o'clock.

SEREBRAKOFF. It is stifling in here. Sonia, hand me that bottle on the table.

SONIA. Here it is.

[*She hands him a bottle of medicine.*

SEREBRAKOFF. [*Crossly.*] No, not that one! Can't you understand me? Can't I ask you to do a thing?

SONIA. Please don't be captious with me. Some people may like it, but you must spare me, if you please, because I don't. Besides, I haven't the time; we are cutting the hay to-morrow and I must get up early.

[VOITSKI *comes in dressed in a long gown and carrying a candle.*

VOITSKI. A thunderstorm is coming up. [*The lightning flashes.*] There it is! Go to bed, Helena and Sonia. I have come to take your place.

SEREBRAKOFF. [*Frightened.*] No, no, no! Don't leave me alone with him! Oh, don't. He will begin to lecture me.

VOITSKI. But you must give them a little rest. They have not slept for two nights.

SEREBRAKOFF. Then let them go to bed, but you go away too! Thank you. I implore you to go. For the sake of our former friendship do not protest against going. We will talk some other time——

VOITSKI. Our former friendship! Our former——

SONIA. Hush, Uncle Vanya!

SEREBRAKOFF. [*To his wife.*] My darling, don't leave me alone with him. He will begin to lecture me.

VOITSKI. This is ridiculous.

[MARINA *comes in carrying a candle.*

SONIA. You must go to bed, nurse, it is late.

MARINA. I haven't cleared away the tea things. Can't go to bed yet.

SEREBRAKOFF. No one can go to bed. They are all worn out, only I enjoy perfect happiness.

MARINA. [*Goes up to* SEREBRAKOFF *and speaks tenderly.*] What's the matter, master? Does it hurt?

My own legs are aching too, oh, so badly. [*Arranges his shawl about his legs.*] You have had this illness such a long time. Sonia's dead mother used to stay awake with you too, and wear herself out for you. She loved you dearly. [*A pause.*] Old people want to be pitied as much as young ones, but nobody cares about them somehow. [*She kisses* SEREBRAKOFF'S *shoulder.*] Come, master, let me give you some linden-tea and warm your poor feet for you. I shall pray to God for you.

SEREBRAKOFF. [*Touched.*] Let us go, Marina.

MARINA. My own feet are aching so badly, oh, so badly! [*She and* SONIA *lead* SEREBRAKOFF *out.*] Sonia's mother used to wear herself out with sorrow and weeping. You were still little and foolish then, Sonia. Come, come, master.

[SEREBRAKOFF, SONIA, *and* MARINA *go out.*

HELENA. I am absolutely exhausted by him, and can hardly stand.

VOITSKI. You are exhausted by him, and I am exhausted by my own self. I have not slept for three nights.

HELENA. Something is wrong in this house. Your mother hates everything but her pamphlets and the professor; the professor is vexed, he won't trust me, and fears you; Sonia is angry with her father, and with me, and hasn't spoken to me for two weeks! I am at the end of my strength, and have come near bursting into tears at least twenty times to-day. Something is wrong in this house.

VOITSKI. Leave speculating alone.

HELENA. You are cultured and intelligent, Ivan, and you surely understand that the world is not destroyed by villains and conflagrations, but by hate and malice and all this spiteful tattling. It is your duty to make peace, and not to growl at everything.

VOITSKI. Help me first to make peace with myself. My darling! [*Seizes her hand.*

HELENA. Let go! [*She drags her hand away.*] Go away!

VOITSKI. Soon the rain will be over, and all nature will sigh and awake refreshed. Only I am not refreshed by the storm. Day and night the thought haunts me like a fiend, that my life is lost forever. My past does not count, because I frittered it away on trifles, and the present has so terribly miscarried! What shall I do with my life and my love? What is to become of them? This wonderful feeling of mine will be wasted and lost as a ray of sunlight is lost that falls into a dark chasm, and my life will go with it.

HELENA. I am as it were benumbed when you speak to me of your love, and I don't know how to answer you. Forgive me, I have nothing to say to you. [*She tries to go out.*] Good-night!

VOITSKI. [*Barring the way.*] If you only knew how I am tortured by the thought that beside me in this house is another life that is being lost forever—it is yours! What are you waiting for? What accursed philosophy stands in your way? Oh, understand, understand——

HELENA. [*Looking at him intently.*] Ivan, you are drunk!

VOITSKI. Perhaps. Perhaps.

HELENA. Where is the doctor?

VOITSKI. In there, spending the night with me. Perhaps I am drunk, perhaps I am; nothing is impossible.

HELENA. Have you just been drinking together? Why do you do that?

VOITSKI. Because in that way I get a taste of life. Let me do it, Helena!

HELENA. You never used to drink, and you never used to talk so much. Go to bed, I am tired of you.

VOITSKI. [*Falling on his knees before her.*] My sweetheart, my beautiful one——

HELENA. [*Angrily.*] Leave me alone! Really, this has become too disagreeable.

[HELENA *goes out. A pause.*

VOITSKI. [*Alone.*] She is gone! I met her first ten years ago, at her sister's house, when she was seventeen and I was thirty-seven. Why did I not fall in love with her then and propose to her? It would have been so easy! And now she would have been my wife. Yes, we would both have been waked to-night by the thunderstorm, and she would have been frightened, but I would have held her in my arms and whispered: "Don't be afraid! I am here." Oh, enchanting dream, so sweet that I laugh to think of it. [*He laughs.*] But my God! My head reels! Why am I so old? Why won't she understand me? I hate all that rhetoric of hers, that morality of indolence, that absurd talk about the destruction of the world—— [*A pause.*] Oh, how I have been deceived! For years I have worshipped that miserable gout-ridden professor. Sonia and I have squeezed this estate dry for his sake. We have bartered our butter and curds and peas like misers, and have never kept a morsel for ourselves, so that we could scrape enough pennies together to send to him. I was proud of him and of his learning; I received all his words and writings as inspired, and now? Now he has retired, and what is the total of his life? A blank! He is absolutely unknown, and his fame has burst like a soap-bubble. I have been deceived; I see that now, basely deceived.

[ASTROFF *comes in. He has his coat on, but*

*is without his waistcoat or collar, and is slightly drunk.* TELEGIN *follows him, carrying a guitar.*

ASTROFF. Play!

TELEGIN. But every one is asleep.

ASTROFF. Play!

[TELEGIN *begins to play softly.*

ASTROFF. Are you alone here? No women about?

[*Sings with his arms akimbo.*

"The hut is cold, the fire is dead;
Where shall the master lay his head?"

The thunderstorm woke me. It was a heavy shower. What time is it?

VOITSKI. The devil only knows.

ASTROFF. I thought I heard Helena's voice.

VOITSKI. She was here a moment ago.

ASTROFF. What a beautiful woman! [*Looking at the medicine bottles on the table.*] Medicine, is it? What a variety we have; prescriptions from Moscow, from Kharkoff, from Tula! Why, he has been pestering all the towns of Russia with his gout! Is he ill, or simply shamming?

VOITSKI. He is really ill.

ASTROFF. What is the matter with you to-night? You seem sad. Is it because you are sorry for the professor?

VOITSKI. Leave me alone.

ASTROFF. Or in love with the professor's wife?

VOITSKI. She is my friend.

ASTROFF. Already?

VOITSKI. What do you mean by "already"?

ASTROFF. A woman can only become a man's friend after having first been his acquaintance and then his beloved—then she becomes his friend.

VOITSKI. What vulgar philosophy!

ASTROFF. What do you mean? Yes, I must confess I am getting vulgar, but then, you see, I am drunk. I usually only drink like this once a month. At such times my audacity and temerity know no bounds. I feel capable of anything. I attempt the most difficult operations and do them magnificently. The most brilliant plans for the future take shape in my head. I am no longer a poor fool of a doctor, but mankind's greatest benefactor. I evolve my own system of philosophy and all of you seem to crawl at my feet like so many insects or microbes. [*To* TELEGIN.] Play, Waffles!

TELEGIN. My dear boy, I would with all my heart, but do listen to reason; everybody in the house is asleep.

ASTROFF. Play!

[TELEGIN *plays softly.*

ASTROFF. I want a drink. Come, we still have some brandy left. And then, as soon as it is day, you will come home with me.

[*He sees* SONIA, *who comes in at that moment.*

ASTROFF. I beg your pardon, I have no collar on.

[*He goes out quickly, followed by* TELEGIN.

SONIA. Uncle Vanya, you and the doctor have been drinking! The good fellows have been getting together! It is all very well for him, he has always done it, but why do you follow his example? It looks dreadfully at your age.

VOITSKI. Age has nothing to do with it. When real life is wanting one must create an illusion. It is better than nothing.

SONIA. Our hay is all cut and rotting in these daily rains, and here you are busy creating illusions! You have given up the farm altogether. I have done all the work alone until I am at the end of my strength—— [*Frightened.*] Uncle! Your eyes are full of tears!

VOITSKI. *Tears?* Nonsense, there are no tears in my

eyes. You looked at me then just as your dead mother used to, my darling—— [*He eagerly kisses her face and hands.*] My sister, my dearest sister, where are you now? Ah, if you only knew, if you only knew!

SONIA. If she only knew what, Uncle?

VOITSKI. My heart is bursting. It is awful. No matter, though. I must go. [*He goes out.*

SONIA. [*Knocks at the door.*] Dr. Astroff! Are you awake? Please come here for a minute.

ASTROFF. [*Behind the door.*] In a moment.

[*He appears in a few seconds. He has put on his collar and waistcoat.*

ASTROFF. What do you want?

SONIA. Drink as much as you please yourself, if you don't find it revolting, but I implore you not to let my uncle do it. It is bad for him.

ASTROFF. Very well; we won't drink any more. I am going home at once. That is settled. It will be dawn by the time the horses are harnessed.

SONIA. It is still raining; wait till morning.

ASTROFF. The storm is blowing over. This is only the edge of it. I must go. And please don't ask me to come and see your father any more. I tell him he has gout, and he says it is rheumatism. I tell him to lie down, and he sits up. To-day he refused to see me at all.

SONIA. He has been spoilt. [*She looks in the sideboard.*] Won't you have a bite to eat?

ASTROFF. Yes, please. I believe I will.

SONIA. I love to eat at night. I am sure we shall find something in here. They say that he has made a great many conquests in his life, and that the women have spoiled him. Here is some cheese for you.

[*They stand eating by the sideboard.*

ASTROFF. I haven't eaten anything to-day. Your

father has a very difficult nature. [*He takes a bottle out of the sideboard.*] May I? [*He pours himself a glass of vodka.*] We are alone here, and I can speak frankly. Do you know, I could not stand living in this house for even a month? This atmosphere would stifle me. There is your father, entirely absorbed in his books, and his gout; there is your Uncle Vanya with his hypochondria, your grandmother, and finally, your step-mother——

SONIA. What about her?

ASTROFF. A human being should be entirely beautiful: the face, the clothes, the mind, the thoughts. Your step-mother is, of course, beautiful to look at, but don't you see? She does nothing but sleep and eat and walk and bewitch us, and that is all. She has no responsibilities, everything is done for her—am I not right? And an idle life can never be a pure one. [*A pause.*] However, I may be judging her too severely. Like your Uncle Vanya, I am discontented, and so we are both grumblers.

SONIA. Aren't you satisfied with life?

ASTROFF. I like life as life, but I hate and despise it in a little Russian country village, and as far as my own personal life goes, by heaven! there is absolutely no redeeming feature about it. Haven't you noticed if you are riding through a dark wood at night and see a little light shining ahead, how you forget your fatigue and the darkness and the sharp twigs that whip your face? I work, that you know—as no one else in the country works. Fate beats me on without rest; at times I suffer unendurably and I see no light ahead. I have no hope; I do not like people. It is long since I have loved any one.

SONIA. You love no one?

ASTROFF. Not a soul. I only feel a sort of tenderness for your old nurse for old-times' sake. The peasants are all alike; they are stupid and live in dirt, and the educated people are hard to get along with. One gets tired of them. All our good friends are petty and shallow and see no farther than their own noses; in one word, they are dull. Those that have brains are hysterical, devoured with a mania for self-analysis. They whine, they hate, they pick faults everywhere with unhealthy sharpness. They sneak up to me sideways, look at me out of a corner of the eye, and say: "That man is a lunatic," "That man is a wind-bag." Or, if they don't know what else to label me with, they say I am strange. I like the woods; that is strange. I don't eat meat; that is strange, too. Simple, natural relations between man and man or man and nature do not exist.

[*He tries to go out;* SONIA *prevents him.*

SONIA. I beg you, I implore you, not to drink any more!

ASTROFF. Why not?

SONIA. It is so unworthy of you. You are well-bred, your voice is sweet, you are even—more than any one I know—handsome. Why do you want to resemble the common people that drink and play cards? Oh, don't, I beg you! You always say that people do not create anything, but only destroy what heaven has given them. Why, oh, why, do you destroy yourself? Oh, don't, I implore you not to! I entreat you!

ASTROFF. [*Gives her his hand.*] I won't drink any more.

SONIA. Promise me.

ASTROFF. I give you my word of honor.

SONIA. [*Squeezing his hand.*] Thank you.

ASTROFF. I have done with it. You see, I am perfectly sober again, and so I shall stay till the end of my life. [*He looks at his watch.*] But, as I was saying, life holds nothing for me; my race is run. I am old, I am tired, I am trivial; my sensibilities are dead. I could never attach myself to any one again. I love no one, and—never shall! Beauty alone has the power to touch me still. I am deeply moved by it. Helena could turn my head in a day if she wanted to, but that is not love, that is not affection——

[*He shudders and covers his face with his hands.*

SONIA. What is it?

ASTROFF. Nothing. During Lent one of my patients died under chloroform.

SONIA. It is time to forget that. [*A pause.*] Tell me, doctor, if I had a friend or a younger sister, and if you knew that she, well—loved you, what would you do?

ASTROFF. [*Shrugging his shoulders.*] I don't know. I don't think I should do anything. I should make her understand that I could not return her love—however, my mind is not bothered about those things now. I must start at once if I am ever to get off. Good-bye, my dear girl. At this rate we shall stand here talking till morning. [*He shakes hands with her.*] I shall go out through the sitting-room, because I am afraid your uncle might detain me. [*He goes out.*

SONIA. [*Alone.*] Not a word! His heart and soul are still locked from me, and yet for some reason I am strangely happy. I wonder why? [*She laughs with pleasure.*] I told him that he was well-bred and handsome and that his voice was sweet. Was that a mistake? I can still feel his voice vibrating in the air; it caresses me. [*Wringing her hands.*] Oh! how terrible it is to be plain! I am plain, I know it. As I came out of church last Sunday I overheard a woman say, "She is a dear, noble girl, but what a pity she is so ugly!" So ugly!

[HELENA *comes in and throws open the window.*

HELENA. The storm is over. What delicious air! [*A pause.*] Where is the doctor?

SONIA. He has gone. [*A pause.*

HELENA. Sonia!

SONIA. Yes?

HELENA. How much longer are you going to sulk at me? We have not hurt each other. Why not be friends? We have had enough of this.

SONIA. I myself—— [*She embraces* HELENA.] Let us make peace.

HELENA. With all my heart. [*They are both moved.*

SONIA. Has papa gone to bed?

HELENA. No, he is sitting up in the drawing-room. Heaven knows what reason you and I had for not speaking to each other for weeks. [*Sees the open sideboard.*] Who left the sideboard open?

SONIA. Dr. Astroff has just had supper.

HELENA. There is some wine. Let us seal our friendship.

SONIA. Yes, let us.

HELENA. Out of one glass. [*She fills a wine-glass.*] So, we are friends, are we?

SONIA. Yes. [*They drink and kiss each other.*] I have long wanted to make friends, but somehow, I was ashamed to. [*She weeps.*

HELENA. Why are you crying?

SONIA. I don't know. It is nothing.

HELENA. There, there, don't cry. [*She weeps.*] Silly! Now I am crying too. [*A pause.*] You are angry with me because I seem to have married your father for his money, but don't believe the gossip you hear. I swear to you I married him for love I was fascinated by his fame and learning. I know now that it was not real love, but it seemed real at the time. I am innocent, and yet your clever, suspicious eyes have been punishing me for an imaginary crime ever since my marriage.

SONIA. Peace, peace! Let us forget the past.

HELENA. You must not look so at people. It is not becoming to you. You must trust people, or life becomes impossible.

SONIA. Tell me truly, as a friend, are you happy?

HELENA. Truly, no.

SONIA. I knew it. One more question: do you wish your husband were young?

HELENA. What a child you are! Of course I do. Go on, ask something else.

SONIA. Do you like the doctor?

HELENA. Yes, very much indeed.

SONIA. [*Laughing.*] I have a stupid face, haven't I? He has just gone out, and his voice is still in my ears; I hear his step; I see his face in the dark window. Let me say all I have in my heart! But no, I cannot speak of it so loudly. I am ashamed. Come to my room and let me tell you there. I seem foolish to you, don't I? Talk to me of him.

HELENA. What can I say?

SONIA. He is clever. He can do everything. He can cure the sick, and plant woods.

HELENA. It is not a question of medicine and woods, my dear, he is a man of genius. Do you know what that means? It means he is brave, profound, and of clear insight. He plants a tree and his mind travels a thousand years into the future, and he sees visions of the happiness of the human race. People like him are rare and should be loved. What if he does drink and act roughly at times? A man of genius cannot be a saint in Russia. There he lives, cut off from the world by cold and storm and endless roads of bottomless mud, surrounded by a rough people who are crushed by poverty and disease, his life one continuous struggle, with never a day's respite; how can a man live like that for forty years and keep himself sober and unspotted? [*Kissing* SONIA.] I wish you happiness with all my heart; you deserve it. [*She gets up.*] As for me, I am a worthless, futile woman. I have always been futile; in music, in love, in my husband's house—in a word, in everything. When you come to think of it, Sonia, I am really very, very unhappy. [*Walks excitedly up and down.*] Happiness can never exist for me in this world. Never. Why do you laugh?

SONIA. [*Laughing and covering her face with her hands.*] I am so happy, so happy!

HELENA. I want to hear music. I might play a little.

SONIA. Oh, do, do! [*She embraces her.*] I could not possibly go to sleep now. Do play!

HELENA. Yes, I will. Your father is still awake. Music irritates him when he is ill, but if he says I may, then I shall play a little. Go, Sonia, and ask him.

SONIA. Very well.

[*She goes out. The* WATCHMAN'S *rattle is heard in the garden.*

HELENA. It is long since I have heard music. And now, I shall sit and play, and weep like a fool. [*Speaking out of the window.*] Is that you rattling out there, Ephim?

VOICE OF THE WATCHMAN. It is I.

HELENA. Don't make such a noise. Your master is ill.

VOICE OF THE WATCHMAN. I am going away this minute. [*Whistles a tune.*

SONIA. [*Comes back.*] He says, no.

[*The curtain falls.*]

## ACT THIRD

*The drawing-room of* SEREBRAKOFF'S *house. There are three doors: one to the right, one to the left, and one in the center of the room.* VOITSKI *and* SONIA *are sitting down.* HELENA *is walking up and down, absorbed in thought.*

VOITSKI. We were asked by the professor to be here at one o'clock. [*Looks at his watch.*] It is now a quarter to one. It seems he has some communication to make to the world.

HELENA. Probably a matter of business.

VOITSKI. He never had any business. He writes twaddle, grumbles, and eats his heart out with jealousy; that's all he does.

SONIA. [*Reproachfully.*] Uncle!

VOITSKI. All right. I beg your pardon. [*He points to* HELENA.] Look at her. Wandering up and down from sheer idleness. A sweet picture, really.

HELENA. I wonder you are not bored, droning on in the same key from morning till night. [*Despairingly.*] I am dying of this tedium. What shall I do?

SONIA. [*Shrugging her shoulders.*] There is plenty to do if you would.

HELENA. For instance?

SONIA. You could help run this place, teach the children, care for the sick—isn't that enough? Before you and papa came, Uncle Vanya and I used to go to market ourselves to deal in flour.

HELENA. I don't know anything about such things, and besides, they don't interest me. It is only in novels that women go out and teach and heal the peasants; how can I suddenly begin to do it?

SONIA. How can you live here and not do it? Wait awhile, you will get used to it all. [*Embraces her.*] Don't be sad, dearest. [*Laughing.*] You feel miserable and restless, and can't seem to fit into this life, and your restlessness is catching. Look at Uncle Vanya, he does nothing now but haunt you like a shadow, and I have left my work to-day to come here and talk with you. I am getting lazy, and don't want to go on with it. Dr. Astroff hardly ever used to come here; it was all we could do to persuade him to visit us once a month, and now he has abandoned his forestry and his practice, and comes every day. You must be a witch.

VOITSKI. Why should you languish here? Come, my dearest, my beauty, be sensible! The blood of a Nixey runs in your veins. Oh, won't you let yourself be one? Give your nature the reins for once in your life; fall head over ears in love with some other water sprite and plunge down head first into a deep pool, so that the Herr Professor and all of us may have our hands free again.

HELENA. [*Angrily.*] Leave me alone! How cruel you are! [*She tries to go out.*

VOITSKI. [*Preventing her.*] There, there, my beauty, I apologize. [*He kisses her hand.*] Forgive me.

HELENA. Confess that you would try the patience of an angel.

VOITSKI. As a peace offering I am going to fetch some flowers which I picked for you this morning: some autumn roses, beautiful, sorrowful roses. [*He goes out.*

SONIA. Autumn roses, beautiful, sorrowful roses!

[*She and* HELENA *stand looking out of the window.*

HELENA. September already! How shall we live

through the long winter here? [*A pause.*] Where is the doctor?

SONIA. He is writing in Uncle Vanya's room. I am glad Uncle Vanya has gone out, I want to talk to you about something.

HELENA. About what?

SONIA. About what?

[*She lays her head on* HELENA'S *breast.*

HELENA. [*Stroking her hair.*] There, there, that will do. Don't, Sonia.

SONIA. I am ugly!

HELENA. You have lovely hair.

SONIA. Don't say that! [*She turns to look at herself in the glass.*] No, when a woman is ugly they always say she has beautiful hair or eyes. I have loved him now for six years; I have loved him more than one loves one's mother. I seem to hear him beside me every moment of the day. I feel the pressure of his hand on mine. If I look up, I seem to see him coming, and as you see, I run to you to talk of him. He is here every day now, but he never looks at me, he does not notice my presence. It is agony. I have absolutely no hope, no, no hope. Oh, my God! Give me strength to endure. I prayed all last night. I often go up to him and speak to him and look into his eyes. My pride is gone. I am not mistress of myself. Yesterday I told Uncle Vanya. I couldn't control myself, and all the servants know it. Every one knows that I love him.

HELENA. Does he?

SONIA. No, he never notices me.

HELENA. [*Thoughtfully.*] He is a strange man. Listen, Sonia, will you allow me to speak to him? I shall be careful, only hint. [*A pause.*] Really, to be in uncertainty all these years! Let me do it!

[SONIA *nods an affirmative.*

HELENA. Splendid! It will be easy to find out whether he loves you or not. Don't be ashamed, sweetheart, don't worry. I shall be careful; he will not notice a thing. We only want to find out whether it is yes or no, don't we? [*A pause.*] And if it is no, then he must keep away from here, is that so?

[SONIA *nods.*

HELENA. It will be easier not to see him any more. We won't put off the examination an instant. He said he had a sketch to show me. Go and tell him at once that I want to see him.

SONIA. [*In great excitement.*] Will you tell me the whole truth?

HELENA. Of course I will. I am sure that no matter what it is, it will be easier for you to bear than this uncertainty. Trust to me, dearest.

SONIA. Yes, yes. I shall say that you want to see his sketch. [*She starts out, but stops near the door and looks back.*] No, it is better not to know—and yet—there may be hope.

HELENA. What do you say?

SONIA. Nothing. [*She goes out.*

HELENA. [*Alone.*] There is no greater sorrow than to know another's secret when you cannot help them. [*In deep thought.*] He is obviously not in love with her, but why shouldn't he marry her? She is not pretty, but she is so clever and pure and good, she would make a splendid wife for a country doctor of his years. [*A pause.*] I can understand how the poor child feels. She lives here in this desperate loneliness with no one around her except these colorless shadows that go mooning about talking nonsense and knowing nothing except that they eat, drink, and sleep. Among them appears from time to time this Dr. Astroff, so different, so handsome, so interesting, so charming. It is like seeing the moon rise on a dark night. Oh, to surrender oneself to his embrace! To lose oneself in his arms! I am a little in love with him myself! Yes, I am lonely without him, and when I think of him I smile. That Uncle Vanya says I have the blood of a Nixey in my veins: "Give rein to your nature for once in your life!" Perhaps it is right that I should. Oh, to be free as a bird, to fly away from all your sleepy faces and your talk and forget that you have existed at all! But I am a coward, I am afraid; my conscience torments me. He comes here every day now. I can guess why, and feel guilty already; I should like to fall on my knees at Sonia's feet and beg her forgiveness, and weep.

[ASTROFF *comes in carrying a portfolio.*

ASTROFF. How do you do? [*Shakes hands with her.*] Do you want to see my sketch?

HELENA. Yes, you promised to show me what you had been doing. Have you time now?

ASTROFF. Of course I have!

[*He lays the portfolio on the table, takes out the sketch and fastens it to the table with thumb-tacks.*

ASTROFF. Where were you born?

HELENA. [*Helping him.*] In St. Petersburg.

ASTROFF. And educated?

HELENA. At the Conservatory there.

ASTROFF. You don't find this life very interesting, I dare say?

HELENA. Oh, why not? It is true I don't know the country very well, but I have read a great deal about it.

ASTROFF. I have my own desk there in Ivan's room. When I am absolutely too exhausted to go on I drop everything and rush over here to forget myself in this work for an hour or two. Ivan and Miss Sonia sit rattling at their counting-boards, the cricket chirps, and I sit beside them and paint, feeling warm and peaceful. But I don't permit myself this luxury very often, only once a month. [*Pointing to the picture.*] Look there! That is a map of our country as it was fifty years ago. The green tints, both dark and light, represent forests. Half the map, as you see, is covered with it. Where the green is striped with red the forests were inhabited by elk and wild goats. Here on this lake lived great flocks of swans and geese and ducks; as the old men say, there was a power of birds of every kind. Now they have vanished like a cloud. Beside the hamlets and villages, you see, I have dotted down here and there the various settlements, farms, hermit's caves, and water-mills. This country carried a great many cattle and horses, as you can see by the quantity of blue paint. For instance, see how thickly it lies in this part; there were great herds of them here, an average of three horses to every house. [*A pause.*] Now, look lower down. This is the country as it was twenty-five years ago. Only a third of the map is green now with forests. There are no goats left and no elk. The blue paint is lighter, and so on, and so on. Now we come to the third part; our country as it appears to-day. We still see spots of green, but not much. The elk, the swans, the black-cock have disappeared. It is, on the whole, the picture of a regular and slow decline which it will evidently only take about ten or fifteen more years to complete. You may perhaps object that it is the march of progress, that the old order must give place to the new, and you might be right if roads had been run through these ruined woods, or if factories and schools had taken their place. The people then would have become better educated and healthier and richer, but as it is, we have nothing of the sort. We have the same swamps and mosquitoes; the same disease and want; the typhoid, the diphtheria, the burning villages. We are confronted by the degradation of our country, brought on by the fierce struggle for existence of the human race. It is the consequence of the ignorance and unconsciousness of starving, shivering, sick humanity that, to save its children, instinctively snatches at everything that can warm it and still its hunger. So it destroys everything it can lay its hands on, without a thought for the morrow. And almost everything has gone, and nothing has been created to take its place. [*Coldly.*] But I see by your face that I am not interesting you.

HELENA. I know so little about such things!

ASTROFF. There is nothing to know. It simply isn't interesting, that's all.

HELENA. Frankly, my thoughts were elsewhere. Forgive me! I want to submit you to a little examination, but I am embarrassed and don't know how to begin.

ASTROFF. An examination?

HELENA. Yes, but quite an innocent one. Sit down. [*They sit down.*] It is about a certain young girl I know. Let us discuss it like honest people, like friends, and then forget what has passed between us, shall we?

ASTROFF. Very well.

HELENA. It is about my step-daughter, Sonia. Do you like her?

ASTROFF. Yes, I respect her.

HELENA. Do you like her—as a woman?

ASTROFF. [*Slowly.*] No.

HELENA. One more word, and that will be the last. You have not noticed anything?

ASTROFF. No, nothing.

HELENA. [*Taking his hand.*] You do not love her. I see that in your eyes. She is suffering. You must realize that, and not come here any more.

ASTROFF. My sun has set, yes, and then I haven't the time. [*Shrugging his shoulders.*] Where shall I find time for such things? [*He is embarrassed.*

HELENA. Bah! What an unpleasant conversation! I am as out of breath as if I had been running three miles uphill. Thank heaven, that is over! Now let us forget everything as if nothing had been said. You are sensible. You understand. [*A pause.*] I am actually blushing.

ASTROFF. If you had spoken a month ago I might perhaps have considered it, but now—— [*He shrugs his shoulders.*] Of course, if she is suffering—but I cannot understand why you had to put me through this examination. [*He searches her face with his eyes, and shakes his finger at her.*] Oho, you are wily!

HELENA. What does this mean?

ASTROFF. [*Laughing.*] You are a wily one! I admit that Sonia is suffering, but what does this examination of yours mean? [*He prevents her from retorting, and goes on quickly.*] Please don't put on such a look of surprise; you know perfectly well why I come here every day. Yes, you know perfectly why and for whose sake I come! Oh, my sweet tigress! don't look at me in that way; I am an old bird!

HELENA. [*Perplexed.*] A tigress? I don't understand you.

ASTROFF. Beautiful, sleek tigress, you must have your victims! For a whole month I have done nothing but seek you eagerly. I have thrown over everything for you, and you love to see it. Now then, I am sure you knew all this without putting me through your examination. [*Crossing his arms and bowing his head.*] I surrender. Here you have me—now, eat me.

HELENA. You have gone mad!

ASTROFF. You are afraid!

HELENA. I am a better and stronger woman than you think me. Good-bye. [*She tries to leave the room.*

ASTROFF. Why good-bye? Don't say good-bye, don't waste words. Oh, how lovely you are—what hands!

[*He kisses her hands.*

HELENA. Enough of this! [*She frees her hands.*] Leave the room! You have forgotten yourself.

ASTROFF. Tell me, tell me, where can we meet to-morrow? [*He puts his arm around her.*] Don't you see that we must meet, that it is inevitable?

[*He kisses her.* VOITSKI *comes in carrying a bunch of roses, and stops in the doorway.*

HELENA. [*Without seeing* VOITSKI.] Have pity! Leave me. [*Lays her head on* ASTROFF'S *shoulder.*] Don't! [*She tries to break away from him.*

ASTROFF. [*Holding her by the waist.*] Be in the forest to-morrow at two o'clock. Will you? Will you?

HELENA. [*Sees* VOITSKI.] Let me go! [*Goes to the window deeply embarrassed.*] This is appalling!

VOITSKI. [*Throws the flowers on a chair, and speaks in great excitement, wiping his face with his handkerchief.*] Nothing—yes, yes, nothing.

ASTROFF. The weather is fine to-day, my dear Ivan; the morning was overcast and looked like rain, but now the sun is shining again. Honestly, we have had a very fine autumn, and the wheat is looking fairly well. [*Puts his map back into the portfolio.*] But the days are growing short. [*Exit.*

HELENA. [*Goes quickly up to* VOITSKI.] You must do your best; you must use all your power to get my husband and myself away from here to-day! Do you hear? I say, this very day!

VOITSKI. [*Wiping his face.*] Oh! Ah! Oh! All right! I—Helena, I saw everything!

HELENA. [*In great agitation.*] Do you hear me? I must leave here this very day!

[SEREBRAKOFF, SONIA, MARINA, *and* TELEGIN *come in.*

TELEGIN. I am not very well myself, your Excellency. I have been limping for two days, and my head——

SEREBRAKOFF. Where are the others? I hate this house. It is a regular labyrinth. Every one is always scattered through the twenty-six enormous rooms; one never can find a soul. [*Rings.*] Ask my wife and Madame Voitskaya to come here!

HELENA. I am here already.

SEREBRAKOFF. Please, all of you, sit down.

SONIA. [*Goes up to* HELENA *and asks anxiously.*] What did he say?

HELENA. I'll tell you later.

SONIA. You are moved. [*Looking quickly and inquiringly into her face.*] I understand; he said he would not come here any more. [*A pause.*] Tell me, did he?

[HELENA *nods.*

SEREBRAKOFF. [*To* TELEGIN.] One can, after all, become reconciled to being an invalid, but not to this country life. The ways of it stick in my throat and I feel exactly as if I had been whirled off the earth and landed on a strange planet. Please be seated, ladies and gentlemen. Sonia! [SONIA *does not hear. She is standing with her head bowed sadly forward on her breast.*] Sonia! [*A pause.*] She does not hear me. [*To* MARINA.] Sit down too, nurse. [MARINA *sits down and begins to knit her stocking.*] I crave your indulgence, ladies and gentlemen; hang your ears, if I may say so, on the peg of attention. [*He laughs.*

VOITSKI. [*Agitated.*] Perhaps you do not need me —may I be excused?

SEREBRAKOFF. No, you are needed now more than any one.

VOITSKI. What is it you want of me?

SEREBRAKOFF. You—but what are you angry about? If it is anything I have done, I ask you to forgive me.

VOITSKI. Oh, drop that and come to business; what do you want? [MME. VOITSKAYA *comes in.*

SEREBRAKOFF. Here is mother. Ladies and gentlemen, I shall begin. I have asked you to assemble here, my friends, in order to discuss a very important matter. I want to ask you for your assistance and advice, and knowing your unfailing amiability I think I can count on both. I am a book-worm and a scholar, and am unfamiliar with practical affairs. I cannot, I find, dispense with the help of well-informed people such as you, Ivan, and you, Telegin, and you, mother. The truth is, *manet omnes una nox,* that is to say, our lives are in the hands of God, and as I am old and ill, I realize that the time has come for me to dispose of my property in regard to the interests of my family. My life is nearly over, and I am not thinking of myself, but I have a young wife and daughter. [*A pause.*] I cannot continue to live in the country; we were not made for country life, and yet we cannot afford to live in town on the income derived from this estate. We might sell the woods, but that would be an expedient we could not resort to every year. We must find some means of guaranteeing to ourselves a certain more or less fixed yearly income. With this object in view, a plan has occurred to me which I now have the honor of presenting to you for your consideration. I shall only give you a rough outline, avoiding all details. Our estate does not pay on an average more than two per cent on the money invested in it. I propose to sell it. If we then invest our capital in bonds, it will earn us four to five per cent, and we should probably have a surplus over of several thousand roubles, with which we could buy a summer cottage in Finland——

VOITSKI. Hold on! Repeat what you just said; I don't think I heard you quite right.

SEREBRAKOFF. I said we would invest the money in bonds and buy a cottage in Finland with the surplus.

VOITSKI. No, not Finland—you said something else.

SEREBRAKOFF. I propose to sell this place.

VOITSKI. Aha! That was it! So you are going to sell the place? Splendid. The idea is a rich one. And what do you propose to do with my old mother and me and with Sonia here?

SEREBRAKOFF. That will be decided in due time. We can't do everything at once.

VOITSKI. Wait! It is clear that until this moment I have never had a grain of sense in my head. I have always been stupid enough to think that the estate belonged to Sonia. My father bought it as a wedding present for my sister, and I foolishly imagined that as our laws were made for Russians and not Turks, my sister's estate would come down to her child.

SEREBRAKOFF. Of course it is Sonia's. Has any one denied it? I don't want to sell it without Sonia's consent; on the contrary, what I am doing is for Sonia's good.

VOITSKI. This is absolutely incomprehensible. Either I have gone mad or—or——

MME. VOITSKAYA. Jean, don't contradict Alexander. Trust to him; he knows better than we do what is right and what is wrong.

VOITSKI. I shan't. Give me some water. [*He drinks.*] Go ahead! Say anything you please—anything!

SEREBRAKOFF. I can't imagine why you are so upset.

I don't pretend that my scheme is an ideal one, and if you all object to it I shall not insist. [*A pause.*

TELEGIN. [*With embarrassment.*] I not only nourish feelings of respect toward learning, your Excellency, but I am also drawn to it by family ties. My brother Gregory's wife's brother, whom you may know; his name is Constantine Lakedemonoff, and he used to be a magistrate——

VOITSKI. Stop, Waffles. This is business; wait a bit, we will talk of that later. [*To* SEREBRAKOFF.] There now, ask him what he thinks; this estate was bought from his uncle.

SEREBRAKOFF. Ah! Why should I ask questions? What good would it do?

VOITSKI. The price was ninety-five thousand roubles. My father paid seventy and left a debt of twenty-five. Now listen! This place could never have been bought had I not renounced my inheritance in favor of my sister, whom I deeply loved—and what is more, I worked for ten years like an ox, and paid off the debt.

SEREBRAKOFF. I regret ever having started this conversation.

VOITSKI. Thanks entirely to my own personal efforts, the place is entirely clear of debts, and now, when I have grown old, you want to throw me out, neck and crop!

SEREBRAKOFF. I can't imagine what you are driving at.

VOITSKI. For twenty-five years I have managed this place, and have sent you the returns from it like the most honest of servants, and you have never given me one single word of thanks for my work, not one—neither in my youth nor now. You allowed me a meager salary of five hundred roubles a year, a beggar's pittance, and have never even thought of adding a rouble to it.

SEREBRAKOFF. What did I know about such things, Ivan? I am not a practical man and don't understand them. You might have helped yourself to all you wanted.

VOITSKI. Yes, why did I not steal? Don't you all despise me for not stealing, when it would have been only justice? And I should not now have been a beggar!

MME. VOITSKAYA. [*Sternly.*] Jean!

TELEGIN. [*Agitated.*] Vanya, old man, don't talk in that way. Why spoil such pleasant relations? [*He embraces him.*] Do stop!

VOITSKI. For twenty-five years I have been sitting here with my mother like a mole in a burrow. Our every thought and hope was yours and yours only. By day we talked with pride of you and your work, and spoke your name with veneration; our nights we wasted reading the books and papers which my soul now loathes.

TELEGIN. Don't, Vanya, don't. I can't stand it.

SEREBRAKOFF. [*Wrathfully.*] What under heaven do you want, anyway?

VOITSKI. We used to think of you as almost superhuman, but now the scales have fallen from my eyes and I see you as you are! You write on art without knowing anything about it. Those books of yours which I used to admire are not worth one copper kopeck. You are a hoax!

SEREBRAKOFF. Can't any one make him stop? I am going!

HELENA. Ivan, I command you to stop this instant! Do you hear me?

VOITSKI. I refuse! [SEREBRAKOFF *tries to get out of the room, but* VOITSKI *bars the door.*] Wait! I have not done yet! You have wrecked my life. I have never lived. My best years have gone for nothing, have been ruined, thanks to you. You are my most bitter enemy!

TELEGIN. I can't stand it; I can't stand it. I am going. [*He goes out in great excitement.*

SEREBRAKOFF. But what do you want? What earthly right have you to use such language to me? Ruination! If this estate is yours, then take it, and let me be ruined!

HELENA. I am going away out of this hell this minute. [*Shrieks.*] This is too much!

VOITSKI. My life has been a failure. I am clever and brave and strong. If I had lived a normal life I might have become another Schopenhauer or Dostoieffski. I am losing my head! I am going crazy! Mother, I am in despair! Oh, mother!

MME. VOITSKAYA. [*Sternly.*] Listen, Alexander!

[SONIA *falls on her knees beside the nurse and nestles against her.*

SONIA. Oh, nurse, nurse!

VOITSKI. Mother! What shall I do? But no, don't speak! I know what to do. [*To* SEREBRAKOFF.] And you will understand me!

[*He goes out through the door in the center of the room and* MME. VOITSKAYA *follows him.*

SEREBRAKOFF. Tell me, what on earth is the matter? Take this lunatic out of my sight! I cannot possibly live under the same roof with him. His room [*He points to the center door*] is almost next door to mine. Let him take himself off into the village or into the wing of the house, or I shall leave here at once. I cannot stay in the same house with him.

HELENA. [*To her husband.*] We are leaving to-day; we must get ready at once for our departure.

SEREBRAKOFF. What a perfectly dreadful man!

SONIA. [*On her knees beside the nurse and turning*

*to her father. She speaks with emotion.*] You must be kind to us, papa. Uncle Vanya and I are so unhappy! [*Controlling her despair.*] Have pity on us. Remember how Uncle Vanya and Granny used to copy and translate your books for you every night—every, every night. Uncle Vanya has toiled without rest; he would never spend a penny on us, we sent it all to you. We have not eaten the bread of idleness. I am not saying this as I should like to, but you must understand us, papa, you must be merciful to us.

HELENA. [*Very excited, to her husband.*] For heaven's sake, Alexander, go and have a talk with him—explain!

SEREBRAKOFF. Very well, I shall have a talk with him, but I won't apologize for a thing. I am not angry with him, but you must confess that his behavior has been strange, to say the least. Excuse me, I shall go to him. [*He goes out through the center door.*

HELENA. Be gentle with him; try to quiet him.

[*She follows him out.*

SONIA. [*Nestling nearer to* MARINA.] Nurse, oh, nurse!

MARINA. It's all right, my baby. When the geese have cackled they will be still again. First they cackle and then they stop.

SONIA. Nurse!

MARINA. You are trembling all over, as if you were freezing. There, there, little orphan baby, God is merciful. A little linden-tea, and it will all pass away. Don't cry, my sweetest. [*Looking angrily at the door in the center of the room.*] See, the geese have all gone now. The devil take them!

[*A shot is heard.* HELENA *screams behind the scenes.* SONIA *shudders.*

MARINA. Bang! What's that?

SEREBRAKOFF. [*Comes in reeling with terror.*] Hold him! hold him! He has gone mad!

[HELENA *and* VOITSKI *are seen struggling in the doorway.*

HELENA. [*Trying to wrest the revolver from him.*] Give it to me; give it to me, I tell you!

VOITSKI. Let me go, Helena, let me go! [*He frees himself and rushes in, looking everywhere for* SEREBRAKOFF.] Where is he? Ah, there he is! [*He shoots at him. A pause.*] I didn't get him? I missed again? [*Furiously.*] Damnation! Damnation! To hell with him!

[*He flings the revolver on the floor, and drops helpless into a chair.* SEREBRAKOFF *stands as if stupefied.* HELENA *leans against the wall, almost fainting.*

HELENA. Take me away! Take me away! I can't stay here—I can't!

VOITSKI. [*In despair.*] Oh, what shall I do? What shall I do?

SONIA. [*Softly.*] Oh, nurse, nurse!

[*The curtain falls.*]

## ACT FOURTH

VOITSKI'S *bedroom, which is also his office. A table stands near the window; on it are ledgers, letter scales, and papers of every description. Near by stands a smaller table belonging to* ASTROFF, *with his paints and drawing materials. On the wall hangs a cage containing a starling. There is also a map of Africa on the wall, obviously of no use to anybody. There is a large sofa covered with buckram. A door to the left leads into an inner room; one to the right leads into the front hall, and before this door lies a mat for the peasants with their muddy boots to stand on. It is an autumn evening. The silence is profound.* TELEGIN *and* MARINA *are sitting facing one another, winding wool.*

TELEGIN. Be quick, Marina, or we shall be called away to say good-bye before you have finished. The carriage has already been ordered.

MARINA. [*Trying to wind more quickly.*] I am a little tired.

TELEGIN. They are going to Kharkoff to live.

MARINA. They do well to go.

TELEGIN. They have been frightened. The professor's wife won't stay here an hour longer. "If we are going at all, let's be off," says she, "we shall go to Kharkoff and look about us, and then we can send for our things." They are traveling light. It seems, Marina, that fate has decreed for them not to live here.

MARINA. And quite rightly. What a storm they have just raised! It was shameful!

TELEGIN. It was indeed. The scene was worthy of the brush of Aibazofski.

MARINA. I wish I'd never laid eyes on them. [*A pause.*] Now we shall have things as they were again: tea at eight, dinner at one, and supper in the evening; everything in order as decent folks, as Christians like to have it. [*Sighs.*] It is a long time since I have eaten noodles.

TELEGIN. Yes, we haven't had noodles for ages. [*A pause.*] Not for ages. As I was going through the village this morning, Marina, one of the shop-keepers called after me, "Hi! you hanger-on!" I felt it bitterly.

MARINA. Don't pay the least attention to them, master; we are all dependents on God. You and Sonia and all of us. Every one must work, no one can sit idle. Where is Sonia?

TELEGIN. In the garden with the doctor, looking for Ivan. They fear he may lay violent hands on himself.

MARINA. Where is his pistol?

TELEGIN. [*Whispers.*] I hid it in the cellar.

[VOITSKI *and* ASTROFF *come in.*

VOITSKI. Leave me alone! [*To* MARINA *and* TELEGIN.] Go away! Go away and leave me to myself, if but for an hour. I won't have you watching me like this!

TELEGIN. Yes, yes, Vanya. [*He goes out on tiptoe.*

MARINA. The gander cackles; ho! ho! ho!

[*She gathers up her wool and goes out.*

VOITSKI. Leave me by myself!

ASTROFF. I would, with the greatest pleasure. I ought to have gone long ago, but I shan't leave you until you have returned what you took from me.

VOITSKI. I took nothing from you.

ASTROFF. I am not jesting, don't detain me, I really must go.

VOITSKI. I took nothing of yours.

ASTROFF. You didn't? Very well, I shall have to wait a little longer, and then you will have to forgive me if I resort to force. We shall have to bind you and search you. I mean what I say.

VOITSKI. Do as you please. [*A pause.*] Oh, to make such a fool of myself! To shoot twice and miss him both times! I shall never forgive myself.

ASTROFF. When the impulse came to shoot, it would have been as well had you put a bullet through your own head.

VOITSKI. [*Shrugging his shoulders.*] Strange! I attempted murder, and am not going to be arrested or brought to trial. That means they think me mad. [*With a bitter laugh.*] Me! I am mad, and those who hide their worthlessness, their dullness, their crying heartlessness behind a professor's mask, are sane! Those who marry old men and then deceive them under the noses of all, are sane! I saw you kiss her; I saw you in each other's arms!

ASTROFF. Yes, sir, I did kiss her; so there.

[*He puts his thumb to his nose.*

VOITSKI. [*His eyes on the door.*] No, it is the earth that is mad, because she still bears us on her breast.

ASTROFF. That is nonsense.

VOITSKI. Well? Am I not a madman, and therefore irresponsible? Haven't I the right to talk nonsense?

ASTROFF. This is a farce! You are not mad; you are simply a ridiculous fool. I used to think every fool was out of his senses, but now I see that lack of sense is a man's normal state, and you are perfectly normal.

VOITSKI. [*Covers his face with his hands.*] Oh! If you knew how ashamed I am! These piercing pangs of shame are like nothing on earth. [*In an agonized voice.*] I can't endure them! [*He leans against the table.*] What can I do? What can I do?

ASTROFF. Nothing.

VOITSKI. You must tell me something! Oh, my God! I am forty-seven years old. I may live to sixty; I still have thirteen years before me; an eternity! How shall I be able to endure life for thirteen years? What shall I do? How can I fill them? Oh, don't you see? [*He presses* ASTROFF'S *hand convulsively.*] Don't you see, if only I could live the rest of my life in some new way! If I could only wake some still, bright morning and feel that life had begun again; that the past was forgotten and had vanished like smoke. [*He weeps.*] Oh, to begin life anew! Tell me, tell me how to begin.

ASTROFF. [*Crossly.*] What nonsense! What sort of a new life can you and I look forward to? We can have no hope.

VOITSKI. None?

ASTROFF. None. Of that I am convinced.

VOITSKI. Tell me what to do. [*He puts his hand to his heart.*] I feel such a burning pain here.

ASTROFF. [*Shouts angrily.*] Stop! [*Then, more gently.*] It may be that posterity, which will despise us for our blind and stupid lives, will find some road to happiness; but we—you and I—have but one hope, the hope that we may be visited by visions, perhaps by pleasant ones, as we lie resting in our graves. [*Sighing.*] Yes, brother, there were only two respectable, intelligent men in this county, you and I. Ten years or so of this life of ours, this miserable life, have sucked us under, and we have become as contemptible and petty as the rest. But don't try to talk me out of my purpose! Give me what you took from me, will you?

VOITSKI. I took nothing from you.

ASTROFF. You took a little bottle of morphine out

of my medicine-case. [*A pause.*] Listen! If you are positively determined to make an end to yourself, go into the woods and shoot yourself there. Give up the morphine, or there will be a lot of talk and guesswork; people will think I gave it to you. I don't fancy having to perform a post-mortem on you. Do you think I should find it interesting? [SONIA *comes in.*

VOITSKI. Leave me alone.

ASTROFF. [*To* SONIA.] Sonia, your uncle has stolen a bottle of morphine out of my medicine-case and won't give it up. Tell him that his behavior is—well, unwise. I haven't time, I must be going.

SONIA. Uncle Vanya, did you take the morphine?

ASTROFF. Yes, he took it. [*A pause.*] I am absolutely sure.

SONIA. Give it up! Why do you want to frighten us? [*Tenderly.*] Give it up, Uncle Vanya! My misfortune is perhaps even greater than yours, but I am not plunged in despair. I endure my sorrow, and shall endure it until my life comes to a natural end. You must endure yours, too. [*A pause.*] Give it up! Dear, darling Uncle Vanya. Give it up! [*She weeps.*] You are so good, I am sure you will have pity on us and give it up. You must endure your sorrow, Uncle Vanya; you must endure it.

[VOITSKI *takes a bottle from the drawer of the table and hands it to* ASTROFF.

VOITSKI. There it is! [*To* SONIA.] And now, we must get to work at once; we must do something, or else I shall not be able to endure it.

SONIA. Yes, yes, to work! As soon as we have seen them off we shall go to work. [*She nervously straightens out the papers on the table.*] Everything is in a muddle!

ASTROFF. [*Putting the bottle in his case, which he straps together.*] Now I can be off.

[HELENA *comes in.*

HELENA. Are you here, Ivan? We are starting in a moment. Go to Alexander, he wants to speak to you.

SONIA. Go, Uncle Vanya. [*She takes* VOITSKI'S *arm.*] Come, you and papa must make peace; that is absolutely necessary.

[SONIA *and* VOITSKI *go out.*

HELENA. I am going away. [*She gives* ASTROFF *her hand.*] Good-bye.

ASTROFF. So soon?

HELENA. The carriage is waiting.

ASTROFF. Good-bye.

HELENA. You promised me you would go away yourself to-day.

ASTROFF. I have not forgotten. I am going at once. [*A pause.*] Were you frightened? Was it so terrible?

HELENA. Yes.

ASTROFF. Couldn't you stay? Couldn't you? To-morrow—in the forest——

HELENA. No. It is all settled, and that is why I can look you so bravely in the face. Our departure is fixed. One thing I must ask of you: don't think too badly of me; I should like you to respect me.

ASTROFF. Ah! [*With an impatient gesture.*] Stay, I implore you! Confess that there is nothing for you to do in this world. You have no object in life; there is nothing to occupy your attention, and sooner or later your feelings must master you. It is inevitable. It would be better if it happened not in Kharkoff or in Kursk, but here, in nature's lap. It would then at least be poetical, even beautiful. Here you have the forests, the houses half in ruins that Turgenieff writes of.

HELENA. How comical you are! I am angry with

you and yet I shall always remember you with pleasure. You are interesting and original. You and I will never meet again, and so I shall tell you—why should I conceal it?—that I am just a little in love with you. Come, one more last pressure of our hands, and then let us part good friends. Let us not bear each other any ill will.

ASTROFF. [*Pressing her hand.*] Yes, go. [*Thoughtfully.*] You seem to be sincere and good, and yet there is something strangely disquieting about all your personality. No sooner did you arrive here with your husband than every one whom you found busy and actively creating something was forced to drop his work and give himself up for the whole summer to your husband's gout and yourself. You and he have infected us with your idleness. I have been swept off my feet; I have not put my hand to a thing for weeks, during which sickness has been running its course unchecked among the people, and the peasants have been pasturing their cattle in my woods and young plantations. Go where you will, you and your husband will always carry destruction in your train. I am joking of course, and yet I am strangely sure that had you stayed here we should have been overtaken by the most immense desolation. I would have gone to my ruin, and you—you would not have prospered. So go! É finita la commèdia!

HELENA. [*Snatching a pencil off* ASTROFF's *table, and hiding it with a quick movement.*] I shall take this pencil for memory!

ASTROFF. How strange it is. We meet, and then suddenly it seems that we must part forever. That is the way in this world. As long as we are alone, before Uncle Vanya comes in with a bouquet—allow me—to kiss you good-bye—may I? [*He kisses her on the cheek.*] So! Splendid!

HELENA. I wish you every happiness. [*She glances about her.*] For once in my life, I shall! and scorn the consequences! [*She kisses him impetuously, and they quickly part.*] I must go.

ASTROFF. Yes, go. If the carriage is there, then start at once. [*They stand listening.*

ASTROFF. É finita!

[VOITSKI, SEREBRAKOFF, MME. VOITSKAYA *with her book,* TELEGIN, *and* SONIA *come in.*

SEREBRAKOFF. [*To* VOITSKI.] Shame on him who bears malice for the past. I have gone through so much in the last few hours that I feel capable of writing a whole treatise on the conduct of life for the instruction of posterity. I gladly accept your apology, and myself ask your forgiveness.

[*He kisses* VOITSKI *three times.* HELENA *embraces* SONIA.

SEREBRAKOFF. [*Kissing* MME. VOITSKAYA'S *hand.*] Mother!

MME. VOITSKAYA. [*Kissing him.*] Have your picture taken, Alexander, and send me one. You know how dear you are to me.

TELEGIN. Good-bye, your Excellency. Don't forget us.

SEREBRAKOFF. [*Kissing his daughter.*] Good-bye, good-bye all. [*Shaking hands with* ASTROFF.] Many thanks for your pleasant company. I have a deep regard for your opinions and your enthusiasm, but let me, as an old man, give one word of advice at parting: do something, my friend! Work! Do something! [*They all bow.*] Good luck to you all.

[*He goes out followed by* MME. VOITSKAYA *and* SONIA.

VOITSKI. [*Kissing* HELENA'S *hand fervently.*] Good-bye—forgive me. I shall never see you again!

HELENA. [*Touched.*] Good-bye, dear boy.

[*She lightly kisses his head as he bends over her hand, and goes out.*

ASTROFF. Tell them to bring my carriage around too, Waffles.

TELEGIN. All right, old man.

[ASTROFF *and* VOITSKI *are left behind alone.* ASTROFF *collects his paints and drawing materials on the table and packs them away in a box.*

ASTROFF. Why don't you go to see them off?

VOITSKI. Let them go! I—I can't go out there. I feel too sad. I must go to work on something at once. To work! To work!

[*He rummages through his papers on the table. A pause. The tinkling of bells is heard as the horses trot away.*

ASTROFF. They have gone! The professor, I suppose, is glad to go. He couldn't be tempted back now by a fortune. [MARINA *comes in.*

MARINA. They have gone.

[*She sits down in an arm-chair and knits her stocking.*

[SONIA *comes in wiping her eyes.*

SONIA. They have gone. God be with them. [*To her uncle.*] And now, Uncle Vanya, let us do something!

VOITSKI. To work! To work!

SONIA. It is long, long, since you and I have sat together at this table. [*She lights a lamp on the table.*] No ink! [*She takes the inkstand to the cupboard and fills it from an inkbottle.*] How sad it is to see them go! [MME. VOITSKAYA *comes slowly in.*

MME. VOITSKAYA. They have gone.

[*She sits down and at once becomes absorbed in her book.*

[SONIA *sits down at the table and looks through an account book.*

SONIA. First, Uncle Vanya, let us write up the accounts. They are in a dreadful state. Come, begin. You take one and I will take the other.

VOITSKI In account with——

[*They sit silently writing.*

MARINA. [*Yawning.*] The sand-man has come.

ASTROFF. How still it is. Their pens scratch, the cricket sings; it is so warm and comfortable. I hate to go. [*The tinkling of bells is heard.*

ASTROFF. My carriage has come. There now remains but to say good-bye to you, my friends, and to my table here, and then—away!

[*He puts the map into the portfolio.*

MARINA. Don't hurry away; sit a little longer with us.

ASTROFF. Impossible.

VOITSKI. [*Writing.*] And carry forward from the old debt two seventy-five——

[WORKMAN *comes in.*

WORKMAN. Your carriage is waiting, sir.

ASTROFF. All right. [*He hands the* WORKMAN *his medicine-case, portfolio, and box.*] Look out, don't crush the portfolio!

WORKMAN. Very well, sir.

SONIA. When shall we see you again?

ASTROFF. Hardly before next summer. Probably not this winter, though, of course, if anything should happen you will let me know. [*He shakes hands with them.*] Thank you for your kindness, for your hospitality, for everything! [*He goes up to* MARINA *and kisses her head.*] Good-bye, old nurse!

MARINA. Are you going without your tea?

ASTROFF. I don't want any, nurse.

MARINA. Won't you have a drop of vodka?

ASTROFF. [*Hesitatingly.*] Yes, I might.

[MARINA *goes out.*

ASTROFF. [*After a pause.*] My off-wheeler has gone lame for some reason. I noticed it yesterday when Peter was taking him to water.

VOITSKI. You should have him re-shod.

ASTROFF. I shall have to go around by the blacksmith's on my way home. It can't be avoided. [*He stands looking up at the map of Africa hanging on the wall.*] I suppose it is roasting hot in Africa now.

VOITSKI. Yes, I suppose it is.

[MARINA *comes back carrying a tray on which are a glass of vodka and a piece of bread.*

MARINA. Help yourself. [ASTROFF *drinks.*

MARINA. To your good health! [*She bows deeply.*] Eat your bread with it.

ASTROFF. No, I like it so. And now, good-bye. [*To* MARINA.] You needn't come out to see me off, nurse.

[*He goes out.* SONIA *follows him with a candle to light him to the carriage.* MARINA *sits down in her arm-chair.*

VOITSKI. [*Writing.*] On the 2d of February, twenty pounds of butter; on the 16th, twenty pounds of butter again. Buckwheat flour——

[*A pause. Bells are heard tinkling.*

MARINA. He has gone. [*A pause.*

[SONIA *comes in and sets the candle-stick on the table.*

SONIA. He has gone.

VOITSKI. [*Adding and writing.*] Total, fifteen—twenty-five——

[SONIA *sits down and begins to write.*

MARINA. [*Yawning.*] Oh, ho! The Lord have mercy.

[TELEGIN *comes in on tiptoe, sits down near the door, and begins to tune his guitar.*

VOITSKI. [*To* SONIA, *stroking her hair.*] Oh, my child, I am so miserable; if you only knew how miserable I am!

SONIA. What can we do? We must live our lives. [*A pause.*] Yes, we shall live, Uncle Vanya. We shall live through the long procession of days before us, and through the long evenings; we shall patiently bear the trials that fate imposes on us; we shall work for others without rest, both now and when we are old; and when our last hour comes we shall meet it humbly, and there, beyond the grave, we shall say that we have suffered and wept, that our life was bitter, and God will have pity on us. Ah, then, dear, dear Uncle, we shall see that bright and beautiful life; we shall rejoice and look back upon our sorrow here; a tender smile—and—we shall rest. I have faith, Uncle, fervent, passionate faith. [SONIA *kneels down before her uncle and lays her head on his hands. She speaks in a weary voice.*] We shall rest. [TELEGIN *plays softly on the guitar.*] We shall rest. We shall hear the angels. We shall see heaven shining like a jewel. We shall see all evil and all our pain sink away in the great compassion that shall enfold the world. Our life will be as peaceful and tender and sweet as a caress. I have faith; I have faith. [*She wipes away her tears.*] My poor, poor Uncle Vanya, you are crying! [*Weeping.*] You have never known what happiness was, but wait, Uncle Vanya, wait! We shall rest. [*She embraces him.*] We shall rest. [*The*

WATCHMAN'S *rattle is heard in the garden;* TELEGIN *plays softly;* MME. VOITSKAYA *writes something on the margin of her pamphlet;* MARINA *knits her stocking.*] We shall rest.

[*The curtain slowly falls.*]